The Middle East as Middle Ground?
Cultural Interaction in the ancient Middle East revisited

edited by
Julia Hoffmann-Salz

Cover Image: View of the theatre of Palmyra, photo taken by J. Hoffmann-Salz in 2005

Owner and publisher:
Verlag Holzhausen GmbH, Leberstraße 122, 1110 Vienna, Austria

Place of publication: Vienna, Austria
Place of production: Vienna, Austria
Printed in the EU

1. Edition 2021
ISBN: 978-3-903207-56-1
© Verlag Holzhausen GmbH, 2021

Bibliographic information of the Austrian National Library and the German National Library: The ÖNB and the DNB list this publication in their national bibliographic; detailed bibliographic data can be found on the internet: For the Austrian National Library: http://onb.ac.at, for the German National Library: http://dnb.ddb.de

All rights, in particular the rights to reproduction and distribution as well as translation are reserved by the publisher. No part of this work may be reproduced in any form (photocopy, microfilm, or any other method) without written permission from the publisher or electronically stored, processed, duplicated or distributed.

www.verlagholzhausen.at

Table of Content

Preface 7

Julia Hoffmann-Salz
The Middle East and the Middle Ground – An Introduction................9

Katharina Knäpper
„Wie es Euch gefällt". Hellenistische Könige und die Asylie
Kleinasiatischer Städte 19

Peter Franz Mittag
Seleukidisches auf den postseleukidischen Münzen Mesopotamiens.......37

Achim Lichtenberger
Viele Mütter. Zu den quasi-municipalen seleukidischen Lokalbronzen
im hellenistischen Phönikien..65

Corinne Bonnet
La place et le rôle de l'agôn dans le middle ground phénicien à
l'époque hellénistique et romaine..87

Julia Hoffmann-Salz
The Ituraeans as a Hellenistic Dynasty – Working the Middle Ground
in Hellenistic Syria..101

Annie Sartre-Fauriat
L'épigraphie du Hauran, reflet des mixités culturelles au
Proche-Orient romain...117

Rubina Raja
Negotiating social and cultural interaction through priesthoods.
The iconography of priesthood in Palmyra................................129

David Graf
The Nabataean Ruler Cult and Ptolemaic Egypt...........................147

Benedikt Eckhardt
The Gymnasium of Jerusalem – a Middle Ground?...........................179

Edward Dąbrowa
The origins and functions of Hellenistic patterns in the Hasmonean
kingship...199

Sabine Müller
Lukian von Samosata und das hellenistische Erbe.........................213

David Engels
Hellenisierung, Sinisierung und Arabisierung - Komparatistische
Überlegungen zu historischen Assimilationsphänomenen 231

Indices...267

Preface

This volume presents the majority of papers given at the conference "The Middle East as Middle Ground? Cultural Interaction in the Ancient Middle East revisited" held at Schloss Wahn at Cologne, Germany, in April 2017. I would like to thank all participants for their contributions and our lively discussions: Corinne Bonnet, Hannah Cotton, Edward Dąbrowa, Lucinda Dirven, David Engels, Bettina Fischer-Genz, David Graf, Katharina Knäpper, Achim Lichtenberger, Peter F. Mittag, Sabin Müller, Paul Newson, Rubina Raja, Annie Sartre-Fauriat. With great pleasure we welcome the additional contribution of Benedikt Eckhardt to this volume.

The conference was made possible through the generous support of the NetEx-Initiative of Cologne University, travel grants from the Global South Study Center of Cologne University, the Rector of Cologne University and Peter F. Mittag, who not only offered his resources, but also provided invaluable advice and support for the conference and the volume.

I am indebted to Torben Godosar and Mario Landsmann for their support during the conference at Schloss Wahn. Katharina Kostopoulos kindly assisted in the compilation of this volume. Torben Godosar and Oliver Steinert thankfully took on the creation of the indices.

I would also like to express my gratitude to Stefan R. Hauser for his consistent support and advice in many preparatory stages of this volume. Special thanks also go to Werner Eck for his invaluable help.

And finally, I thank Gabriele Ambros and the team at Holzhausen Verlag for their help in publishing this volume.

Cologne, March 2021

The Middle East as Middle Ground?
Cultural Interaction in the Ancient Middle East revisited –
An Introduction

Julia Hoffmann-Salz

It is a truth universally acknowledged, that contact between communities leads to the exposure to different behaviours, ideas and artefacts.[1] While peaceful contact, such as trade, intermarriage or joint participation in festivals, brings about voluntary engagement with what is perceived to be different, violent contact, that is conquest, turns this engagement into a power discourse. In this power discourse, adaptation, assimilation, resistance or active promotion of the new order are part of a process of ongoing negotiation between each individual member of a community as well as the community as a whole with the dominant power and its representatives.[2]

In his famous study "The Middle Ground: Indians, Empires and Republics in the Great Lakes region 1650–1815", White was able to show that the contact between a native people and European traders and conquerors was not only a story of unilateral aggression and dominance by the Europeans. In contrast, because of the precarious situation of the Europeans in an alien and hostile environment where they were outnumbered, they were in fact dependent on negotiating with the native population and on finding a common framework for cooperation. He calls this realm the Middle Ground:

> "The Middle Ground is the place in between: in between cultures, peoples, and in between empires and the nonstate world of villages. [...] On the Middle Ground diverse peoples adjust their differences through what amounts to a process of creative, and often expedient, misunderstandings. People try to persuade others who are different from themselves by appealing to what they perceive to be the values and practices of those others. They often misinterpret and distort both the values and the practices of those they deal with, but from these misunderstandings arise new meanings and through them new practices – the shared meanings and practices of the Middle Ground."[3]

---

[1] This sentence is of course inspired by the famous opening line of Jane Austen's Pride and Prejudice, London 1813. On the effects of contact to alien peoples on social organization, architecture, technology etc. compare e.g. Cook 2017, 102–103.

[2] Compare the ideas in the introduction to MacDonald 2014.

[3] White 1991, xxvi.

The idea of the frontier being a place of reciprocal input from both the native population and the European invaders had already been expressed by Turner in his ground-breaking contribution "The significance of the frontier in American History" from 1893.[4] The importance of White's study, however, lies in the conceptualization of the Middle Ground as the place of cultural "accommodation", which he contrasts with the concept of "acculturation [...] in which a dominant group is largely able to dictate correct behaviour to a subordinate group. [But] accommodation took place because for long periods of time in large parts of the colonial world whites could neither dictate to Indians nor ignore them."[5] There is, of course, a very strong economic motivation for this accommodation that in turn facilitated the creation of acceptable negotiation practices. In this vein, Colchester and MacKay argue for modern Middle Grounds:

> "The Middle Ground was created because both parties wanted to trade, neither had a monopoly on power, and they had to find mutually intelligible and acceptable means of dealing with each other. [...] An essential element of the Middle Ground was thus the mutual acceptance of means of dispute settlement. [This] highlights two of the main challenges of the Middle Ground, first, the need for indigenous societies to agree means to represent their own collectivities and, secondly, for mutually agreed negotiating processes so that indigenous peoples can treat with industrial societies without being divided and ruled."[6]

But the Middle Ground not only challenged communities, it also affected individuals. Thus, Bahr uses the concept of Middle Ground or Middle Course as a framework for the individual decisions actively taken by native students in a state boarding school "to maintain the integrity of their native culture while making accommodations that allowed them to succeed in school. [...] [T]hey made decisions and took actions that allowed them to cope with the confrontations between white and native cultures."[7] In this, she also engages with two other concepts of individual accommodation and negotiation: the idea of "cultural brokers" expressed by Connell Szazs and that of "turning the power" put forward by Trafzer and Loupe. For Connell Szazs, Natives that had successfully adapted to the new cultural environment of a post-con-

---

4   Jackson Turner 1921, chapter 1. Other modern scholarship already using the term Middle Ground include Fields 1985. He takes the idea of a Middle Ground as a place of political compromise between two opposing ideologies that creates an uneasy balance in the geographical Middle between the adherents to these ideologies.

5   White 1991, xxvi.

6   Colchester and MacKay 2004, 3–6.

7   Bahr 2014, 6.

quest world could act as guides or 'cultural brokers' helping their community to adapt, too.[8] Trafzer and Loupe highlight, that native students educated in state schools could use their understanding of white culture to use this to their own advantage in creating the best possible path for their own future – and thereby "turn the power".[9]

The Middle Ground originally established between Natives and Europeans came to an end when the balance of power between the actors changed because the Europeans no longer needed the support of the Native communities.[10]

Many of the ideas expressed in the Middle Ground discourse – and its larger framework of frontier studies – have long been part of the discourse on the world of ancient Greece and Rome as well. In his study "The Creation of the Roman Frontier" from 1985, Dyson already stressed the need for cooperation between Roman conquerors and Natives in frontier regions and the role of trade in the formation of a new social reality.[11] Elton conceptualizes the frontier of the Roman empire "as a series of overlapping zones" were "political, social, ethnic, religious, linguistic, economic and military boundaries all overlap."[12] More recently, Sommer used the theoretical framework of frontier zone studies to elucidate characteristics of the Roman Middle East.[13]

The ancient Middle East with its rich history of conquest and changing political allegiances and the ensuing impact on populations, languages, trade, art, dress etc. has for a long time attracted scholars of cultural interaction. This Middle East roughly corresponds with the area affected by the conquest of Alexander the Great between Asia Minor and the Hindukush. However, this volume will focus on only a small part of this world, that is Syria and its environs. Chronologically, the main body of papers will focus on the period of political transition from the late Seleucid Empire to the Roman takeover.[14] This is hoped to allow for a more cohesive insight into the Middle Ground in this region.

Seen from the West, contact between the Greek world and the Middle East is visible in literature and material culture since the 8th century BCE.[15] It was to have a lasting impact on Rome and through Rome on the Europe

---

[8]   Connell Szasz 2001, 22–23.
[9]   Trafzer and Loupe 2012, 27.
[10] White 1991, xxxi.
[11] Dyson 1985, 4–5, 273–276.
[12] Elton 1996, 4.
[13] Sommer 2006, 17f.
[14] On the geographical and chronological definition of the ancient Middle East see Kuhrt 2007, 617 with a slightly different chronological frame, but see her thoughts on 618; and the introduction in Kuhrt 1995.
[15] Compare Dihle 2009, 10–14; van Dongen 2007, 13–49.

of today.[16] This contact and its consequences on both the native and the alien societies has been variously described. Ever since Droysen wrote about the „Vermischung des abend- und morgenländischen Lebens"[17], hellenization has been the term to conceptualize this intermingling of cultures. Many discussions have enfolded subsequently, focussing e.g. on the sources for this concept and their correct interpretation, the impact of hellenism on identity or the limits of cultural interaction.[18] Other terms – such as acculturation or hybridisation[19] – have also been put forward to more accurately describe what Wallace-Hadrill calls a "vigorous and continuous process of dialogue" of the cultures.[20] Particularly in art and architecture, concepts of eclecticism and bricolage have been put forward to analyse the visual aspects of cultural interaction.[21]

Scholars have also discussed possible means by which this cultural interaction could have taken place. Like with the American frontier, emphasis is often laid on economic exchange and infrastructure, such as in the seminal study "The corrupting Sea. A Study of Mediterranean History" by Horden and Purcell.[22] Malkin already used the idea of a Middle Ground to explain the cultural contact between Greeks and Phoenicians. He writes:

> "Both Greeks and Phoenicians of the Archaic period explored maritime routes, traded, and established emporia and territorial colonies. Cultural borrowings among them and the native populations soon transcended any particular point of trade or settlement, to create a web that crisscrossed the spaces of the ancient Mediterranean. [...] This was the context for the emergence of a colonial Middle Ground that greatly facilitated cultural exchange."[23]

More recently, Bonnet has used White's ideas to explain the cultural interaction of the Phoenicians with the Greek world, stressing that the Middle Ground is "espace de mediation et entre-deux créatif où les cultures se

---

[16] Compare Ball 2001, 1–2.

[17] Droysen 1836, V.

[18] On the problem of hellenization in Syria and particularly the problem of finding sources and understanding them see Millar 1987, 110–133. In their introduction to Kuhrt and Sherwin-White 1987, both editors also stress the need to go beyond the 'Greek-centrism' in order to understand all sides of the interaction. On Hellenism and identity e.g. Mairs, 2010. On the limits e.g. Momigliano 1971.

[19] On the theory of acculturation and a critique of this approach in the introduction of Versluys 2017; on hybridisation e.g.: Kouremenos et al. 2011; Fludernik and Gehrke (edd.) 2004.

[20] Wallace-Hadrill 2008, 23.

[21] E.g. Versluys 2017.

[22] Horden and Purcell 2000.

[23] Malkin 2005, 238. Other uses of the concept e.g. Woolf 2009.

croisent, apprennent à se comprendre et entrelacent leur destin."[24] In this debate, the role of local / native elites as agents between the cultures – or in fact 'cultural brokers', even though the term has so far not been used here – has already received scholarly attention.[25]

White's ideas of the Middle Ground offer two obvious advantages when looking at cultural interaction in the ancient Middle East that allow to leave behind the conceptual problems of the hellenization vs. acculturation dichotomy: the stress on agency of the native population and the idea of misunderstandings as a driving force in finding a common framework for interaction. In White's Middle Ground, Natives are not only the downtrodden victims of conquest but conscious agents of their own destiny – even if this means creating new social structures to enable the community to negotiate this destiny as argued by Colchester and MacKay. The second aspect of misunderstandings as a means of negotiating between native and alien communities is also of obvious importance. Famous examples as Herod Agrippa I.'s assembly of kings in Tiberias in 42 CE that was quickly disbanded by a furious Roman governor underline the many difficulties of the negotiation process between local and foreign actors.[26]

However, the idea of the Middle Ground only offers one model of conceptualization for cultural interaction – amongst many others. The papers of this volume, that originated in a conference in Cologne in 2017, thus show not only the possibilities of using the Middle Ground concept, but also allow the development of other ideas on cultural contact in a changing world.

In her paper on Hellenistic kings and *asylia* in the cities of Asia Minor Katharina Knäpper illuminates the attitudes of Ptolemaic, Seleucid and Antigonid kings towards this privilege. Looking at Smyrna, Kos, Magnesia on the Meander, Teos and Kyzikos, Knäpper can show that the Seleucids were particularly active in issuing a grant of *asylia* as part of their diplomatic repertoire to further geostrategic interests. As a classic Greek diplomatic instrument, these grants underlined the Seleucid's 'Greekness' while the Seleucid kings also adopted 'oriental' elements into their rule.

Discussing the coins minted in Parthia, Elymais and Charakene, Peter Franz Mittag concludes that both continuing and discontinuing Seleucid minting tradition were conscious political choices, reflecting the ruler's awareness of his subject's habits regarding the design of coins, the degree of hellenization of the subjects as well as the political and military situation at the time. Though misunderstandings and misinterpretations of designs may have occurred, the overall picture suggests that the rulers of the three kingdoms

---

[24] Bonnet 2015, 523.
[25] See e.g. Dreyer and Mittag 2011; Lavan, Payne and Weisweiler 2016.
[26] Sartre 2001, 501.

had a profound understanding of the ideological messages of Seleucid coin designs and knew how to use them.

Achim Lichtenberger studies the quasi-municipal local bronze coins of Phoenician cities under Antiochos IV, which were issued jointly by the king and the cities. He can show that even though the legends in both Greek and Phoenician and the depiction of local gods were used as distinct identity markers of a Phoenician or Hellenistic identity, the concept of 'mother city' of neighbouring rivals expressed on the coins was mutually comprehensible. Rather than visualising a Middle Ground between two cultures, the coins testify to the political intentions of the local actors.

In her contribution on the role of the *agón* in Hellenistic Phoenicia, Corinne Bonnet underlines the dynamic and nuanced character of the Middle Ground. She stresses that not all aspects of an indigenous culture were up for negotiations with a foreign power, while simultaneously, local actors in the Phoenician cities were happy to embrace those elements of Greek culture that they could utilize for self-promotion and distinction – a development that started long before the actual Macedonian conquest but was considerably intensified through it. In this sense, hellenization is not a means of subjugation but rather of appropriation and utilization in the creation of the Middle Ground.

Discussing the coins of the Ituraean dynast Ptolemy son of Mennaios as his only surviving self-document, Julia Hoffmann-Salz stresses the intentionally Hellenistic choices this dynast made to legitimize his rule. These choices were determined by his need to negotiate with various stakeholders with often opposing or competing interest towards whom Ptolemy nonetheless had to present a relatable language of power to maintain his position. His success in this venture is also a success in negotiating a 'Middle Ground' within a volatile political landscape.

Anni Sartre-Fauriat studies the epigraphy of the Roman Hauran, a region in Southern Syria that offers a unique insight into its cultural heritage due to over 4000 inscriptions collected to date and recently published in new editions of the much valued IGLS. These inscriptions show a region well integrated into the political and economic landscape of the Roman Near East but also allow glimpses of the indigenous identity underneath. Here, Sartre-Fauriat can show how multi-facetted local self-definitions within the framework of the 'Middle Ground' can be.

The representation of Palmyrene priests in funerary portraits, portraits from the public sphere and the banqueting tesserae form the body of evidence for Rubina Raja's study on the negotiation of a Middle Ground in the oasis city of Palmyra. Raja stresses that even though the city is commonly considered to be a place where various cultural influences were adapted due to the city's role in international commerce, the portraits of priests remain remarkably unchanged during time. As members of the local elite, their dress and attributes must therefore be considered as a link tying together local tradition and foreign influences.

Re-evaluating the evidence on the ruler cult of the Nabataean kings against the background of developments in Ptolemaic Egypt, David Graf demonstrates that these had an important influence on Nabataea. This can be traced in the cult for Obodas the god, the representation of the royal family in statues, the depiction of the rulers on coins, their royal title and epithets and the use of basileophoric names, all of which testifying to a divinization of the Nabataean kings. In adopting these Ptolemaic influences and adapting them to their needs, the Nabataeans also seem to foreshadow developments in the Seleucid realm.

The famous establishment of a *gymnasion* in Jerusalem by the high priest Jason is the focus of the paper of Benedikt Eckhardt, who debates the potential role of this institution as a Middle Ground for both the transmission of cultural ideas as well as the brokering of positions of power for the members of the local elite. Comparing the situation of the *gymnasion* in Jerusalem with that at Sardis and Limyra, Toriaion and Babylon, Eckhardt shows that Jason's ultimate failure was not the result of a cultural conflict but of the mechanisms of the Middle Ground itself.

Edward Dąbrowa analyses the Hellenistic elements of Hasmonaean kingship in connection with both the secular and religious authority the Hasmonaeans claimed over their state. After describing those Hellenistic elements, he points to the lack of two important elements of Hellenistic ruler activities: promotion of Greek culture and urbanization. Dąbrowa concludes that the Hasmonaean kingship was only marginally modelled after Hellenistic ruler ideals and that those Hellenistic elements actually incorporated by the Hasmoneans were used to highlight the distinction between their secular and religious authority, which was expressed in purely indigenous terms.

Discussing Hellenistic legacy in Lukian, Sabine Müller portraits the writer as an individual example of cultural accommodation since he, as a non-native speaker of Greek and self-styled barbarian, became such an erudite scholar of classical and Hellenistic Greek cultural heritage. By wilfully distorting and ridiculing stories from the past, he commented on contemporary issues and tried to highlight moral shortcomings of people of his own time. Since in order to understand his point, a deep knowledge of Hellenistic heritage was indispensable, his work can be understood as a discourse on the intellectual Middle Ground between contemporary scholarship and its Hellenistic legacy.

In his paper on Hellenization, Sinicization and Arabization, David Engels asks fundamental questions about the meaning of cultural assimilation and appropriation between 19th century romanticism and modern scepticism.

Comparing the process of Hellenization with the Sinicization of East Asia in the 4th and 3rd centuries BC and the Arabization of the Middle East in the 7th and 8th century CE, he looks at aspects of control and assimilation, autonomy and integration, tolerance and conversion as well as civilization and 'barbarianism'. Engels concludes that all three processes show surprising similarities making apparent that they were less determined by local and cultural factors than by a historical dynamic in which acculturation was an unforeseen by-product of military expansion.

As a collection, the papers can illuminate how native communities utilized contacts to other and often dominant groups to express their own identities and formulate their interests in a mutually communicable framework. Conquest and expansion of dominant groups like the Hellenistic monarchies or the Roman Empire created a need for local partners who were then able to use this position of strength to negotiate such a communicable framework even if this process involved a risk of frequent misunderstandings. The Hellenistic Middle East can thus be shown to be a Middle Ground – a place where various actors from different cultures negotiated what White called "shared meanings and practices".[27]

---

[27] White 1991, xxvi.

Introduction

Bibliography

Bahr, D.M. 2014. The Students of Sherman Indian School: Education and Native Identity since 1892. Norman.

Ball, W. 2001. Rome in the East. London and New York.

Bonnet, C. 2015. Les enfants de Cadmos. Le paysage religieux de la Phénicie hellénistique. Paris.

Colchester, M. and F. MacKay (edd.) 2004. In Search of Middle Ground. Indigenous Peoples, Collective Representation and the Right to Free, Prior and Informed Consent. Moreton-in-Marsh.

Connell Szasz, M. 2001. Between Indian and White Worlds: The Cultural Broker. Norman.

Cook, R.A. 2017. Continuity and Change in the Native American Village. Multicultural Origins and Descendants of the Fort Ancient Culture. Cambridge.

Dihle, A. 2009. Hellas und der Orient. Phasen wechselseitiger Rezeption. Berlin and New York.

van Dongen, E. 2007. classical Contacts between pre- Greece and the Near East in the context of cultural influences: An overview, in: R. Rollinger and A. Luther and J. Wiesehöfer with the support of B. Gufler (edd.), Getrennte Wege? Kommunikation, Raum und Wahrnehmung in der Alten Welt, Frankfurt a.M.,13–49.

Dreyer, B. and P. F. Mittag (Edd.) 2011. Lokale Eliten und hellenistische Könige. Zwischen Kooperation und Konfrontation. Frankfurt a.M.

Droysen, J.G. 1836. Geschichte des Hellenismus, Vol. 1: Geschichte der Nachfolger Alexanders. Hamburg.

Dyson, S. L. 1985. The Creation of the Roman Frontier. Princeton.

Elton, E. 1996. Frontiers of the Roman Empire. London.

Fields, B. J. 1985. Slavery and Freedom on the Middle Ground: Maryland during the Nineteenth Century. Yale.

Fludernik, M. and H.-J. Gehrke (edd.) 2004. Normen, Ausgrenzung, Hybridisierungen und 'Acts of Identity'. Würzburg.

Horden, P. and N. Purcell 2000. The Corrupting Sea. A Study of Mediterranean History. Malden and Oxford.

Jackson Turner, F. 1921. The frontier in American History. New York.

Kouremenos, A. et al. (edd.) 2011, From Pella to Gandhara. Hybridisation and Identity in the Art and Architecture of the Hellenistic East. Oxford.

Kuhrt, A. 2007. 'Ex Oriente Lux': How we may widen our perspectives on ancient history, in: R. Rollinger and A. Luther and J. Wiesehöfer with the support of B. Gufler (edd.), Getrennte Wege? Kommunikation, Raum und Wahrnehmung in der Alten Welt, Frankfurt a.M., 617–631.

Kuhrt, A. 1995. The Ancient Near East c. 3000- 330 BC, Vol. 1. London.

Lavan, M. and R.E. Payne and J. Weisweiler (edd.), Cosmopolitanism and Empire. Universal Rulers, Local Elites, and Cultural Intergration in the Ancient Near East and Mediterranean, Oxford 2016.

MacDonald, P.K. 2014. Networks of Domination. The Social foundations of Peripheral Conquest in International Politics. Oxford and New York.

Mairs, R. 2010. An 'identity crisis'? Identity and its Discontents in Hellenistic Studies, in: Bollettino di Archeologia Online I, 55–62.

Malkin, I. 2005. Herakles and Melqart: Greeks and Phoenicians in the Middle Ground, in: E.S. Gruen (ed.), Cultural Borrowings and Ethnic Appropriations in Antiquity. Stuttgart, 238–258.

Millar, F. 1987. The problem of Hellenistic Syria, in: A. Kuhrt and S. Sherwin-White (edd.), Hellenism in the East. The interaction of Greek and non-Greek civilizations from Syria to Central Asia after Alexander, London, 110–133.

Momigliano, A. 1971. Alien Wisdom: The Limits of Hellenization. Cambridge.

Sartre, M. 2001. D'Alexandre à Zénobie. Histoire du Levant antique Ive siècle av. J.-C. – IIIe siècle ap. J.-C. Paris.

Sommer, M. 2006. Der römische Orient. Darmstadt.

Trafzer, C. E. and L. Loupe. 2012. From Perris Indian School to Sherman Institute, in: C.E. Trafzer and M.S. Gilbert and L. Sisquoc (edd.), The School on Magnolia Avenue: Voices and Images of Sherman Institute. Corvallis.

Versluys, M.J. 2017. Visual Style and Constructing of Identity in the Hellenistic World. Nemrud Dağ and Commagene under Antiochos I. Cambridge.

Wallace-Hadrill, A. 2008. Rome's Cultural Revolution. Cambridge.

White, R. 1991. The Middle Ground: Indians, Empires, and Republics in the Great Lakes region, 1650–1815. Cambridge.

Woolf, G. 2009. Cruptorix and his kind. Talking ethnicity on the middle ground, in: T. Derks and N. Roymans (edd.), Ethnic Constructs in Antiquity, Amsterdam, 207–218.

„Wie es Euch gefällt."
Hellenistische Könige und die Asylie kleinasiatischer Städte[*]

Katharina Knäpper

1. Einleitung

Smyrna, im Jahre 246 v. Chr.: Das Heiligtum der Aphrodite Stratonikis und die Stadt werden von Seleukos II. und der Delphischen Amphiktyonie für heilig und unverletzlich erklärt, just zu dem Zeitpunkt als nach dem Tode Antiochos' II. der 3. Syrische Krieg, der sogenannte Laodike-Krieg, um die Nachfolge des Königs entbrennt. Diese Tatsache ist über die delphische Anerkennungsinschrift sowie Hinweise auf die bestehende Asylie Smyrnas in weiteren Inschriften überliefert.[1] Es handelt sich dabei um die zweite[2] überhaupt belegte Anerkennung ortsgebundener Asylie, die erste für eine kleinasiatische Polis und die erste seitens eines Königs.

Die Interpretation dieser Asylieanerkennung für Smyrna, ihre ereignishistorische Einordnung und ihre Position innerhalb der königlichen Asy-

---

[*] Bei diesem Aufsatz handelt es sich um eine überarbeitete Fassung meines Vortrags auf der in diesem Sammelband präsentierten Konferenz. Für Anregungen und Hinweise danke ich den Teilnehmern und Veranstaltern, aber vor allem Corinne Bonnet und Julia Hoffmann-Salz.

[1] Rigsby 1996, Nr. 7; in Delphi gefunden (bei Asylieinschriften wird grundsätzlich auf das Corpus von Rigsby verwiesen, sofern keine neueren und maßgeblich modifizierten Editionen vorliegen); ferner wird im Isopolitievertrag zwischen Smyrna und Magnesia am Sipylos (I.Magnesia Sip. 1 I, ca. 243 v. Chr.) und in der smyrnaischen Anerkennung der Aitolischen Soteria (I.Smyrna 1, 574, 245 v. Chr.) auf die bestehende Asylie Smyrnas verwiesen; vgl. darüber hinaus die von Meyer 2010, bes. 31–51, vorgeschlagene Deutung zeitgenössischer Münzen aus Smyrna mit mauerbekröntem Frauenkopf als Aphrodite Stratonikis nach erhaltener Asylie.

[2] Erstmalig ist territoriale Asylie im Jahre 266 (Datierung nach Dreyer 1999, bes. 404f., Anm. 147; 364; 374) für das Heiligtum der Athene Itonia in Koroneia seitens der Delphischen Amphiktyonie über eine ebenfalls in Delphi gefundene Inschrift belegt. Es kann nicht ausgeschlossen werden, dass in den 20 Jahren zwischen den Anerkennungen für Koroneia und Smyrna weitere Asylieanerkennungen stattgefunden haben, von den sich keine Zeugnisse erhalten haben. Dafür spräche die Ausweitung der Asylie von Koroneia nach Smyrna: Koroneia lag in Boiotien und war knappe 60 km von Delphi entfernt; Smyrna hingegen lag in der Asia Minor. Dagegen spräche, dass in beiden Fällen die Delphische Amphiktyonie zentral eingebunden war, die Asylieanerkennung mit einem pythischen Jahr zusammenfiel und beide Inschriften in Delphi, also nicht in einem städtischen Dossier, gefunden wurden. Zudem war die politische Lage – mit dem Chremonideischen Krieg im Falle Koroneias und dem 3. Syrischen Krieg im Falle Smyrnas – vergleichbar angespannt, so dass eine Übertragung des noch neuen Phänomens denkbar wäre.

lieanerkennungen dienen als Ausgangspunkt des vorliegenden Beitrags. Eine Analyse dieser Dokumentgruppe erlaubt aber nicht nur, den Blick auf den *modus operandi* der hellenistischen Monarchen bezüglich der territorialen Asylie zu lenken, sondern offenbart auch zu einem gewissen Teil die königliche Perspektive auf Asylie, und damit auf zwischen Poleis stattfindende diplomatische Kontakte.

Des Weiteren scheint es bedeutsam, einerseits darzulegen, durch welche Charakteristika sich königliche Asylieverleihungen auszeichneten und andererseits zu prüfen, ob und gegebenenfalls welche Unterschiede es bei der Anerkennung der Asylie seitens verschiedener Monarchen gab. Eine der Kernfragen zielt in diesem Zusammenhang auf mögliche Spezifika seleukidischer, antigonidischer, ptolemäischer Asylieanerkennungen oder derjenigen der sogenannten ‚hellenisierten' Herrscher. Ferner gilt es zu überlegen, ob sich festgestellte Gemeinsamkeiten und/oder Unterschiede aus der Befolgung spezifisch griechischer beziehungsweise nicht-griechischer Verhaltensmuster erklären lassen und was das einerseits für die Aushandlung der Zugehörigkeit zur griechischen Kulturkoiné und andererseits für die monarchische Sicht auf die territoriale Asylie in der ausgedehnten Oikumene der späteren hellenistischen Zeit bedeutete.

2. Königliche Asylieanerkennungen

Aus der Hochphase der territorialen Asylie im 3. und 2. Jh. v. Chr.[3] sind – bisweilen mit gewissen Fragezeichen – neunzehn königliche Asylieanerkennungen bezeugt, dabei sind die Seleukiden mit bis zu acht Anerkennungen durch drei Monarchen, Seleukos II., Antiochos III. und seinen Sohn Antiochos, gegenüber sechs Poleis, nämlich Smyrna, Kos, Magnesia am Mäander, Teos sowie mit hoher Wahrscheinlichkeit Amyzon und eventuell Xanthos, am prominentesten vertreten.[4] Von den Antigoniden sind vier Asylieanerkennungen, für Kos, Magnesia am Mäander, Teos und Kyzikos, durch zwei Mo-

---

[3] Zur territorialen Asylie als eigenständigem Phänomen der hellenistischen Zeit vgl. Knäpper 2018, bes. 11–18.

[4] Seleukidische Asylieanerkennungen: Seleukos II.: Smyrna, 246 v. Chr. (Rigsby 1996, Nr. 7); Kos, 242 v. Chr. (IG XII 4, 1, 210 = Rigsby 1996, Nr. 9); Antiochos III.: Magnesia am Mäander, 221/208 v. Chr. (Rigsby 1996, Nr. 69); Teos, ausgehendes 3. Jh. v. Chr. (SEG 41, 1003; vgl. auch Herrmann 1965, 1–4 mit Übersetzung und ausführlichem Kommentar; Rigsby 1996, 281–283); Amyzon, ausgehendes 3. Jh. v. Chr. (J. und L. Robert 1983, Nr. 12; Nr. 13; vgl. ferner Piejko 1988, 613); Xanthos, ausgehendes 3. Jh. v. Chr. (Rigsby 1996, Nr. 164); Antiochos, S. Antiochos' III.: Magnesia, 208 v. Chr. (Rigsby 1996, Nr. 70); Amyzon, ausgehendes 3. Jh. v. Chr. (J. und L. Robert 1983, Nr. 12; 13; vgl. ferner Piejko 1988, 613).

Hellenistische Könige und Asylie in kleinasiatischen Städten

narchen, Antigonos Gonatas und Philipp V., erhalten;[5] für die Ptolemäer Ptolemaios III. und Ptolemaios IV. ist jeweils eine Asylieanerkennung, für Kos beziehungsweise Magnesia am Mäander, bekannt.[6] Daneben liegt eine Asylieanerkennung Attalos' I. für Magnesia am Mäander sowie – und das ist eine Besonderheit innerhalb des Materials – ein Asylie*gesuch* seitens Eumenes II. für das Nikephorion in Pergamon vor.[7] Darüber hinaus sind jeweils einmalige Asylieanerkennungen hellenisierter Monarchen für Kos – Ziaëlas von Bithynien, Alexander II. von Epeiros, Spartokos IV. vom Regnum Bosporanum – und der Athamanischen Könige, Amynandros und Theodoros, für Teos bezeugt.[8]

Allen königlichen Anerkennungen ist gemein, dass sie, anders als die große Masse der Asyliedokumente, in Briefform überliefert sind und stärker auf die eigenen Anerkennungsmotive der Monarchen als auf die Wiedergabe der Bewerberargumente fokussieren. Den Kern der auf uns gekommenen Quellen zur territorialen Asylie bilden allerdings zwischen Poleis ausgehandelte Anerkennungsbeschlüsse, die sowohl die Argumente der Bewerber als auch der Verleiher wiedergeben und über das vorhergehende diplomatische Prozedere Auskunft gewähren.[9] Diese Zeugnisse prägten daher auch die Inhalte sowie die relativ egalitäre, nicht zwingend politische Machtgefälle repräsentierende Diktion des Phänomens Asylie, die sich bis zu einem gewissen Grad auch in den königlichen Anerkennungsbriefen spiegeln.[10]

---

[5] Antigonidische Asylieanerkennungen: Antigonos Gonatas: Kos, 242 v. Chr. (IG XII 4, 1, 208 = Rigsby 1996, Nr. 10); Philipp V.: Magnesia am Mäander, 208 v. Chr. (Frustrum einer Königsinschrift, Rigsby 1996, Nr. 72; Asylieempfehlung an Chalkis, Rigsby 1996, Nr. 97, 1-8); Teos, ausgehendes 3. Jh. v. Chr. (indirekt bezeugt über die Verbreitung der teischen Asylie durch seinen Gesandten Perdikkas, Rigsby 1996, Nr. 140; Nr. 141; Nr. 142; Nr. 148; Nr. 149; Nr. 150; Nr. 151; Nr. 152); Kyzikos, ca. 180 v. Chr. (Aufforderung Philipps V. an die Bürger von Dion, die Asylie von Kyzikos anzuerkennen, SEG 48, 785 = Pandermalis 1997).

[6] Ptolemäische Asylieanerkennungen: Ptolemaios III.: Kos, 242 v. Chr. (IG XII 4, 1, 212 = Rigsby 1996, Nr. 8); Ptolemaios IV.: Magnesia am Mäander, 208 v. Chr. (Rigsby 1996, Nr. 71).

[7] Attalidische Asylieanerkennung: Attalos I.: Magnesia am Mäander, 208 v. Chr. (Rigsby 1996, Nr. 68). Attalidisches Asyliegesuch: Eumenes II., 182 v. Chr. (Rigsby 1996, Nr. 176; Nr. 177.).

[8] Ziaëlas von Bithynien: Kos, 242 v. Chr. (IG XII 4, 1, 209 = Rigsby 1996, Nr. 11); Alexander II. von Epeiros: Kos, 242 v. Chr. (IG XII 4, 1, 211); Spartokos IV. vom Regnum Bosporanum: Kos, 242 v. Chr. (IG XII 4, 1, 213 = Rigsby 1996, Nr. 12); Amynandros und Theodoros von Athamanien: Teos, ausgehendes 3. Jh. v. Chr. (Rigsby 1996, Nr. 135).

[9] Zu den Strukturtypen von Asylieanerkennungen vgl. Knäpper 2018, 79–81.

[10] Vgl. dazu Hofmann 2015, 143-150, die Prozedere und schriftliche Fixierung der Kommunikation zwischen König und Stadt *en detail* darstellt; vgl. auch Ma 2003, bes. 21–24; zur Ausdifferenzierung der Asyliespezifika über mitgeführte Psephismata, vgl. Chaniotis 1999, bes. 54–56, 60f.

3. Die Beispiele Smyrna und Kos

Wie eingangs zitiert, ereignete sich die erste Asylieanerkennung für eine klein-asiatische Polis unter seleukidischer Beteiligung: wahrscheinlich 246 v. Chr.[11] wurden das Heiligtum der Aphrodite Stratonikis[12] und die Stadt Smyrna für heilig und unverletzlich erklärt. Die historische Situation hinter diesem Ereignis ist besonders komplex. Nach seinem plötzlichen Tod in Ephesos im Juli[13] hinterließ Antiochos II. zwei Söhne, Seleukos (II.) und Antiochos (Hierax), aus der Ehe mit Laodike sowie einen Sohn, den Knaben Antiochos, aus der am Ende des 2. Syrischen Kriegs zu Gunsten einer Verbindung mit den Ptolemäern eingegangenen Ehe mit Berenike Phernephoros. Entgegen der in einigen Quellen belegten Verabredung, nach der Laodike in den Stand einer Konkubine gefallen und ihre Söhne in der Thronfolge hinter Berenikes Sohn gerückt wären, erhob der König kurz vor seinem Tod seinen ältesten Sohn Seleukos zum Mitregenten.[14] Diese problematische Konstellation führte in der Folge zum 3. Syrischen Krieg zwischen Seleukiden und Ptolemäern, da beide Königinnen den Thronanspruch ihrer Kinder durchzusetzen versuchten, wobei Berenike und ihr Sohn trotz anfänglicher Erfolge und des zur Hilfe herbeigerufenen Bruders Ptolemaios' III. noch vor Eintreffen desselben ermordet wurden.[15]

Die Situation nach dem Tod Antiochos' II. eskalierte so schnell, dass der junge König Seleukos II., der, im Osten des Reiches befindlich, wohl erst im September vom Tod des Vaters erfahren hatte,[16] Probleme bekam das

---

[11] Zur Datierung s. Anm. 19.

[12] Es ist strittig, ob es sich beim Epitheton Stratonikis um einen Verweis auf eine Apotheose Stratonikes oder auf eine ‚kriegerische' Aphrodite handelt. Dafür wird zumeist angeführt, dass auch im Isopolitievertrag zwischen Smyrna und Magnesia am Sipylos (I.Magnesia Sip. 1 I, ca. 243 v. Chr.) Stratonike, die Mutter Antiochos II., mit kultischen Ehren bedacht wird. Mit der Wurzel *strat-* gebildete Epiklesen der Aphrodite sind aber auch anderswo, gerade in Kleinasien (I.Mylasa I 203, 5; 204, 3; I.Iasos II 222f.; I.Erythrai II 207, 10), belegt, vgl. dazu Rigsby 1996, 96–99; Wallensten 2003, 199–201; Pironti 2005, 172–174 mit einer Materialsammlung und Literatur; zur numismatischen Interpretation vgl. ferner Meyer 2010, bes. 45f.

[13] Zur Chronologie der Ereignisse mit gründlicher Aufbereitung der Quellen und Literatur, vgl. Coşkun 2016, (hier: 120, bes. Anm. 58) mit kritischer Durchsicht von Quellen und Literatur.

[14] Coşkun 2016, bes. 114–122, charakterisiert diese Quellentendenz als ptolemäische Propaganda. Er betont ferner, Antiochos II. habe nie den Plan gehegt, seine erste Ehe aufzulösen oder seinen ‚traditionellen' erstgeborenen Nachfolger zu benachteiligen.

[15] Zum Thronfolgeproblem und den folgenden Kriegen, vgl. Piejko 1990; Ma 2000, 43–45; Chaniotis 2005, 110f.; Grainger 2010, 153–194; jüngst Coşkun 2016, bes. 110–112; vgl. ferner Ihnken in I.Magnesia Sip., S. 33, der jedoch annimmt, die Streitigkeiten zwischen Seleukos II. und Antiochos Hierax hätten ebenfalls bereits 246 v. Chr. eingesetzt.

[16] Zu den babylonischen Belegen für die Chronologie dieser Ereignisse vgl. Coşkun 2016, 120f., bes. Anm. 57 und 63.

Hellenistische Könige und Asylie in kleinasiatischen Städten 23

Reich zusammenzuhalten. So waren die oberen Satrapien sowie einige Städte Kleinasiens bereits früh auf die Seite Berenikes und ihres Sohnes gewechselt[17] und es war abzusehen, dass Ptolemaios III. in den Konflikt eingreifen würde. In diese Zeit fällt Seleukos' Asylieanerkennung für Smyrna und es ist plausibel, anzunehmen, dass er Städte privilegiert hätte, die ihn als König anerkannten. Damit wären die Verleihung der Asylie an Smyrna und das Heiligtum der Aphrodite Stratonikis sowie die gleichzeitige Freiheitsproklamation und Tributsbefreiung für die Stadt, wie wir sie in der delphischen Inschrift fassen können,[18] als Gegenleistungen für Gunstbeweise anlässlich seiner Inthronisation zu verstehen. Eine relativ zügige Ereignisfolge lässt sich, wie eingangs geschildert, aus den Erwähnungen bestehender Asylie in der auf 245 v. Chr. datierten smyrnaischen Anerkennung der Aitolischen Soteria sowie im auf ca. 243 v. Chr. datierten Isopolitievertrag zwischen Smyrna und Magnesia am Sipylos rekonstruieren.[19]

    Ob die Smyrnaier aber um diese Asylieverleihung des Königs gebeten haben, wie es in Asylieinitiativen üblich wäre, wird nicht erwähnt. Sie haben zwar eigene Gesandte nach Delphi geschickt,[20] aber ob sie zuvor an Seleukos II. herangetreten sind, lässt sich nicht mehr eruieren. Um festzustellen auf wessen Initiative die Asylie Smyrnas erklärt wurde, gilt es zwei alternative Szenarien zu prüfen:

---

[17] Vgl. Plischke 2014, 223–225, die die Designation Seleukos' II. zum Mitregenten für unzureichend belegt hält und die Nachfolgefrage als offen ansieht; Coşkun 2016, 118–122, mit Betonung der Mitregentschaft Seleukos' II.; vgl. ferner Grainger 2010, 153f., 161–164.

[18] Rigsby 1996, Nr. 7, 3–8.

[19] I.Smyrna 1, 574, 21f.; I.Magnesia Sip. 1 I, 12f.; Rigsby 1996, 101, betont hingegen, eine rasante Ereignisfolge ergäbe sich grundsätzlich aus der in der delphischen Inschrift genannten Belobigung des Verhaltens des Königs durch die Theoren, die im Frühjahr zur Verkündung der Pythien aufbrachen (Rigsby 1996, Nr. 7, 14–16). Er nimmt an, es könnten nur die Pythien desselben Jahres gemeint sein. Dafür ignoriert er allerdings – bewusst – die babylonischen Belege für Seleukos' II. Anwesenheit in Babylon im Sommer 246 v. Chr., die in Kombination mit der Nennung der pythischen Theoren in der delphischen Inschrift durchaus ein chronologisches Problem darstellen: Wenn Seleukos II. im Sommer in Babylon und erst im September wieder unterwegs nachhause gewesen ist, kann er nicht noch vor dem Frühjahr die Asylie Smyrnas anerkannt und verbreitet haben. Der *terminus ante quem* der Asylieanerkennung Seleukos' II. für Smyrna ist allerdings durch die vorbenannten Inschriften bezüglich der Aitolischen Soteria sowie der Isopolitie Magnesias am Sipylos und Smyrnas ohnehin mit 245 v. Chr. gegeben und mit 243 v. Chr. abgesichert. Die Nennung der pythischen Theoren in der delphischen Anerkennung könnte, um alle Informationen schlüssig zusammenzuführen, auf Gesandte des kommenden Zyklus bezogen sein. In Anbetracht des – auf das Jahr gesehen – späten Bekanntwerdens des Todes Antiochos' II. im September 246 v. Chr. wäre eine gewisse Dichte der Ereignisse dennoch zu betonen.

[20] Rigsby 1996, Nr. 7, 9–10.

Entweder bedachte Seleukos II. Smyrna ungefragt mit Asylie, etwa als Dank für die Parteinahme zu seinen Gunsten im Rahmen der Thronfolgekonflikte. Dagegen spräche einerseits, dass die Asylie zu diesem Zeitpunkt ein Novum darstellte. Smyrna war die zweite Stadt, die überhaupt territoriale Asylie erhielt, zudem die erste in Kleinasien beziehungsweise im seleukidischen Machtbereich und es lagen keine Vorbilder für königliche Beteiligung an diesem Phänomen vor. Wenn der König also von sich aus aktiv geworden wäre, bliebe zu klären, aus welchem Anlass er zu einem neuen Privileg gegriffen hätte. Es hätten traditionellere Methoden zur Verfügung gestanden, auf städtische Ehrungen zu reagieren. So haben beispielsweise die Milesier Huldadressen an den König gesandt, worauf dieser den Bürgern mit einer Krone des didymäischen Apollon dankte, wie ein Antwortschreiben Seleukos' II. belegt.[21] Das Beispiel Milets verdeutlicht also, dass eine Anerkennung der Asylie nicht unbedingt zum Standardrepertoire des Seleukos in Antwort auf städtische Huldigungen in Zusammenhang mit den Nachfolgestreitigkeiten gehörte.

Oder aber – und hier sind wir beim zweiten Szenario – Seleukos II. reagierte 246 v. Chr. auf ein Anliegen der Smyrnaier, das entweder ihm sehr bald nach seiner Inthronisation vorgebracht wurde, vermutlich aber bereits seinem Vater und möglicherwiese sogar ihm selbst als Mitregenten vorgelegen hat. Dafür, dass das Asyliebegehren der Smyrnaier bereits Antiochos II. bekannt war, spricht die zügige Ereignisfolge zwischen Seleukos' II. Mitregentschaft, dem Tod des Vaters und der Asylieanerkennung Smyrnas, aber auch die grundsätzlich guten Beziehungen zwischen Antiochos II. und Smyrna.[22] Die Smyrnaier hätten in diesem Falle ob der generellen politischen Unsicherheiten um Asylie angefragt und möglicherweise wäre sogar eine Antwort Antiochos' II. bereits in Planung/in Arbeit gewesen, als der König in recht jungem Alter verstarb. Als Seleukos II. sich nun – aus den oberen Satrapien zurückkehrend –[23] den vielfachen Krisenherden gegenüber sah, beantwortete er das Asyliegesuch der Smyrnaier. Einerseits hätte er sich damit einen Partner in der Region um Magnesia am Sipylos verschaffen können, das, wie wir aus dem Isopolitievertrag zwischen Smyrna und Magnesia am Sipylos

---

[21] I.Didyma 49. Diese Inschrift wurde zwar bereits von den Herausgebern mit einer Asylieverleihung in Zusammenhang gebracht, allerdings lassen sich – ohne Zirkelschlüsse auf Smyrna – keinerlei Hinweise für diese Annahme finden; zur Diskussion mit ablehnendem Standpunkt vgl. Boffo 1985, 181; vgl. auch Rigsby 1996, 174. Möglicherweise gehört ferner auch die Abtretung Stratonikeias an die Rhodier in diesen Kontext, vgl. dazu von Steuben und Bringmann 1995, Nr. 206.

[22] Orth 1977, 134–137.

[23] Coşkun 2016, 121f.

Hellenistische Könige und Asylie in kleinasiatischen Städten   25

wissen, im 3. Syrischen Krieg auf Seiten der Ptolemäer agierte.[24] Andererseits böte die Anerkennung eines Privilegs, was bereits dem Vater vorgelegen hätte, die Möglichkeit, die eigene Eignung zum König zu beweisen. Die Annahme eines an Antiochos II. adressierten Asyliegesuchs und eines bereits durchdachten Antwortschreibens würde die Schnelligkeit der Reaktion Seleukos' II. erklären, aber auch sein überaus engagiertes Verhalten in Sachen der Asylie Smyrnas zu einem Zeitpunkt, als Herrschaftssicherung das wichtigste Unterfangen gewesen sein musste.

Da sich eine Entscheidung zwischen den beiden vorgeschlagenen Szenarien auf die Abwägung von Informationen stützt, scheint ein Vergleich mit der zweiten für Seleukos II. belegten Asylieanerkennung, nämlich der für Kos aus dem Jahre 242 v. Chr., vielversprechend. Die Koer hatten ihr *oikumene*-umspannendes Asyliegesuch – das erste seiner Art – geplant und vermittels von zumindest acht Gesandtschaften geordnet durchgeführt. Die jeweiligen Reiserouten lassen sich an Hand von Gesandtennennungen innerhalb des Antwortdossiers feststellen[25] und darüber hinaus sind Reste eines Dekrets, das die Aussendung der Theoren beschließt, erhalten.[26] Neben zahlreichen Städten erkannten sechs Herrscher – Seleukos II., Antigonos Gonatas, Ptolemaios III., Ziaëlas von Bithynien, Spartokos IV. vom Regnum Bosporanum sowie Alexander II. von Epeiros –[27] die Asylie der Stadt Kos und des Heiligtums des Asklepios an, so dass in diesem Fall Vergleichsmaterial zur Kontextualisierung der seleukidischen Anerkennung vorliegt.

In seinem nicht vollständig erhaltenen Brief fokussiert Seleukos II. nach einem Hinweis auf die normenkonforme Religionsausübung der Koer (Z. 1–4) auf die bei ihm eingetroffene Gesandtschaft mit der Bitte um Asylie (Z. 4–12). Er lobt die Koer und betont, er habe Diogeitos, den Gesandten der Koer, empfangen, weil er das Beste für seine Polis wolle (Z. 12–21). Darauf hält der König fest, dass er die Asylie „καθότι ὁ δῆμος ἠξίωσεν" ‚wie das Volk es erbat' anerkennt (Z. 21–23) und unterstreicht für die Zukunft, „δὲ πειρασόμεθα |τῶν καθ᾽ ἡμᾶς ὄντων ἐν ἡ- | συχίαι μὴ ἀχαριστεῖν ἡμῖν | ἐν

---

[24]   Vgl. dazu den Kommentar zu StV III 492; vgl. dagegen I.Magnesia Sip., 34–36, wo Ihnken annimmt, Antiochos Hierax sei bereits zu diesem Zeitpunkt der Gegenspieler Seleukos' II.

[25]   Eine Auflistung der koischen Gesandtschaften bietet Hallof in IG XII 4, 1, 206f.

[26]   IG XII 4, 1, 207; zur Inschrift vgl. ferner Rigsby 2004.

[27]   Nur Ptolemaios III. und Ziaëlas von Bithynien sind aus dem jeweiligen Königsbrief zu bestimmen. Die Zuordnung der übrigen Inschriften erfolgte nach text- beziehungsweise dossierimmanenten Kriterien, wobei die Zuordnungen der Briefe des Antigonos' Gonatas, Alexanders II. von Epiros und Seleukos' II. hohe Sicherheit beanspruchen dürfen; die Zuordnung des Briefes Spartokos' IV. wird stärker diskutiert. Vgl. dazu die jeweiligen Kommentare von IG XII 4, 1, 210 (Seleukos II.), IG XII 4, 1, 211 (Alexander II. von Epeiros) und IG XII 4, 1, 213 (Spartokos IV. vom Regnum Bosporanum); vgl. ferner Knäpper 2018, 99–103, mit Literatur.

τοῖς ἀξιουμένοις" ‚und wir werden versuchen, wenn es bei uns friedlich bleibt, Euch nicht ungefällig zu sein, bei dem, was Ihr erbittet.' (Z. 24–27). Dieser zwischen Asylieanerkennung und Abschiedsformel platzierte Einschub, scheint auf den 242 v. Chr. noch immer nicht beendeten 3. Syrischen Krieg gegen Ptolemaios III. sowie möglicherweise auch den bereits schwelenden Konflikt mit seinem Bruder Antiochos Hierax anzuspielen.[28]

In ihrer Gesamtheit aber fällt die Antwort Seleukos' II. in Bezug auf die Asylie von Kos deutlich weniger proaktiv aus als im Falle von Smyrna. Weder berichtet der König davon – und der Anerkennungsteil der Inschrift ist zur Gänze erhalten –, die Asylie in ‚seinen' Städten empfehlen zu wollen, noch werden weitere politisch wie finanziell relevante Privilegien verliehen. Ferner wird künftige Unterstützung an die Stabilität der politischen Lage geknüpft, und das obwohl die Situation für Seleukos II. 242 v. Chr. gegenüber der von 246 v. Chr. sogar weniger belastend gewesen sein dürfte.

Die Erwiderung eines Asyliegesuchs durch einen König hängt also von verschiedenen Faktoren ab. Zum einen spielt dabei das Verhältnis zur betreffenden Stadt eine Rolle, zum anderen aber auch inwiefern eine Asylieverleihung seinen strategischen Erwägungen dienlich wäre. Während Seleukos II. in den Wirren um die Nachfolge seines Vaters viele Gründe gehabt zu haben scheint, die Asylie Smyrnas gepaart mit einer Befreiung von Tributsleistungen und der Erklärung allgemeiner Freiheit anzuerkennen und zu forcieren, liegt der Fall in Kos anders.

Die Stadt gehörte generell zum ptolemäischen Einflussbereich und wurde gerade von Ptolemaios' III. Vater, Ptolemaios II. Philadelphos, zu Beginn und gegen Mitte des 3. Jh. gefördert.[29] In Bezug auf Kos waren es also die Ptolemäer, die eine engere Verbindung zur Insel aufwiesen, auch wenn die Insel zum Zeitpunkt des Asyliegesuchs eher dem (erweiterten) Machtbereich der Antigoniden angehörte.[30] So überrascht es nicht, dass eine von lediglich zwei bekannten Asylieanerkennungen der Ptolemäer[31] Kos betrifft.[32]

---

[28] Die zeitliche Fixierung der Auseinandersetzungen zwischen den Brüdern ist sehr voraussetzungsreich und nicht unumstritten; Ihnken (I.Magnesia Sip., 34–36) nimmt an, der Bruderkrieg sei zeitgleich mit dem 3. Syrischen Krieg von Statten gegangen; so auch Coşkun 2016, 122 zumindest mit Bezug auf die Sardeis-Episode; vgl. ferner Ma 1999, 46f.; zur Verzahnung mit den Ereignissen in den oberen Satrapien vgl. Plischke 2014, 217f., 223–225.

[29] Von Steuben und Bringmann 1995, Nr. 422; Nr. 423; wobei Nr. 423 auch Ptolemaios III. zugeordnet werden könnte.

[30] Vgl. dazu Dreyer 1999, 416–419; Grainger 2010, 124f.

[31] Die aus Ägypten bekannten Asyldeklarationen seitens der ptolemäischen Könige stellen ein im Detail von den hier betrachteten Asylieverleihungen zu trennendes Phänomen dar, vgl. dazu etwa von Woeß 1923 mit Quellenanhang; vgl. ferner von Woeß 1926; Dunand 1972; Dunand 1980; Palme 2003 mit einem Schwerpunkt auf den Asylbriefen der Kaiserzeit; Traulsen 2004, 241–248.

[32] IG XII 4, 1, 212 = Rigsby 1996, Nr. 8.

Hellenistische Könige und Asylie in kleinasiatischen Städten 27

Darin verkündet Ptolemaios III., von Gesandten aufgesucht, über den Kultvollzug informiert und um die Anerkennung der Asylie des Asklepieions gebeten worden zu sein (Z. 3–8), wie sie auch die Amphiktyonen sowie andere Könige, Bünde und Poleis anerkannt hätten (Z. 8–13). Er schließt an, er erkenne wegen des Gottes und der Politen „τὴν τε δὴ θυσίαν καὶ τὴν [πα]νήγυριν καὶ τὴν τοῦ ἱεροῦ ἀσυλί[αν" ‚die Asylie des Opfers und der Prozession und des Heiligtums' an (Z. 13–16) und bemerkt, er habe die ihm zu Ehren aufgestellte Statue[33] sowie die Anerkennung der Spiele in Hiera Nesos zur Kenntnis genommen (Z. 16–19). Mehr erfahren wir nicht; weder Empfehlungen noch Weiterverbreitung der Asylie werden erwähnt.

Für die Antigoniden ist ebenfalls eine fragmentarische Asylieanerkennung des Asklepieions in Kos überliefert.[34] Antigonos Gonatas erkennt darin die Asylie im Rahmen der gesetzten Grenzsteine an (Z. 12–14) und verlautet ferner, er werde die Asylie in seinen Städten weiterempfehlen (Z. 10–12), was wiederum durch Dekrete aus Städten des antigonidischen Kerngebiets, nämlich Kassandreia, Amphipolis und Philippi, belegt ist.[35] Antigonos Gonatas fördert die Asylie von Kos in seinem Einflussgebiet also in ähnlicher Art und Weise, wie Seleukos II. die Smyrnas. Diese Förderung darf aber nicht als königlicher Zwang ausgelegt werden, wie Ben Raynor es kürzlich herausgearbeitet hat; vielmehr lässt sich gerade auch für die Poleis im makedonischen Kerngebiet eine gewisse Autonomie in Asyliefragen nachweisen.[36]

Der Vollständigkeit halber ist an dieser Stelle auf die Asylieanerkennungen des bithynischen Monarchen Ziaëlas, des Bosporaners Spartokos IV. sowie Alexanders II. von Epeiros zu verweisen,[37] wobei letztere auf Grund des extrem fragmentarischen Zustands lediglich über eine erwähnte königliche Empfehlung in der leukadischen Asylieanerkennung identifiziert wird.[38] Die Inschriften des Bithyniers und des Bosporaners hingegen erweisen sich als verhältnismäßig lang. Ziaëlas betont, er fördere die Freunde seines Vaters und erkenne die Asylie auch an, da er mit Ptolemaios verbündet sei (Z. 23–25), während Spartokos IV. auf eine bereits auf seinen Vater zurückgehende

---

[33] Von einer begünstigten Poleis zuvor dargebrachte Statuen sind auch aus Teos für Antiochos III. und Laodike bekannt, vgl. SEG 41, 1003 I 40–55; ferner sind in Asyliedokumenten Statuen verzeichnet, die von der Delphischen Amphiktyonie und vom Aitolischen Bund an die asylie*ersuchenden* Eumenes II. und seine Familie gestiftet wurden (Rigsby 1996, Nr. 178, 12–14; Nr. 179, 21–23); zur Ausdeutung des Herrscherkults mit Fokus auf die teische Inschrift vgl. Ma 1999, 219–226; zum städtischen Herrscherkult vgl. dazu Habicht 1956, 230–242; vgl. ferner Dreyer 2007, 252f., 315–320.

[34] IG XII 4, 1, 208 = Rigsby 1996, Nr. 10.

[35] IG XII 4, 1, 220 I (= Rigsby 1996, Nr. 25), 5-7; IG XII 4, 1, 220 II (= Rigsby 1996, Nr. 26), 32; IG XII 4, 1, 220 III (= Rigsby 1996, Nr. 27), 48.

[36] Raynor 2016, bes. 227, 256f., 259–262.

[37] IG XII 4, 1, 209 = Rigsby 1996, Nr. 11; IG XII 4, 1, 213 = Rigsby 1996, Nr. 12; IG XII 4, 1, 211.

[38] IG XII 4, 1, 220 V 66–68, 72.

Verquickung freundschaftlicher und verwandtschaftlicher Bande mit den Hellenen abhebt (Z. 24–35). Beiden ist folglich gemein, dass sie zu erklären trachten, warum sie die koische Asylie überhaupt anerkennen und damit an einem – aus ihrer Warte – dezidiert griechischen Phänomen partizipieren.[39] Damit aber arbeiteten sie sich an der Bestimmung dessen ab, was sie als genuin Griechisch wahrnahmen und konstruierten aus ihrer Position als ‚hellenisierte' Monarchen heraus einen Teil der zeitgenössischen Vorstellung von Gräzität. Sie inszenierten sich durch die Unterstützung der Asyliegesuche einerseits gegenüber den anderen Akteuren der hellenistischen Oikumene als an der Kulturkoiné Beteiligte; andererseits konnte das aus der Partizipation an der Asylie resultierende ‚internationale Renommee', visualisiert über die inschriftlich publizierten Briefe und verbreitet über die zahlreichen Gesandtschaften, auch zur Legitimation im eigenen indigenen Herrschaftsraum genutzt werden.

Abschließend gilt festzuhalten, dass neben der bereits festgestellten Tatsache, dass das königliche Engagement in Bezug auf die territoriale Asylie einer Polis / eines Heiligtums von unterschiedlichen Faktoren abhing, die sich nicht lediglich auf die Absicherung des Territoriums beziehungsweise von Einflusssphären reduzieren lassen, die königlichen Antworten auf das Koer Asyliegesuch verdeutlichen, dass schon vier Jahre nach der ersten königlichen Partizipation am Asyliephänomen, systematisches Ansuchen um Asylie vor Königen Realität wurde. Gerade die Allgegenwärtigkeit der Initiative der Bürger von Kos im Koer Gesuch spricht im Rekurs auf die Abwägung zwischen den zwei für Smyrna vorgestellten Szenarien eher für eine Seleukos II. entweder kurzfristig vorgelegte oder bereits dem Vater präsentierte Asyliebitte der Smyrnaier, denn für eine unaufgeforderte Asylieverleihung des jungen Königs.

4. Die Beispiele Magnesia am Mäander, Teos und Kyzikos

Auch wenn die Beispiele aus Smyrna und Kos zu demonstrieren scheinen, dass sich königliche Partizipation am Asyliephänomen proportional zur faktischen Einbindung der Region in den jeweiligen Einflussbereich entwickelte, darf diese Facette königlicher Anerkennungsmotive nicht überbewertet werden. Dafür scheint das Exemplum Magnesias am Mäander geeignet. Die Stadt war lange Zeit eine grundsätzlich dem seleukidischen Aktionsraum zugerechnete Stadt, wenn auch nach 241 v. Chr. unter Vorherrschaft des Antiochos Hierax. Dieser focht in den 230er Jahren vielfache Kämpfe gegen Attalos I. aus, was zu verheerenden seleukidischen Landverlusten in Kleinasien und

---

[39] Vgl. dazu Michels 2009, 42–49, der den Brief Ziaёlas' von Bithynien geradezu als Modell einer philhellenischen Aktion deutet.

Hellenistische Könige und Asylie in kleinasiatischen Städten

späterer Rückeroberung führte. Magnesia am Mäander scheint in dieser Situation unabhängig geblieben zu sein.[40]

Die Magnesier haben gegen Ende des 3. Jh.s das zweite große Asyliegesuch der hellenistischen Welt initiiert. In zwei Serien aus den Jahren 221 v. Chr. und 208 v. Chr. wurde die Asylie des Heiligtums der Artemis Leukophryene und der Polis bei Poleis, Bünden und Königen umworben.[41] Auch hier antworten fünf hellenistische Monarchen – Antiochos III. und sein Sohn, Philipp V., Ptolemaios IV. und Attalos I.

Im Zuge ihres wiederholten Asyliegesuchs des Jahres 208 v. Chr. haben die Magnesier einen weiten Weg auf sich genommen, um Antiochos III. und seinen Sohn in Antiocheia in der Persis anzutreffen.[42] Zahlreiche auf dem Wege liegende und ansonsten nicht am Phänomen der territorialen Asylie partizipierende Städte sind so zu Interaktionspartnern der Magnesier geworden.[43] Die beiden seleukidischen Könige antworteten den Magnesiern mit Briefen, die nahelegen, dass mit einem städtischen Psephisma ausgestattete Gesandte die Bitte um die Statuserhöhung des lokalen Agons vorgetragen hätten (A. III. Z. 13–16, A. Z. 10–15). Beide Herrscher – und darin liegt ein Hinweis auf die bereits im ersten Gesuch des Jahres 221 v. Chr. anerkannte Asylie –[44] erkannten nur die Erhöhung des magnesischen Agons, nicht aber die Asylie an (A. III. Z. 21–25, A. Z. 17–23): die Vermutung, Antiochos III. hätte die Asylie bereits beim ersten Gesuch vor seinem Aufbruch nach Syrien anerkannt, liegt nahe; für seinen Sohn wäre unter dieser Prämisse Nachahmung des Vaters anzunehmen.[45]

Attalos I. gewährte den Magnesiern ebenfalls nur die Statuserhöhung des Agons (Z. 5–10), gab aber an, Briefe an die ihm unterstehenden Städte ausgesandt zu haben (Z. 19f.), mit der Aufforderung, es ihm gleichzutun. Ob er mit dieser Einflussnahme Erfolg hatte, lässt sich nicht klären, denn die erhaltenen Asylieanerkennungen attalidischer Städte für Magnesia datieren später und fallen so in die Regentschaft der Nachfolger Attalos' I.[46]

---

[40] Ma 1999, 45–48.

[41] Das Problem der Historizität zweier magnesischer Asyliegesuche habe ich anderswo besprochen, vgl. Knäpper 2018, 113–117; unter den aktuellsten Beiträgen zu dieser Fragestellung vgl. etwa Slater-Summa 2006; Thonemann 2007; vgl. dagegen Sosin 2009.

[42] Antiochos III.: Rigsby 1996, Nr. 69; Antiochos S. Antiochos' III.: Rigsby 1996, Nr. 70.

[43] Die Unterschriften dieser Städte sind der Asylieanerkennung aus Antiocheia in der Persis angeschlossen, Rigsby 1996, Nr. 111, 100–111; in zwei Kolumnen, der Platz reicht für zumindest acht Namen.

[44] Vgl. Knäpper 2018, 116f. Die Zugehörigkeit der hier diskutierten Dokumente zum Asyliematerial ergibt sich bereits aus der Publikation im magnesischen Asyliedossier.

[45] Dafür spricht auch, dass in der Asylieanerkennung aus Antiocheia in der Persis die Asylieanerkennung ebenfalls fehlt. Man könnte diese Übereinstimmung mit gemeinsamer Ausfertigung der Dokumente erklären.

[46] Rigsby 1996, Nr. 128; Nr. 130; Nr. 131.

Darüber hinaus ist die Asylie- und Agonerhöhungsanfrage an Ptolemaios IV. zu nennen.[47] Diese wurde vollumfänglich – also inklusive Asylie – gewährt (Z. 7, 12–15), jedoch ohne auf jedwede Art von Förderung der Asylie zu verweisen.

Zuletzt bleibt das Frustrum einer Königsinschrift zu erwähnen, die Philipp V. zugeordnet wird.[48] Die Inschrift ist zwar fast zur Gänze verloren, die chalkidische Anerkennung verweist jedoch auf einen Brief Philipps V., der die Asylieanerkennung vollzogen und ebendies den Politen von Chalkis nahegelegt hätte.[49]

Für die Asylieanerkennung Magnesias ist also zu konstatieren, dass trotz vielfacher Beteiligung von Monarchen, und zweifach ausgesprochener Empfehlung der Asylie keine Korrelationen zwischen königlichem Engagement und der Zugehörigkeit der Stadt zum Einflussgebiet des jeweiligen Monarchen festgestellt werden kann. Es sind gerade die Ptolemäer, die ausführlich auf das Asylieansinnen der Magnesier antworten und es sind die Antigoniden, die eine weitreichende Asylieempfehlung brieflich verbreiten. Attalos I. verweist zwar für die Attaliden, die bekanntermaßen mit den Seleukiden im Clinch um die betreffende Region lagen, auf Briefe an seine Städte; aber erhalten hat sich von dieser Initiative nichts. Auch Antiochos III. und sein Sohn scheinen die Asylie Magnesias nicht gesondert zu fördern, obwohl die Region zum Zeitpunkt des zweiten magnesischen Gesuchs wieder in den Fokus der Seleukiden gerückt war.

Die Förderung eines Asyliegesuchs durch einen hellenistischen Monarchen hing folglich nicht von der Zugehörigkeit zum eigenen Einflussgebiet ab; vielmehr rekurrierte die Promotion bestimmter Asylievorhaben wohl auf für relevant gehaltene Kriterien. So lässt sich für Antiochos III. kurze Zeit nach der Anerkennung des magnesischen Asyliegesuchs ein gänzlich anderes Verhalten im Falle der teischen Bitte um Anerkennung der Asylie feststellen. Es liegen einige Hinweise vor, dass Antiochos III. als Urheber der Asylieanerkennung von Teos fungierte.[50] Im ersten Ehrendekret der Stadt an Antiochos III. wird beschrieben, dass der König Teos – nach der Eroberung der Stadt aus dem pergamenischen Machtbereich wegen der Eusebie gegenüber Dionysos und seines Wunsches, die Dionysischen Techniten wie die Teier von den hohen Beiträgen, die sie leisten mussten, zu befreien (Z. 10–16) – die Asylie verlieh und die Stadt auch vom Tribut gegenüber Attalos I. befreite:

„ἀνῆκε τὴ[ν] πόλιν καὶ τὴγ χώραν ἡμῶν ἱερὰν καὶ ἄσυλον καὶ ἀφορολό- | γητον κ[αὶ] τῶν ἄλλων ὧν ἐφέρομεν συντάξεων βασιλεῖ Ἀττά- | λωι

---

[47] Rigsby 1996, Nr. 71.

[48] Rigsby 1996, Nr. 72.

[49] Rigsby 1996, Nr. 97, 1–8.

[50] SEG 41, 1003 I; vgl. auch Herrmann 1965, Nr. 1 mit Übersetzung und ausführlichem Kommentar.

ὑπεδέξατο ἀπολυθήσεσθαι ἡμᾶς δι᾽ αὐτοῦ" (Z. 18–20). Das habe sich als eine wohlstandsbringende Sicherheitsgarantie ausgewirkt (Z. 20–22).

Es wird deutlich, dass Antiochos III., zumindest von den Teiern, als Urheber der Asylie angesehen wurde. Seine Wohltaten garantierten der Stadt Prosperität und wurden auch als Begründung zur Einrichtung des Herrscherkults für Antiochos und seine Gemahlin Laodike[51] und der Stiftung zahlreicher Statuen für das Herrscherpaar herangezogen.[52]

Wie Seleukos II. als Protektor von Smyrna unternahm Antiochos III. darauf zahlreiche Bemühungen zur Verbreitung der teischen Asylie. So begleitete ein königlicher Gesandter, Hagesandros, die Teier im Rahmen ihrer Asyliewerbung auf Kreta[53] und ein weiterer Gesandter, Menippos, trat selbstständig für die Sache der Teier in Rom ein.[54]

Das teische Asyliansinnen wurde – neben den wohl eher zufällig ins Boot geholten Athamanischen Königen[55] – auch von Philipp V. anerkannt wie unterstützt. Auch er ließ seinen Gesandten Perdikkas die Teier zu den Poleis des Kretischen Koinons, der damaligen Geißel der Ägäis, namentlich Oaxos, Sybrita, Lato, Lato bei Kamara, Istron, dem Sitz des Stammes der Arkader und Allaria, begleiten.[56]

Diese Vermittlung Antiochos' III. wie Philipps V. auf Kreta hatte realpolitisches Gewicht; vielfache Asylieanerkennugen fokussieren auf die vermittelnde Rolle der Gesandten und belegen, dass die erfolgten Asylieanerkennungen ursächlich mit den Gesandten in Zusammenhang gebracht wurden. Die Seleukiden und Antigoniden stützten im Falle von Teos folglich auf sehr proaktive Weise das Asyliegesuch einer westkleinasiatischen Polis. Die Ptolemäer für ihren Teil wurden seitens der Teier nicht einmal angefragt, was mit dem zusehends weiter zurückgedrängten Einfluss derselben in der Ägäis korrespondiert.

Schließlich gilt es an dieser Stelle den einzigen erhaltenen Brief eines hellenistischen Monarchen mit einer Asylieempfehlung einzubringen. Aus den 180er Jahren v. Chr. ist eine Asylieanerkennung für Kyzikos belegt. Neben Asylieanerkennungen aus Rhodos, Medion und zweier nicht sicher zu lokalisierender dorischer Poleis liegt eine Aufforderung Philipps V. an die

---

[51] Sie war seine Kusine, nicht Schwester.

[52] Vgl. Ma 1999, 219–226; zum städtischen Herrscherkult vgl. dazu Habicht 1956, 230–242; vgl. ferner Dreyer 2007, 252f., 315–320, s. auch Anm. 33.

[53] Rigsby 1996, Nr. 138, 9; Nr. 143, 9; Nr. 149, 14.

[54] Rigsby 1996, Nr. 153; zur Diskussion der römischen Asylie Teos' vgl. jüngst Hofmann 2014, 203–213, mit Wiederabdruck, Übersetzung und intensiver Diskussion der Inschrift.

[55] Rigsby 1996, Nr. 135.

[56] Rigsby 1996, Nr. 140, 12; Nr. 141, 3; Nr. 142, 22; Nr. 148, 19; Nr. 149, 18; Nr. 150, 20; Nr. 151, 15; Nr. 152, 19.

Bürger von Dion vor, die Asylie von Kyzikos anzuerkennen.[57] Diese Asylieempfehlung ist die dritte, die sich für Philipp V. anführen lässt. Er scheint Asylieanerkennungen also eher proaktiv begegnet zu sein.

5. Facetten monarchischer Teilhabe an der territorialen Asylie

Gerade im Vergleich der Handlungen Seleukos' II. und Antiochos' III. lässt sich festhalten, dass Asyliegewährungen seitens königlicher Interaktionspartner keinem Automatismus im Sinne eines normierten euergetischen Verhaltenskodex' folgten. Für Seleukos II. sind mit Smyrna und Kos und für Antiochos III. mit Magnesia und Teos je zwei recht zeitnahe Asylieanerkennungen bekannt, die aber hinsichtlich des königlichen Engagements abhängig von kurz- und mittelfristigen strategischen Erwägungen differieren. Dabei ist die Opportunität der Einbindung in ein Asylienetzwerk von zetraler Bedeutung – es scheint, dass gerade die Absteckung eines neuen, in der aktuellen politischen Welt umkämpften ‚Claims' dabei relevanter für die Ausgestaltung und Intensität der Asylieanerkennung war, als eine althergebrachte Zugehörigkeit zum Einflussgebiet des jeweiligen Monarchen. Das bestätigen auch die analysierten Asylieanerkennungen der Ptolemäer, Attaliden und Antigoniden.

Der Grad des an den Tag gelegten königlichen Bemühens um die Asylie einer Polis/eines Heiligtums konnte dabei von der bloßen Anerkennung, über die Empfehlung dieser im eigenen Kerngebiet bis zum diplomatischen Einsatz für die jeweilige Asylie jenseits direkter eigener Einflusssphären oder der Kopplung an weitere Privilegien reichen. Seleukos II. und Antiochos III. wurden dabei *de facto* zum Motor der territorialen Asylie in Smyrna und Teos.

Unter den hellenistischen Herrschern nutzten die Seleukiden territoriale Asylie – das von den griechischen Poleis entwickelte Mittel der *peer polity interaction*[58] also – besonders intensiv. Offenbar stellten sie die erste um Asylie angefragte Dynastie dar und versammelten darüber hinaus die meisten asylieverleihenden Könige auf sich. In ähnlicher Weise, wenn auch deutlich weniger ausgeprägt, traten die Attaliden auf, für die sogar ein eigenes Asyliegesuch überliefert ist. Die Attaliden aber haben den Umgang mit territorialer Asylie mit hoher Wahrscheinlichkeit von den kooperierenden/konkurrierenden Seleukiden gelernt und in der Auseinandersetzung mit

---

[57]   SEG 48, 785 = Pandermalis 1997; die Asylieanerkennung in Antwort auf diesen Brief soll in Dion gefunden worden sein, ist aber bislang nicht publiziert, vgl. Hatzopoulos 2009, 54 (= Hatzopoulos 1996, Nr. 32 = Rigsby 1996, Nr. 171; alle ohne Text).

[58]   Zum diplomatischen Charakter der Asylie vgl. auch Ma 2003, bes. 21–24; Raynor 2016, 255f.; Knäpper 2018, 243–248.

Hellenistische Könige und Asylie in kleinasiatischen Städten 33

denselben um Asia Minor entwickelt. Der attalidische Umgang mit der Asylie könnte sich also aus dem seleukidischen erklären lassen.

Daneben ist nur noch für die Antigoniden eine den Seleukiden vergleichbare, intensive Nutzung der territorialen Asylie auszumachen. Bereits Antigonos Gonatas verbreitete anerkannte Asylie weiter, Philipp V. agierte in gleich drei Fällen proaktiv und unterstützte gerade die Teier mannigfaltig – es scheint also ein gewisses Muster vorzuliegen.

Die Ptolemäer traten in Sachen Asylie deutlich seltener und weniger engagiert in Aktion, auch wenn sie die territoriale Asylie (im griechischen Sinne) kannten und anwendeten.

Betrachtet man die Partizipation der hellenistischen Dynastien an der Asylie, als einem der Gräzität verpflichteten Instrument der Polisdiplomatie, so drängt sich die Frage auf, warum die stärksten Ähnlichkeiten zwischen Seleukiden und Antigoniden zu konstatieren sind. Man könnte eine gemeinsame(re) Linie der gemeinhin als ‚orientalisierter‘ wahrgenommenen Seleukiden und Ptolemäer erwarten. Schließlich wurde sowohl für die Seleukiden, als auch Ptolemäer konstatiert, dass sie sich besonders stark von den Gepflogenheiten des Ostens beziehungsweise Ägyptens haben beeinflussen lassen.[59] Doch während die Seleukiden sich stark in Sachen Asylie einsetzten und darin den Antigoniden glichen, blieben die Ptolemäer, selbst zu Zeiten stärkeren Einflusses in der Ägäis, zurückhaltend.

Damit aber fügt die Auswertung der königlichen Verhaltensmuster in Zusammenhang mit der Gewährung der territorialen Asylie ein Mosaiksteinchen zur differenzierteren Betrachtung der Aufnahme und Perpetuierung östlicher und westlicher Muster durch hellenistische Könige hinzu.[60] Die königliche Anwendung griechischer oder außergriechischer Gepflogenheiten folgte Opportunitäts- und Praktikabilitätserwägungen: Antiochos III. etwa konnte sich βασιλεὺς Ἀντίοχος Μέγας nennen,[61] seine Frau als Schwestergemahlin konzeptualisieren[62] und ein achaimenidischen Mustern folgendes Hofzeremoniell vorziehen;[63] zeitgleich aber konnte er ebenso auf dezidiert griechische Weise an der zwischenstaatlichen Diplomatie der kleinasiatischen Poleis partizipieren, indem er territoriale Asylie verlieh und dabei weitaus mehr Gemeinsamkeiten mit den Antigoniden als mit den Ptolemäern an den Tag legte. Mit anderen Worten: ihr monarchisches Selbstverständnis erlaubte den Seleukiden, und auch den Attaliden, die in dieser Hinsicht von den ersteren ge-

---

[59] Zur Entwicklung seleukidischer Muster nach ptolemäischem Vorbild, vgl. Dreyer 2007, 315f.; zu vorderorientalischen Traditionen der Seleukiden vgl. Beaulieu 2014; Plischke 2014, 325–334.

[60] Zu methodischen Erwägungen in diesem Zusammenhang vgl. mit Fokus auf Babylonien Mittag 2014.

[61] Vgl. dazu die Zusammenstellung und Diskussion der Zeugnisse bei Ma 1999, 272–276.

[62] SEG 41, 1003 I 36, 46f.; II 11f., 64, 71.

[63] Vgl. Wiesehöfer 1996, 30f.; vgl. jüngst auch Richter 2017.

lernt haben, jedes notwendige diplomatische Parkett zu bedienen – das ‚orientalische‘ wie das griechische – um die eigenen (geo)strategischen Interessen und Pläne geschickt zu realisieren, während die Antigoniden und Ptolemäer in diesem Zusammenhang eher zum ‚Reintypus‘ griechischen beziehungsweise außergriechischen Verhaltens tendierten.

Darüber hinaus erlauben die Asylieanerkennungen hellenisierter Monarchen – von der anderen Seite her betrachtet – einen Einblick in die Art und Weise, wie die mit dem Hellenentum in Kontakt gekommenen ‚indigenen‘ Könige die Asylie verstanden und damit auch, wie sie das Verhältnis zwischen formal freien Poleis und Königen werteten und für sich nutzbar machten. Sie konnten sich überdies, neben all den auch für sie relevanten (geo)strategischen Interessen, als Privilegienverleiher in einem griechischen Referenzrahmen inszenieren, was sicher auch in ihrem eigenen Wirkungskreis positive Effekte barg.

Zudem lassen die Asyliegesuche auch einen spezifischen Einblick in die von diplomatischen Kontakten ausgelösten Prozesse von kulturellem Austausch zwischen den weiter östlich gelegenen Poleis und der ‚griechischen Welt‘ zu. Dabei wurden, gerade in Kleinasien, wirkmächtige kulturelle wie politische Vorstellungen der Griechen, wie etwa ein zumindest dem Anschein nach freies und auf Egalität ausgerichtetes Agieren der Poleis auf der politischen Bühne, aber auch die Bedeutsamkeit der überregionalen Heiligtümer und Agone bedient, was die Asyliegesuche und -anerkennungen zu einem Mittel der Etablierung der griechischen Kultur als gemeinsame Grundlage, als ‚Middle Ground‘, des Kontaktes zwischen den vielen, kulturell unterschiedlich geprägten Akteuren, und zwar jenseits indigener Eigenheiten, ermöglichte.

Bibliographie

Boffo, L. 1985. I re ellenistici e i centri religiosi dell' Asia minore. Florenz.

Chaniotis, A. 1999. „Empfängerformular und Urkundenfälschung. Bemerkungen zum Urkundendossier von Magnesia am Mäander", in: R.G. Khoury (Hg.), Urkunden und Urkundenformulare im Klassischen Altertum und in den orientalischen Kulturen, Heidelberg, 51–69.

Chaniotis, A. 2005. War in the Hellenistic World. A Social and Cultural History. Malden.

Coşkun, A. 2016. Laodike I, Berenike Phernophoros, Dynastic Murders, in: A. Coşkun und A. McAuley (Hgg.), Seleukid Royal Women. Creation, Representation and Distortion of Hellenistic Queenship in the Seleukid Empire, Stuttgart, 107–134.

Dreyer, B. 1999. Untersuchungen zur Geschichte des spätklassischen Athen (322– ca. 230 v. Chr.). Stuttgart.

Dreyer, B. 2007. Die römische Nobilitätsherrschaft und Antiochos III. Hennef.

Dunand, F. 1972. Droit d'asile et refuge dans les temples en Égypte lagide, in: Hommages à la mémoire de Serge Sauneron II, 77–97.

Dunand, F. 1980. L'exode rural en Égypte hellénistique, in : Ktema 5, 137–150.

Grainger, J. D. 2010. The Syrian Wars. Leiden.

Herrmann, P. 1965. Antiochos der Große und Teos, in: Anadolu 9, 29–160.

Hofmann, V. 2014. Mimesis vel aemulatio? Die hellenistischen Anfänge der offiziellen römischen Epistolographie und ihre machtpolitischen Implikationen, in: ZRG RA 131, 177–215.

Hofmann, V. 2015. Communications between City and King in the Hellenistic East, in: S. Procházka und L. Reinfandt und S. Tost (Hgg.), Official Epistolography and the Language(s) of Power, Wien, 139–152.

Knäpper, K. 2018. HIEROS KAI ASYLOS. Die territoriale Asylie im Hellenismus in ihrem historischen Kontext. Stuttgart.

Ma, J. 2000. Antiochos III. and the Cities of Western Asia Minor. Oxford.

Ma, J. 2003. Peer Polity Interaction in the Hellenistic Age, in: Past & Present 180, 9–39.

Meyer, M. 2010. Die Aphrodite Stratonikis in Smyrna und die Asylie der Stadt, in: Jahrbuch für Numismatik und Geldgeschichte 60, 35–70.

Michels, C. 2009. Kulturtransfer und monarchischer ‚Philhellenismus'. Bithynien, Pontos und Kappadokien in hellenistischer Zeit. Göttingen.

Orth, W. 1977. Königlicher Machtanspruch und städtische Freiheit. Untersuchungen zu den politischen Beziehungen zwischen den ersten Seleukidenherrschern und den Städten des westlichen Kleinasiens. München.

Pandermalis, D. 1997, Dion, in : AEMΘ 11, 234–235.

Piejko, F. 1988. Rez. von: J. und L. Robert, Fouilles d'Amyzon en Carie I. Exploration, monnaies et inscriptions, in : Gnomon 57, 608–621.

Piejko, F. 1990. Episodes from the Third Syrian War in a Gurob Papyrus, 246 B.C., in: APF 36, 13–27.

Rigsby, K. J. 1996. Asylia. Territorial Inviolability in the Hellenistic World. Berkeley u.a.

Palme, B. 2003. Asyl und Schutzbrief im spätantiken Ägypten, in: M. Dreher (Hg.), Das antike Asyl. Kultische Grundlagen, rechtliche Ausgestaltung und politische Funktion, Köln, 203–236.

Pironti, G. 2005. Aphrodite dans le domaine d'Arès. Éléments pour un dialogue entre mythe et culte, in : Kernos 18, 167–184.

Plischke, S. 2014. Die Seleukiden und Iran. Die seleukidische Herrschaftspolitik in den östlichen Satrapien. Wiesbaden.

Raynor, B. 2016. *Theorodokoi, Asylia*, and Makedonian Cities, in: GRBS 56, 225–262.

Richter, S. 2017. Persianism under the early Seleukid Kings? The Royal Title 'Great King', in: M.J. Versluys und R. Strootman (Hgg.), Persianism in Antiquity, Stuttgart, 155–168.

Robert, J. und L. 1983. Fouilles d'Amyzon en Carie. Paris.

Slater, W. J. und D. Summa. 2006. Crowns at Magnesia, in: GRBS 46, 275–299.

Sosin, J.D. 2009. Magnesian Inviolability, in: TAPHA 139, 369–410.

von Steuben, H. und K. Bringmann (Hgg.). 1995. Schenkungen hellenistischer Herrscher an griechische Städte und Heiligtümer I. Zeugnisse und Kommentare. Berlin.

Thonemann, P. 2007. Magnesia and the Greeks of Asia (I. Magnesia 16.16), in: GRBS 47, 151–160.

Traulsen, C. 2004. Das sakrale Asyl in der Alten Welt. Zur Schutzfunktion des Heiligen von König Salomo bis zum Codex Theodosianus.Tübingen.

Wallensten, J. 2003. ΑΦΡΟΔΙΤΗΙ ΑΝΕΘΗΚΕΝ ΑΡΞΑΣ. A Study of Dedications to Aphrodite from Greek Magistrates. Lund.

Wiesehöfer, J. 1996. Discordia et Defectio – Dynamis kai Pithanourgia. Die frühen Seleukiden und Iran, in: B. Funck (Hg.), Hellenismus. Beiträge zur Erforschung von Akkulturation und politischer Ordnung in den Staaten des hellenistischen Zeitalters, Tübingen, 29–56.

von Woeß, F. 1923. Das Asylwesen Ägyptens in der Ptolemäerzeit und die spätere Entwicklung. Eine Einführung in das Rechtsleben Ägyptens, besonders der Ptolemäerzeit. München.

von Woeß, F. 1926. ἀσυλία, in: ZRG R.A. 46, 32–67.

Zu den postseleukidischen Münzen im südlichen Zweistromland

Peter Franz Mittag

Kurz nach der Mitte des 2. Jhs. v. Chr. verloren die Seleukiden in verschiedenen Schritten die Kontrolle über das südliche Zweistromland, das seit 312 v. Chr. eine Kernregion des Seleukidenreiches gebildet hatte und durch die Gründung von griechischen *poleis* erkennbar hellenisiert worden war. Insbesondere Seleukeia am Tigris ist hier hervorzuheben, aber auch altehrwürdige Städte wie Babylon oder Susa beherbergten Bürger mit griechischem Bürgerrecht.[1] Es ist daher zunächst nicht weiter erstaunlich, dass die von den politischen Nachfolgern der Seleukiden geprägten Münzen viele hellenistische bzw. seleukidische Elemente aufweisen.[2] Ein weiterer Grund für diesen im Folgenden näher zu untersuchenden Befund liegt im primären Zweck der Münzen: Sie sollten den Zahlungsverkehr vereinfachen bzw. gewährleisten und Abweichungen von der üblichen Gestaltung konnten die Akzeptanz der Münzen durchaus negativ beeinträchtigen. Ähnlich gelagerte Fälle radikaler politischer Umbrüche zeigen dies mit aller wünschenswerten Deutlichkeit. Das vielleicht drastischste Beispiel sind die Münzen, die die Yuèzhī nach der Eroberung Baktriens prägen ließen und die in ihrer Gestaltung weitgehend denjenigen der von ihnen besiegten baktrischen Könige angeglichen wurden.[3] Ein weiteres Beispiel bilden die von den Römern nach der Provinzialisierung Syriens dort geprägten Tetradrachmen, die bis auf zusätzliche Monogramme den als Vorbilder dienenden Tetradrachmen des längst verstorbenen seleukidischen Königs Philippos I. zum Verwechseln ähneln.[4]

Auch wenn diese Beispiele in ihren jeweiligen Kontexten sicher Extreme darstellen, so gilt es doch auch bei den Münzen, die nach dem Ende der seleukidischen Herrschaft im südlichen Zweistromland geprägt wurden, stets zu berücksichtigen, inwieweit auch hier (Seh-)Gewohnheiten die Gestaltung der postseleukidischen Münzen beeinflusst haben könnten. Interessanterweise lassen sich in den einzelnen Regionen sehr unterschiedliche Entwicklungen feststellen. Ein Überblick über die jeweiligen Prägungen soll dies

---

[1] Zu Babylon s. etwa Boiy 2004, 206–209; zu Susa: Le Rider 1965; Dąbrowa 1998, 419; Martinez-Sève 2002, 31–54; Canali de Rossi 2004, Nr. 204–223 (griechische Inschriften aus arsakidischer Zeit); van't Hoff 2006, 5. Neben Susa (Antiocheia am Eulaios) zog sicher auch Seleukeia am Hedyphon griechische Siedler an: Cohen 1978, 18; Sherwin-White und Kuhrt 1993, 20; Dąbrowa 1998, 418.

[2] Die neuen Herren nahmen dezidiert Rücksicht auf die bestehenden Strukturen, was sich im Bereich der Verwaltung, aber auch der Religion und Kunst greifen lässt; vgl. stellvertretend den Brief Artabanos' II. an Susa (Rougemont 2012, no. 3), siehe grundsätzlich die knappen Bemerkungen bei Kosmin 2014, 256–258.

[3] Bopearachchi 1991, Hermaios Sér. 10–22.

[4] RPC 4124; zu den Vorbildern s. SC 2459–2470.

Peter Franz Mittag

zunächst verdeutlichen. Anschließend wird – ausgehend von Richard Whites *middle ground*-Theorie – eine Deutung dieses Befundes versucht.

1. Überblick über die postseleukidischen Münzen im südlichen Zweistromland

Die Herrschaft im südlichen Zweistromland wurde nach der Zurückdrängung der Seleukiden aus dieser Region von drei Königreichen beansprucht: von den Arsakiden, den Kamnaskiriden, die in der Elymais herrschten, und den sogenannten Königen der Charakene, mit einem Machtzentrum in der ehemaligen seleukidischen Satrapie Mesene. Insbesondere die 140er und 130er Jahre waren geprägt von wechselnden Herrschaftsverhältnissen. In diesem Zeitraum gelang es mehrfach Königen verschiedener Herrscherhäuser, sich der gleichen Prägestätten zu bemächtigen. Den Arsakiden kommt zweifellos der größte Anteil am Zusammenbruch der seleukidischen Herrschaft in Mesopotamien zu, dennoch soll aus chronologischen Gründen mit den Kamnaskiriden begonnen werden.

1.1. Münzprägung der Kamnaskariden

Auch wenn die Quellenlage zur Geschichte der Elymais keineswegs als gut bezeichnet werden kann, so sind die wichtigsten Aspekte doch weitgehend klar. Um 147 v. Chr. gelang es Kamnaskires, den seleukidischen Satrapen zu vertreiben.[5] 145 v. Chr. operierte Kamnaskires erfolgreich in Babylonien,[6] wurde aber bereits 145/4 v. Chr. von Demetrios II. wieder zurückgedrängt[7]; nach dessen Gefangennahme durch die Arsakiden konnte Kamnaskires die Kontrolle über Susa zurückgewinnen und im Dezember 141 v. Chr. auch Apameia am Silhu einnehmen[8]. Bis zum endgültigen Sieg der Arsakiden über die elymaischen Könige im Jahr 133/132 v. Chr.[9] scheinen auch Okkonapses und Tigraios jeweils kurzzeitig in Susa geherrscht zu haben.[10] Die arsakidische Oberhoheit über die Susiana konnte um 127/6 v. Chr. anscheinend Dareios

---

[5]   Le Rider 1965, 35.
[6]   Sachs und Hunger 1996, -144 obv. 18' und -144 rev. 20–22; hierzu und zu den folgenden Ereignissen: Potts 2002, 349–362.
[7]   van't Haaff 2007, 4 f.
[8]   Sachs und Hunger 1996 -140 C obv. 35–38 und -140 rev. 30'–35'
[9]   Sachs und Hunger 1996, -132 D ‚obv.' 8'–10': „That month, I heard ... Susa they made, and killed many troops of the Elamite in figthing, and the ... they ...".
[10] Die Datierung von Okkonapses und Tigraios ist umstritten. Assar 2006, 93 Anm. 19 datiert die Herrschaft des Okkonapses in die Jahre 144/3 v. Chr., Le Rider 1965, 68 und 346–7 sprach sich noch für eine Datierung um 162/1 v. Chr. aus (dort wegen der Münzlegenden als Hyknapses bezeichnet).

nochmals in Frage stellen.[11] Während von diesen Herrschern Münzen existieren, scheint Pittit, gegen den die Arsakiden 125/124 v. Chr. einen Feldzug unternahmen,[12] keine eigenen Münzen geprägt zu haben.

Die elymaischen Münzen entstanden durchweg in der Münzstätte Susa, die bereits in seleukidischer Zeit tätig war, und sind sehr eng an seleukidische Vorbilder angelehnt. So zeigt die Vorderseite jeweils den Kopf des Königs mit Diadem nach rechts. Für die Gestaltung der Rückseiten griff man bei den Tetradrachmen auf die beiden seleukidischen Haupttypen Zeus Nikephoros und Apollon zurück, wobei Apollon deutlich häufiger erscheint (Abb. 2-4). Auch die letzten seleukidischen Tetradrachmen im Namen des Demetrios II., die in Susa geprägt wurden, zeigen Apollon auf dem Omphalos sitzend mit Pfeil und Bogen (Abb. 1),[13] so dass sich ein nahtloser Übergang feststellen lässt.

Abb. 1: Demetrios II., Tetradrachme, Susa, SC 1995; CNG, Triton XVIII, 6.1.2015, no. 165

Abb. 2: Kamnaskires I., Tetradrachme, Susa, van't Haaff 2.1; CNG, Triton VII, 12.1.2004, no. 518

Abb. 3: Kamnaskires II., Tetradrachme, Susa, van't Haaff 2.1; H. D. Rauch, Auktion 88, 7.5.2011, Nr. 211

Abb. 4: Dareios, Tetradrachme, 127/6 v. Chr., van't Haaff 6.1; Peus, Auktion 368, 25.4.2001, Nr. 330

---

11 Zur problematischen Rekonstruktion der Ereignisse siehe van't Haaf 2007, 5; Assar 2006, 108 (vielleicht nutzte Dareios die arsakidische Schwäche, die mit der Eroberung Babyloniens durch Hyspaosines einherging); Alram 1986, 138 f.; die älteren Ansätze und Argumente bietet Mørkholm 1965, 148–152.
12 Sachs und Hunger 1996 -124 B obv. 19', -124 B rev. 12'–14' und 17'–18'.
13 Houghton und Lorber 2002 und 2008 (im Folgenden = SC), 1995; vgl. entsprechend SC 1867: Tetradrachmen des Alexander Balas, ca. 150–147 v. Chr.

Die Drachmen zeigen in der Regel ebenfalls Apollo, in einem Fall auch Artemis/Ischtar.[14] Die Variationsbreite ist auf den Buntmetallmünzen deutlich höher, doch auch hier dominieren seleukidische Vorbilder.[15]

Abb. 5: Kamnaskires III., Tetradrachme, 82–74 v. Chr., van't Haaff 7.1; Lanz, Auktion 162, 6.6.2016, Nr. 178

Abb. 6: Kamnaskires IV., Tetradrachme, van't Haaff 8.1; Hirsch, Auktion 323, 22.9.2016, Nr. 2234

Abb. 7: Kamnaskires V., Tetradrachme, 46/5 v. Chr., van't Haaff 9.1; Roma Numismatics Ltd, Auktion XII, 29.9.2016, Nr. 413

Wie bereits betont, verloren die elymaischen Könige abgesehen von den kurzen Zwischenspielen des Dareios, der vielleicht zu dieser Dynastie gehörte, und Pittit im Jahr 133/132 v. Chr. die Herrschaft über Susa und damit auch ihre einzige Münzprägestätte. Als um 80 v. Chr. die Münzprägung im Namen elymaischer Könige fortgesetzt wurde, hatten sich die Rahmenbedingungen bereits maßgeblich geändert und die Vorbilder der Münzen bildeten in starkem Maß die arsakidischen Prägungen. Die Könige trugen nun *torques* und bestickte Kleidung. Allerdings verzichteten sie auf die Tiara, die die Arsakiden zu dieser Zeit meist trugen, und die Rückseitengestaltung orientierte sich weiterhin an hellenistischen Vorbildern; hier erscheint unter Kamnaskires III. (ca. 82/1–73/2 v. Chr.) und Kamnaskires IV. (ca. 63/2–54/3 v. Chr.) Zeus Nikephoros (Abb. 5–6), vielleicht in Anlehnung an die Tetradrachmen

---

[14] Van't Haaff 2007, type 2.2.

[15] Pferdekopf (van't Haaff 2.3 und 4.2), Stierkopf (van't Haaff 4.4), Anker (van't Haaff 2.4), Dreifuß (van't Haaff 2.5), Füllhorn (van't Haaff p 2.6), Adler (van't Haaff 2.7 und 5.5), Köcher und Bogen (van't Haaff 2.8-9), Tyche (van't Haaff 2.10), Nike (van't Haaff 2.11; vgl. SC 1995A), Elefant (van't Haaff S. 55); Apollon (van't Haaff 3.2), Eberkopf (van't Haaff 5.4), Hermes (van't Haaff 4.5), Herme (van't Haaff 5.6), Palmzweig (van't Haaff 5.7), Göttin mit langem Zepter (van't Haaff 4.3) und Blitzbündel (van't Haaff 5.3). Lediglich Artemis/Ischtar (van't Haaff 5.2; vgl. SC 1868: Alexander Balas, ca. 150–147 v. Chr.) fällt aus dem rein hellenistischen Rahmen.

Antiochos' IV.[16] Manche Tetradrachmen tragen zudem auf der Vorderseite einen Anker, das seleukidische Erkennungszeichen schlechthin. Noch häufiger als auf den Münzen Kamnaskires' III. findet sich der Anker auf den Prägungen Kamnaskires' V. (ca. ca. 54/3–33/2 v. Chr.), dessen Rückseiten nun nicht mehr Zeus Nikephoros tragen, sondern eine diademierte und drapierte Büste seines Vorgängers (Abb. 7).[17] In der Folgezeit verwilderte dieser Münztyp und wurde im frühen zweiten Jh. n. Chr. durch einen neuen, nun völlig unhellenistischen Münztyp ersetzt.

1.2. Die Münzprägung der Arsakiden

Die Arsakiden eroberten ab den 240er Jahren v. Chr. zunehmend Teile des zentralen Seleukidenreiches. Da sie vorher keine eigenen Münzen geprägt hatten, orientierten sie sich von Beginn an an seleukidischen Vorbildern, kopierten diese jedoch nicht einfach, sondern wandelten sie in wesentlichen Punkten ab.

Abb. 8: Arsakes I., Drachme, Nisa(?), Sellwood 2.1; CNG, Triton XIII, 5.1.2010, no. 502

Die Vorderseite der frühesten arsakidischen Münzen zeigt einen Kopf mit Diadem nach rechts (später nach links), die Rückseite eine nach links sitzende männliche Gestalt, die einen Bogen hält und damit an die typische seleukidische Münzdarstellung des auf dem Omphalos sitzenden Apollon erinnert, der Pfeil und Bogen trägt (Abb. 8, vgl. Abb. 1). Zudem ist die Legende wie bei den seleukidischen Münzen (mehr oder weniger) vertikal links und rechts des Rückseitenbildes angebracht; allerdings lautet die Legende zunächst wohl ΑΡΣΑΚΟΥ (zuweilen mit dem aramäischen Zusatz krny = Befehlshaber) bzw. ΑΡΣΑΚΟΥ ΑΥΤΟΚΡΑΤΟΡΟΣ, die Arsakiden verzichteten also bewusst auf den Königstitel, den die Seleukiden stets trugen.[18] Trotz der Ähnlichkeiten zu den Prägungen der Seleukiden, zeigen sich weitere signifikante Unterschiede. Der Kopf der Vorderseite trägt unter dem Diadem einen *baschlik*, eine

---

[16] Van't Haaf 2007, type 7.1–8.3.
[17] Van't Haaf 2007, type 9.1–9.2.
[18] Sellwood ²1980, 1.1–4.1; entgegen der Annahme von Sellwood dürfte die Legende ΑΡΣΑΚΟΥ älter sein als diejenigen mit dem Zusatz *autokrator*; vgl. etwa Curtis 2012, 68.

kapuzenartige Haube mit langen Wangenlaschen; zudem besitzt er einen Ohrring.[19] Die Gestalt der Rückseite trägt offenbar keine griechische Kleidung und sitzt nicht wie Apollon auf dem *omphalos*, sondern auf einem Hocker. Daher wurde zuweilen angenommen, sowohl die Vorder- als auch die Rückseite zeigten den arsakidischen Herrscher oder ein Mitglied der herrscherlichen Familie. Häufig wird die Figur der Rückseite als der Stammvater der Arsakiden, Arsakes, gedeutet.[20] In der neueren Forschung wurden einige der nicht-griechischen Bildelemente auf achaimenidische Vorbilder zurückgeführt. Rolf Strootman, verbandt die Kopfbedeckung mit Satrapendarstellungen des 4. Jhs. aus Kleinasien und leitete daraus ab, dass ähnlich wie diese Satrapen auch die Arsakiden die Oberherrschaft des Großkönigs, nun also der Seleukiden, anerkannt hätten.[21] Die große zeitliche und geographische Distanz sowie deutliche ikonographische Unterschiede zwischen den kleinasiatischen Satrapenkappen und dem arsakidischen *baschlik* nähren aber Zweifel an einem so weitreichenden Schluss. Zwar soll damit keineswegs ausgeschlossen werden, dass sich die Arsakiden an älteren – und wohl auch achaimenidischen – Vorbildern orientierten, da Darstellungen einer ‚echten' arsakidischen Tracht jedoch fehlen, lässt sich nicht mehr entscheiden, was an den Münzdarstellungen Arsakes' I. arsakidisch und was achaimenidisch ist.

Die Drachmen des Nachfolgers, Arsakes' II. (ca. 211–191 v. Chr.), verzichten auf den Titel *autokrator* und die Rückseitendarstellung wurde entgegen der seleukidischen Tradition nach rechts gedreht (Abb. 9).[22] Trüge der Kopf der Vorderseite kein Diadem und wäre die Legende nicht auf Griechisch verfasst, würde nichts mehr an die seleukidischen Münzen erinnern. Das ist im Vergleich mit der Münzprägung der Kamnaskiriden eine bemerkenswert schnelle Entwicklung zur Eigenständigkeit.

Abb. 9: Arsakes II., Drachme, Rhagai(?), 211–191 v. Chr., Sellwood 6.1; CNG, Triton XIII, 5.1.2010, no. 507

Abb. 10: Mithradates I., Drachme, Hekatompylos, Sellwood 10.1; Hess Divo AG, Auktion 327, 22.10.2014, Nr. 81

---

19 Sellwood 1.1.
20 Vgl. etwa Günther 2012, 59.
21 Strootman 2017, 187–190. Vgl. auch Sinisi, 2012, 280.
22 Sellwood 5.1–6.1.

Abb. 11: Mithradates I., Drachme, Nisa,
Sellwood 11.3; CNG, Triton XIII, 5.1.2010, no. 529

Deutliche Entwicklungsschübe erfuhr die arsakidische Münzprägung nach einer Pause von mindestens 20 Jahren erst wieder unter Mithradates I. (ca. 171–138[23] v. Chr.), der das arsakidische Herrschaftsgebiet deutlich ausweiten konnte. Nun wurden – zumeist in den neu eroberten Münzstätten wie Ekbatana und Susa – auch verstärkt Bronzemünzen und kleinere Silbermünzen als Drachmen geprägt, für die Entwicklung entscheidend blieben aber die Drachmen. Zunächst folgten die Drachmen weitgehend dem Erscheinungsbild aus der Zeit Arsakes' II., allerdings sitzt die Gestalt der Rückseite nun nicht mehr auf einem Stuhl, sondern auf einem *omphalos* (Abb. 10).[24] Insofern orientierten sich die Münzen nun stärker an seleukidischen Vorbildern. Ab einem unbekannten Zeitpunkt wurde die Legende zudem von ΑΡΣΑΚΟΥ zu ΑΡΣΑΚΟΥ ΒΑΣΙΛΕΩΣ erweitert,[25] Mithradates I. nutzte nun also den (hellenistischen) Königstitel, den seine Vorgänger bisher vermieden hatten. Wohl nach der Eroberung von Ekbatana nahm der König sogar den Titel Großkönig (Münzlegende: ΑΡΣΑΚΟΥ ΒΑΣΙΛΕΩΣ ΜΕΓΑΛΟΥ) sowie die Epitheta *theos* und *theopator* an.[26] Zwar verzichtet Mithradates I. später auf den *baschlik* und erscheint nun nur noch mit Diadem, doch trägt er einen deutlichen *torques* und bestickte Kleidung, ist also vom Kinn abwärts 'unseleukidisch' (Abb. 11). Zudem zeigen seine Münzen einen vergleichsweise langen Bart, der in dieser Form auf keine hellenistischen Vorbilder zurückzuführen ist.[27] Selbst nach der Eroberung von Seleukeia am Tigris und der Übernahme der dortigen Prägetätigkeit

---

[23] Assar 2006, 87–158, hier: 94–98, hält einen Tod Mithradates I. im Jahr 132 v. Chr. für wahrscheinlicher.
[24] Sellwood 7.1–8.1. Die Darstellung erinnert abgesehen von der Sitzgelegenheit nun stärker an achaimenidische Vorbilder, insbesondere an die Datames-Prägungen des 4. Jhs. v. Chr. Ob damit allerdings eine direkte Anlehnung an die Achaimeniden propagiert werden sollte, scheint eher unwahrscheinlich zu sein, da Datames Satrap in Kilikien und Kappadokien war und seine Münzen im Mesopotamien des fortgeschrittenen 2. Jhs. v. Chr. nicht soweit bekannt gewesen sein dürften, als dass man durch eine Bezugnahme eine Botschaft hätte verbreiten können, die von den Nutzern hätte verstanden werden können. Vgl. auch Wick 2008, 12–15.
[25] Sellwood 9.1.
[26] Sellwood 10.
[27] Seleukidische Könige trugen zwar gelegentlich Bärte. In der Regel waren diese aber vergleichsweise kurz. Die einzige Ausnahme bildet Houghton und Lorber 2002, 685–6 und 711–2 (Seleukos II. mit langem Bart). Siehe hierzu Mittag 2021.

(5.7.141 v. Chr.) behielt Mithradates den langen Bart bei, obwohl er auf den *torques* und auf die bestickte Kleidung verzichtete sowie sich hinsichtlich der Rückseitenmotive stärker an seleukidische Vorbilder anlehnte.

Abb. 12: Mithradates I., Tetradrachme, Seleukeia am Tigris, 141–139/8 v. Chr.; Sellwood 13.2; Peus, Auktion 413, 29.10.2014, Nr. 139

Abb. 13: Mithradates I., Drachme, Seleukeia am Tigris, ca. 141–139/8 v. Chr.; Sellwood 13.10 (Zeus *aetophoros*); CNG, Triton XIII, 5.1.2010, no. 534

Die in Seleukeia hergestellten Tetradrachmen zeigen auf den Rückseiten einen nach links stehenden, nackten Herakles mit Trinkgefäß, Löwenfell und Keule sowie das zusätzliche Epitheton *philhellen*, die Drachmen den thronenden Zeus *aetophoros* (Abb. 12–13).[28] Es lässt sich somit mit zunehmendem Vorstoß Mithradates' I. in das südliche Zweistromland eine verstärkte Adaption hellenistischer Traditionen feststellen, allerdings fanden mit dem stehenden Herakles und dem Epitheton *philhellen* auch neue nicht-seleukidische Elemente Eingang in die arsakidische Münzprägung, insofern ergibt sich ein komplexes Gesamtbild. Dieser Trend setzt sich unter Phraates II. fort, dem es 133/2 v. Chr. gelang, Susa zu erobern.[29]

Abb. 14: Phraates II., Tetradrachme, Susa, 132–127 v. Chr., Sellwood 14.2; Assar 2006, Abb. 5

Abb. 15: Phraates II., Tetradrachme, Seleukeia am Tigris, Sellwood 17.1; CNG, Triton V, 15.1.2002, no. 1561

---

[28] Sellwood 13.
[29] Schuol 2000, 274.

Postseleukidische Münzen im südlichen Zweistromland 45

Abb. 16: Demetrios I., Tetradrachme, Antiocheia am Orontes, 162–156 v. Chr.; SC 1635; Hess-Divo AG, Auktion 328, 22.5.2015, Nr. 69

Abb. 17: Phraates II., Drachme, Nisa, Sellwood 16.6; Peus, Auktion 376, 29.10.2003, Nr. 595

Die dort produzierten Münzen sind so 'seleukidisch' wie keine vorangegangenen (und folgenden) arsakidischen Münzen. Die Tetradrachmen zeigen auf der Vorderseite den 'klassischen' diademierten Kopf nach rechts mit kurzem Wangenbart, wie er auch auf kurz darauf geprägten seleukidischen Münzen zu finden ist,[30] die Rückseite ziert ein auf dem *omphalos* sitzender Apollo mit Pfeil und Bogen (Abb. 14), ebenso wie bei den vorangehenden kamnaskiridischen Münzen aus Susa (s.o.).[31] Etwas weniger 'seleukidisch' sind die Münzen aus Seleukeia am Tigris, die vielleicht im Herbst 129 v. Chr. entstanden (Abb. 15)[32]: Der Bart ist hier etwas länger, der König trägt einen Ohrring und die seit Demetrios I. zuweilen zu findende thronende Tyche (Abb. 16) ist durch eine ähnlich gestaltete, aber sicher männliche Gottheit ersetzt (siehe hierzu unten).[33] In den nördlichen Prägestätten folgen seine Münzen jedoch dem dort üblichen Schema und zeigen auf den Rückseiten die arsakidische Gestalt mit Bogen auf einem *omphalos* sitzend (Abb. 17).[34] In den unterschiedlichen Prägestätten wurden unter Phraates II. also sehr verschiedene Bildmotive verwendet.

Abb. 18: Artabanos I., Tetradrachme, Susa, 125 v. Chr.; Assar 2006, fig. 22

Abb. 19: Artabanos I., Tetradrachme, Seleukeia am Tigris, 125 v. Chr., Sellwood 21.1; CNG, Triton XX, 10.1.2017, no. 418

---

[30] Vgl. etwa die Münzen Antiochos' IX. der Jahre 114/3 v. Chr.: SC 2346 f.
[31] Sellwood 14.
[32] Zur Datierung s. Assar 2006, 101 und 105.
[33] Sellwood 17.
[34] Sellwood 16.

Interessanterweise übernahm sein Nachfolger Artabanos I. (126–122 v. Chr.) nach der erneuten Eroberung von Susa 126/5 v. Chr. für die in seinem Namen dort geprägten Tetradrachmen als Rückseitenmotiv wieder Apollo (Abb. 18). Der bisherige Pfeil wurde jedoch gegen einen Palmzweig ausgetauscht, der wohl als Hinweis auf die Wiedereroberung der Stadt gedeutet werden kann. Auch in Seleukeia am Tigris sind zumindest die Rückseiten nun völlig seleukidisch, da sie die 'traditionelle' Tyche zeigen (Abb. 19). Allerdings werden auf der Vorderseite im Vergleich zu Phraates II. die nicht-seleukidischen Elemente verstärkt: Der König trägt nun neben dem Ohrring einen mehrfachen Halsring und ein verziertes Obergewand.[35] Arsakes X. (122/1 v. Chr.) und Mithradates II. (121–91 v. Chr.) setzten diese zweigesichtige Münzprägung (Vorderseite stark 'arsakisiert'; Rückseite rein seleukidisch) in Susa fort (Abb. 20). Mithradates II. nutzte aber ab dem Jahr 109/8 v. Chr. den Großkönigtitel (ΒΑΣΙΛΕΩΣ ΒΑΣΙΛΕΩΝ ΑΡΣΑΚΟΥ)[36], gegen Ende seiner Herrschaft den erweiterten Titel ΒΑΣΙΛΕΩΣ (ΒΑΣΙΛΕΩΝ) ΜΕΓΑΛΟΥ ΑΡΣΑΚΟΥ ΕΠΙΦΑΝΟΥΣ und trug eine Tiara sowie ein Diadem (Abb. 21)[37]. In Seleukeia am Tigris führte er zudem das klassische arsakidische (Drachmen-)Rückseitenmotiv ein (Abb. 22).[38] Damit waren die wesentlichen Entwicklungsschritte weg von den seleukidischen Vorbildern vollzogen. Abgesehen vom Diadem, das der Herrscher nach wie vor trägt, und der griechischen Legende erinnert auf den Tetradrachmen aus Seleukeia am Tigris nichts mehr an seleukidische Münzen. Die weitere Entwicklung der arsakidischen Münzprägung war von seleukidischen Vorbildern nicht mehr direkt beeinflusst und kann daher hier außer Acht gelassen werden.

Abb. 20: Mithradates II., Tetradrachme, Susa, Sellwood -, Assar 2006 fig. 30; CNG, auction 103, 14.9.2016, no. 444

Abb. 21: Mithradates II., Aes, Susa, Sellwood 28.21; Rauch, GmbH 94, 9.4.2014 Nr. 494

---

[35] Sellwood 21.
[36] Sellwood 27.14–27; zur Datierung: Assar 2006, 141.
[37] Sellwood 28.18–23. Zu den verschiedenen Diademformen und weiteren ikonographischen Entwicklungen unter Mithradates II. s. etwa Magub 2017, 609–613.
[38] Sellwood 24.1.

Abb. 22: Mithradates II., Tetradrachme, Seleukeia am Tigris, Sellwood 24.1; CNG, Triton VI, 14.1.2003, no. 505

Dieser knappe Überblick sollte verdeutliche, wie vielschichtig und komplex die Entwicklung der arsakidischen Münzgestaltung bis zum Ende des 1. Jhs. v. Chr. ist.

1.3. Die Münzprägung der Charakene

Der Loslösungsprozess der Satrapie Mesene aus dem seleukidischen Herrschaftsverband verlief über einen längeren Zeitraum, wobei der Status des Hyspaosines, der vielleicht bereits von Antiochos IV. zum Ethnarchen der Region eingesetzt worden war, wechselte.[39] Während des Arsakidenfeldzuges Demetrios' II. stand Hyspaosines vielleicht auf der Seite des Seleukiden.[40] 133 v. Chr. unternahm er einen Feldzug Richtung Babylonien;[41] spätestens im Jahr 129/8 v. Chr. nahm er den Königstitel an[42] und scheint Babylonien erobert zu haben, verlor diese Region 127/6 v. Chr. jedoch wieder an die

---

[39] Plin. nat. hist. 6.139; s. zum langsamen Loslösungsprozess der Mesene aus dem seleukidischen Herrschaftsverband Schuol 2000, 291–294; Gregoratti 2011, 212.

[40] Nodelman 1959/60, 87 datierte frühe Prägungen des Hyspaosines, die Aes-Münzen des Demetrios II. kopieren, die zwischen 141 und 139 in Seleukeia am Tigris geprägt wurden, in exakt diesen Zeitraum: Hyspaosines „must have issued his coins between these dates. Certainly he would not have done so later, when Demetrius was defeated and discredited." Vgl. auch Alram 1987, 124 (Weiternutzung der seleukidischen Ära). Die Datierung dieser Münzen in die Jahre 141 bis 139 v. Chr. ist aber keineswegs sicher oder zwingend. Nodelman 1959/60, 89 leitet aus der Tatsache, dass Babylon unter seiner Herrschaft zur seleukidischen Datierung zurückkehrte und nicht zur Datierung nach Hyspaosines wechselte, eine große Seleukidenfreundlichkeit des Hyspaosines ab; vgl. Tarn 1971, 578, der vermutet, die griechische Bevölkerung könne Kamnaskires gegen die Arsakiden unterstützt haben. Zur Münzprägung der Charakene siehe auch Le Rider 1959, 229–253.

[41] Sachs/Hunger 1996, -132 B Rev. 18–20: „That month, I heard as follows: the forces of Aspasinē, the enemy from the environs(?) of Messene(?), a friend of the Elamite enemy, came and fell on the harbor of ships in the Tigris and plundered this harbor of ships together with their possessions."

[42] Assar 2006, 106. Die Königserhebung könnte mit dem Tod Antiochos' VII. im Jahr 129 v. Chr. in Verbindung stehen.

Arsakiden.[43] Einzige Münzstätte in dem hier behandelten Zeitraum war Antiocheia am Persischen Golf (das für die Region Charakene namengebende Spasinu Charax).[44] Die letzten seleukidischen Tetradrachmen, die in Antiocheia am Persischen Golf geprägt wurden, zeigen stets Apollon auf dem Omphalos sitzend mit Pfeil und Bogen.[45] Interessanterweise bilden aber nicht die seleukidischen Prägungen die ikonographischen Vorbilder der Tetradrachmen des Hyspaosines, sondern die Münzen des baktrischen Königs Euthydemos I. (Abb. 23–24).[46]

Abb. 23: Euthydemos I., Tetradrachme, Bop. Ser. 12; Gorny und Mosch, Auktion 215, 13.10.2013, Nr. 918

Abb. 24: Tetradrachme, Hyspaosines, 129/8 v. Chr., Seleukeia am Tigris(?), Alram 491 var.; Peus, Auktion 386, 26.4.2006, Nr. 373

Auf den Bronzemünzen des Hyspaosines findet sich auf den Vorderseiten zuweilen ein gestaffeltes Doppelporträt, das Hyspaosines und vielleicht seinen Vater Sagdodonakos darstellt (Alram 493 f.). Die Rückseiten der Bronzemünzen zeigen ein geflügeltes Blitzbündel (Alram 492), Athena (Alram 493) und Artemis (Alram 494) und stehen damit in bester hellenistischer Tradition.

---

[43] Sachs/Hunger 1996, -126 A obv. 6'–9': „That month, on the 4th, Timarkusu, who previously from the side of the king Arsaces was appointed the guard commander and who in month IV had escaped from Aspasinē, came from the side of Indupanē with troops of Media; they entered Babylon"; vgl. -125 A obv. 20; Schuol 2000, 294 f.; Assar 2006, 113; Gregoratti 2011, 212 f.

[44] Erst im 2. Jh. n. Chr. unter Meredates und Orobazes II. finden sich Münzen mit deutlich abweichendem Stil, was auf eine Verlegung der Münzprägestätte hinweisen könnte; Nodelman 1959/60, 113 brachte eine Verlegung von Charax nach Forat ins Spiel; vgl. auch Alram 1986, 155).

[45] SC 1866: Alexander Balas, 150-145 v. Chr.; 1993 f.: Demetrios II., 145–144 v. Chr.

[46] Alram 1986, Nr. 491.

Abb. 25: Apodakos, Tetradrachme, 104/3 v. Chr., Alram 496; Roma Numismatics Ltd, Auktion XII, 29.9.2016, Nr. 409

Abb. 26: Tiraios I., Tetradrachme, 95/4 v. Chr., Alram 498; CNG, mail bid sale 58, 19.9.2001, no. 805

122/1 v. Chr. wurde die Charakene Teil des arsakidischen Reiches, erlangte aber scheinbar recht schnell eine gewisse Unabhängigkeit.[47] Auch die in der Folgezeit geprägten Münzen zeigen zunächst den sitzenden Herakles (Abb. 25). Einzig Tiraios I. tauschte diesen Typus in den Jahren 95/4 bis 90/89 v. Chr. gegen eine nach links thronende Göttin mit Nike und Füllhorn aus, die ein wenig an die Tyche aus Seleukeia am Tigris erinnert (Abb. 26; vgl. Abb. 16).[48] Im Gegensatz zu den Kamnaskiriden, die sich seit der zweiten Prägeperiode deutlich an arsakidische Vorbilder anlehnten, behielten die charakenischen Könige die 'klassische' hellenistische diademierte Rechtsbüste bei, auch wenn die Haar- und Bartmode seit Tiraios II. (79/8–49/8 v. Chr.) an arsakidische Vorbilder angelehnt wurde (Abb. 27–29).[49]

---

[47] Schuol 2000, 298; Gregoratti 2011, 213.
[48] Nodelman 1959/60, 92f. brachte diesen Typenwechsel mit dem Sieg Tiraios' I. über Gotarzes I., einen Gegenkönig gegen den Arsakidenkönig Mithradates II., in Verbindung
[49] Darauf wies schon Alram 1986, 154 hin. Vgl. Nodelman 1959/60, 94 (unter Tiraios II. Orientalisierung des Münzporträts, erste aramäische Gegenstempel) und 95 (unter Attambelos: „all Greek influence is gone from the portraiture, which is perfectly oriental").

Abb. 27: Tiraios II., Tetradrachme, 71/0 v. Chr.; Hess-Divo AG, Auktion 320, 26.10.2011, Nr. 253

Abb. 28: Attambelos I., 47/6–25/4 v. Chr., Tetradrachme, 40/39 oder 38/7 v. Chr., BMC 4; CNG, electronic auction, 8.4.2015, no. 385

Abb. 29: Abinergaos II., Bronze-Tetradrachme, ca. 165–180 n. Chr., BMC 302, 2; Peus, Auktion 405, 2.11.2011, Nr. 2371

2. Interpretation dieses Befundes

Die im Kontext mit diesem Band vielleicht wichtigste Frage lautet: Kann der Befund mit dem Konzept des middle ground erklärt werden? Der Begriff wurde von Richard White eingeführt und von ihm verkürzt wie folgt definiert: „The middle ground is the place in between: in between cultures, peoples, and in between empires and the nonstate world of villages. ... On the middle ground diverse peoples adjust their differences through what amounts to a process of creative, and often expedient, misunderstandings. People try to persuade others who are different from themselves by appealing to what they perceive to be the values and practices of those others. They often misinterpret and distort both the values and the practices of those they deal with,

Postseleukidische Münzen im südlichen Zweistromland

but from these misunderstandings arise new meanings and through them new practices – the shared meanings and practices of the middle ground."[50] Bei allen Vorbehalten gegenüber der Übertragung eines Konzeptes, das für die Untersuchung der nordamerikanischen Geschichte entwickelt wurde, auf die Verhältnisse des südlichen Zweistromlandes im 2. Jhs. v. Chr., so erscheint doch zumindest der Aspekt, mit Hilfe der Werte und Praktiken einer fremden Kultur, andere beeinflussen zu wollen (um es einmal so schwach zu formulieren), bedenkenswert. Es sind vor allem zwei Grundfragen, die in diesem Kontext essentiell sind:

1. Wer traf die Entscheidung über die Gestaltung der Münzen?
2. Welche Botschaften sollten mithilfe der hellenistischen Bilder und Legenden der postseleukidischen Münzen vermittelt werden bzw. ist ggf. mit Fehlinterpretationen bzw. Uminterpretationen zu rechnen?

2.1. Die Entscheidung über die Münzgestaltung

Nichtnumismatische Zeugnisse zur Organisation der Münzprägung fehlen, so dass Informationen allein aus den Münzen selbst bzw. über Analogieschlüsse gezogen werden können. Lassen sich auf diese Weise zumindest in Ansätzen einige Indizien zu den technischen Abläufen der Münzprägung gewinnen, so bleibt auch dann weitgehend unklar, wer die Münzgestaltung maßgeblich beeinflusste. Die folgenden Überlegungen sollen einige Antwortmöglichkeiten eröffnen. Grundsätzlich sind dabei drei Entscheidungsebenen denkbar: (1) der königliche Hof, (2) der Satrap, (3) die Münzstättenleitung.

Wie vielschichtig die Entscheidungsprozesse im Einzelnen sein konnten, mag ein Blick auf die seleukidischen Verhältnisse verdeutlichen. Viele Seleukiden entschieden sich offenbar bewusst dafür – auch in Abgrenzung zu ihren Vorgängern –, Rückseitenmotive, Epitheta, Diademformen etc. auf ihren Münzen individuell zu gestalten. Antiochos IV. ist hierbei vielleicht das prominenteste Beispiel, denn er bevorzugte als Rückseitenmotiv seiner Tetradrachmen Zeus – und nicht wie seine Vorgänger Apollon –, propagierte neue Epitheta und trug als erster Seleukide auf einigen Nominalen ein Strahlendiadem. Auffallend ist in diesem Kontext allerdings, dass diese individuellen Änderungen nicht in allen seleukidischen Münzstätten umgesetzt wurden, sondern sich vielfach nur in einzelnen Orten, vor allem in der bevorzugten Residenz Antiocheia am Orontes, feststellen lassen.[51] Was bedeutet das? Wollte oder konnte Antiochos IV. bzw. seine Administration diese Änderungen nicht andernorts durchsetzen? Gegen die Annahme einer Unfähigkeit zur Durchsetzung spricht, dass derselbe Antiochos IV. durchaus in der Lage war,

---

[50] White ²2011, xxvi.
[51] SC 1396 f. (Zeus Nikephoros); andernorts wurde (zunächst) weiterhin der traditionelle Apollon-Typ geprägt (etwa in Ake-Ptolemais: SC 1472–75).

in vielen Städten seines Herrschaftsgebietes eine Kleingeldreform durchzu-
führen, in deren Rahmen nicht nur viele neue Prägestätten aktiv wurden, sondern auch auf eine weitgehend einheitliche Vorderseitengestaltung geachtet
wurde. Allem Anschein nach handelte es sich um eine einheitlich geplante
Maßnahme, deren Umsetzung keine erkennbaren Probleme bereitete.[52]
Wenn demgegenüber die für die Selbstdarstellung des Königs sicher weitaus
wichtigeren, weil für die Bezahlung der herrschaftsrelevanten Soldaten essen-
tiellen und durch den Handel überregional umlaufenden Silbermünzen keinem einheitlichen Schema folgten, scheint dies zumindest nicht an der man-
gelnden Durchsetzbarkeit gelegen zu haben. Dieser Befund könnte das Ergebnis eines bewussten Entscheidungsprozesses oder aber auch eines Desin-
teresses des Königs bzw. seines administrativen Apparates an einer reichsweiten Einheitlichkeit sein.

Da die Strukturen der Finanzadministration des spätantiken römischen Reiches vergleichsweise besser bekannt sind als die entsprechenden
Strukturen hellenistischer Reiche, sei zur Konkretisierung dieser 'Frage' ein
Blick auf die dortigen Entscheidungsstrukturen geworfen. Johannes Wienand
konnte überzeugend herausarbeiten, dass Entscheidungen über die Gestaltung der Münzen auf drei Ebenen erfolgten, die mit den gerade genannten
drei Ebenen in hellenistischen Reichen vergleichbar sind:[53] „Weitreichende
Richtungswechsel in der Gestaltung der Münzen" seien demnach wahrscheinlich im direkten Umfeld des Kaisers getroffen worden, „auf einer …
Verwaltungsebene mit überregionaler Geltung" seien Elemente wie Beizeichen bestimmt worden, „Offizins- und Münzstättensiglen sowie die emissi-
onskritischen Beizeichen" hätten in der Entscheidungsgewalt der Münzstätten gelegen.

Übertragen auf die hier zu untersuchenden Verhältnisse würde dies
bedeuten, dass ein neues grundsätzliches Münzaussehen auf der Ebene des
königlichen Hofes festgelegt worden sein könnte.[54] Allerdings beziehen sich
die Überlegungen Wienands verständlicherweise nur auf Änderungen, die
vorgenommen wurden. Gilt dies auch im Fall einer Beibehaltung von Münz-
typen? Muss man annehmen, dass solche Entscheidungen ebenfalls auf der
obersten Ebene getroffen wurden, oder könnte man sich nicht auch vorstellen, dass ein Desinteresse im Umfeld des Königs dazu geführt haben könnte,
dass ältere Darstellungen einfach beibehalten wurden?

Gerade in Susa könnte man sich die Situation so vorstellen, dass
Kamnaskires – und später die Arsakiden – letztlich nichts an den vorgefundenen Strukturen, dem Personal und den Darstellungskonventionen änderten

---

[52] Siehe hierzu den Beitrag von Lichtenberger in diesem Band.
[53] Wienand 2012, 53 f.
[54] Beizeichen und münzstätteninternen Zeichen kommt bei den hier zu untersuchenden As-
      pekten der mesopotamischen Münzprägung keine Rolle zu.

Postseleukidische Münzen im südlichen Zweistromland 53

und die jeweiligen Prägestätten daher einfach weiterarbeiteten, wie sie es gewohnt waren. Lediglich das Vorderseitenporträt und die Legende wurden den geänderten politischen Verhältnissen angepasst, ohne dass die jeweiligen Könige oder deren direktes Umfeld hierbei eine aktive Entscheidungsrolle übernommen haben mussten. Andererseits könnten grundsätzliche Veränderungen analog zu den seleukidischen und spätrömischen Verhältnissen am Hof entschieden worden sein – etwa der Austausch des Pfeiles durch einen Palmzweig unter Artabanos I.

Interessanterweise zeigen die Münzen aus Kupferlegierungen sowohl in der Elymais als auch bei den Arsakiden rein griechische Rückseiten, egal welcher Herrscher an der Macht war.[55] Es scheint so, als hätte diese Kleingeldprägung in der Zuständigkeit der jeweiligen Städte gelegen. Es ist allerdings bemerkenswert, dass diese Städte, die zum Teil sehr alte vorhellenistische Traditionen besaßen, stets griechische Legenden und Motive nutzten und in keinem Fall auf ältere Kulte oder Traditionen verwiesen, wie es einige Städte des Seleukidenreiches taten.[56]

2.2. Sein oder Schein

Angesichts der Tatsache, dass nicht geklärt ist, welche Personen mit welchem Bildungshintergrund sich an den einzelnen Höfen der postseleukidischen Herrscher aufhielten, ist die Frage, welche nicht-hellenistischen Ideen in vordergründig hellenistischem Gewand auf den neugestalteten Münzen Eingang gefunden haben könnten, nur schwer zu beantworten. Natürlich ist es grundsätzlich denkbar, dass beispielsweise die beiden unterschiedlichen Herakles-Rückseiten des arsakidischen Seleukeia am Tigris und der charakenischen Münzen wirklich den griechischen Gott Herakles darstellen sollten, der von den Rezipienten in den Prägeorten auch in diesem Sinn verstanden wurde. Ebenso denkbar ist aber auch, dass Herakles jeweils ganz andere nicht-hellenistische Gottesvorstellungen repräsentierte – beispielsweise Verethragna.[57] Zudem ist nicht auszuschließen, dass Münzbilder politische Statements bilden sollten. So könnte man annehmen, Hyspaosines habe angesichts der Übernahme eines baktrischen Rückseitenmotivs enge Beziehungen zu

---

[55] Für die in Susa geprägten Münzen s. oben Anm. 15, zu den arsakidischen Münzen siehe Sellwood 6.2, 7.2, 8.2–3, 11.6–7, 12.9–29, 14.3–6, 15.5–7, 16.26–30, 17.5, 18.3, 20.7, 21.5–9, 23.4–10, 24.33–46, 26.25–33, 27.6–28 und 28.8–23.

[56] Vgl. etwa die Bronzemünzen aus Byblos aus der Zeit Antiochos IV., die auf ihren Rückseiten u.a. Kronos-El zeigen (SC 1443 f.).

[57] Vgl. Bonnet 1992, 184 f. Für eine besondere Verehrung des Herakles in der Charakene spricht auch eine in der zweiten Hälfte des 2. Jhs. v. Chr. dort geweihte bronzene Heraklesstatue; hierzu: Schuol 2000, 297 und Canali de Rossi 2004, Nr. 86. Nach Nodelman 1959/60, 96 bevorzugte Hyspaosines Bel (allerdings mit falschem Hinweis auf Weissbach 1931, 1095).

Baktrien gepflegt. Baktrische Münzen fanden nachweislich ihren Weg in die Region[58] und konnten auch aus anderen Gründen als Vorbilder gedient haben – etwa weil sie als besonders silberhaltig und hochgewichtig angesehen wurden und daher beliebt waren. Um einer Antwort auf diese Fragen näherzukommen, scheint ein Blick auf die seltsame Mischgestalt auf den Tetradrachmen Phraates' II. aus Seleukeia am Tigris hilfreich zu sein.

Abb. 30: Demetrios II., Tetradrachme, Seleukeia am Tigris, 145–141 v. Chr., SC 1984, 30 mm; A. Tkalec AG, Auktion Mai 2005, Nr. 92

Abb. 31: Phraates II., Tetradrachme, Seleukeia am Tigris, Sellwood 17.1; CNG, Triton V, 15.1.2002, no. 1561

Auf den ersten Blick ist die Darstellung nur eine Variante der seit Demetrios I. in Seleukeia am Tigris geläufigen Tetradrachmenrückseite, die eine nach links sitzende Tyche zeigt, die in der vorgestreckten rechten Hand ein kurzes Zepter und im linken Arm ein Füllhorn hält (Abb. 30–31). Arm- bzw. Handhaltung, Sitzrichtung, Gewand und Füllhorn sind auf den Tetradrachmen Phraates' II. nahezu identisch, jedoch zeigen sich vier Abweichungen: (1) die Gestalt hält in der rechten Hand eine Nikestatuette, (2) sie sitzt auf einem andersartigen Möbelstück, (3) sie trägt eindeutig einen Bart und (4) auf dem Kopf befindet sich ein *kalathos*. Offenbar ist einerseits ikonographische Nähe zur traditionellen Tychedarstellung beabsichtigt, andererseits zeigt auch ein nur wenig konzentrierter Blick sofort die Unterschiede. Sowohl die Nike, als

---

[58] Le Rider 1965, Nr. 485f. (jeweils eine Tetradrachme in einem Schatzfund aus der zweiten Hälfte des 2. Jhs. bzw. um 140 v. Chr.) und 442 f.

Postseleukidische Münzen im südlichen Zweistromland 55

auch das Sitzmöbel und der *kalathos* können der hellenistischen Bilderwelt zugeordnet werden, eine bärtige Gestalt in Frauenkleidung ist jedoch sehr ungewöhnlich.[59] Es scheint keine bildliche Parallele zu geben. Erkennbar wird mit Bildelementen gearbeitet, die dem Betrachter grundsätzlich bekannt vorkommen mussten, doch ist die Zusammenstellung einzigartig. Der Verfasser eines Auktionskataloges aus dem Jahr 2003 hat es im Sinne von White wie folgt auf den Punkt gebracht: „One wonders if the artist was intent on rendering a Persian god in Greek guise, or simply misunderstood the types he was copying."[60]

Letzteres, also ein Missverständnis, ist unwahrscheinlich, denn angesichts der Tatsache, dass Seleukeia am Tigris ein kulturelles Zentrum darstellte, standen Phraates II. sicher genug Personen als Berater zur Verfügung, die bei der Gestaltung der Münzrückseite behilflich sein konnten. Alle anderen Bild- und Textelemente sind tadellos und die handwerkliche Ausführung lässt keine Wünsche offen, so dass zumindest auf dieser Ebene gut ausgebildete Personen tätig waren. Nicht zuletzt daher dürfte die ja ganz gezielt neu geschaffene Ikonographie nicht das Ergebnis von Unverständnis und/oder Dilettantismus sein, sondern eine gut überlegte Neuschöpfung, die bewusst mit bestehenden Bildtraditionen spielte. Nur weil dem modernen Betrachter der ikonographische Kontext fehlt, muss man nicht das Gegenteil unterstellen. Es lässt sich heute nicht mehr rekonstruieren, welche (prominenten) Statuen oder bildlichen Darstellungen sich in dieser Zeit in Seleukeia am Tigris befanden, so dass nicht auszuschließen ist, dass die neuen Münzen eine stadtbekannte Darstellung aufgriffen.

Abgesehen von der Frage nach nicht bekannten ikonographischen Parallelen kann man die Darstellung aber auch politisch lesen, indem man den Sieg (Nikestatuette) einer Zwittergestalt(?) mit der sich daraus ergebenden Prosperität (Füllhorn) verbindet.[61] Ein Identifizierung der Zwittergestalt mit Inanna-Ishtar wäre vielleicht zu überlegen, die sowohl eine weibliche als auch eine männliche Seite besaß.[62] In jedem Fall ließe sich aus der Darstellung

---

[59] Zuweilen wurde die Gestalt als Dionysos gedeutet; vgl. Hill 1927, 206. Als möglicher Interpretationsansatz aus dem griechischen Kulturkreis kommt vielleicht auch das Fest des Aphroditos in Betracht, bei dem Männer in Frauenkleidung und Frauen in Männerkleidung opferten; vgl. Tümpel 1894, 2794 f.

[60] CNG, mail bid sale 63, 21.5.2003, no. 871.

[61] Die Nikestatuette wendet sich der sitzenden Gestalt zu; hätte konkreter die Sieghaftigkeit des Königs thematisiert werden sollen, hätte die Nikestatuette den Königsnamen Arsakes bekränzen können/müssen.

[62] Vgl. Harris 1991, 261–278, insbes.: 268–270 und Groneberg 1986, 25–46; Dayet 1925, 63–66, hier: 64 vermutete, es handele sich um Phraates II., sah sich aber gleichzeitig genötigt, die ungewöhnliche Darstellung eines Königs zu erklären (1. Kreation eines griechischen Künstlers, um den König lächerlich zu machen oder 2. Versuch eines arsakidischen Künstlers, der das Original missverstand, oder 3. Anweisung des Königs).

eine klare politische Botschaft Phraates' II. an die Einwohner Seleukeias ablesen: die kurz zuvor erfolgte Eroberung der Stadt durch die Arsakiden bedeutete kein Ende der wirtschaftlichen Blüte – ganz im Gegenteil. Die Kontinuität wurde noch durch die für die bisherige arsakidische Münzprägung ungewöhnlich hellenistische Gestaltung der Vorderseite unterstrichen. So stehen die Gesichtszüge des Königs und der kurze ‚griechische' Bart deutlich stärker in seleukidischer Tradition als die Münzvorderseiten seines Vorgängers aus der gleichen Stadt. Sollte diese Deutung richtig sein, kann nicht von einem Missverstehen seitens des arsakidischen Hofes ausgegangen werden, sondern muss eine ganz gezielte Gestaltung der Tetradrachmen mit klarer Botschaft angenommen werden, die bewusst auf eine griechische oder hellenisierte Bevölkerung abgestimmt war.

Man darf daher wohl auch bei den anderen Münzen annehmen, dass jeweils sehr bewusste Entscheidungen für eine ganz bestimmte Münzgestaltung getroffen wurden. Wenn dem so sein sollte, liegen fünf – sich zum Teil ergänzende – Annahmen nahe, die es anhand des oben dargestellten Befundes zu überprüfen gilt:

1. Es handelt sich grundsätzlich um eine Rücksichtnahme auf (Seh-)Gewohnheiten der Untertanen.
2. Je höher der Grad der Hellenisierung der Untertanen oder der Anteil der griechischen Bevölkerung war, desto höher war der Grad der seleukidischen Übernahmen.
3. Die Münzen spiegeln die politisch-militärischen Verhältnisse.
4. Je länger die Herrschaft dauerte, desto weniger Rücksicht auf seleukidische Traditionen wurde genommen.
5. Je stärker ein Herrscher war – respektive sich fühlte –, desto weniger Rücksicht musste er nehmen.

2.2.1. Rücksichtnahme auf (Seh-)Gewohnheiten der Untertanen

Die Tatsache, dass alle drei Königreiche die Münzprägung nach seleukidischen Gewichtsstandards aufnahmen, muss als Rücksichtnahme auf die bestehende Geldwirtschaft gedeutet werden, deren Abschaffung kaum im Sinn der jeweiligen neuen Machthaber gewesen sein dürfte.[63] Eingangs war bereits darauf hingewiesen worden, dass an anderen Orten und zu anderen Zeiten zuweilen die Münzprägung der fremden Vorgänger exakt kopiert wurde, um die Umlauffähigkeit der Münzen zu gewährleisten. Allerdings hat keines der hier behandelten drei Königreiche ältere Münzen einfach kopiert. In allen Fällen wurden die Vorderseitenporträts abgewandelt – entweder an das

---

[63] Auch Alram 1986, 137 weist auf die „wirtschaftliche(r) Notwendigkeit" hin.

Postseleukidische Münzen im südlichen Zweistromland 57

vermeintliche Aussehen des neuen Herrschers angeglichen oder wie im Fall der frühen arsakidischen Münzen wohl idealisiert. Darüber hinaus trugen alle Könige nicht-seleukidische Herrschernamen.

Der obige Überblick hat deutlich gemacht, dass daneben der Grad der Abweichungen von den seleukidischen Vorbildern sehr unterschiedlich hoch sein konnte. Keiner der Prägeherren verzichtete jedoch auf die Darstellung des Königsdiadems. Selbst die frühen arsakidischen Münzen, die nicht den Königstitel aufweisen, zeigen dieses Detail. Das Diadem kann geradezu als hellenistisches Herrschaftszeichen par excellence betrachtet werden.[64] Zudem tragen alle Münzen, die in Mesopotamien geprägt wurden, den Königstitel. Damit sind die wesentlichen beiden Marker autonomer Herrschaft präsent, wie sie stets auch von den Seleukiden verwendet wurden. Haartracht, Barttracht, Kleidung und Schmuck kam demgegenüber eine geringere Bedeutung zu. Auch die Seleukiden konnten unterschiedliche Bärte tragen, ohne dass es zu Auswirkungen auf die Akzeptanz ihrer Herrschaft oder ihrer Münzen gekommen wäre.[65] Zudem besaß jeder Seleukide eine individuelle Frisur. Auch wenn die seleukidischen Könige in der Regel keine Gewandbüsten nutzten, konnte aber dieser Fall ebenfalls auftreten.[66] Zuweilen trugen Seleukiden auch Ohrringe,[67] doch müssen sowohl die elaborierten Gewänder der arsakidischen Könige als auch deren Hals- und Ohrschmuck als 'unseleukidisch' empfunden worden sein. Im Gegensatz dazu bemühten sich die Könige der Elymais und der Charakene anscheinend ganz bewusst um ein möglichst 'seleukidisches' Erscheinungsbild. Ähnliches lässt sich in Bezug auf die Rückseiten feststellen. Während in Susa und Spasinou Charax die Rückseiten der Silbermünzen jeweils ein festes rein hellenistisches Vorbild kopierten, zeigen die Münzen der Arsakiden eine größere Bandbreite.

Im Sinne von White könnte man annehmen, dass einige der Übernahmen lediglich den Versuch darstellen, sich des Mediums und der 'Sprache' der Seleukiden zu bedienen, wobei auch "misunderstandings" und "misinterpretations" vorliegen könnten. Die oben behandelten Tetradrachmen Phraates' II. aus Seleukeia am Tigris weisen aber in eine andere Richtung und auch die gezielte und richtige Verwendung von Epitheta scheint die Annahme zu bestätigen, dass die Schöpfer der Münzen durchaus verstanden, mit der seleukidischen Bild- und Formensprache richtig umzugehen.

Die Könige der Elymais und der Charakene übernahmen ein beschränktes Set an seleukidischen Epitheta (Soter, Nikephoros und Euergetes) und thematisierten damit ihre Sieghaftigkeit und ihre Wohltaten gegenüber

---

[64] Siehe etwa Haake 2012, 293–313.
[65] Vgl. etwa SC 1992 (Demetrios II, erste Regierungszeit) oder SC 2345–2400 (Antiochos IX. mit zum Teil sehr unterschiedlichen Bartformen).
[66] Beispielsweise unter Antiochos Hierax: SC 855 und 914
[67] Ehling 2005, 41 ff.

den Untertanen, wobei die frühen Kamnaskiriden nur ihre Sieghaftigkeit betonten und die Könige der Charakene erst ab Tiraios I. die Wohltaten, danach immer Sieghaftigkeit und Wohltaten hervorhoben (siehe Tabelle 1). Ebenso wie ihre Tetradrachmen stets die gleiche Rückseite tragen, folgen auch die Epitheta anscheinend recht starren Regeln. Bei den Arsakidenn zeigt sich dagegen ein viel komplexeres Bild. Zum einen wurden nicht nur 'seleukidische' Epitheta verwendet, zum anderen trug fast jeder arsakidische König ein anderes Set an Epitheta. Auffallend ist einerseits, dass erst nach der Eroberung Mesopotamiens überhaupt Epitheta verwendet wurden, und andererseits, dass das Philhellenentum in der Hälfte der Fälle betont wurde. Das führt fast automatisch zur zweiten oben formulierten Annahme.

2.2.2. Bedeutung des Hellenisierungsgrades der Bevölkerung

Eine enge Relation zwischen dem Hellenisierungsgrad der Bevölkerung und dem Grad der Übernahme seleukidischer Elemente in der Münzprägung scheint vor allem im arsakidischen Reich bestanden zu haben, denn die Münzen in den stärker hellenisierten Regionen sind viel 'seleukidischer' als die aus den frühen arsakidischen Prägestätten (Hekatompylos, Nisa, Rhagai), die vergleichsweise wenig hellenisiert waren und schnell 'arsakidisiert' wurden (Nisa wurde in Mithradakart umbenannt, Rhagai in Arsakeia).[68] Zudem scheinen abgesehen von sehr ungewöhnlichen Blei-Tetradrachmen und -Drachmen, die in Nisa vielleicht aus Silbermangel entstanden,[69] in keiner der drei Städte seleukidische Münzen geprägt worden zu sein, so dass hier keine Prägestätten bestanden, die traditionsbildend hätten wirken können.

Andererseits waren aber Susa und Spasinou Charax sicher nicht stärker hellenisiert als Seleukeia am Tigris. Die Münzen beider Städte sind aber deutlich stärker an seleukidischen Vorbildern orientiert als die frühen arsakidischen Münzen aus Seleukeia am Tigris; ja Mithradates II., der in Seleukeia am Tigris die traditionelle arsakidischen Rückseitendarstellung einführte, behielt in Susa die dort etablierte Apollondarstellung bei. Die Münzen der (bestenfalls) teilhellenisierten Stadt Susa sind also ‚seleukidischer' als diejenigen der seleukidischen Neugründung Seleukeia am Tigris. Der Grad der Hellenisierung allein kann den numismatischen Befund daher kaum erklären. Vielleicht können politische und/oder militärische Umstände zum Verständnis beitragen.

---

[68] Cohen 2013, 209 f. (zu Rhagai), 210–214 (zu Hekatompylos), 220 f. (zu Nisaia; offenbar wurden dort kaum Bronzemünzen gefunden, was gegen eine starke Monetarisierung des lokalen Handels und damit gegen einen starken griechischen Bevölkerungsanteil spricht).

[69] Houghton und Lorber 2002, 98 und 466.

Postseleukidische Münzen im südlichen Zweistromland

Arsakiden			Elymais			Charakene		
Arsakes I.	247–217							
Arsakes II.	217–191							
Phriapatios	191–176							
Phraates I.	176–171							
Mithradates I.	171–132	Philhellen	Kamnaskires I./II.	ca. 147–139	Soter, Nikephoros			
			Okkonapses	ca. 144/3 o. 139	Soter			
			(Phraates)	ca. 139/8				
Phraates II.	139/8–127	Nikephoros	Tigraios	ca. 138/7–133/2	Soter			
Bagasis	127/6	Theopator	Dareios	127/6				
Artabanos I.	126–122	Philadelphos, Theopator				Hyspaosines	129/8–124	
Arsakes X.	122/1	Epiphanes, Philhellen				Apodakos	124–104/3	
Mithradates II.	121–91	Epiphanes, Philhellen				Tiraios I.	95/4–90/89	Euergetes
						Tiraios II.	79/8–49/8	Soter kai Euergetes
Gotarzes I.	88–81/0	Theopator, Nikator	Kamnaskires III.	ca. 82/1–73/2				
Orodes I.	81/0–76/5	Philopator, Epiphanes, Philhellen						
Sinatrukes	78/7–71/0	Theopator, Nikator						
Phraates III.	71/0–57	Philopator, Euergetes, Epiphanes, Philhellen	Kamnaskires IV.	ca. 63/2–54/3		Artabazos I.	49/8–48/7	
Mithradates III.	57–55	Autokrator, Philopator, Epiphanes, Philhellen	Kamnaskires V.	ca. 54/3–33/2		Artembelos I.	ca. 47/6–25/4	Soter kai Euergetes
Orodes II.	57–38	Dikaios, Epiphanes, Philhellen				Theonesios I.	ca. 19/8	Soter kai Euergetes
Phraates IV.	38–2	Dikaios, Euergetes, Epiphanes, Philhellen				Artembelos II.	17/6 v.–8/9 n.	Soter kai Euergetes

Tabelle 1: Epitheta der hier behandelten Könige

2.2.3. Bedeutung der politisch-militärischen Verhältnisse

Die Tatsache, dass die Kamnaskiriden die seleukidischen Traditionen nahtlos fortsetzten und später demonstrativ den 'seleukidischen' Anker verwendeten, scheint darauf hinzudeuten, dass die neuen Herrscher darin einen herrschafts-stabilisierenden Faktor erblickten. Kamnaskires I. etablierte seine Herrschaft in einer Phase des Zusammenbruches der seleukidischen Suprematie und der arsakidischen Eroberungen im Zweistromland. Der dezidierte Anschluss an die seleukidischen Traditionen könnte die Rivalität zu den Arsakiden wider-spiegeln. Nachweislich bildeten die Kamnaskiriden – und vielleicht auch die Könige der Charakene – mit Demetrios II. eine Koalition gegen die Arsaki-den.[70]

Hyspaosines, der noch von Antiochos IV. eingesetzt worden war und nur schrittweise in die Position eines eigenständigen Königs hineingewachsen zu sein scheint, stand in ständiger Rivalität mit den Arsakiden. In dieser Situation wählte er zumindest im Münzbild zwar keinen direkten Anschluss an die seleukidische Herrschaft, durch die Verwendung eines rein hellenistischen Bildes (auch wenn sich dahinter vielleicht andere Gottesvorstellungen verbargen) konnte die Abgrenzung zu den Arsakiden aber zum Ausdruck gebracht werden. Insofern lag es für diese beiden kleineren Königreiche, zu deren Bewohnern auch hellenisierte Indigene und angesiedelte Griechen und Makedonen zählten, allein aus politischen Erwägungen heraus offenbar nahe, Kontinuität einer potentiellen arsakidischen Eroberung entgegenzuhalten. Die in Mesopotamien eingedrungenen arsakidischen Fremdherrscher konnten dagegen nicht zuletzt aufgrund ihrer militärischen Stärke von Beginn an in deutlicherem Maß ihre Fremdartigkeit betonen. Zudem war deren Dynastie seit Jahrzehnten etabliert, während die Kamnaskiriden und die Könige der Charakene erst neue Dynastien zu etablieren versuchten. Das führt zu der vierten Annahme.

2.2.4. Bedeutung der Herrschaftsdauer

Ganz so einfach ist die Sache aber nicht, denn die arsakidischen Münzen durchlaufen zumindest in Seleukeia am Tigris einen anderen Zyklus. Unter Mithridates I. findet sich – ähnlich wie in der Charakene – mit Herakles zwar eine hellenistische, aber eine eher 'unseleukidische' Rückseitengestaltung, die unter Phraates II. abgewandelt wurde. Nun erscheint auf den Reversen der Tetradrachmen aus Seleukeia eine sitzende Gestalt, die stark an frühere Tychedarstellungen erinnert, auch wenn sie im Detail abgewandelt ist (s.o.). Artabanos I. kehrte vollends zu den seleukidischen Vorbildern zurück, so

---

[70] Vgl. Just. 36, 1, 4; vgl. auch 30, 10, 5; Schuol 2000, 271.

Postseleukidische Münzen im südlichen Zweistromland

dass hier eine zunehmende Annäherung an Seleukidisches festzustellen ist. Erst Mithradates II. beendete dieses pseudo-seleukidische Zwischenspiel, indem er die 'traditionelle' arsakidische Rückseite mit dem sitzenden Bogenschützen auch in Seleukeia am Tigris einführte. Gerade der Vergleich zwischen den genannten vier arsakidischen Herrschern führt zur fünften Annahme.

2.2.5. Rolle der individuellen Stärke des Herrschers

Mithradates II. war im Vergleich mit seinen direkten Vorgängern ein extrem erfolgreicher König, der sein Herrschaftsgebiet deutlich stabilisieren und ausweiten konnte. Das könnte die Abkehr von stark an seleukidischen Vorbildern orientierten Rückseitenmotiven in Seleukeia am Tigris erklären. Nach der Eroberung von Susa zeigen die dort in seinem Namen geprägten Tetradrachmen – wie bereits mehrfach betont – jedoch das grundsätzlich gleiche Erscheinungsbild wie unter den Kamnaskiriden. Lediglich das Vorderseitenporträt und der Königsname wurden angepasst und der Pfeil – wie bereits bei Artabanos I. – gegen einen Palmzweig ausgetauscht. Allein der Hinweis auf eine relative Stärke eines Königs kann diesen Befund nicht erklären, was wiederum zurückführt zu den anderen Annahmen, insbesondere zu den Fragen nach der Dauer der Herrschaft (hier: in der Region), nach den Entscheidungsträgern für die Gestaltung der Münzen aus Susa und schließlich zu der ganz grundsätzlichen Frage nach Sicherung der Akzeptanz von Münzen als Zahlungsmittel durch die Nutzung traditioneller Bildmotive. In diesen und in anderen Fällen scheint die Gestaltung der Münzen also das Ergebnis eines komplexen Entscheidungsprozessen gewesen zu sein, wobei die jeweiligen Nachfolger der Seleukiden mithilfe der Münzen deren Nutzer von der Rechtmäßigkeit und dem Erfolg ihrer Herrschaft zu überzeugen suchten und hierzu auf die Sehgewohnheiten der Nutzer sehr flexibel Rücksicht nahmen. Insofern ist vielleicht zumindest ein Teilaspekt von White's Ansatz auf die hier behandelten Münzen anwendbar: „People try to persuade others who are different from themselves by appealing to what they perceive to be the values and practices of those others."[71]

3. Fazit

Die Münzprägung der drei Königreiche im postseleukidischen südlichen Zweistromland schließt in ganz unterschiedlicher Weise an die seleukidischen Traditionen an bzw. zeigt sehr individuelle Neuentwicklungen. Hierbei verfügten die für die Gestaltung der Münzen zuständigen Personen durchaus

---

[71] White 2011, xxvi.

über das notwendige Wissen, um mit den hellenistischen Bild- und Texttraditionen verständnisvoll umzugehen. Fehlinterpretationen scheinen in keinem Fall vorzuliegen, vielmehr zeigen gerade die innovativen Elemente, dass das übernommene Repertoire sehr zielgenau entsprechend den jeweiligen politischen und militärischen Verhältnissen eingesetzt wurde. Aspekte der Akzeptanzsicherung der Münzen als Zahlungsmittel durch traditionelle Bildmotive, des Hellenisierungsgrades einer Region, des Etablierungsstandes einer Dynastie, der Stärke einzelner Herrscher und politische Positionierungen bestimmten in hohem Maß die Münzgestaltung. In der arsakidischen Münzprägung spiegeln insbesondere die sich immer wieder verändernden Tetradrachmen aus Seleukeia am Tigris diese Aspekte geradezu idealtypisch wider. Die Könige des Elymais und der Charakene waren demgegenüber viel stärker traditionsbehaftet. In Susa und Spasinou Charax wurden über Jahrzehnte hinweg immer die gleichen Rückseitenmotive verwendet. In Susa fügten sich auch starke arsakidische Könige weitgehend diesen Traditionen. Erst die längere arsakidische Herrschaft über die Elymais führte zu einer deutlichen 'Arsakidisierung' der dortigen Münzprägung. In der Charakene, die auch über den Handel nach wie vor eine starke 'Westbindung' besaß,[72] hielten sich die hellenistischen – und damit vielleicht auch antiarsakidischen – Traditionen viel stärker.

Die wahrscheinlich stärker in der Kontrolle der einzelnen Städte liegende Buntmetallprägung zeigt ein völlig anderes Bild. Fas alle Münzen tragen auf ihren Rückseiten rein griechische Darstellungen und eine griechische Legende und stellen sich damit in viel stärkerem Maß in seleukidische Traditionen als die Silbermünzen. Das ist insofern überraschend, als im seleukidischen Reich in dieser Phase nicht nur die Buntmetall-, sondern auch die Silbermünzen häufig Darstellungen mit Bezug auf vorhellenistische lokale Kulte tragen.

---

[72] Vgl. etwa die guten Handelsbeziehungen zu Palmyra, die sich auch in Inschriften greifen lassen: Canali de Rossi 2004, Nr. 148–150, 153–157 und 159–165.

Bibliographie

Alram, M. 1986. Nomina Propria Iranica in Nummis (IPNB IV). Wien.

Alram, M. 1987. Die Vorbildwirkung der arsakidischen Münzprägung, in: LNV 3, 116–147.

Assar, G. F. 2006. A revised Parthian chronology of the period 165–91 BC, in: Electrum 11, 87–15.

Boiy, T. 2004. Late Achaemenid and Hellenistic Babylon. Leuven et al.

Bonnet, C. 1992. Héraclès en Orient: interprétations et syncrétismes, in: C. Bonnet und C. Jourdain-Annequin (Hgg.), Héraclès. D'une rive à l'autre de la Méditerranée. Bilan et perspectives, Brüssel, 165–198.

Bopearachchi, O. 1991. Monnaies gréco-bactriennes et indo-grecques. Catalogue raisonné. Paris.

Canali de Rossi, F. 2004. Iscrizioni dello estremo oriente greco. Bonn.

Cohen, G.M. 1978. The Seleucid Colonies. Studies in Founding, Administration and Organization. Wiesbaden.

Cohen, G.M. 2013. The Hellenistic Settlements in the East from Armenia and Mesopotamia to Bactria and India. Berkeley.

Curtis, V. S. 2012. Parthian Coins: Kingship and Divine Glory, in: P. Wick und M. Zehnder (Hgg.), The Parthian Empire and its Religions. Studies in the Dynamics of Religious Diversity, Gutenberg, 67–81.

Dąbrowa, E. 1998. Zeugnisse zur Geschichte der parthischen Susiane und Elymais, in: J. Wiesehöfer (Hg.), Das Arsakidenreich und seine Zeugnisse, Stuttgart, 417–424.

Ehling, K. 2005. Der Herr der Ringe: Seleukos I. und andere Könige mit Ohrringen, in: E. Dąbrowa (Hg.), Festschrift für J. Wolksi, Electrum 10, 41–48.

Gregoratti, L. 2011. A Parthian Port on the Persian Gulf: Characene and its Trade, in: Anabasis 2, 209–229.

Groneberg, B. 1986. Die sumerisch-akkadische Inanna/Ištar: Hermaphroditos?, in: Die Welt des Orients 17, 25–46.

Günther, L.-M. 2012. Seleukidische Vorbilder der parthischen Münzikonographie, in: P. Wick und M. Zehnder (Hgg.), The Parthian Empire and its Religions. Studies in the Dynamics of Religious Diversity, Gutenberg, 53–66.

Dayet, M. 1925. Un tétradrachme arsacide inédit, in: Arethuse 7, 63–66.

Haake, M. 2012. Diadem und *basileus*. Überlegungen zu einer Insignie und einem Titel in hellenistischer Zeit, in: A. Lichtenberger und K. Martin und H. Nieswand und D. Salzmann, Das Diadem der hellenistischen Herrscher. Übernahme, Transformation oder Neuschöpfung eines Herrschaftszeichens?, Bonn, 293–313.

Harris, R. 1991. Inanna-Ishtar as Paradox and a Coincidence of Opposites, in: History of Religions 30/3, 261–278.

Hill, G. F. 1927. Greek Coins Aquired by the British Museum in 1926, in: NC, 193–208.

Houghton, A. and C. Lorber 2002. Seleucid Coins. A comprehensive catalogue. New York.

Kosmin, P. J. 2014. The Land of the Elephant Kings. Harvard.

Le Rider, G. 1959. Monnaies de Characène, in: Syria 36, 1959, 229–253.

Le Rider, G. 1965. Suse sous les Séleucides et les Parthes. Les trouvailles monétaires et l'histoire de la ville.

Magub, A. 2017. Coins of Mithradates II of Parthia (c. 121–91 BC), in: M. Caccamo Caltabiano (Hg.), Proceedings of the XVth International Numismatic Congress, Rom, 609–613.

Martinez-Sève, L. 2002. La ville de Suse à l'époque hellénistique, in : Revue Archéologique 1, 31–54.

Mittag, P.F. 2021. Bedeutungslose Bärte? Einige Bemerkungen zu ungewöhnlichen Münzdarstellungen seleukidischer Könige des 3. Jhs. v. Chr., in: Jörn Lang und Carmen Marcks-Jacobs (Hgg.), Arbeit am Bild. Festschrift Dietrich Boschung, Regensburg, 208–213.

Mørkholm, O. 1965. A Greek Coin Hoard from Susiana, in: ActaA 36, 127–156.

Nodelman, S. A. 1959/60. A preliminary history of Characene, in: Berytus 13, 83–121.

Potts, D.T. 2002. Five Episodes in the History of Elymais, 145–124 B.C.: New Data from the Astronomical Diaries, in: Cahiers de Studia Iranica 25, 349–362.

Rougemont, G. 2012. Inscriptions grecques d'Iran et d'Asie centrale. London.

Sachs, A.J. und H. Hunger 1996. Astronomical Diaries and Related Texts from Babylon, Vol. III, Diaries from 164 B.C. to 61 B.C. Wien.

Schuol, M. 2000. Die Charakene. Ein mesopotamisches Königreich in hellenistisch-parthischer Zeit. Stuttgart.

Sellwood, D. ²1980. An Introduction to the Coinage of Parthia. London.

Sherwin-White, S. and A. Kuhrt 1993. From Sarmarkhand to Sardis. A new approach to the Seleucid Empire. Berkeley.

Sinisi, F. 2012. The Coinage of the Parthians, in: W.E. Metcalf (Hg.), The Oxford Handbook of Greek and Roman Coinage, Oxford, 275–294.

Strootmann, R. 2017. Imperial Persianism: Seleukids, Arsakids and *Fratarakā*, in: R. Strootman und M.J. Versluys (Hgg.), Persianism in Antiquity, Stuttgart, 177–200.

Tarn, W.W. 1971. Parthia, in: CAH IX, 574–613.

Tümpel, K. 1894. s.v. Aphroditos, RE I,2, Sp. 2794 f.

van't Haaff, P. A. 2007. Catalogue of Elymaean Coinage, ca. 147 B.C. – A.D. 228. Lancaster und London.

Wick, P. 2008. Hellenistische Münzen aus dem Osten. Spiegel religiöser Dynamiken im kulturellen Austausch zwischen Ost und West. Bochum.

Wienand, W. 2012. Der Kaiser als Sieger. Metamorphosen triumphaler Herrschaft unter Constantin I. Berlin.

White, R. ²2011. The Middle Ground. Indians, Empires, and Republics in the Great Lakes region, 1650–1815. Cambridge.

Viele Mütter. Zu den quasi-municipalen seleukidischen Lokalbronzen im hellenistischen Phönikien

Achim Lichtenberger

1. Einleitung

Unter dem Seleukidenkönig Antiochos IV. (175–164 v. Chr.) kommt es zu einer bemerkenswerten Prägung von Bronzen in einigen Städten Phönikiens.[1] Byblos, Berytos, Sidon und Tyros geben Münzen aus, die auf der Vorderseite das Bild des Königs zeigen und auf der Rückseite lokale Themen abbilden. Auf der Rückseite werden sowohl der Königsname als auch der Name der emittierenden Stadt genannt, so dass diese Gepräge von der Forschung als „quasi-municipal" bezeichnet werden.[2] Von der Prägeautorität her sind diese Münzen Zwitter, da sie weder nur städtisch noch nur königlich sind und es sich auch nicht einfach um eine königliche Münzprägestätte in einer Stadt handelt, sondern als Prägeherr tritt die Stadt neben dem König auf. Neben diesen Münzen haben die Städte eigene Bronzemünzen ausgegeben, die auf der Vorderseite das Bild der städtischen Tyche zeigten und als Prägeautorität nur die Stadt angaben. Diese rein-städtischen Bronzen setzen vielleicht schon unter Antiochos IV. ein (Sidon?), oftmals aber erst deutlich später (Tyros, 126/5 v. Chr.; Berytos, ab 102/1 v. Chr.; Byblos, ab 101/0 v. Chr.).[3]

Die quasi-municipalen Münzen wurden in allen vier Städten in einem gemeinsamen Nominalsystem geprägt, weshalb eine Form der zentralen, d.h. königlichen, Initiative oder Kontrolle dieser Prägungen anzunehmen ist.[4] Die Münzen zeigen auf den Rückseiten lokale Gottheiten, und außerdem sind bei einigen der Gepräge die Legenden auf Griechisch und auf Phönikisch.[5] Solche bilingualen Legenden kennen wir auch von hellenistischen Siegelabdrücken der phönikischen Städte.[6] Neben den vier phönikischen Städten, haben unter Antiochos IV. auch weitere Städte solche Münzen ausgegeben, bei denen lokale Elemente jedoch nicht so stark hervortreten.[7]

Für Anregungen beim Schreiben des Beitrags danke ich B. Morstadt, Bochum und H. Lichtenberger, Tübingen.

[1] Zum historischen Kontext vgl. Bunge 1975, 181–185; Grainger 1991; Mittag 2006.

[2] Mørkholm 1966, 125–130; Hoover 2004, 489–492; Houghton und Lorber und Hoover 2008, 45; Sawaya 2012, 273–274; Lorber 2015, 68–71.

[3] Zur städtischen Münzprägung von Berytos vgl. Sawaya 2008.

[4] Mørkholm 1965.

[5] Eine Transliteration und Transkription des Phönikischen ist nur in Anlehnung zum Hebräischen möglich. Vgl. dazu Segert 1976, 58.

[6] Ariel und Naveh 2003, 64–70 (Tyros); 75–77 (Sidon).

[7] Sawaya 2004, 109–111; Houghton und Lorber und Hoover 2008, 45–46.

Bislang hat sich die Forschung mit diesen Münzen vor allem als Zeugnisse für das mehr und mehr desintegrierende Seleukidenreich beschäftigt: die Münzen zeigten, dass der König den Städten die Möglichkeit gab, selbstbewusst die eigene städtische Identität in Szene zu setzen. Der König erhoffte sich so der Loyalität der Städte und ihrer Flotten zu versichern.[8] Eine solche Interpretation ist vernünftig und insbesondere die phönikischen Legenden unterstreichen den Aspekt, dass es sich bei den Münzen um selbstbewusste Identitätsbekundungen handelt. Zugleich ist bei den Prägungen unter Antiochos IV. bemerkenswert, dass der König mit Strahlenkrone gezeigt wird, ein Motiv, das von den königlichen Edelmetallprägungen nur ausnahmsweise bekannt ist und Teil einer an den König herangetragenen gesteigerten Sakralisierung des Herrschers ist (Abb. 1–8, 10).[9] Möglicherweise dienen hier die phönikischen Städte als Orte, an denen neue – und zwar gesteigerte – Ausdrucksformen der Sakralisierung des Herrscherbildes getestet wurden.

Ein weiterer Aspekt, mit dem sich die Forschung bei diesen Prägungen beschäftigt hat, ist der Umstand, dass die phönikischen Legenden von Tyros und Sidon einen Wettstreit bekunden, und zwar darum, wer die Mutterstadt von wem ist. Peter Franz Mittag spricht in diesem Zusammenhang von einem „Kleinkrieg"[10], den Otto Mørkholm „quite amusing"[11] findet. Dieser Wettstreit zeigt, dass die Münzen nicht allein als Zeugnisse der Kommunikation zwischen Stadt und Herrscher, sondern auch als Zeugnisse der Kommunikation und Konkurrenz zwischen den Nachbarstädten zu lesen sind.

Im Folgenden möchte ich mich mit den Prägungen mit zweisprachigen Legenden beschäftigen und der Frage nachgehen, was diese Legenden bedeuten, weshalb diese Legenden verwendet wurden und wie sie sich zu den Bildern verhalten.[12] Zum Schluss soll dann diskutiert werden, ob diese Münzprägungen mit dem Konzept des *Middle Ground* sinnvoll beschrieben werden.[13] Dazu ist es zunächst notwendig, die numismatischen Zeugnisse unter Antiochos IV. zu besprechen. Die Datierung und die Nominalzuweisung (A-E) der einzelnen Münzen folgt Arthur Houghton, Catherine Lorber und Oli-

---

[8] Vgl. z.B. Hoover 2004, 489–490; Houghton und Lorber und Hoover 2008, 46.

[9] Bunge 1975, 185; Mittag 2006, 130–136. Nur auf Hemidrachmen und Diobolen aus Antiochia tritt die Strahlenkrone in der Edelmetallprägung des Antiochos IV. auf (Le Ridder 1999, 220–221).

[10] Mittag 2006, 189 Anm. 45.

[11] Mørkholm 1963, 65.

[12] Phönikische Legenden wurden in hellenistischer Zeit auch von anderen Städten Phönikiens verwendet, doch gaben die phönikischen Buchstaben dort immer nur Jahreszahlen an. Ein Ethnikon auf Phönikisch wurde nur in den genannten vier Städten geschrieben.

[13] Zum Versuch, das Middle Ground-Konzept auf das hellenistische Phönikien anzuwenden, vgl. Bonnet 2015, 29–34.

Quasi-municipale Lokalbronzen im hellenistischen Phönizien   67

ver Hoover. Die quasi-municipalen Bronzen wurden in den vier Städten auch unter den Nachfolgern des Antiochos IV. geprägt, zuletzt unter Antiochos IX. (114/3–95 v. Chr.).

2. Antiochos IV. (175–164 v. Chr.)

Unter Antiochos IV. haben Byblos, Berytos, Sidon und Tyros quasi-municipale Bronzemünzen ausgegeben, welche phönikische Legenden aufweisen.

    a)   Byblos
Die auf den Rückseiten von Byblos dargestellten Lokalgottheiten sind ägyptisierend und werden ca. 168–164 v. Chr. datiert.

Nominal B (19–23 mm, 3,70–9,31 gr.):
(1) Houghton – Lorber – Hoover 2008, 80 Nr. 1443 (Abb. 1 [20 mm]):
Vs.: Kopf des Antiochos IV. n.r. mit Strahlenkrone und Diadem; *basileos Antiochou*
Rs.: Geflügelte stehende Gottheit n.l.; *lgbl qdš* („l^egubul qudš" – „von Gubul der Heiligen")

(2) Houghton – Lorber – Hoover 2008, 80 Nr. 1444:
Vs.: Kopf des Antiochos IV. n.r. mit Strahlenkrone und Diadem
Rs.: Geflügelte stehende Gottheit n.l.; *basileos Antiochou; lgbl qdš* („l^egubul qudš" – „von Gubul der Heiligen")

Nominal C (16–18 mm, 2,17–4,48 gr.)
(3) Houghton – Lorber – Hoover 2008, 80 Nr. 1445 (Abb. 2 [17 mm]):
Vs.: Kopf des Antiochos IV. n.r. mit Strahlenkrone und Diadem
Rs.: Stehende Isis n.l.; *basileos Antiochou; lgbl* („l^egubul" – „von Gubul")

Kleinere Nominale der Emission zeigen zu dem Bild des Königs auf der Vorderseite auf den Rückseiten Harpokrates und den Kopf eines Apisstiers.[14]
    Die Münzen verweisen in griechischer Sprache darauf, dass sie unter Antiochos IV. geprägt wurden. In phönikischer Sprache wird als Prägeautorität die Stadt mit ihrem alten phönikischen Namen *Gubul*, und dem Zusatz „heilig" genannt.[15] Dieselbe Münzlegende findet sich auch auf städtischen Bronzen von Byblos aus dem 2./1. Jh. v. Chr.[16] Die genaue Bedeutung des Ortsnamens ist unklar. Vielleicht ist er mit dem arabischen *gebel*, „Berg" verwandt und bezieht sich auf einen heiligen Berg, bzw. von dem hebräischen *g^ebul*,

---

[14]   Houghton und Lorber und Hoover 2008, 80–81 Nr. 1446–1447.
[15]   Vgl. dazu und zu den Münzbildern Bonnet 2015, 163–164.
[16]   Hoover 2010, 39–40 Nr. 141–144.

„Grenze, Gebiet"[17], das in einer Nebenbedeutung (Ps 78,54) ebenfalls „Berg" bedeuten kann. Aus dem semitischen Stamm ist dann wohl auch der griechische Ortsname Byblos abgeleitet worden. Die ägyptisierenden Gottheiten verweisen wohl auf die langen Beziehungen von Byblos zu Ägypten.[18]

b) Berytos

Die Münzen von Berytos zeigen auf den Rückseiten lokale Gottheiten in der *interpretatio Graeca* als Poseidon und als weibliche Gottheit. Die Münzen datieren ca. 168–164 v. Chr.

Nominal B (19–22,5 mm, 3,58–8,36 gr.):
(4) Houghton – Lorber – Hoover 2008, 81 Nr. 1448:
Vs.: Kopf des Antiochos IV. n.r. mit Strahlenkrone und Diadem
Rs.: Stehender Poseidon mit Dreizack und Phiale; *basileos Antiochou; ll'dk' 'm bkn'n* („lᵉl'adik'a 'em bᵉkan'an" – „von Laodikeia, Mutter in Kanaan")

(5) Houghton – Lorber – Hoover 2008, 81 Nr. 1449 (Abb. 3 [21 mm]):
Vs.: Kopf des Antiochos IV. n.r. mit Strahlenkrone und Diadem
Rs.: Stehender Poseidon mit Dreizack und Phiale; *basileos Antiochou; ll'dk' 'm bkn'n* („lᵉl'adik'a 'em bᵉkan'an" – „von Laodikeia, Mutter in Kanaan"); *La(odikeia) Ph(oinikia)*

Nominal C (17–18 mm, 2,83–4,28 gr.):
(6) Houghton – Lorber – Hoover 2008, 82 Nr. 1450 (Abb. 4 [18 mm]):
Vs.: Kopf des Antiochos IV. n.r. mit Strahlenkrone und Diadem
Rs.: Stehende weibliche Göttin auf Prora mit Ruder; *basileos Antiochou; ll'dk' 'm bkn'n* („lᵉl'adik'a 'em bᵉkan'an" – „von Laodikeia, Mutter in Kanaan"); *La(odikeia) Ph(oinikia)*

Kleinere Nominale der Emission zeigen zu dem Bild des Königs auf der Vorderseite auf den Rückseiten Ruder und Dreizack gekreuzt oder nur einen Dreizack.[19]

Berytos ist die Gräzisierung eines semitischen Toponyms, das bereits in Ugarit als *Beruta* überliefert ist.[20] Der gräzisierte Name ist spätestens seit Ps.-Skyllax in den 30er Jahren des 4. Jh.s v. Chr. belegt.[21] Unter Seleukos IV.

---

[17] Gesenius 2013, 194. Vgl. auch insgesamt zum westsemitischen Sprachgebrauch des Stamms Jean und Hoftijzer 1965, 47.
[18] Zu den Münzbildern vgl. Babelon 1890, CVIII–CIX; Wright 2009/10, 194; Iossif 2014, 64. Zu Byblos und Ägypten zuletzt Bonnet 2015, 153–196.
[19] Zu den quasi-municipalen Prägungen von Berytos vgl. Moore 1992; Sawaya 2004.
[20] Jidejian 1997, 47–49. Dort auch eine Übersicht zur Geschichte von Berytos.
[21] Ps-Skyllax, Periplous 106.

Quasi-municipale Lokalbronzen im hellenistischen Phönizien 69

oder Antiochos IV. wurde Berytos als „Laodikeia in Phoinikia" neu gegründet.[22] Der Name erscheint in griechischen Inschriften.[23] Es ist bemerkenswert, dass im Fall von Berytos das griechische Toponym Laodikeia phönikisch umgeschrieben wurde, dass das aber nicht mit dem Namenszusatz Phoinikia geschah. Letzterer wurde als Kanaan übersetzt, eine Gleichsetzung, die aus der Septuaginta (Ex 16,35) belegt ist. Offensichtlich war der neue Stadtname Laodikeia so wichtig, dass er transkribiert wurde und es wurde nicht das ältere phönikische Toponym verwendet. Laodikeia in Phoinikia wurde aber zusätzlich als Abkürzung LA und Ph auf die Münzen gesetzt. Auch in einer phönikischen Inschrift des Jahres 132 v. Chr. aus Umm el-Awamid wird Laodikeia auf Phönikisch geschrieben.[24]

Bemerkenswert ist, dass der städtische Titel um „'em", „Mutter" erweitert wurde.[25] Der Grund für diese Erweiterung ist unklar. Denkbar wäre, dass hier eine Übersetzung des griechischen Metropolis-Begriffs intendiert war[26], doch ist – anders als es im Griechischen zu erwarten wäre – nicht der Bezug so zu verstehen, dass Laodikeia die Metropolis „von" Phönikien/Kanaan ist, sondern, wie das Bet anzeigt, „in". Dieses Bet dürfte aber im Sinne von „von" gemeint sein, denn auch auf den hellenistischen münzähnlichen Tesserae aus Tyros wird das Bet zur Anzeige des Verhältnisses von Melqart zu Tyros verwendet.[27]

Vielleicht hat Berytos den Anspruch „Mutter" zu sein, auch von Sidon und Tyros übernommen, die beide die Mutterschaft für andere Städte reklamierten.

Andererseits – und das hat die Forschung bislang nicht gesehen – gibt es aber auch im westsemitischen Sprachgebrauch die Vorstellung, dass eine Stadt „Mutter" in (im Sinne von „von"?) einer Region sein kann, wie 2Sam 20,19 belegt, wo Abel-Bet-Maacha als Mutter in Israel (*am bisrael*) bezeichnet wird[28], eine Wendung, welche die Septuaginta bezeichnenderweise als *metropolis en Israel* übersetzt. Es ist also sehr wohl denkbar, dass sich hier in dem städtischen Mutterkonzept griechische und semitische Vorstellungen trafen.

Zum weiteren Verständnis dieser Münzen ist ein Blick zu den städtischen Bronzemünzen aufschlussreich. Münzen des 2. und frühen 1. Jh.s v.

---

[22] Sawaya 2004, 110 Anm. 7.

[23] OGIS II Nr. 247.

[24] Donner und Röllig 1962, 3–4 Nr. 18. Zur Identifikation des Laodikeias vgl. Donner und Röllig 1964, 26.

[25] Zur Lesart „'em" vgl. die Diskussion bei Moore 1992, 119–120; Sawaya 2004, 129–130; Cohen 2006, 208.

[26] Zum griechischen Metropolis-Apoikie-Konzept siehe z.B. Seibert 1963, 234–235; Leschhorn 1984, 95–98.

[27] Abou Diwan und Sawaya 2011; Bonnet 2015, 293.

[28] Vgl. Gesenius 2013, 69. Vgl. auch Tomback 1978, 23 zu weiteren Belegen aus dem Talmud und dem Arabischen.

Chr. verwenden die phönikische Titulatur „von Laodikeia, Mutter in Kanaan"[29], wobei die bereits bekannten griechischen Beizeichen LA und Ph[30] auf den griechischen Stadtnamen oder (nur auf den städtischen Bronzen belegt) BE und Ph[31] auf den gräzisierten phönikischen Stadtnamen kombiniert mit Teilen des hellenistischen Namens verweisen. Spätestens 87/86 v. Chr. wechselt die phönikische Legende zu *lb'rt* („l[e] Biarut") womit wieder der phönikische Stadtname verwendet wird.[32] In einem Fall wird dieser Name aber wiederum mit den griechischen Buchstaben LA und Ph kombiniert.[33]

Eine der früheren städtischen Münzen kombiniert sogar den phönikischen Titel „von Laodikeia, Mutter in Kanaan" mit dem griechischen *tes metr*[34], was wohl als *tes metropoleos* aufzulösen ist, womit deutlich wird, dass das phönikische Wort „Mutter" als äquivalent zum griechischen Metropolis-Konzept gesehen wurde.

Darüber hinaus unterstreicht die Fülle an Kombinationsmöglichkeiten griechischer und phönikischer Namen und Schrift, dass mit der Verwendung des einen oder des anderen keine Exklusivität einherging und keine Konkurrenz und kein Widerspruch zwischen den verschiedenen Namen bestand.

c) Sidon

Die Münzen von Sidon zeigen auf den Rückseiten entweder maritime Symbolik oder Europa auf dem Stier. Sie datieren auf ca. 168–164 v. Chr.

Nominal B (21–23 mm, 4,78–7,71 gr.):
(7) Houghton – Lorber – Hoover 2008, 83 Nr. 1453 (Abb. 5 [22 mm]):
Vs.: Kopf des Antiochos IV. n.r. mit Strahlenkrone und Diadem
Rs.: Galeere n.l.; *basileos Antiochou, Sidonion; lṣdnm* („l[e]ṣidonim" – „von den Sidoniern")

Nominal C (19–20 mm, 4,54–6,43 gr.):
(8) Houghton – Lorber – Hoover 2008, 83 Nr. 1454 (Abb. 6 [19 mm]):
Vs.: Kopf des Antiochos IV. n.r. mit Strahlenkrone und Diadem; *Basileos Antiochou Sidonion*
Rs.: Ruder; *lṣdnm 'm kmb 'p' kt ṣr* ("l[e]ṣidonim 'em kambe 'ap'a (oder 'ipp'a) kit ṣur" – „von den Sidoniern, Mutter von Kambe, Hippo, Kition, Sur")

---

29   Sawaya 2008, 63–69 série. 1–6; Hoover 2010, 30 Nr. 105–106; 31 Nr. 114.
30   Sawaya 2008, 63–67 série 1–5; Hoover 2010, 30 Nr. 105; 31 Nr. 114.
31   Sawaya 2008, 67–69 série 6; Hoover 2010, 30 Nr. 106.
32   Sawaya 2008, 69–74 série 7–8, 12; Hoover 2010, 30 Nr. 107, 109; 31 Nr. 115. Zur Datierung des Wechsels des Stadtnamens vgl. Sawaya 2004, 130–131.
33   Sawaya 2008, 69–70 série 7; Hoover 2010, 31 Nr. 115.
34   Sawaya 2008, 64 série 2; Hoover 2010, 31 Nr. 114.

Nominal D (17–19 mm, 2,60–3,95 gr.):
(9) Houghton – Lorber – Hoover 2008, 83 Nr. 1455:
Vs.: Kopf des Antiochos IV. n.r. mit Diadem; *Basileos Antiochou*
Rs.: Europa auf dem Stier n.l.; *Sidonion; lṣdnm* („leṣidonim" – „von den Sido-niern")

(10) Houghton – Lorber – Hoover 2008, 83–84 Nr. 1456 (Abb. 7 [17 mm]):
Vs.: Kopf des Antiochos IV. n.r. mit Strahlenkrone und Diadem; *Basileos Antiochou*
Rs.: Europa auf dem Stier n.l.; *Sidonion; lṣdnm* („leṣidonim" – „von den Sido-niern")

Kleinere Nominale der Emission zeigen zu dem Königsporträt auf der Vorderseite Apollon, Dionysos und eine Mänade auf der Rückseite.[35]
     Die Münzen nennen auf Phönikisch und zum Teil auf Griechisch das kollektive städtische Ethnikon und nicht, wie bei den anderen behandelten Prägungen, den Stadtnamen. Die Nennung eines phönikischen Ethnikons ist möglicherweise damit zu erklären, dass bei den größeren Nominalen auch auf Griechisch das Ethnikon und nicht der Stadtname genannt wird, wie es für griechische Münzlegenden üblich ist.[36] Das könnte der Ausgangspunkt für die phönikische Form gewesen sein.[37] Gegen diese Erklärung spricht aber, dass auf den Münzen von Tyros ebenfalls in der phönikischen Legende Sidonier genannt werden, während Tyros auf Phönikisch den Ortsnamen nennt und auf Griechisch das Ethnikon. Daher gibt es wohl andere Gründe, weshalb die Sidonier auf eigenen und auf tyrischen Münzen als Kollektiv und nicht als Ort genannt werden. Phönikische Königsinschriften aus Sidon aus dem 6. und 5. Jh. v. Chr. belegen, dass sich der König immer als König der Sidonier bezeichnet und nicht etwa als König von Sidon.[38] In Byblos dagegen, wird der König seit der Ahiram-Inschrift (ca. 1000 v. Chr.) als König von Byblos bezeichnet.[39] Die Angabe des Ethnikons in der phönikischen Legende ist daher wohl weniger als Aufnahme einer griechischen Praxis zu verstehen, sondern als Fortführung einer traditionellen Kollektivbezeichnung der Sidonier.[40]

---

[35]   Houghton und Lorber und Hoover 2008, 84 Nr. 1457–1460.

[36]   So auch das griechische Ethnikon auf den hellenistischen Siegelabdrücken aus Sidon, während die phönikische Legende den Stadtnamen nennt. Vgl. Ariel und Naveh 2003, 75–77.

[37]   Zur ungewöhnlichen Pluralbildung der Sidonier vgl. Friedrich und Röllig 1999, 34.

[38]   Donner und Röllig 1962, 2–3 Nr. 13–16.

[39]   Donner und Röllig 1962, 1–2 Nr. 1, 4–7, 9–11. So auch in der Münzprägung: Hoover 2010, 37–39 Nr. 130–131, 133–134, 136–140.

[40]   In diesem Zusammenhang ist auch darauf hinzuweisen, dass im Alten Testament Phönikier kollektiv auch als Sidonier bezeichnet wurden: Jinejian 1995, 69. Vgl. auch

Bemerkenswert ist die Münzlegende, in der sich die Sidonier als „Mutter" von Kambe, Hippo, Kition und Tyros bezeichnen: *lṣdnm 'm kmb 'p' kt ṣr* ("l^eṣidonim 'em kambe 'ap'a (oder 'ipp'a) kit ṣur" – „von den Sidonier, Mutter von Kambe, Hippo, Kition, Sur").[41] „Mutter" ist in diesem Kontext trotz der westsemitischen Tradition mit dem griechischen Metropolis, also Mutterstadt, zu vergleichen. Kambe, Hippo, Kition und Tyros werden zu Apoikien, Tochterstädten.

Bereits von Franz Karl Movers wurde vorgeschlagen, in Kambe eine sidonische Vorgängersiedlung oder eine andere Bezeichnung von Karthago zu sehen.[42] Für Karthago gab es in der Antike mehrere alternative Namen.[43] Karthago war bekanntermaßen eine Gründung von Tyros[44], und Sidon würde damit reklamieren, die Mutterstadt der bedeutendsten punischen Stadt zu sein. Auch wenn es Kritik an der Gleichsetzung von Kambe und Karthago gegeben hat,[45] scheint diese Identifikation doch die plausibelste zu sein.

Bei Hippo dürfte es sich um das spätere Hippo Regius oder um Hippo Diarrhytus, beide in Nordafrika handeln[46]. Eines der beiden hat im 2. Jh. v. Chr. auch eigene Münzen geprägt.[47] Beide waren phönikische Gründungen.[48] Die historiographische Überlieferung nennt aber keine Mutterstadt von den beiden Städten, weshalb es nicht möglich ist, den Wahrheitsgehalt des sidonischen Anspruchs zu überprüfen. Corinne Bonnet diskutiert Hippo Regius im Zusammenhang mit der Verbreitung des Melqart-Kults, was ein indirekter Hinweis auf Tyros als Mutterstadt sein könnte.[49] Sollte dies zutreffend sein, würde Sidon also auch eine weitere tyrische Tochterstadt als Mutterstadt reklamieren.

Kition ist die Stadt auf Zypern. Kition war bereits eine alte phönikische Gründung und es war eine Gründung von Tyros.[50] Offensichtlich rekla-

---

Bonnet 2015, 199 (zum homerischen Sprachgebrauch). Für die Nennung des Stadtnamens „Sidon" vgl. allerdings o. Anm. 36.

[41] Zur Lesung der Legende vgl. Movers II.2 1850, 133–146; Babelon 1890, CX.

[42] Movers II.2 1850, 135–144; Babelon 1890, CX; Bunnens 1979, 260–261; Grainger 1991, 112.

[43] Zu den Namen vgl. Huss 1985, 39.

[44] Bunnens 1979, 285–289; Huss 1985, 39–43; Bonnet 1988, 165; Günther 2000; Garbati 2015; Bonnet 2015, 80–92. Vgl. auch Daubner 2009, bes. 181–182, der eine fragmentierte hellenistische Inschrift aus Tyros sogar als Urkunde der Metropolis-Apoikie-Beziehung zwischen Tyros und Karthago rekonstruieren möchte.

[45] Gsell I 1920, 377–379. Vgl. auch Huss 1985, 39 Anm. 5; Abou Diwan 2012, 103 Anm. 30.

[46] Vgl. aber die Skepsis bei Gsell I 1920, 363.

[47] Müller III 1862, 53–57 Nr. 63–65; SNG Kop. 42, 672–675.

[48] Sallust Jugh. 19,1. Siehe dazu Bunnens 1979, 162–165, 374. Vgl. auch Gsell I 1920, 362–363. Zu Hippo Regius: Marec 1954, 8.

[49] Bonnet 1988, 195.

[50] Rey-Coquais 1987, 601; Bonnet 1988, 316.

Quasi-municipale Lokalbronzen im hellenistischen Phönizien 73

mierte auch in diesem Fall Sidon, die Mutterstadt von einer der bedeutendsten Tochterstädte von Tyros zu sein.

Ein solcher Anspruch ist nur möglich, weil Sidon in der Münzlegende auch behauptet, die Mutterstadt von Tyros zu sein. Es bleibt unklar, wie Sidon diesen Anspruch untermauerte, und die dazugehörigen Traditionen sind für uns in der Überlieferung nicht mehr greifbar. Deutlich wird aber, dass sich darin die starke städtische Konkurrenz zwischen Sidon und Tyros manifestiert, eine Konkurrenz, die vom frühen 1. Jahrtausend v. Chr. bis in die römische Kaiserzeit reichte.[51]

Möglicherweise erklärt sich die Zusammenstellung der Liste daraus, dass Sidon hier mehrere bekannte tyrische Gründungen für sich in Anspruch nahm. Allerdings muss eine solche Deutung hypothetisch bleiben, solange unklar bleibt, ob Kambe mit Karthago (oder einer anderen tyrischen Gründung) gleichzusetzen ist und das genannte Hippo tatsächlich eine Gründung von Tyros war. Sollte diese Hypothese aber zutreffen, so wäre offensichtlich, dass die Münzlegende vor allem gegen die Nachbarstadt gerichtet war. Für eine solche Interpretation spricht auch die zeitgleiche tyrische Münzprägung, die genau das Gegenteil behauptete, nämlich, dass Tyros die Mutterstadt von Sidon sei. Auch in der römischen Kaiserzeit wird noch aufwendig die Beziehung zwischen phönikischen Mutterstädten und punischen Tochterstädten gepflegt, wie Inschriften aus Tyros belegen.[52]

Die Konkurrenz zwischen Sidon und Tyros wird auch in der Bildauswahl der sidonischen Bronzen deutlich, die Europa auf dem Stier zeigen. Um diesen Mythos stritten die beiden Städte und beide reklamierten für sich, die Heimat der Europa zu sein.[53] Daher verwundert es auch nicht, dass beide Städte unter Antiochos IV. das Bild der Europa auf ihre Bronzen setzen.[54] Es ist dabei bemerkenswert, dass beide Städte einen griechischen Mythos wählten. Der Europa-Mythos setzt vor allem durch das Wirken des Kadmos, der bei der Suche nach seiner Schwester Europa zu einem wichtigen mythologischen Städtegründer und Kulturbringer wurde, Städtegründungen in Gang, welche gedanklich mit dem Metropolis-Konzept verwandt sind. Somit variiert das Bild des griechischen Mythos den durch die phönikischen Münzlegenden formulierten Metropolis-Anspruch der Städte.[55] Als Vehikel nutzte

---

[51] Bonnet 2015, 410.
[52] Rey-Coquais 1987; Lichtenberger 2008, 159–160; Bonnet 2015, 199–200. Vgl. auch die städtische Bronzemünze von Tyros unter Philippus Arabs: Lichtenberger 2008, 160 Abb. 28.
[53] Bühler 1968, 9–10.
[54] Sawaya 2012, 274.
[55] Die Ansicht von Meyer 2006, 7, das Bild des Europa-Mythos sei die Illustration zum Anspruch Sidons, Mutterstadt von Kambe, Hippo, Kition und Tyros zu sein, geht daher in die falsche Richtung.

74   Achim Lichtenberger

man den griechischen Mythos, auch wenn der Anspruch vor allem auf die phönikische Nachbarstadt abzielte.

Auf städtischen Bronzen von Sidon wurde die einfache phönikische Legende „von den Sidoniern" zusammen mit dem entsprechenden griechischen Ethnikon vom späten 2. Jh. v. Chr. bis in die zweite Hälfte des 1. Jh.s v. Chr. verwendet.[56] Anfangs, wohl in der Zeit von Antiochos IV. oder Demetrios I., wurde auch der lange Titel angegeben: *lṣdnm 'm kmb 'p' kt ṣr* ("leṣidonim 'em kambe 'ap'a (oder 'ipp'a) kit ṣur" – „von den Sidonier, Mutter von Kambe, Hippo, Kition, Sur").[57]

d) Tyros

Ähnlich wie die Münzen von Sidon zeigen auch jene von Tyros auf den Rückseiten entweder maritime Symbolik oder Europa auf dem Stier. Sie sind datiert auf 169/168-164 v. Chr., und von dieser Datierung ist auch die Datierung der entsprechenden Münzen aus Byblos, Berytos und Sidon abhängig.

Nominal B (20–23 mm, 4,35–10,30 gr.):
(11) Houghton – Lorber – Hoover 2008, 86 Nr. 1463:
Vs.: Kopf des Antiochos IV. n.r. mit Diadem und Stern
Rs.: Hinterteil eines Schiffs n.l.; *basileos Antiochou Tyrion; lṣr 'm ṣdnm* („leṣur 'em ṣidonim" – „von Sur, Mutter der Sidonier")

(12) Houghton – Lorber – Hoover 2008, 86 Nr. 1464:
Vs.: Kopf des Antiochos IV. n.r. mit Diadem
Rs.: Hinterteil eines Schiffs n.l.; *basileos Antiochou, Tyrion; lṣr 'm ṣdnm* („leṣur 'em ṣidonim" – „von Sur, Mutter der Sidonier")

(13) Houghton – Lorber – Hoover 2008, 86 Nr. 1465 (Abb. 8 [22 mm]):
Vs.: Kopf des Antiochos IV. n.r. mit Strahlenkrone und Diadem
Rs.: Hinterteil eines Schiffs n.l.; *basileos Antiochou Tyrion; lṣr 'm ṣdnm* („leṣur 'em ṣidonim" – „von Sur, Mutter der Sidonier")

Nominal C (16–18 mm, 2,00–4,57 gr):
(14) Houghton – Lorber – Hoover 2008, 86 Nr. 1466:
Vs.: Kopf des Antiochos IV. n.r. mit Diadem
Rs.: Prora n.l.; *basileos Antiochou Tyrion; lṣr 'm ṣdnm* („leṣur 'em ṣidonim" – „von Sur, Mutter der Sidonier")

---

[56]   Hoover 2010, 77–80 Nr. 281–285, 288–294, 299; Abou Diwan 2012, 94–98.
[57]   Hoover 2010, 78 Nr. 287; 80 Nr. 296; Abou Diwan 2012, 92–94.

Quasi-municipale Lokalbronzen im hellenistischen Phönizien   75

(15) Houghton – Lorber – Hoover 2008, 86 Nr. 1467 (Abb. 9 [16.5 mm]):
Vs.: Kopf des Antiochos IV. n.r. mit Diadem
Rs.: Prora n.l.; *basileos Antiochou, Tyrion; lṣr 'm ṣdnm* („l^eṣur 'em ṣidonim" –
„von Sur, Mutter der Sidonier")

(16) Houghton – Lorber – Hoover 2008, 87 Nr. 1468:
Vs.: Kopf des Antiochos IV. n.r. mit Strahlenkrone und Diadem
Rs.: Prora n.l.; *basileos Antiochou Tyrion; lṣr 'm ṣdnm* („l^eṣur 'em ṣidonim" – „von
Sur, Mutter der Sidonier")

(17) Houghton – Lorber – Hoover 2008, 87 Nr. 1469 (Abb. 10 [18 mm]):
Vs.: Kopf des Antiochos IV. n.r. mit Strahlenkrone und Diadem
Rs.: Europa auf dem Stier n.l.; *basileos Antiochou; lṣr 'm ṣdnm* („l^eṣur 'em ṣido-
nim" – „von Sur, Mutter der Sidonier")

Kleinere Nominale derselben Emission zeigen zum Bild des Königs auf der
Vorderseite auf der Rückseite eine Palme[58] oder eine Keule[59].

Tyros wählt thematisch ähnliche Motive wie Sidon, und auch in Tyros
werden zumeist sowohl das phönikische als auch das griechische Ethnikon
nebeneinander angegeben. Dabei ist zu betonen, dass auf Phönikisch – anders als etwa in Berytos – tatsächlich der ursprüngliche Name Sur genannt
wird und nicht eine phönikische Transkription des griechischen Namens erfolgt.

Tyros nennt sich in der phönikischen Legende konsequent „Mutter
der Sidonier". Dies ist die Kontraposition zu der phönikischen Münzlegende
von Sidon, in der Tyros (und vielleicht seine Tochterstädte) zu einer Tochterstadt von Sidon gemacht wird.

Blicken wir auf die städtischen Bronzen von Tyros in hellenistischer
Zeit, so finden wir auf den Münzen des späten 2. und 1. Jh.s v. Chr. die
schlichte phönikische Ortsbezeichnung *lsr*, „von Sur", die bis in die römische
Kaiserzeit weiter läuft.[60] Seitenhiebe auf Sidon fehlen. Letzteres erklärt sich
vermutlich aus dem zeitlichen Abstand zu den Prägungen unter Antiochos
IV., denn die städtische Münzprägung von Tyros setzt erst nach 126/25 v.
Chr. ein, während die quasi-municipalen und die städtischen Münzen von
Sidon, die den pompösen Metropolisstatus angeben, zuletzt unter Demetrios
I. (162–150 v. Chr.) geprägt wurden.[61] In der Zwischenzeit scheint sich dieser

---

[58] Houghton und Lorber und Hoover 2008, 87 Nr. 1470.
[59] Houghton und Lorber und Hoover 2008, 87 Nr. 1471.
[60] Hoover 2010, 98–99 Nr. 360–365, 367. Zu den kaiserzeitlichen Münzen mit
     phönikischem Ethnikon vgl. Lichtenberger 2008, 152, 156. Zu hellenistischen
     Siegelabdrücken und einem Astragal mit dem phönikischen Toponym vgl. Bordreuil 1996.
[61] Houghton und Lorber und Hoover 2008, 177–178 Nr. 1667.

Wettstreit in der Münzprägung gelegt zu haben. Über die Gründe, weshalb diese Konkurrenz vor allem unter Antiochos IV. bestand und unter Demetrios I. bereits auslief, hat sich die Forschung wenig Gedanken gemacht. Ein Grund könnte sein, dass beide Städte ab Alexander I. Balas (152–145 v. Chr.) mit einer umfangreichen königlichen Silberprägung begannen.[62] Diese schien zwischen den Städten koordiniert zu sein und während der zweiten Herrschaft des Demetrios II. (129–125 v. Chr.) war die Zusammenarbeit sogar so eng, dass ein tyrischer Beamte die Münzprägung von Sidon kontrollierte.[63]

Bei den städtischen Bronzen von Tyros ist im Übrigen bemerkenswert, dass ein griechisches Ethnikon nicht direkt angegeben wird, sondern nur als Monogramm der ersten drei Buchstaben von Tyros erscheint.[64] Dafür wird aber der griechische Ehrentitel *hier(a kai) asy(los)* auf einigen Münzen auf Griechisch angegeben.[65] Auf hellenistischen Tesserae aus Tyros wird der griechische Ehrentitel sogar in phönikischen Buchstaben transkribiert.[66]

3. Antiochos V. (164–162 v. Chr.) – Antiochos IX. (114/3–95 v. Chr.)

Auch unter den auf Antiochos IV. folgenden Seleukidenkönigen wurden in den vier Städten quasi-municipale Münzen ausgegeben, auf denen phönikische Legenden zu finden sind.

a) Byblos

Byblos prägt unter Antiochos V. (164–162 v. Chr.)[67], unter Alexander I. Balas (152–145 v. Chr.)[68] und zuletzt unter Antiochos VII. Sidetes (138–129 v. Chr.)[69] quasi-municipale Bronzen mit phönikischen Legenden. Es handelt sich jeweils um den Typus mit einer geflügelten stehenden Gottheit und der phönikischen Legende *lgbl qdš* („l^{e}gubul qudš" – „von Gubul der Heiligen").

---

[62] Houghton und Lorber und Hoover 2008, 210.

[63] Houghton und Lorber und Hoover 2008, 410.

[64] Hoover 2010, 98–99 Nr. 360–364, 366–368. Vgl. auch die Überlegungen von Hoover 2004, 491–492 zum Ende des Wettstreits. Er ist der Ansicht, die seleukidischen Könige hätten Interesse daran gehabt, dass die Städte ihre Rivalitäten beendeten. Vgl. auch Lorber 2015, 69.

[65] Hoover 2010, 98 Nr. 360–361, 364.

[66] Abou Diwan und Sawaya 2011; Bonnet 2015, 292-294. Nur das *kai* wird durch ein waw übersetzt.

[67] Houghton und Lorber und Hoover 2008, 135 Nr. 1578.

[68] Houghton und Lorber und Hoover 2008, 235 Nr. 1822.

[69] Houghton und Lorber und Hoover 2008, 379 Nr. 2099.

b) Berytos

Berytos prägte quasi-municipale Bronzen mit phönikischer Legende[70] unter Antiochos V. (164–162 v. Chr.)[71], unter Alexander I. Balas (152–145 v. Chr.)[72], unter Antiochos VII. Sidetes (138–129 v. Chr.)[73], in der zweiten Herrschaft des Demetrios II. (129–125 v. Chr.)[74], unter Alexander II. Zabinas (128–122 v. Chr.)[75] sowie unter Antiochos VIII. (121/0–97/6 v. Chr.)[76]. Zumeist handelt es sich bei den Rückseiten um den aus der Zeit Antiochos IV. bekannten stehenden Poseidontypus, der kombiniert ist mit der phönikischen Legende *ll'dk' 'm bkn'n* („l^{e}l'adik'a 'em b^{e}kan'an" – „von Laodikeia, Mutter in Kanaan"). Unter Alexander II. Zabinas kommt es allerdings zu einer ungewöhnlichen Emission. Zum einen wird der Poseidon nun auf eine Quadriga gestellt[77], ein Typus, der später in der städtischen Bronzeprägung der Normaltypus wird (Abb. 11)[78]. Zum anderen taucht auf einer quasi-municipalen Bronze als phönikische Legende wieder der alte Name auf: *lb'rt* („l^e Biarut") (Abb. 12)[79]. Zugleich erfolgt ein Wechsel der Beizeichen von LA und Ph zu BE und RY. Die Gründe für das Auftreten des phönikischen Namens bleiben unbekannt[80].

c) Sidon

Sidon gab quasi-municipale Münzen mit phönikischen Legenden unter Demetrios I. (162–150 v. Chr.)[81], unter Alexander I. Balas (152–145 v. Chr.)[82], in der ersten Herrschaft des Demetrios II. (146–138 v. Chr.)[83], unter Antiochos VII. Sidetes (138–129 v. Chr.)[84], in der zweiten Herrschaft des

---

[70] Vgl. dazu Sawaya 2004, 114–126.

[71] Houghton und Lorber und Hoover 2008, 136 Nr. 1579.

[72] Houghton und Lorber und Hoover 2008, 237 Nr. 1825–1826.

[73] Houghton und Lorber und Hoover 2008, 380 Nr. 2100.

[74] Houghton und Lorber und Hoover 2008, 426 Nr. 2185–2186

[75] Houghton und Lorber und Hoover 2008, 462 Nr. 2250–2252.

[76] Houghton und Lorber und Hoover 2008, 512 Nr. 2326–2328.

[77] Houghton und Lorber und Hoover 2008, 462 Nr. 2250.

[78] Hoover 2010, 30–31 Nr. 105–109, 111–112.

[79] Houghton und Lorber und Hoover 2008, 462 Nr. 2252.

[80] Sawaya nimmt an, dass die Stadt vielleicht kurzzeitig ein Privileg vom König erhielt und deswegen den alten Namen wählte. (Sawaya 2004, 121–122). Unterstützt würde diese Überlegung davon, dass Berytos die einzige Stadt der vier ist, die unter Alexander II. Zabinas Bronzen prägte.

[81] Houghton und Lorber und Hoover 2008, 177–178 Nr. 1666–1668.

[82] Houghton und Lorber und Hoover 2008, 239 Nr. 1833.

[83] Houghton und Lorber und Hoover 2008, 299 Nr. 1957.

[84] Houghton und Lorber und Hoover 2008, 382 Nr. 2104–2106A.

Demetrios II. (129–125 v. Chr.)[85], unter Antiochos VIII. (121/0–97/6 v. Chr.)[86] sowie unter Antiochos IX. (114/3–95 v. Chr.)[87] aus.

Die von Sidon geprägten Typen und Legenden entsprechen jenen unter Antiochos IV. eingeführten. Die Münzen tragen die phönikische Legende *lṣdnm* („l^eṣidonim" – „von den Sidoniern"). Der Typus mit Ruder und der pompösen Legende wurde zuletzt unter Demetrios I. ausgeprägt.[88] Zu den möglichen Gründen, weshalb Sidon nun nicht mehr für sich in Anspruch nahm, Mutterstadt von Tyros und anderen Städten zu sein, siehe oben.

d) Tyros

In Tyros wurden quasi-municipale Bronzen mit phönikischer Legende unter folgenden Königen ausgegeben: Unter Demetrios I. (162–150 v. Chr.)[89], in der ersten Herrschaft des Demetrios II. (146–138 v. Chr.)[90], unter Antiochos VII. Sidetes (138–129 v. Chr.)[91] sowie in der zweiten Herrschaft des Demetrios II. (129–125 v. Chr.)[92].

Die Rückseitentypen entsprechen im Wesentlichen jenen von Antiochos IV. eingeführten. Nur der Typus mit Europa auf dem Stier wird nicht weitergeführt. Außerdem wird die Legende *lṣr 'm ṣdnm* („l^eṣur 'em ṣidonim" – „von Sur, Mutter der Sidonier") zugunsten von *lṣr* („l^eṣur" – „von Sur") aufgegeben. Auch in Tyros zeigt sich in der quasi-municipalen Münzprägung, dass die Konkurrenz mit Sidon um den jeweiligen Mutterstadtstatus über die andere Stadt nicht von langer Dauer ist und hier sogar schon mit dem Ende der Regierungszeit des Antiochos IV. ein Ende findet. Sidon beendet den Streit etwas später nach der Regierungszeit des Demetrios I., in der im übrigen Sidon in der quasi-municipalen Münzprägung auch noch einmal die Europa auf dem Stier ausgibt.[93]

4. Schlussbetrachtung – Bronzemünzen als *Middle Ground*

Die vorgestellten quasi-municipalen Münzprägungen phönikischer Städte unter Antiochos IV. bieten ein Laboratorium zur Betrachtung des *Middle Ground*-Konzepts, wie es in der Nachfolge von Richard White entworfen

---

[85] Houghton und Lorber und Hoover 2008, 427–428 Nr. 2189–2192.
[86] Houghton und Lorber und Hoover 2008, 514 Nr. 2333–2334.
[87] Houghton und Lorber und Hoover 2008, 542 Nr. 2387.
[88] Houghton und Lorber und Hoover 2008, 177–178 Nr. 1667.
[89] Houghton und Lorber und Hoover 2008, 179–180 Nr. 1671–1675.
[90] Houghton und Lorber und Hoover 2008, 303–304 Nr. 1968–1969.
[91] Houghton und Lorber und Hoover 2008, 387–388 Nr. 2112–2114.
[92] Houghton und Lorber und Hoover 2008, 431 Nr. 2198–2199.
[93] Houghton und Lorber und Hoover 2008, 179 Nr. 1668. Das Bild findet sich später öfters in der städtischen Bronzeprägung von Sidon: vgl. Hoover 2010, 78–79 Nr. 284, 286, 290.

Quasi-municipale Lokalbronzen im hellenistischen Phönizien 79

wurde.[94] White hat eine Situation beschrieben, in der es zu einer besonderen kulturellen Ausprägung in einer kolonialen Situation in Nordamerika zwischen 1650 und 1815 kam, als Eingeborene und europäische Kolonialmächte miteinander interagierten. Obwohl die Kolonisten überlegen waren, waren sie doch auf die lokalen Einwohner angewiesen, und wegen dieser instabilen Asymmetrie näherten sich verschiedene Gruppen an, und es entstand für eine gewisse Zeit ein *Middle Ground*, auf dem eine neue Form des Kulturaustauschs erfolgte, der auch von bewusst in Kauf genommenen Missverständnissen geprägt war.

Numismatisch sind die quasi-municipalen Münzen zunächst einmal auf einer sehr basalen Ebene ein eigener *Middle Ground* für die Stadt und den König, etwas „in-between"[95]. Die Prägungen wurden nominell gemeinsam von König und Stadt herausgegeben, keinem gehörten sie alleine und jede Seite brachte etwas ein.

Auch wenn es sich in Phönikien nicht um eine koloniale Situation handelt, so ist doch ein nicht stabil asymmetrisches Machtverhältnis zwischen Städten und Königen gegeben, wobei jeder für sich einen unterschiedlichen kulturellen Hintergrund besaß und dieser durch die Sprachwahl der Münzlegende expliziert wurde.

Städte und Könige stehen für zwei unterschiedliche Gruppen mit nicht vollständig deckungsgleichen kulturellen Wertesystemen: auf der einen Seite alte phönikische Städte mit selbstbewussten Lokaltraditionen (Europa-Mythos, lokale Gottheiten), auf der anderen Seite militärisch überlegene Seleukidenkönige, die sich an griechisch-makedonischer Kultur orientierten. Eine solche Konstellation ist natürlich sehr vereinfacht, waren doch die phönikischen Städte bereits seit mehreren Jahrhunderten griechischen Einflüssen ausgesetzt[96] und haben die Seleukidenkönige durchaus auch ihre makedonischen Wurzeln in einem syrischen Umfeld weiterentwickelt. Dennoch kann man die bilinguen Bronzemünzen gut in ein bipolares Untersuchungsschema setzen, denn mit der unterschiedlichen Sprache ist zunächst einmal ein bewusster kultureller Akt der Distinktion vorgenommen worden.[97]

Für White ist das kulturelle „misunderstanding" eine zentrale Beobachtungskategorie, wobei das „misunderstanding" zu etwas neuem, Gemeinsamem auf dem *Middle Ground* führt.[98] Trifft dies auch für Phönikien zu? Als wichtiges Ergebnis der Diskussion der Bronzeprägungen mit phönikischen Legenden ist festzuhalten, dass etwa die zweisprachige Verwendung

---

[94] White 1991. Zur Übertragung des Modells auf die Altertumswissenschaften vgl. insbesondere Ulf 2009 und Ulf 2014.

[95] White 1991, XXVI.

[96] Grainger 1991, 108–112.

[97] Vgl. auch Iossif 2014, 73.

[98] White 1991, XXVI.

des „Mutter"-Konzepts zunächst zwar zwei unterschiedliche Hintergründe hat, dass aber das was Richard White als bewusstes oder unbewusstes „misunderstanding" sieht, hier nicht vorliegt, sondern das Mutterkonzept für Städte jeweils anschlussfähig ist.

Angesichts der Austauschbarkeit der griechischen und der phönikischen Legenden – wie wir das etwa in Berytos gesehen haben – und angesichts der Leichtigkeit der Übersetzungen, scheint es fraglich, ob ein besonderer *Middle Ground* notwendig war, damit phönikische Städte und hellenistische Herrscher zusammenkamen. Das bedeutet selbstverständlich nicht, dass es nicht vielleicht auch unterschiedliche Interessen der beiden gegeben hat, doch sind diese eher politisch zu sehen, als dass sie tiefgreifende kulturelle Alteritäten betreffen (wie sie etwa Europäer und nordamerikanische Ureinwohner potentiell erfuhren). Trotzdem werden Identitätsmarker wie Sprache und lokale Götterbilder in der Münzprägung eingesetzt. Die realpolitischen Gründe dahinter dürften, wie die Forschung schon lange erkannt hat, darin liegen, dass die Könige den Städten Freiräume geben wollten, um sie und ihre Flotten für sich zu gewinnen.[99] Diese Form der ungleichen Machtverhältnisse, die aber nicht stabil sind, und bei denen auch der vermeintlich stärkere Partner auf den schwächeren angewiesen ist, ist typisch für die *Middle Ground*-Situation, wie sie von White beschrieben wird.

Allerdings darf auch ein anderer Aspekt nicht außer Acht gelassen werden. Die Bronzemünzen wurden vor allem für den lokalen Geldumlauf benötigt[100] und die lokale Akzeptanz erhöhte sich, wenn bekannte oder lokale Bilder gewählt wurden[101]. Auch dieser nominalspezifische Grund könnte hinter den lokalen phönikischen Bildern stehen und in jedem Fall sollte man nicht einen Kulturkonflikt hinter den Bildern und den Legenden vermuten. Dafür gab es einfach schon zu lange einen intensiven mediterranen Kulturkontakt, als dass in Phönikien schwere Missverständnisse wie im kolonialen Amerika entstehen konnten. Daher ist es doch zweifelhaft, ob das Konzept des *Middle Grounds* wirklich die Situation der bemerkenswerten phönikischen Prägungen unter Antiochos IV. sinnvoll beschreibt.

---

[99] Vgl. jetzt aber Iossif 2014, 79–81.

[100] Vgl. zum erhöhten Bedarf von Bronzegeld im 2. Jh. v. Chr. in der Levante: Houghton 2004, 62–64.

[101] Zu dem Aufkommen der lokalen Bilder zunächst in Tyros vgl. Hoover 2004, 486–488.

Quasi-municipale Lokalbronzen im hellenistischen Phönizien   81

Bibliographie

Abou Diwan, G. 2012. Le monnayage civique non datée de Sidon: Opportunisme civique et pragmatisme royal (169/8–111/0 av. J.–C.), in: American Journal of Numismatics 24, 91–121.

Abou Diwan, G. und Z. Sawaya. 2011. Les tessères monétiformes de « Melqart à Tyr », in : Syria 88, 265–283.

Ariel, D.T. und J. Naveh. 2003. Selected Inscribed Sealings from Kedesh in the Upper Galilee, in: BASOR 329, 61–80.

Babelon, E. 1890. Rois de Syrie, d'Arménie et de Commagène. Paris.

Bonnet, C. 1988. Melqart. Cultes et mythes de l'Héraclès tyrien en méditerranée. Leuven.

Bonnet, C. 2015. Les enfants de Cadmos. Le paysage religieux de la Phénicie hellénistique. Paris.

Bordreuil, P. 1996. Bulles et poids de Tyr, in: E. Aquaro (Ed.), Alle soglie della classicità. Il Mediterraneo tra tradizione e innovazione. Studi in onore die Sabatino Moscati, I, Pisa, 47–58.

Bühler, W. 1968. Europa. Ein Überblick über die Zeugnisse des Mythos in der antiken Literatur und Kunst. München.

Bunge, J.G. 1975. 'Antiochos-Helios'. Methoden und Ergebnisse der Reichspolitik Antiochos' IV. Epiphanes von Syrien im Spiegel seiner Münzen, in: Historia 24, 164–188.

Bunnens, G. 1979. L'expansion phénicienne en méditerranée. Brüssel.

Cohen, G.M. 2006. The Hellenistic Settlements in Syria, the Red Sea Basin, and North Africa. Berkeley.

Daubner, F. 2009. Eine *apoikia* in einer hellenistischen Inschrift aus Tyros, in: ZPE 168, 177–182.

Donner, H. und W. Röllig. 1962/64. Kanaanäische und aramäische Inschriften, I–II. Wiesbaden.

Friedrich, J. und W. Röllig. [3]1999. Phönizisch-punische Grammatik. Rom.

Garbati, G. 2015. Le relazioni tra Cartagine e Tiro in età ellenistica. Presente e memoria nel *tophet* di Salambmô, in: Topoi Suppl. 13, 335–353.

Gesenius, W. [18]2013. Hebräisches und Aramäisches Handwörterbuch über das Alte Testament. Berlin.

Grainger, J. D. 1991. Hellenistic Phoenicia. Oxford.

Gsell, S. [4]1920. Histoire ancienne de l'Afrique du Nord, I. Paris.

Günther, L.-M. 2000. Legende und Identität: die 'Verwandtschaft' zwischen Karthago und Tyros, in: Actas del IV Congreso Internacional de Estudios Fenicios y Púnicos, 161–165.

Hoover, O.D. 2004. *Ceci n'est pas l'autonomie*. The Coinage of Seleucid Phoenicia as Royal and Civic Power Discourse, in: Topoi Suppl. 6, 485–507.

Hoover, O.D. 2010. Handbook of Coins of the Southern Levant. Phoenicia, Southern Koile Syria (including Judaea), and Arabia. Fifth to First Centuries BC. Lancaster.

Houghton, A. 2004. Seleucid Coinage and Monetary Policy of the 2nd Century BC, in: Topoi Suppl. 6, 49–79.

Houghton, A. and C. Lorber and O.D. Hoover. 2008, Seleucid Coins. A Comprehensive Catalogue. Part II. Seleucus IV through Antiochus XIII. New York.

Huss, W. 1985. Geschichte der Karthager. München.

Iossif, P.P. 2014. The Last Seleucids in Phoenicia: Juggling Civic and Royal Identity, in: American Journal of Numismatics 26, 61–87.

Jean, C.F. und J.Hoftijzer 1965. Dictionnaire des inscriptions sémitiques de l'ouest. Leiden.

Jidejian, N. 1995. Sidon a travers les ages. Beirut.

Jidejian, N. 1997. Beirut through the Ages. Beirut.

Le Rider, G. 1999. Antioche de Syrie sous les Séleucides. Corpus des monnaies d'or et d'argent. I. De Séleucos I à Antiochos V. Paris.

Leschhorn, W. 1984.„Gründer der Stadt". Studien zu einem politisch-religiösen Phänomen der griechischen Geschichte. Stuttgart.

Lichtenberger, A. 2008. Tyros und Berytos. Zwei Fallbeispiele städtischer Identitäten in Phönikien, in: M. Blömer und M. Facella und E. Winter (Hgg.), Lokale Identität im Römischen Nahen Osten. Kontexte und Perspektiven, 151–175.

Lorber, C.C. 2015. Royal Coinage in Hellenistic Phoenicia: Expressions of Continuity, Agents of Change, in: Topoi Suppl. 13, 55–88.

Marec, E. 1954. Hippone. Antique Hippo Regius. Algier.

Meyer, M. 2006. Sehen – Lesen – Wissen. Zu Bild, Schrift und Bildträger am Beispiel späthellenistischer Stadtprägungen in der Levante (https://www.uni-giessen.de/fbz/fb04/institute/altertum/philologie/dokumentationen/ikono texte-duale-mediensituationen/ikonotexte%20programm/ sehen-lesen-wissen) [zuletzt abgerufen: 18.4.2017].

Mittag, P.F. 2006. Antiochos IV. Epiphanes. Eine politische Biographie. Berlin.

Moore, W. 1992. Berytos-Laodicea Revisited, in: Schweizer Münzblätter 42, 117–125.

Mørkholm, O. 1965. The Municipal Coinages with Portrait of Antiochos IV of Syria, in: Congresso Internazionale di Numismatica. Roma 11–16 settembre 1961, II, 63–67.

Mørkholm, O. 1966. Antiochus IV of Syria. Kopenhagen.

Movers, F.K. 1850. Die Phönizier. Band II.2. Das phönizische Altertum: Geschichte der Kolonien. Bonn.

Müller, L. 1862. Numismatique de l'ancienne Afrique, III. Kopenhagen.

Rey-Coquais, J.-P. 1987. Une double dédicace de Lepcis Magna à Tyr, in : L'Africa Romana 4, 597–602.

Sawaya, Z. 2004. Le Monnayage Municipal Séleucide de Bérytos (169/8–114/3 ? av. J.-C.), in : Numismatic Chronicle 164, 109–146.

Sawaya, Z. 2008. Les monnaies civiques non datées de Bérytos, in : Numismatic Chronicle 168, 61–109.

Sawaya, Z. 2012. Tyr à l'époque hellénistique de la conquête macédonienne à l'autonomie (332–126/5 av. J.–C.) : histoire et monnaie, in : BAAL. Hors-Série VIII, 269–284.

Segert, S. 1976. A Grammar of Phoenician and Punic. München.

Seibert, J. 1963. Metropolis und Apoikie. Historische Beiträge zur Geschichte ihrer gegenseitigen Beziehungen. Würzburg.

Tomback, R.S. 1978. A Comparative Semitic Lexicon of the Phoenician and Punic Languages. Missoula.

Ulf, C. 2009. Rethinking Cultural Contacts, in: Ancient West and East 8, 81–132.

Ulf, C. 2014. Eine Typologie von kulturellen Kontaktzonen („Fernverhältnisse" – Middle Grounds – dichte Kontaktzonen), oder: *Rethinking Cultural Contacts* auf dem Prüfstand, in: R. Rollinger und K. Schnegg (Hgg.), Kulturkontakte in antiken Welten: Vom Denkmodell zum Fallbeispiel, Leuven, 469–504.

White, R. 1991. The Middle Ground. Indians, Empires, and Republics in the Great Lakes Region, 1650–1815. Cambridge.

Wright, N.L. 2009/10. Non-Greek Religious Imagery on the Coinage of Seleucid Syria, in: Mediterranean Archaeology 22/23, 193–206.

Abbildungen

Abb. 1-10 s. o. (alle Nachweise nach Houghton und Lorber und Hoover 2008).

Abb. 11 [19 mm] Städtische Bronzeprägung von Berytos, 87/6–82/1 v. Chr. (Hoover 2010, 30 Nr. 109).

Abb. 12 [18 mm] Quasi-municipale Bronze von Berytos unter Alexander II. Zabinas (Houghton und Lorber und Hoover 2008, 462 Nr. 2252).

Abb. 1: Vs.: Kopf des Antiochos IV. n.r. mit Strahlenkrone und Diadem; *basileos Antiochou*
Rs.: Geflügelte stehende Gottheit n.l.; *lgbl qdš* („lᵉgubul qudš" – „von Gubul der Heiligen")

Abb. 2: Vs.: Kopf des Antiochos IV. n.r. mit Strahlenkrone und Diadem
Rs.: Stehende Isis n.l.; *basileos Antiochou; lgbl* („lᵉgubul" – „von Gubul")

Abb. 3: Vs.: Kopf des Antiochos IV. n.r. mit Strahlenkrone und Diadem
Rs.: Stehender Poseidon mit Dreizack und Phiale; *basileos Antiochou; ll'dk' 'm bkn'n* („lᵉl'adik'a 'em bᵉkan'an" – „von Laodikeia, Mutter in Kanaan"); *La(odikeia) Ph(oinikia)*

Abb. 4: Vs.: Kopf des Antiochos IV. n.r. mit Strahlenkrone und Diadem
Rs.: Stehende weibliche Göttin auf Prora mit Ruder; *basileos Antiochou; ll'dk' 'm bkn'n* („lᵉl'adik'a 'em bᵉkan'an" – „von Laodikeia, Mutter in Kanaan"); *La(odikeia) Ph(oinikia)*

Quasi-municipale Lokalbronzen im hellenistischen Phönizien 85

Abb. 5: Vs.: Kopf des Antiochos IV. n.r. mit Strahlenkrone und Diadem
Rs.: Galeere n.l.; *basileos Antiochou, Sidonion; lṣdnm* („lᵉṣidonim" – „von den Sidoniern")

Abb. 6: Vs.: Kopf des Antiochos IV. n.r. mit Strahlenkrone und Diadem; *Basileos Antiochou Sidonion*
Rs.: Ruder; *lṣdnm 'm kmb 'p' kt ṣr* ("lᵉṣidonim 'em kambe 'ap'a (oder 'ipp'a) kit ṣur" – „von den Sidoniern, Mutter von Kambe, Hippo, Kition, Sur")

Abb. 7: Vs.: Kopf des Antiochos IV. n.r. mit Strahlenkrone und Diadem; *Basileos Antiochou*
Rs.: Europa auf dem Stier n.l.; *Sidonion; lṣdnm* („lᵉṣidonim" – „von den Sidoniern")

Abb. 8: Vs.: Kopf des Antiochos IV. n.r. mit Strahlenkrone und Diadem
Rs.: Hinterteil eines Schiffs n.l.; *basileos Antiochou Tyrion; lṣr 'm ṣdnm* („lᵉṣur 'em ṣidonim" – „von Sur, Mutter der Sidonier")

Abb. 9: Vs.: Kopf des Antiochos IV. n.r. mit Diadem
Rs.: Prora n.l.; *basileos Antiochou, Tyrion; lṣr 'm ṣdnm* („lᵉṣur 'em ṣidonim" – „von Sur, Mutter der Sidonier")

Abb. 10: Vs.: Kopf des Antiochos IV. n.r. mit Strahlenkrone und Diadem
Rs.: Europa auf dem Stier n.l.; *basileos Antiochou; lṣr 'm ṣdnm* („lᵉṣur 'em ṣidonim" – „von Sur, Mutter der Sidonier")

Abb. 11: Prägung von Berytos mit Poseidon auf der Quadriga

Abb. 12: Prägung von Berytos mit der phönizischen Legende *lb'rt* („lᵉ Biarut")

La place et le rôle de l'*agôn* dans le *middle ground* phénicien à l'époque hellénistique et romaine

Corinne Bonnet

Dans mon récent ouvrage sur la Phénicie hellénistique,[1] j'ai trouvé dans la notion de *middle ground,* empruntée à Richard White,[2] un cadre efficace pour ressaisir la complexité des relations qui s'instaurent entre les différentes composantes d'une société affectée par l'impérialisme gréco-macédonien. Le concept de *middle ground* ne renvoie en effet pas à un univers irénique où tout serait possible, serein et partagé. Il fait référence à un espace qui abrite des transactions, des procédures de négociation, des recherches de compromis, tantôt pacifiques, tantôt violentes et belliqueuses, marquées au sceau de la compréhension mutuelle ou du malentendu, de la bonne foi ou de la ruse, impliquant tout ou partie de la population, des chefs, des élites, des intermédiaires, des hommes ou des femmes, des « citoyens », des étrangers, des métisses, qui mobilisent des mots et des objets, des symboles et des slogans. C'est un espace concret et symbolique d'une grande complexité, rendu nécessaire par l'irruption d'un « autre » ordre politique et culturel. Le *middle ground* est, comme disent les spécialistes de marketing, une *win-win zone*, où les différences de statut, les hiérarchies politiques, sociales, de genre, les asymétries relationnelles s'estompent pour favoriser un « gain » réciproque qui n'efface pas les rapports de force, mais les contournent en quelque sorte. Dans cette *win win zone*, tout n'est cependant pas négociable, ni ajustable. Les travaux des sociologues sur les cultures émergeantes nous apprennent que les produits du multiculturalisme sont passablement imprévisibles, imprédictibles, mais que, pour les acteurs concernés, il est des éléments qui échappent à la négociation.[3] En d'autres termes, au sein du *middle ground*, la part d'*agency*, individuelle ou collective, est importante, mais elle est encadrée par une série de contraintes structurelles, de même qu'elle est rendue nécessaire, utile, créative par une conjoncture historique qui conduit à renégocier les réalisations quotidiennes de ces structures.[4]

On le voit : la notion de *middle ground* est riche en nuances et dynamique. Elle permet de sortir – telle était l'ambition de Richard White – de la dichotomie réductrice entre assimilation/acculturation et résistance. Appliquée au contexte de la Phénicie hellénistique, la notion de *middle ground* permet

---

[1] Bonnet 2014.

[2] White 2009.

[3] Grossetti 2004 ; Latour 2011–12.

[4] Sur ces notions, voir Sahlins 1989 et 1995, entre autres.

de s'interroger sur la manière dont réagirent les populations phéniciennes confrontées à l'arrivée d'Alexandre le Grand en 332 av. J.-C. et à la mise sous tutelle gréco-macédonienne des petits royaumes de la côte, précédemment sous l'emprise des Perses.[5] Quel était l'éventail des possibles face à un pouvoir nouveau qui se présentait en libérateur du joug achéménide, mais imposait ensuite le sien ? Quelle capacité de réaction avaient les Phéniciens qui connaissaient et fréquentaient les Grecs en Méditerranée depuis des siècles ? Parmi les cités phéniciennes, les unes accueillent le fils de Philippe II en « libérateur »,[6] là où les Tyriens, face à sa volonté hautement symbolique de sacrifier à l'Héraclès local, Melqart, le Baal de Tyr, dont il prétendait être, par le biais de l'Héraclès argien, un descendant, lui interdisent l'accès au sanctuaire insulaire et tente, non sans ruse, de le réorienter vers le sanctuaire continental.[7] Le lieu de culte, dont Hérodote affirme qu'il est contemporain de la fondation de la ville,[8] est envisagé par Alexandre comme un possible *middle ground* susceptible de favoriser un rapprochement, voire une « entente » autour du principe de *syngeneia*,[9] entre Alexandre et les Tyriens, par le truchement de leur dieu, mais il échoue et provoque un siège long et sanglant, de sept mois, l'un des plus terribles de l'Antiquité. De toute évidence, le sanctuaire insulaire ne se prête pas à devenir un lieu de partage ; ce n'est pas un espace négociable. L'impérialisme gréco-macédonien se déploie alors dans toute sa « splendeur » et, au terme du siège qui met un terme à la fière insularité de Tyr,[10] Alexandre exhibe logiquement les symboles de sa domination. Il surimpose ostentatoirement « son » Héraclès au Baal local qui ne disparaît cependant pas pour autant.[11] S'intéresser au *middle ground* ne signifie donc pas, comme le montre cet exemple, sous-estimer les logiques impériales ou impérialistes qui accompagnent l'intégration de la Phénicie dans le *new deal* politique, économique et culturel. Or, dans leur volume intitulé *Empires in World History. Power and the Politics of Differences*,[12] Burbank et Cooper insistent sur la capacité des empires à gérer « a vast and complex web of different territories and peoples united

---

[5]   Cf. Bonnet 2014 pour une étude approfondie des « paysages religieux » qui résultent de ces importantes mutations.

[6]   C'est le cas d'Arados, Byblos et Sidon, si l'on en croit les sources : cf. Arrien 2, 13–15; Diodore 17, 46–47; Quinte-Curce 4, 1, 6 et 15–26 ; Justin 11, 10. Pour l'analyse de ces divers récits, ainsi que les relations entre eux, voir Bonnet 2014, 58–59.

[7]   Cf. Arrien 2, 15 ; Diodore 17, 40 ; Quinte-Curce 4, 2, 2 ; Justin 11, 10. Pour toute la bibliographie relative au siège de Tyr, cf. Bonnet 2014, 41–106. Voir aussi Bonnet 2015.

[8]   Hérodote 2, 44.

[9]   Sur l'importance de la logique de « parenté » dans les relations diplomatiques à l'époque hellénistique, voir en dernier lieu Stavrianopoulou 2013.

[10]   Cf. Bonnet sous presse.

[11]   Cf. Bonnet 2014, 276–327, pour les nombreuses traces de la pérennité de son culte, jusqu'à l'époque romaine.

[12]   Burbank et Cooper 2011.

by force and ambition » et à façonner « an all-encompassing order » alliant centralisation et pluralisme, global et local, avec l'aide d'« imperial intermediaries » et d'« imperial imaginaries » vecteurs de légitimité et de valeurs partagées. C'est précisément dans ce registre de l'imaginaire, mais aussi des pratiques sociales qui en découlent que mon analyse se situe. Je souhaite en effet montrer que la notion grecque d'*agôn*, qui renvoie à l'émulation, à la compétition, mais aussi à la gloire et à la distinction, a non seulement été sollicitée par les nouveaux maîtres de la Phénicie pour asseoir et qualifier leur domination, mais qu'elle a aussi fait l'objet d'appropriations créatives de la part d'acteurs locaux qui s'en sont servi pour se singulariser et pour tisser ou rénover des liens au sein du *new deal* hellénistique. Dans un premier temps, je montrerai comment Alexandre et son entourage ont tiré profit de la notion d'émulation, et tout spécialement du lien entre Héraclès et l'*agôn*, pour asseoir symboliquement leur triomphe, en particulier à Tyr. Dans un second temps, en passant du registre de l'« impérialisme » à celui du *middle ground* et des transferts culturels, j'analyserai quelques inscriptions en rapport avec les pratiques agonistiques, comme révélatrices d'une articulation subtile entre local et global, identité et altérité. Ce dossier sera l'occasion de questionner la notion problématique d'« hellénisation » traditionnellement invoquée pour rendre compte d'une acculturation grecque des populations conquises, qui ne rend pas suffisamment justice aux stratégies mises en place de part et d'autre.

1. L'*agôn* comme symbole de la nouvelle domination

Après un accueil somme toute bienveillant – Arrien, Diodore, Quinte-Curce, Plutarque et Justin concordent sur ce point[13] – à Arados, Byblos et Sidon, Alexandre fait face à Tyr à une crispation qui se concentre autour d'un enjeu symbolique de taille : le culte du dieu tutélaire, Melqart, le Baal de Tyr. Ce qu'Alexandre vise, en voulant lui offrir un sacrifice, c'est une véritable *investiture* locale. En effet, honorer le dieu des Tyriens, c'est s'immiscer dans le réseau symbolique qui fait du roi « historique » un héritier direct du roi « mythique », puisque, faut-il le rappeler, le nom de Melqart fait de lui le « Roi de la Ville » (*milk qart*).[14] Le refus farouche, et presque insensé, des Tyriens montre bien que l'enjeu relève de cette association intime entre le religieux et le politique, entre le dieu tutélaire et l'identité, voire l'existence même du groupe. C'est donc au nom d'Héraclès que l'assaut à l'île prétendument inexpugnable est lancé. Les Tyriens bombardent leurs ennemis de balles de plomb

---

13 Cf. *supra*, note 6.
14 Sur Melqart, son culte et son rôle dans l'imaginaire tyrien, en métropole comme dans la diaspora, voir notamment Bonnet 1988 et 2009.

portant l'inscription phénicienne « Melqart a vaincu »,[15] tandis qu'Alexandre rêve qu'Héraclès en personne l'accueille sous les murs de Tyr, lui serre la main et l'introduit dans la ville.[16]

Au terme d'un siège féroce, en juillet 332, Alexandre, qui a transformé le paysage tyrien en reliant l'île au continent, entre enfin dans la cité et peut s'adresser sans aucun obstacle à l'Héraclès local. Dans son sanctuaire, de manière tout à fait symptomatique, se sont réfugiés le roi de Tyr et les ambassadeurs carthaginois présents sur place au début des hostilités, qui ont tous la vie sauve.[17] L'appropriation du culte du Baal de Tyr se fait alors massivement, ostentatoirement, sous la bannière de l'Héraclès argien dont Alexandre l'Argéade prétend descendre,[18] le fondateur des Jeux Olympiques. Alexandre organise une procession militaire en son honneur, une parade navale et un défilé au flambeau ; il fait également célébrer des *agones*.[19] Partout où il passe, il est vrai, Alexandre met à l'honneur le dieu tutélaire ou souverain du lieu, un choix qui pourrait entrer en résonance avec la célébration des *basileia* macédoniennes, mais aussi favoriser un rapprochement entre le conquérant et la divinité locale dans le but de légitimer son emprise sur le territoire.[20]

Une inscription métrique d'Amphipolis commémore, en deux distiques, la double victoire d'un *hetairos* macédonien d'Alexandre à la course armée et à la course du stade aux jeux de Tyr en 332 :[21]

> « Après qu'Alexandre eut détruit l'île de Tyr à la force de la lance et qu'il eut exalté Héraclès par des honneurs (*timais*) porteurs de prix, Antigone, fils de Kallas, premier parmi ses compagnons, remporta alors une double couronne, à la course de l'hoplite et à celle du stade. »

Le texte figure sur une base de statue (perdue) en marbre, qui devait représenter le vainqueur et qui avait été érigée à son retour en Macédoine, peutêtre dans le sanctuaire local d'Héraclès ou au gymnase. L'insistance sur la destruction de l'île de Tyr et l'exaltation d'Héraclès, deux événements corrélés, semblent tout à fait significatives. Les compétitions instituées à Tyr par Alexandre eurent en tout cas une postérité remarquable. En outre, dès le début du IIe siècle av. J.-C., on possède une trace épigraphique de l'existence

---

[15] Cf. Bordreuil 2000. Pour la mise en relation avec le siège de Tyr, Bonnet 2014, 72–73.

[16] Arrien 2, 18, 1 ; Plutarque, Vie d'Alexandre 24, 5-6. Sur le sens de cette gestuelle, voir Bonnet 2014, 75–76.

[17] Arrien 2, 24, 5 ; Quinte-Curce 4, 2, 10–12 et 4, 3, 19–23.

[18] Mitchell 2006.

[19] Arrien 2, 24, 6.

[20] Sur cette hypothèse, voir Lindsay Adams 2006 et Caneva 2012.

[21] Cf. Koukouli-Chrysanthaki 1971 (pl. 26–27); Moretti 1976, n° 113 ; cf. BE 1973, 286.

L'Agôn dans le *middle ground* phénicien

d'un gymnase à Tyr. Sur un autel prismatique à base moulurée, on lit en effet une dédicace grecque émanant d'un éphèbe vainqueur à la lutte :[22]

OYTI
ος Δηητρίο[υ]
ἐφήβους πάλη[ν νι] –
[κ]ήσας Βασιλεῖ Μεγάλωι
Ἀντιόχωι καὶ τῶι υἱῶ
Βασιλεῖ Σελεύκωι Ἑρμεῖ
Ἡρακλεῖ

« ------
fils de Démétrios
ayant été vainqueur à la lutte dans la catégorie des éphèbes
au Grand Roi Antiochos et à son fils
le roi Séleucos à Hermès et à Héraclès. »

Le bénéficiaire de l'offrande est Antiochos III, qui avait associé au pouvoir son fils Séleucos IV, ce qui situe la dédicace en 188/7 av. J.-C. Le vainqueur anonyme, dont le patronyme est bien grec, associe les deux Séleucides aux dieux du gymnase, Hermès et Héraclès.

Ceux-ci sont également attestés, un siècle et demi plus tard, en 25/4 av. J.-C., à Arados, dans une inscription bilingue grecque et phénicienne provenant également d'un gymnase,[23] mais, chose intéressante, la partie grecque les désigne comme « Hermès Héraclès », là où le phénicien exprime une offrande « à Hermès (…) à Melqart », (L'RM … LMLQRT), avec une transcription phonétique du grec pour le premier, mais une « traduction » ou *interpretatio* pour le second. Ces micro-écarts renvoient indubitablement à des stratégies et à des degrés d'intégration ou d'appropriation, mais aussi de résistance culturelles et linguistiques variables. Melqart, plus de trois cents ans après avoir pris la tête de la révolte tyrienne, résiste encore aux assauts de l'Héraclès grec.

Les documents à peine mentionnés témoignent en tout cas de l'importance du gymnase dans le nouveau paysage civique et cultuel : lieu de formation des éphèbes et de transmission de la *paideia* grecque,[24] c'est aussi un espace de sociabilité entre les différentes composantes « ethniques » de la société, en particulier ses élites. Enfin, comme l'indique l'inscription de l'autel

---

[22] Cf. Rey-Coquais 2006, n° 1, 17-18, fig. 1a–b.

[23] Musée du Louvre, AO 7676 = IGLS VII 4001, p. 25-26 ; cf. Yon et Caubet 1993, 55–56, n° 8, pl. III ; Briquel-Chatonnet 2012, 628–634, avec d'excellentes photos et un estampage (fig. 1-5, 630–632) ; Briquel-Chatonnet 2019.

[24] Cf. Chankowski 2010.

prismatique de Tyr, le gymnase fait aussi fonction de sanctuaire du culte royal,[25] un autre élément remarquable du paysage religieux issu du *middle ground* placé sous la houlette grecque. La présence d'un gymnase à Tyr a donc dû contribuer à la diffusion de ce que l'on pourrait appeler l'« hellénisme » entendu comme *ethos*, ou mode de vie grec au sens large. On connaît du reste deux gymnasiarques tyriens, l'un exerçant à Alexandrie, l'autre à Tyr. [26]

Ces charges ne sont sans doute pas sans rapport avec les concours athlétiques placés sous le patronage d'Héraclès et institués par Alexandre pour célébrer sa victoire, qui furent pérennisés.[27] Les Jeux Héracléens de Tyr prirent même une dimension internationale : tous les quatre ans, des délégations d'origine très variée se rendaient à Tyr pour y participer ;[28] à l'époque impériale, ils furent même proclamés panhelléniques. Les *agones* servirent donc à désenclaver les cités phéniciennes et à les inscrire dans des réseaux internationaux d'inspiration grecque, puis gréco-romaine, au même titre que d'autres régions périphériques du nouvel espace hellénistique. En d'autres termes, à travers ces pratiques agonistiques, c'est la *koinè* culturelle que l'on construit à l'échelle de la Méditerranée.[29] Les récents travaux d'Onno van Nijf et Christina Williamson, à Groningen, ont remarquablement exploré cette dimension, et continuent de le faire. Il s'agit, à travers ces grands événements centripètes, d'activer, de faire vivre et résonner, de donner à voir concrètement, dans toute sa splendeur, l'immense réseau des tribus grecques et assimilées, un monde connecté, sous la tutelle des grandes dynasties hellénistiques, puis du pouvoir romain, et sous la protection des dieux « indigènes », désormais valorisés à une échelle globale. Ces stratégies raffinées impliquent à la fois les autorités, les élites locales et le « grand public » avide de fêtes et autres déploiements fastueux, bienfaisants et joyeux, qui donnaient du lustre à leur « petite patrie ». Le 2e Livre des Maccabées, en évoquant la mission mandatée à Tyr par Jason, le grand-prêtre de Jérusalem, en 172 av. J.-C., pour prendre part aux Jeux Héracléens, mentionne la présence sur place d'Antiochos IV.[30] Ces festivals étaient donc aussi l'occasion de voir, de toucher, d'interagir avec le pouvoir « central », autant que de faire de la cité organisatrice, l'espace des Jeux, le

---

[25]   Cf. Virgilio 2003.

[26]   Cf. Rey-Coquais 1989, n° 2.2, 617–618.

[27]   Tous les témoignages relatifs à ces Jeux ont été utilement rassemblés par Abou Diwan et Sawaya 2011, 276–278.

[28]   Cf. Robert 1990, 704. Pour les traces épigraphiques de ces concours et de leur rayonnement, voir Rey-Coquais 2006, n° 57–75, 55–60.

[29]   Williamson et van Nijf 2016.

[30]   2 Macc. 4, 18–20 : « Comme on célébrait à Tyr les jeux quadriennaux en présence du roi, l'impur Jason envoya des représentants des Antiochiens de Jérusalem portant avec eux trois cents drachmes d'argent pour le sacrifice à Héraclès ». Sur ce passage, cf. Nodet 2005, 34, 144, 230.

centre du réseau. Le faste et la renommée des Jeux Héracléens de Tyr n'empêchèrent cependant pas les délégués de Jérusalem, dans un sursaut identitaire, tel qu'il est mis en scène par le rédacteur nationaliste du 2e Livre des Maccabées, de refuser de consacrer leur dotation au sacrifice en l'honneur du dieu de Tyr.

Tyr ne constitue nullement un exemple isolé en ces matières : Sidon aussi accueillit des *agones* à l'époque hellénistique, desquels, cependant, on ignore la genèse. Une inscription du IIIe siècle av. J.-C. mentionne une compétition en l'honneur d'Apollon *delphikos*[31]; un certain Abdoubastios y signale sa victoire à la lutte, alors qu'était agonothète Apollophanès, fils d'Abduzmounos, avec deux anthroponymes théophores qui renvoient l'un à Apollon, l'autre à Eshmoun. Le grand sanctuaire de Bostan esh-Sheikh, dans la périphérie de Sidon, où étaient vénérés Eshmoun et Astarté, mais où Apollon figure aussi en très bonne place, notamment sur la célèbre « Tribune d'Eshmoun » dont il occupe le centre,[32] a en outre livré des vases de pierre faisant fonction d'urne votive et portant des inscriptions agonistiques fragmentaires[33]. L'exemplaire le mieux conservé, datant de 43/2 av. J.-C., porte le texte suivant : « L'an 68, Sôsas, fils de Zénon, pour sa victoire, a dédié à Asclépios »,[34] Asclépios étant l'*interpretatio graeca* usuelle d'Eshmoun. L'urne, outre qu'elle évoque les procédures de déroulement des concours et le prix remporté, fait aussi allusion au rôle de l'eau dans le culte d'Eshmoun « à la source Ydal » et dans celui d'Astarté.[35] Comme a Tyr, les *agones* sidoniens se prolongèrent à l'époque romaine.[36] On voit aussi des Sidoniens participer aux *agones* en l'honneur d'Apollon délien à Délos, comme c'est le cas de Sillis qui prit part au concours de pugilat dès 270/69 av. J.-C.[37]

Initiés et promus par le nouveau pouvoir en place, les festivals agonistiques tissent leur toile à l'échelle de la Méditerranée, favorisant à la fois l'intégration des différentes composantes de l'empire à l'échelle globale et l'exaltation des spécificités civiques à l'échelle locale. Par ailleurs, le climat d'émulation inhérent aux concours, qui trouve son origine dans l'*ethos* épique

---

[31] Waddington 1870, n° 1866c; cf. BE 1977, 537. Sur le devenir des compétitions sidoniennes à l'époque romaine, voir Robert 1936. Cf. Robert 1990, 704. Pour les traces épigraphiques de ces concours et de leur rayonnement, voir Rey-Coquais 2006, n° 57–75, 55-60; Williamson et van Nijf 2016.

[32] Cf. Bonnet 2014, 231–245.

[33] Cf. Soyez 1972.

[34] *Ibidem*, 167-168 ; SEG 26, 1646.

[35] Cf. Groenewoud 2001.

[36] Pour les développements romains des concours sidoniens, voir Apicella 2002, 129–130. On possède plusieurs listes de vainqueurs, y compris des étrangers. Voir en dernier lieu Yon et Aliquot et al. 2016.

[37] IG XI 2, 203 A, l. 68–69.

Corinne Bonnet

et aristocratique, caractérisé par des valeurs telles que l'*aretè*, la *timè*, le *kleos*, etc.,[38] est de nature à servir les élites émergentes, avides de saisir cette occasion pour se distinguer localement, mais aussi aux yeux du pouvoir dominant. L'autocélébration de la cité, de ses dieux et des « meilleurs » parmi ses citoyens, en symbiose avec la glorification des nouvelles dynasties et de leurs glorieuses origines, finit par servir les intérêts de tous et par renforcer le « tricotage » des liens politiques, sociaux, culturels et religieux.[39]

Donnons à présent la parole à Diotimos, un éminent Sidonien, vainqueur aux Jeux Néméens, près d'Argos, honoré à son retour victorieux par la cité de Sidon tout entière. [40] Ce document ouvre une fenêtre extraordinaire sur les stratégies du *middle ground* phénicien autour de 200 av. J.-C. et implique, dans une relation féconde, l'individu et la cité, le passé et le présent, les pratiques et l'imaginaire sociaux.

2. L'*agôn* au service du *middle ground*

Diotimos est un membre de l'élite sidonienne, que son inscription désigne comme un *dikastès*, un terme grec qui renvoie sans doute à une charge institutionnelle locale que l'on nommait « suffète » en phénicien, un terme qui renvoie précisément à l'idée de « juger ». [41] Diotimos était peut-être une sorte de « gouverneur » local dans une cité désormais sans roi, puisque, assez rapidement, les autorités grecques mirent un terme aux dynasties locales. L'inscription honorifique, entièrement grecque, élégante bien que tissée de lieux communs, figurait sur le socle d'un monument érigé par la cité pour célébrer la prestigieuse victoire d'un des siens à la course de chars à Némée, en terre grecque. Le bloc de marbre (54 x 152 x 51 cm), découvert par Ernest Renan à Saïda en 1862, est aujourd'hui perdu :

> « La cité des Sidoniens (a honoré) Diotimos, fils de Dionysios, juge
> qui a remporté la victoire à la course de chars aux concours néméens.
> Timocharis d'Eleutherna a fait (cette statue).
> Le jour où, dans la plaine argolique, tous les compétiteurs,
> de leurs sièges, lancèrent pour le concours
> leurs rapides chevaux, c'est à toi Diotimos,

---

[38] Cf. Argyriou-Casmeridis 2016.

[39] Cf. Chaniotis 1995 ; Van Bremen 2007.

[40] Cf. Bonnet 2014, 260–265, 332–343, avec toute la bibliographie antérieure. *L'editio princeps*, due à E. Bikerman, date de 1939. Récemment voir aussi Couvenhes et Heller 2006, 35–38 ; Gruen 2006, 306 ; Stavrianopoulou 2013, 177–178.

[41] Flavius Josèphe C.Ap. 1, 157, témoigne de cet usage. Le titre de suffète est aussi attesté à Tyr à l'époque hellénistique. Cf. Apicella et Briquel-Chatonnet 2015, avec une interprétation de cette charge à laquelle je n'adhère pas.

que le peuple de Phoronis a décerné une belle gloire,
et tu as reçu des couronnes d'éternelle mémoire.
Car, le premier parmi les citoyens, de l'Hellade
tu as rapporté la gloire d'une victoire hippique
dans la maison des nobles Agénorides.
Exulte aussi Thèbes, la ville sainte cadméenne,
à la vue de sa métropole illustrée par ces victoires.
Pour Dionysios, ton père, est accompli son vœu pour le concours,
puisque l'Hellade a fait retentir cette clameur :
'Tu n'excelles pas seulement par tes navires, ô fière Sidon,
mais aussi par les attelages qui remportent le prix'. »[42]

L'artiste qui a réalisé la statue, actif notamment à Rhodes aux alentours de 200 av. J.-C., de même que le poète anonyme qui a composé l'épigramme sont des représentants de cet hellénisme est-méditerranéen, qui trouve volontiers ses modèles dans le grand réservoir de la *paideia* classique.[43] L'ombre de Pindare se devine aisément derrière l'épigramme de Diotimos. Comme dans les *Néméennes* du poète thébain, l'actualité de la victoire s'entrelace avec les allusions mythologiques pour terminer sur la célébration du lauréat et de sa cité d'origine, nouant ainsi les fils entre passé et présent, références mythologiques et constructions identitaires.[44] Rien n'interdit de penser que le poète fût sidonien, ou plus généralement phénicien, membre d'un des cercles littéraires de langue grecque qui fleurirent alors à Tyr, Gaza, Ascalon ou Gadara, dont Méléagre est le fleuron le plus connu.[45]

De même que jadis Alexandre avait augmenté la *timè* d'Héraclès en l'honorant à Tyr, de même la victoire de Diotimos aux prestigieux *agones* de Némée rejaillit-elle sur toute la cité de Sidon, et même au-delà. La mise en avant, dans le texte, des liens de parenté avec la Grèce, par le truchement d'Agénor et de Cadmos, apporte un surcroît de légitimé à l'intégration des

---

[42] Σιδωνίων ἡ πόλις Διότιμον Διονυσίου δικαστὴν / νικήσαντα Νέμεια ἅρμοτι / Τιμόχα[ρι]ς Ἐλευθερναῖος ἐποίησε / Ἀργολικοῖς ὅκα πάντες ἐ[ν ἄγκεσιν ὠκεὰς ἵππους] / ἤλασαν ἐκ δίφρων εἰς ἔριν ἀντ[ίπαλοι], / σοὶ καλόν, ὦ Διότιμε, Φορωνίδος [ὤπασε λαός] / κῦδος, ἀειμνάστους δ'ἦλθεν ὑπὸ στεφ[άνους], / ἀστῶγ γὰρ πρᾶτιστος ἀφ' Ἑλλάδος ἱππικὸν [ε]ὖχος / ἄγαγες εἰς ἀγαθῶν οἶκον Ἀγηνοριδᾶν. / Αὐχεῖ καὶ Θήβας Καδμηίδος ἱερὸν ἄστυ / δερκόμενον νίκαις εὐκλέα ματρόπολιν / πατρὶ δὲ σῶι τελέ[θ]ει Διονυσί[ωι εὖχος ἀ]γῶνος / Ἑλλὰς ἐπεὶ τρανῇ τόνδ' ἐβόασε [θρόον] ·/ οὐ μόνον ἐν ναυσὶν μεγαλύνε[αι ἔξοχα, Σιδών], / ἀλλ' ἔτι καὶ ζευκτοῖς ἀθλοφ[όροις ἐν ὄχοις]. Traduction personnelle.

[43] Sur ces milieux, en particulier en Palestine, voir Geiger 2014.

[44] Cf. Kurke 1991; Hornblower et Morgan 2007. Je note que le personnage de Cadmos et l'entité désignée comme les « Cadméens », ses descendants, sont présents à plusieurs reprises dans les *Néméennes* (1, 51 ; 4, 20–21 ; 8, 51).

[45] Cf. Gutzwiller 2013, parmi de nombreux travaux de l'Auteur sur Méléagre.

Sidoniens dans le grand circuit des festivals internationaux ou « panhellé-niques », puisque la tribu des Hellènes[46] s'étend désormais de la Macédoine à l'Indus. Avec habileté, l'épigramme suggère une reconfiguration spatiale par rapport aux mutations issues de la conquête : désormais, ce ne sont plus tant les Grecs qui s'imposent, victorieux, en Phénicie, mais aussi les Phéniciens, en l'occurrence les Sidoniens, qui conquièrent la gloire en Grèce et sont dou-blement honorés par les Grecs d'Argolide et de Béotie, outre que par leurs propres concitoyens.

Les références mythologiques, tournant autour du thème de la *syn-geneia*, un puissant opérateur pour penser les nouveaux réseaux relationnels,[47] visent à souligner un renversement de perspective, ou un rééquilibrage que l'espace agonistique et le savoir-faire de Diotimos ont rendu possibles. C'est pourquoi, dans la foulée, le texte rappelle, qu'avant même l'arrivée d'Alexandre et la soumission des royaumes phéniciens au pouvoir gréco-ma-cédonien, les Phéniciens avaient apporté en Grèce un don majeur : les *phoi-nikeia grammata*, symbole d'une certaine primauté culturelle des enfants de Cadmos et, en tout cas, d'un prestige doublement mérité.[48] Le succès de Dio-timos résonne d'autant plus que le fondateur des compétitions en l'honneur de Zeus Néméen n'était autre qu'Héraclès qui avait étouffé là-bas, de ses mains nues, un lion malfaisant. Si la conquête d'Alexandre avait bien soumis les Phéniciens aux Grecs, les Phéniciens veillaient à rappeler aux mêmes Grecs ce qu'ils leur devaient. Ils actualisaient dès lors, par le biais de la victoire de Diotimos et de l'épigramme l'honorant, un *kleos* ancestral. En reliant sub-tilement le présent et le passé mythique, cette inscription contribue à repenser la rhétorique de l'identité et de l'altérité, puisque la frontière entre Grecs et non-Grecs semble se diluer dans un espace aux contours renégociés, y com-pris sous le signe de l'émulation[49].

Les élites urbaines phéniciennes, issues en bonne partie de l'époque précédente[50], occupent donc habilement le *middle ground*. Ils adhèrent au mo-dèle grec de l'*agôn*, source de distinction, d'auto-célébration et de prestige so-cial – un modèle d'origine aristocratique dont les tyrans de l'époque archaïque avaient usé et abusé. Diotimos et ses pairs sont ainsi des acteurs déterminants et efficaces de la scène locale/régionale et internationale, où ils déploient des

---

[46] Dans la même direction, du point de vue des Ptolémées, voir Kainz 2016.

[47] Cf. *supra*, note 9.

[48] Cf. Hérodote V, 58.

[49] On peut envisager d'avoir recours ici au concept de contre-acculturation, comme dans Couvenhes et Heller 2006, 35–38.

[50] Sur le lien possible de Diotimos avec la famille royale sidonienne déchue, cf. Bonnet 2014, 205, 206, 347.

stratégies de médiation politique « gagnant-gagnant ». Quant aux « micro-identités » locales, enracinées dans des traditions que l'on redécouvre et remet à l'honneur, comme celles qui touchent à Cadmos et sa fratrie, elles trouvent dans l'hellénisme une caisse de résonnance appréciable, qui favorise l'adhésion à l'habitus grec – *agôn, syngeneia* – tout en mettant à l'honneur une certaine forme de « patriotisme » ou de « localisme » (re)naissant qui traduit, dans des formes renouvelées, l'appartenance à une Phénicie imaginaire ou mémorielle.[51]

En conclusion, même si les documents que nous avons examinés traduisent la forte emprise de la culture grecque, de l'« hellénisme », sur la Phénicie à l'époque hellénistique, ils donnent aussi à voir la capacité des acteurs à ne pas *subir* cette emprise, mais à s'en emparer et à s'approprier, de manière créative, voire paradoxale, les outils, les codes et les références d'un hellénisme qui fut initialement conquérant, voire impérialiste. La pénétration de ces « marqueurs » grecs – langue, style, goût, etc. – est d'ailleurs largement antérieure à l'arrivée d'Alexandre et connaît, après la conquête, une indubitable extension et intensification. Il n'en reste pas moins vrai que le concept d'« hellénisation », avec ce qu'il implique de vision à sens unique, avec la charge historiographique « coloniale » qui est la sienne, ne rend pas justice à la complexité et à la subtilité de ce qui se joue après 332. La notion de *middle ground* apporte, dans l'appréhension de ces processus, fluidité, dynamique, finesse aussi, pour appréhender et rendre compte des interactions qui se nouent après la conquête d'Alexandre. Au sein du *middle ground* phénicien, la *mètis* culturelle se concrétise notamment dans le cadre des pratiques agonistiques et à la faveur de nouvelles formes d'émulation culturelle, qui transforment les paysages, les modes d'agir et de penser, les actions et les discours.

---

[51] La conclusion d'E. Bikerman, dès 1939 (Bikerman 1939, 99), esquisse des perspectives intéressantes lorsqu'il estime que l'hellénisation dont témoigne l'inscription s'apparente au mode de vie « à la française » de l'Europe du XVIIIᵉ siècle.

Bibliographie

Diwan, A. et Z. Sawaya. 2011. Les tessères monétiformes de 'Melqart à Tyr', in: Syria 88, 265–283.

Apicella, C. 2002. *Sidon* aux époques hellénistique et romaine, thèse soutenue sur la dir. de M. Sartre.

Apicella, C. et F. Briquel-Chatonnet 2015. La transition institutionnelle dans les cités phéniciennes, des Achéménides à Rome, in : J. Aliquot et C. Bonnet (ed.), La Phénicie hellénistique, (Topoi suppl. 13), Paris, 9–29.

Argyriou-Casmeridis, A. 2016. Victories and Virtues: The Epigraphic Evidence for Hellenistic Athletes as Models of *arête*, in: C. Mann et S. Remijssen et S. Scharff (edd.), Athletics in the Hellenistic world, Stuttgart, 153–179.

Bonnet, C. 1988. Melqart. Cultes et mythes de l'Héraclès tyrien en Méditerranée. Leuven.

Bonnet, C. 2009. L'identité religieuse des Phéniciens dans la diaspora. Le cas de Melqart, dieu ancestral des Tyriens, in : N. Belayche et S. Mimouni (ed.), Entre lignes de partage et territoires de passage. Les identités religieuses dans les mondes grec et romain, Paris et Louvain, 295–308.

Bonnet, C. 2014. Les enfants de Cadmos. Le paysage religieux de la Phénicie hellénistique. Paris.

Bonnet, C. 2015. Le siège de Tyr par Alexandre et la mémoire des vainqueurs, in: J. Aliquot et C. Bonnet (Edd.), La Phénicie hellénistique (Topoi suppl. 13), Paris, 315–334.

Bonnet, C. sous presse. 'Ton territoire est au cœur des mers' (Ezéchiel 27, 4). Regards croisés sur l'insularité de Tyr, in: E. Guillon et B. Costa (edd.), Insularité, îléité, insularisation en Méditerranée phénicienne et punique. Ibiza.

Bordreuil, P. 2000. Nouveaux documents phéniciens inscrits, in: Atti del IV Congresso di studi fenici e punici, I, 205–215.

Briquel-Chatonnet, F. 2012. Les inscriptions phénico-grecques et le bilinguisme des Phéniciens, in : CRAI, 619–638.

Briquel-Chatonnet, F. 2019. À propos de l'inscription bilingue d'Arados, in : La vie, la mort et la religion dans l'univers phénicien et punique. Actes du VIIe Congrès d'études phéniciennes et puniques, Tunis, 65–72.

Burbank, J. et F. Cooper 2011. Empires. De la Chine ancienne à nos jours. Paris.

Caneva, S. 2012. D'Hérodote à Alexandre. L'appropriation gréco-macédonienne d'Ammon de Siwa, entre pratique oraculaire et légitimation du pouvoir, in: C. Bonnet et A. Declercq et I. Slobodzianek (edd.), Les représentations des dieux des autres, Caltanissetta, 193–219.

Chaniotis, A. 1995. Sich selbst feiern? Städtische Feste des Hellenismus im Spannungsfeld von Religion und Politik, in: M. Wörrle et P. Zanker (edd.), Stadtbild und Bürgerbild im Hellenismus, München, 147–169.

Chankowski, A.S. 2010. L'éphébie hellénistique. Étude d'une institution civique dans les cités grecques des îles de la Mer Égée et de l'Asie Mineure. Paris.

Couvenhes, J.C. et A. Heller 2006. Les transferts culturels dans le monde institutionnel des cités et des royaumes à l'époque hellénistique, in:

J.-C. Couvenhes et B. Legras (edd.), Transferts culturels et politique dans le monde hellénistique, Paris, 15–49.

Geiger, J. 2014. Hellenism in the East: Studies on Greek Intellectuals in Palestine. Stuttgart.

Groenewoud, E.M.C. 2001. Use of Water in Phoenician Sanctuaries, in: ANES, 38, 139–159.

Grossetti, M. 2004. Sociologie de l'imprévisible. Dynamiques de l'activité et des formes sociales. Paris.

Gruen, E. 2006. Greeks and non-Greeks, in: G.R. Bugh (ed.), The Cambridge Companion to the Hellenistic World, Cambridge, 295–314.

Gutzwiller, K. 2013. Genre and Ethnicity in the Epigrams of Meleager, in: S. Ager et R. Faber (edd.), Belonging and Isolation in the Hellenistic World, Toronto, 47–69.

Hornblower, S. et C. Morgan 2007. Pindar's Poetry, Patrons, and Festivals. From Archaic Greece to the Roman Empire. Oxford.

Kainz, L. 2016. 'We are the Best, We are One, and We are Greeks!' Reflections on the Ptolemies' Participation in the *agones*, in: C. Mann et S. Remijssen et S. Scharff (edd.), Athletics in the Hellenistic world, Stuttgart, 331–353.

Koukouli-Chrysanthaki, C. 1971. Αγωνιστικη επιγραφη εκ Αμφιπολεως, in: Archaiologikon Deltion 26, 120–127.

Kurke, L. 1991. The Traffic in Praise: Pindar and the Poetics of Social Economy. Berkeley.

Latour, B. 2011–12. Il n'y a pas de monde commun : il faut le composer, in: Multitudes 45, 38–41.

Lindsay Adams, W. 2006. The Games of Alexander the Great, in: W. Heckel et L. Tritle et P. Wheatley (edd.), Alexander's Empire. Formulation to Decay, Claremont (Ca.), 125–138.

Mitchell, L. 2006. Born to Rule? Succession in the Argead Royal House, in: W. Heckel et L. Tritle et P. Wheatley (edd.), Alexander's Empire. Formulation to Decay, Claremont (Ca.), 61–74.

Moretti, L. 1976. Iscrizioni storiche ellenistiche II, Grecia centrale e settentrionale. Florence.

Nodet, É. 2005. La crise maccabéenne : historiographie juive et traditions bibliques. Paris.

Rey-Coquais, J.-P. 1989. Apport d'inscriptions inédites de Syrie et de Phénicie aux listes de divinités ou à la prosopographie de l'Égypte hellénistique ou romaine, in: L. Criscuolo et G. Geraci (edd.), Egitto e storia antica dall'ellenismo all'età araba. Bilancio di un confronto, Bologna, 614–617.

Rey Coquais, J.-P. 2006. Inscriptions grecques et latines de Tyr (Baal III, h. s.). Beyrouth.

Robert, L. 1936. Notes de numismatique et d'épigraphie grecque. VIII. Fêtes de Sidon, in : Revue de Numismatique 39, 274–278 (repris dans Opera minora selecta, II, 1990, 1029–1033).

Robert, L. 1990. Opera minora selecta, VII. Amsterdam.

Sahlins, M. 1989. Des îles dans l'histoire, (éd. or. Chicago 1985).

Sahlins, M. 1995. How « Natives » think. About Captain Cook, for Example. Chicago.

Soyez, B. 1972. Le bétyle dans le culte de l'Astarté phénicienne, in : MUSJ 47, 149–169.

Stavrianopoulou, E. 2013. Hellenistic world(s) and the elusive concept of 'Greekness', in: Ead. (ed.), Shifting Social Imaginaries in the Hellenistic Period. Narrations, Practices, and Images, Leiden, 177–205.

Van Bremen, R. 2007. The Entire House is Full of Crowns: Hellenistic *Agōnes* and the Commemoration of Victory, in: S. Hornblower et C. Morgan (edd.), Pindar's Poetry, Patrons, and Festivals. From Archaic Greece to the Roman Empire, Oxford, 345–375.

Virgilio, B. 2003. Epigrafia e culto dei re seleucidi, in: Studi epigrafici e linguistici sul Vicino Oriente antico 20, 39–50.

White, R. 2009. Le Middle Ground. Indiens, empires et républiques dans la région des Grands Lacs, 1650–1815. Cambridge.

Waddington, W.-H. 1870. Inscriptions grecques et latines de Syrie. Paris.

Williamson, C. et O. van Nijf. 2016. Connecting the Greeks: Festival networks in the Hellenistic world, in: C. Mann et S. Remijssen et S. Scharff (edd.), Athletics in the Hellenistic world, Stuttgart, 43–71.

Yon, J.-B. et J. Aliquot et al. 2016. Inscriptions grecques et latines du Musée national de Beyrouth (Baal h. s. XII). Beyrouth.

Yon, J.-B. et A. Caubet 1993. Arouad et Amrit VIIIe-Ier siècles av. J.-C., in: Transeuphratène 6, 47–67.

The Ituraeans as a Hellenistic Dynasty –
Working the Middle Ground in Hellenistic Syria

Julia Hoffmann-Salz

The final decades of the Seleucid Empire are depicted as a somewhat desperate affair in our literary sources: several pretenders to the throne from within the Seleucid family struggled for power and in order to succeed, at least the final generation of Seleucids chose some apparently unsavoury allies – local Arab dynasts. This is the picture that emerges from Diodorus:

> "Pinning all his hopes on the alliance with Sampsigeramus, he sent for him to come with his army. He, however, having made a secret agreement with Azizus to do away with the kings, came with his army and summoned Antiochus to his presence. When the king, knowing nothing of this, complied, Sampsigeramus acted the part of a friend but placed him under arrest, and though for the time being he merely held him closely guarded in chains, he later had him put to death. So too, in accordance with the agreement to divide up the kingdom of Syria, Azizus intended to assassinate Philip, but Philip got wind of the plot and fled to Antioch."[1]

The beginnings of the Ituraean principality in and around the Beka-Valley are to be placed in this context of these emerging local dynasties carving principalities out of the failing Seleucid Empire.[2] To understand this particular historic milieu, the concept of the Middle Ground as developed by White has much to offer. As already stated in the introduction to this volume, White's concept of a Middle Ground is about stressing the mutual dependence of the agents negotiating political, cultural and economic contact. As long as there is a balance of power between these agents, a true Middle Ground as a common framework for interaction can be established and maintained, even if misunderstandings occur.[3] A balance of power was created in the frontier regions of North America because the European immigrants needed the Natives to survive in an unknown environment and the Natives needed the Europeans to enhance their position in intertribal conflicts. In this interdependent relationship, negotiating a Middle Ground became possible. But the balance was disrupted with the arrival of more and more Europeans, their

---

[1] Diod. 40, 1b.
[2] Kosmin 2014, 250.
[3] Cf. White 2011, xxvi.

adaptation to the life in North America and their increasing manipulation of intertribal struggles in their favour.[4]

Late Seleucid Syria also was a region in which various powers tried to struggle for supremacy within a volatile landscape of power: The Seleucid pretenders – like the European immigrants – faced imminent threats to their existence and needed allies to survive. Local dynasts, like the Natives of North America, offered support in exchange for privileges, that enhanced their own standing in the region, much like the native tribes of North America used European support for their internal rivalries.[5] Misunderstandings occurred on both sides, when agents did not interpret the balance of power correctly – and this worked both ways, as the story from Diodorus quoted above shows: obviously the Seleukid pretenders considered themselves to be 'natural' sovereigns whereas the local chiefs believed to have enough 'indigenous' authority to do away with them and thus questioned the validity of Seleucid kingship as a reference framework for their own power.

At least some of the negotiation process of native elites with superior 'external' powers can be glimpsed in the 'state formation' of the Ituraeans. Ptolemy, Son of Mennaeus, is the first leader of an Ituraean principality mentioned in the sources around 85 BCE, when he tried to conquer Damascus. He managed to enforce his position as a local leader during the invasion of Syria by Tigranes of Armenia 73/72 BCE. In 63 BCE Pompey confirmed this after Ptolemy paid him 1.000 talents.[6] Ptolemy's successor and son Lysanias supported the Parthians and was executed in 36 BC after their withdrawal from Syria – apparently at the insistence of Cleopatra.[7] However, after Actium, there was still an Ituraean tetrarchy under one Zenodorus, who was successively divested of parts of his territory, until after his death his remaining territories were given over to Herod in 20 BCE.[8] Until the mid-1st century CE smaller Ituraean principalities existed around Abila and Arca, which were successively transferred to Herodian princes before they were finally incorporated into the Roman province of Syria.[9] This paper will focus on Ptolemy, son of Mennaeus, and his negotiation of power between his local base and subsequent external powers in order to show by which means he established himself as a Hellenistic dynast.

---

[4] White 2011, xxxi.

[5] Cf. Sartre 2001, 380–383. The idea of this ‚exchange principle‘ is already expressed in Diod. 33,4: "Hence at any moment there were struggles and continual wars in Syria, as the princes of each house constantly lay in wait for one another. The populace, in fact, welcomed the dynastic changes since each king on being restored sought their favor."

[6] Flav.Jos. ant. Jud. 13, 15, 1–2; 13, 16, 3–4; 14, 3, 2.

[7] Diod. 49, 32, 4–5.

[8] Flav.Jos. ant. Jud. 15, 10, 2.

[9] On the history of the Ituraean principality see especially Aliquot 1999–2003; Myers 2010.

The starting point of an analysis of the Ituraeans must be their coins as their only surviving self-document. Ptolemy, son of Mennaeus, issued a series of bronze coins in 73/72 BCE, as some are dated to the year 240, assumed to be calculated to the Seleucid era. He minted coins that may reflect three nominations.[10] The heaviest coins depicted a bearded Zeus with a laurel wreath and on the reverse two men in armour standing next to each other – probably the Dioscuri (Fig. 1). The coins of middle weight have Artemis and on the reverse Nike with a wreath in her right hand and a palm branch behind her shoulder (Fig. 2). The smallest coins show Hermes with a winged helmet and on the reverse a winged caduceus on a club framed by loop bows.[11]

Though there is no proof in the documentary sources that Tigranes authorized Ptolemy's minting activity after his conquest of Syria, a connection between the two events is nonetheless likely, since Tigranes himself also minted coins at Damascus in these years.[12] These activities may thus be part of the administrative measures Tigranes introduced to his new territories and probably saw Ptolemy, son of Mennaeus, gaining recognition as a local authority.[13] But Ptolemy's minting activity must also be understood as a deliberate attempt at making a point. Various reasons for minting coins have been put forward in the scholarly literature such as military activities, victories, supra-regional competitions and games, building projects or a simple need for cash in local markets.[14] For the Hellenistic East, bronze coinage of local authorities such as cities is explained either by an economic demand for coins, as a political statement of independence or both.[15] These motives may also have played a role for Ptolemy, son of Mennaeus: economically, supplying coins to his principality not only facilitated market exchange but also brought revenue in different forms.[16] Politically, minting coins was both an advertisement of his new status and an act of proving that he was capable of fulfilling his new role to his subjects and neighbours. Since he minted bronze coins, it can be assumed that these were meant specifically for his own principality and the surrounding region, where he was competing with other power

---

[10]   Kindler 1990; Herman 2006, 52.

[11]   Ptolemy coined in two emissions 73/72 and 63/63 BCE nine different coin types, Lysanias three types of which some are dated to 41/40 BCE, Zenodorus seven types from two dated emissions from 31/30 and 26/25 BCE as well as undated coins. Only for three of these coins there is a known provenance from official excavations: Two coins of Ptolemy have been found in Gamala on the Golan and Bir En-Suba on the Hermon range, one coin of Lysanias was recovered on Tel Anafa. Ituraean coins have a number of counter-marks and monograms whose meaning is unclear: Herman 2006, 52–53.

[12]   Meyers 2010, 156–157.

[13]   Sartre 2001, 432.

[14]   Mittag 2016, 218–219.

[15]   Meadows 2001, 55–61.

[16]   Compare OGIS 339 where the citizens of Sestos proclaim to gain revenue from minting their own coins.

players.[17] As Kropp has already pointed out, coins and other monuments were testaments of propaganda for the local audience of a ruler creating new meanings by combining identifiable elements "designed to highlight social superiority and enhance royal prestige".[18] In the same vein, Butcher believes that coins were "an expression of identity" and continues "it is less likely that they were intended primarily to represent the public face of that community among other communities, […], and that instead they were chosen to represent the community to itself, or individuals to themselves etc., so that the symbols affirm rather than provide information."[19] He stresses that particularly gods and symbols were important indicators for the identity of a group.[20]

In order to be accepted, these coins of course had to correspond to people's expectations of how coins should look like. Therefore, the motives Ptolemy chose for his coins hint at how he interpreted the cultural Middle Ground in between the Greek Seleucid heritage, Tigranes as the new Armenian master and his own 'indigenous' legitimization. Zeus, the Dioscuri, Artemis, Nike and Hermes stress respect for and alignment with the Greek/Seleucid heritage – and possibly the military potential of the new principality.

After Pompey confirmed his position, Ptolemy, son of Mennaeus, apparently issued a second series of coins around 63/62 BCE with the legend *Ptolemaiou tetrarchou kai archiereos* in 12 spelling variants and substantial weight variation. The heaviest coins again depict Zeus, this time without a beard and on the reverse a flying eagle carrying a wreath (Fig. 3). The middle nomination shows Artemis with her hair in a pigtail and on the reverse a striding Nike with a wreath in her hand and a palm branch behind her shoulder. The Hermes-coin, too, is minted again. There is also an undated emission of coins with Pallas Athene wearing a Corinthian Helmet and, on the reverse, the Dioscuri in arms leaning on spears (Fig. 4). They have no legend but some of the monograms of these coins are also found on the coins of Ptolemy with legends.[21] From the numbers of coins on sale on numismatic platforms in the last few years, Ptolemy's emissions must have been quite substantial.

There is some debate as to the exact meaning of Ptolemy's title. The title *tetrarch* itself had been used by Pompey since arriving in Asia Minor as a title for local dynasts whose position was accepted by Rome.[22] Wright has argued that since tetrarch literally means leader of 'a fourth part', Ptolemy was only one of four leaders within the Ituraean dominion.[23] However, Coşkun

---

[17] Cf. Meadows 2014, 191–2; Bernholz and Vaubet 2014, 1: "competition among rulers strengthens the incentive to improve social arrangements and public institutions".

[18] Kropp 2013, 8–10, 382–384, quotation 384.

[19] Butcher 2005, 147.

[20] Butcher 2005, 151–153.

[21] Herman 2006, 64.

[22] Vollmer, 1991, 436–441; Baltrusch 2012, 69–70; cf. App. Syr. 8, 50.

[23] Wright 2013, 55–71.

The Ituraeans as a Hellenistic Dynasty 105

maintains that the concept of a partial sovereignty should be abandoned and the chronology revised. In his view, Ptolemy, son of Mennaios, acted as a local king under Pompey and was only later relegated to being a mere tetrarch under Marc Antony. For Coşkun, the dating 'year 2' on the coins of Ptolemy with the legend tetrarch and high priest refer to an era after Philippi and thus the year 41/40 BCE, shortly before Ptolemy's death. His successor Lysanias quickly returned to dating after the Seleucid era and kept the title tetrarch and high priest.[24] This reasoning is attractive, but one wonders why Ptolemy should have chosen not to put his name and royal title on his earlier coins only to then mint coins with a lesser title in the 40ies. If it is correct to assume that his coins are also a political statement advertising his status and its acceptance by the various superpowers active in the region, putting his name and a title such as tetrarch and high priest on his coins was meant to enhance his status, not broadcast a 'downgrading' from king to tetrarch. And Ptolemy, son of Mennaeus, had good reasons to represent his rank as gloriously as possible, as he was faced with severe competition.

But before discussing this, it is necessary to look at the second part of Ptolemy's title, high priest. Other local dynasts also called themselves high priests, such as the Hasmonaeans who were ethnarchs and high priests[25], or the dynasts of Olba in Cilicia, who were toparchs and high priests[26], or even the kings of the Phoenician cities, who also were kings and priests.[27] And they not only acted as political leaders but also as 'proper' priests in cultic activities of their communities. Some scholars therefore believe that the title of Ptolemy, son of Mennaeus, also implies a real double role as a political and religious authority in his principality and claim that he must have been high priest for a highest god of the Ituraeans.[28] A second group of scholars, however, considers the title tetrarch and high priest as a variant of the Ptolemaic and Seleucid title of the provincial governor of Syria, *strategos kai archiereus*. His position was not that of a priest proper but of a supervisor of all temples and cultic aspects in his province. His title as high priest only identified this specific right to access all sanctuaries and their resources.[29]

Adherents of the first thesis see Ptolemy as the Ituraean high priest, who – in the tradition of a Bedouin sheik – was both the political and religious leader of his community.[30] Correspondingly, the gods that are represented on the coins of Ptolemy are interpreted as Hellenistic variants of a local Ituraean

---

[24] Coşkun 2015, 172–188.
[25] Eckhardt 2013, 299.
[26] Hill 1899, 194ff; cf. Kropp 2013, 8–10; Capdetrey 2007, 168.
[27] Schwentzel 2009, 66.
[28] Hermann 2002, 90–91; Grainger 2015, 144.
[29] Tscherikower 1937, 38 from OGIS 230, cf. Meyers 2010, 101.
[30] Schottroff 1982, 138–139; Knauf 1998, 273.

triad, Zeus, Artemis and Hermes. These are then equated with the famous alleged triad of Heliopolis, Jupiter, Venus and Mercury.[31] Arguments have been put forward against this. Kropp, though in favour of associating Ptolemy's Zeus with Heliopolitan Jupiter and his Hermes with Mercury, has argued that there was no triad in Heliopolis.[32] Aliquot has surveyed the religious landscape of the Ituraean principality and even though most of the inscriptions offering information on the gods worshiped in this region are from the period of Roman rule, it becomes clear that there is no distinct triad at the top of the regional pantheon. He can also show that the gods of the Ituraean principality have both a strong Aramaean and a visible Arabic heritage, thereby making it impossible to take them as markers of 'ethnic' identity.[33] A further argument against an identification of these three gods as the highest gods of an Ituraean pantheon and also the gods to whom a priesthood of Ptolemy, son of Mennaeus, was connected, could be that they do not appear on all coin series of the Ituraean rulers: Ptolemy's successor Lysanias also minted coins. They show a 'royal portrait' of Lysanias on the averse and Athena with a Nike standing on her hand on the reverse. There are also coins with Nike, a veiled woman or a double *cornucopia* on the reverse. The third tetrarch Zenodorus minted coins, too. They have a portrait of the young Octavian on the averse and a bust of Zenodorus on the reverse. But he also continued issues of his predecessors with the bust of Zeus, Nike or the Athena from the reverses of Lysanias' coins.[34] If a triad of Zeus, Artemis and Hermes had been the highest gods of the Ituraean pantheon and the cult to which the Ituraean rulers were high priests, it would be surprising that they did not continuously depict them on their coins.

This is not to say, however, that Zeus in particular may not be the Greek version of a local highest god. After all, the only securely located capital of the descendants of Ptolemy, Abila of Lysanias, has a temple for Zeus and Cronus, the hellenized 'version' of the Aramean highest god El.[35] Diodorus equates El with Cronus, but also with Helios and Saturn.[36] This offers obvious links to Helios/Jupiter Heliopolitanus in Heliopolis and also to the temple of Saturn in Majdal Anjar, one of the possible locations for Chalcis, the so far not located capital of Ptolemy's principality. Kropp believes that Ptolemy was *archiereus* to a cult of a local Zeus, the Baal of Heliopolis/Baalbek,

---

[31] Hermann 2002, 91.

[32] Kropp 2013, 239–240.

[33] Aliquot 2009, 183–187.

[34] Schwentzel 2009, 69–72.

[35] Gatier 2003, 120ff.

[36] Diod. 2, 30, 3-4. On the analogy of Baal Hammon – El – Cronus – Saturn – Pluto see Theuer 2000, 316. On Zeus and Helios Merkelbach 2001, 78–79.

since he only uses this title on his heaviest coins depicting Zeus.[37]A highest god connected to the sun or the sky in general would fit in with trends in the region, where Niehr sees a widespread popularity of a highest celestial god with solar qualities fed by Aramaic, Achaemenid and Hellenistic traditions. Niehr even believes the Ituraeans to be the transmitters of this trend from Mesopotamia and central Syria to the Phoenician coast.[38] More importantly, he stresses that this god is closely associated with the ruling houses as the gods ruled the universe and pantheon just like the kings ruled their territories.[39] Even though the idea of a Seleucid patronage of Zeus in order to assimilate this Syrian tradition is contested in scholarship, Zeus was still depicted on Seleucid coins and could have been interpreted in the context of this association of highest celestial god and kingship by the local population.[40] Thus, when Wright maintains that Zeus and Tyche/a female goddess that replace Apollo as the preferred motive on silver coins of the late Seleucids "almost certainly represent the Syrian gods Ba'al Hadad and Atargatis in Hellenic guise"[41], this may have been an intentional policy of offering a Middle Ground but could also be the result of very different developments unknown to us. However, their frequency on Seleucid coins must have inextricably linked them to Seleucid royal power for their subjects and users of the coins. The same may be said about the other gods popular on Seleucid coins, which were – apart from Zeus – particularly Athena, Apollon and Artemis. Apollon seems to have been associated with Helios, bringing us back to the El – Cronus – Helios – analogy.[42] Additionally, Hermes was also depicted on late Seleucid coins, such as on the reverse of a series of coins from the Damascus mint under Demetrios III Eukarios.[43] Ptolemy may thus have chosen to use Zeus and his official title on his heaviest coins precisely because he could then tap into this perceived tradition of Seleucid power imagery.

It becomes obvious that the gods chosen by Ptolemy, son of Mennaeus, for his coins were selected because they could be 'read' by different

---

[37] Kropp 2013, 30. Similar connection between the priesthood of Ptolemy and Heliopolis/Baalbek e.g. in Herman, 90–91.

[38] Niehr 2003, 51, 85, 87. Compare Aristoph. Peace 406–413 on the importance of Sun and Moon for the Persians; Luk. de Dea Syria 34 on Sun/Helios and Moon/Selene for Syria.

[39] Niehr 2003, 35.

[40] On Zeus and the Seleucids cf. Dowden 2006, 78; Erickson 2013, 119; Mastrocinque 2002, 368 *non vidi*, against a use of Zeus as an integrative figure for the local gods see Mittag 2006, 139–145.

[41] Wright 2009/10, 200.

[42] Lorber and Iossif 2009, 21, 32. See also the Seleucid coins from Susa depicting Artemis, Apollon, Athena, the Dioscuri, Hermes and possibly Zeus and Herakles: Frye 1984, 157.

[43] 97/6–98/7 BCE, SC 2456.2; HGC 9, 1312.

groups and because they were closely associated with kingship and power.[44] And this is also true for the one motive on Ituraean coins that has been considered to be Ptolemy's most individual choice: the Dioscuri. Divine twins, associated with the Morning and the Evening Star and the Moon, are common elements of both Aramaic and Arabic religion. Thus, the famous Zakkur inscription names divine twins apparently in place of the moon god[45] and they were also popular in supposedly Arabic contexts in Palmyra, Emesa and Edessa under a variety of names.[46] Their association with the Moon also makes possible a connection with Artemis, who is sometimes linked to the moon.[47] Again, however, it is important to highlight that the Dioscuri were equally a not uncommon motive on coins in late Hellenistic Syria either as portraits or as their symbols.[48] And again, the Dioscuri are a motive that is 'relatable' to all the various audiences that Ptolemy's coins could meet: the local Aramaic and Arabic populations, the Phoenician and Hellenistic neighbours, probably even the Armenian invaders and later the Romans.

Thus, the choice of gods stresses the political message that Ptolemy wished to promote with his coins – the legitimacy of his rule. Chaniotis sums up the rule of Hellenistic kings as follows: „Hellenistic kings founded the legitimacy of their rule not only on dynastic principles, but also to a great extent on military victories, on a privileged relationship with the divine (usually in the form of the royal cult), and on their role as benefactors."[49] These key aspects – legitimacy, military victory, privileged relationship to the gods and bringer of benefactions – are implicitly 'covered' by Ptolemy's coins. First, legitimacy: at least since the use of the legend of tetrarch and high priest, Ptolemy could boast a legitimized claim to power. References to military success, if not actual victories, are found in the fact that Athena, Artemis and also the Dioscuri have military connotations. The Dioscuri are even depicted

---

[44] Niehr also argues for Baitokaike that it is a regional sanctuary for a league of cities under the control of Arados and that the Zeus of Baitokaike is this league's god, while all cities also venerated their own gods: Niehr 2003, 47–50. In this sense, the gods from the coins of the Ituraeans could also be considered as 'state gods' endorsed by the ruling house to promote the unity of the principality.

[45] Niehr 2014, 169.

[46] Hvidberg-Hansen 2007, 14–15, 36, 96–97.

[47] Take the merging of Artemis and Isis e.g. at Ephesus, where they are the queen of the sky ruling over Sun and Moon or Theokrit's version of a unit of Artemis, Selene and Hecate: von Stuckrad 2000, 597–598; Petrovic 2007, 4ff.

[48] Their portraits are e.g. found on coins from Ake Ptolemais between 132 and 118 BCE: Kadman 1961, 51, 182–183; their caps and stars are depicted on a series of coins of Ptolemy V (204–181 BCE), their portraits on coins from Tripolis 189/88 BCE, the *pilei* again on coins from Beirut under Demetrius I (162–50 BCE), Antiochus VII (138–29 BCE), Antiochus X (94–83 BCE), and during the course of the 1st century BCE: Murray 1991, 54–56. Cf. Lichtenberger 2009, 155.

[49] Chaniotis 2002, 106.

The Ituraeans as a Hellenistic Dynasty 109

in armor. This, again, is not so unusual since the Aramaic weather and moon gods were also portrayed with weapons like bows, swords and lances.[50] Clearly, these gods point to the military prowess of Ptolemy and his army. And they are probably also meant to highlight a privileged connection between Ptolemy and these gods. This has already been argued particularly for the Dioscuri. In Syria, these gods are often called Monimus and Azizus with Ptolemy's father Mennaeus/Monikos potentially being associated with Monimus.[51] This could be considered as a nascent hero/ruler cult, but the evidence is slight.[52] However, Ptolemy's close connection to the gods could also be expressed in his function as *archiereus*, making him the chief intermediary between his community and the gods. This suggests that his title of *tetrarch* and *archiereus* was consciously modelled on the existing titles in the region both from the Phoenician and Hasmonean kings and the Seleucid governors.

Also visible, however, is the Dioscuri's connection to the final element of Hellenistic kingship: the ruler as benefactor. The divine twins are protective gods, particularly of travelers and merchants (and seafarers). This competence was associated with them both in Hellenistic and 'Arabic' tradition.[53] And it may hint at the economic backbone of Ptolemy's rule – trade. Due to the geological conditions in the Near East, there were three distinctive routes for North-South-trade and travel: The 'coastal route' along the Mediterranean coast, the 'valley route' along the Jordan Valley and then up the Beka-Valley, and the 'inland route' sidelining the Jordan Rift and the Antilebanon range on its eastern sides passing via Damascus to Emesa and the North. The Beka-Valley was under Ituraean control and continued to be used as a trade route. Material remains in Kamid el-Loz at the southern end of the Beka-Valley have inspired the archaeologists to claim that the place was a "reloading point in the long-distance trade in the Hellenistic period".[54] Findings from other sites such as Arca, Yanouh or Qalat el Hosn also suggest that the settlements in the area were well connected to regional and supra-regional trade networks.[55] Ptolemy also endeavored to gain control of parts of the other two routes: twice he tried to conquer Damascus[56] and he also attacked cities along the coast and established forts there.[57] Both these activities gain him mentions in the literary sources – and a bad reputation. Thus, Josephus

---

[50] Theuer 2000, 334; Bunnens 2015, 111–116; Will 1947–48, 21–36; Merlat 1951, 229–249.
[51] Cf. Schwentzel 2009, 68.
[52] Kropp 2013, 239.
[53] Hvidberg-Hansen 2007, 14–15, 36, 96–97; Seyrig 1970, 77–111; Gawlikowski 2015, 252–253; Walker 2015, 139–147.
[54] Kulemann-Ossen and Leicht and Heinz 2007/2008, 170–179.
[51] Arca: J.-P. Thalmann 2000, 13; Yanouh: M. Al-Maqdissi 2005, 39; Qalat el Hosn: P. Ghanimé-Marion 2007, 103–139.
[56] Flav. Jos. ant. Jud. 13, 392; bell. Jud. 1, 103.
[57] Strab. 16, 2, 18.

remarks that at Ptolemy's first attack, the Damascenes invited the Nabataean king Aretas to take over their city "because of their hatred against Ptolemy, son of Mennaeus". [58] But if one ignores the slur against Ptolemy, it becomes apparent that he deliberately sought to gain control over the major trade arteries. These routes must have been used to trade many different products and potentially rather valuable ones high in demand everywhere in the ancient world, such as incense.[59] Valuable goods would of course increase the profits for Ptolemy, as he could exact higher customs duties. By choosing the Dioscuri for his coins, Ptolemy may have been alluding to this economic benefit of his rule. A very similar message of economic prosperity, protection of trade and peace may have been the reason to choose Hermes, who is also associated with these aspects.[60]

This again underlines Ptolemy's ambition to proof himself as a 'proper' Hellenistic ruler. As such, he also engaged in diplomatic activities with his neighbours. He cooperated with Marian, the local tyrant of Tyre[61], formed a marriage alliance with Dionysus, the ruler of Tripolis[62], and offered refuge to the surviving children of the Hasmonaean Aristobulos II after he was executed by the Romans. Josephus recounts that Ptolemy later even married one of the Hasmonaean princesses he had rescued.[63] Taken together, these actions show Ptolemy's ambition to be accepted amongst his neighbours.

A multilateral legitimization strategy within a Hellenistic framework becomes apparent here, whereby Ptolemy stresses that his rule and expansion policy bring benefactions to his people and therefore show his support by the gods. Of course, stressing the legitimacy of his rule was relevant both to his subjects and to his neighbours.[64] And both groups of recipients make it obvious why Ptolemy had to take such care with this issue: he faced serious competition from both! From the description of his expansion towards the coast and Damascus it has already become apparent that there was a fierce territorial rivalry between Ptolemy and the surrounding communities – a competition that probably had much to do with the control of the trade routes of the wider region as argued above.

But his rule was also contested within the Ituraean community as there seems to have been a strong local elite or even rival ruling house

---

[58]   Flav. Jos. ant. Jud. 13, 392.
[59]   On the importance of incense as a standard sacrifice to the gods in the Near East cf. Kaizer 2008, 182–183.
[60]   Compare the very similar reasoning behind Augustus' identification with Hermes/Mercury: Chittenden 1945, 42 and 46ff. for the promotion of Hermes by Hellenistic rulers.
[61]   Flav. Jos. ant. Jud. 14, 297.
[62]   Flav. Jos. ant. Jud. 14, 39.
[63]   Flav. Jos. bell. Jud. 1, 185–186; ant. Jud. 14, 125–126.
[64]   Cf. Baltrusch 2012, 235.

The Ituraeans as a Hellenistic Dynasty
111

challenging his position at Arca. This could be inferred from the information in Josephus that Iamblichus of Arca supported Caesar with troops, while Ptolemaios son of Mennaeus had been on Pompey's side.[65] The ruling house at Arca had Semitic names – we know Iamblichus, who actually called his son Ptolemy, and in the next generation there are Soaimus and his son Noarus or Ouarus. Arca would go on to call itself 'Arca of the Ituraeans' on coins of the 2nd century CE.[66] The leading family at Arca thus seems to have used the 'indigenous ticket' to legitimize their position and Ptolemy son of Mennaeus and his family may have chosen the 'Hellenistic' one as an alternative means of justifying their rule.

This strong competition for power both from inside the Ituraean community and from its neighbours may then have been a decisive force for Ptolemy's decision to mint coins. Meadows argues that "the driving forces behind [small-scale coinage] may have been inter-civic competition"[67] and this must surely also apply for 'inter-principality' competition as applicable to the Ituraeans, Hasmonaeans, Nabataeans and the various city states around them. If, as argued above, Ptolemy's main income derived from trade and he was in an economic competition with his neighbours, this would again have been a strong argument in favour of his own currency. Small states dependent on trade profited from a "competitive money" if this could be established as a generally accepted means of payment.[68] To enhance the acceptability of his coins, Ptolemy used a Ptolemaic dating tradition, indicating the date with 'L', which was used in the former Ptolemaic territories in Syria till after the Roman conquest. He seems also to have used a Pompeian era on some of his coin issues.[69] Both measures could be interpreted as attempts to turn his coins into such a 'competitive money'.

In the context of the volatile political landscape of his time, it was important for Ptolemy to demonstrate his power and his legitimacy as ruler in an acceptable and relatable manner. In a very tangible sense, he had to establish a Middle Ground between his indigenous subjects, his various neighbours and the super-powers also meddling in the region. To do so, he heavily relied on a visibly Hellenistic framework that must have appeared advantageous to him at the time. This Middle Ground was the result of an interdependent relationship between Ptolemy, his subjects and the superpowers comparable to the situation White describes for Natives and Europeans in 17th century North America – both in a political and a physical sense. Of course, Seleucid pretenders and Armenian invaders struggled for military and

---

[65] Flav. Jos. ant. Jud. 14, 129.

[66] Starcky 1971, 106–109.

[67] Meadows 2014, 192.

[68] Cf. Bernholz and Vaubel 2014, 2.

[69] Schwentzel 2009, 68.

political dominance, but this was a potentially life-threatening activity, as the quotation at the beginning of the paper makes obvious. Equally, Ptolemy son of Mennaeus schemed to be accepted as a local dynast, but again this was also a potentially fatal game to play, as the fates of his two successors Lysanias and Zenodorus demonstrate. Their stories show how difficult and dangerous negotiating the Middle Ground was for local dynasts – but of course, they were up against the Roman Empire. Misunderstanding and misinterpreting this new situation eventually cost Ptolemy's successors their principality and their lives.

Bibliography

Aliquot, J. 1999-2000. Les Ituréens et la présence arabe au Liban, in : MUSJ 56, 161–290.

Aliquot, J. 2009. La vie religieuse au Liban sous l'Empire Romaine. Paris.

Al-Maqdissi, M. 2005. Les tombeaux dits 'de Yanouh' : un type nouveau, in : P.-L. Gatier and L. Nordiguian (edd.), Yanouh et le Nahr Ibrahim. Nouvelles découvertes archéologiques dans la vallée d'Adonis, Beirut, 20–40.

Baltrusch, E. 2012. Herodes. König im Heiligen Land. Eine Biographie. Munich.

Bernholz, P. and R. Vaubet 2014. The Political Economy of Monetary and Financial Innovation: Introduction and Overview, in: P. Bernholz and R. Vaubet (edd.), Explaining Monetary and Financial Innovation. A historical analysis, Berlin et al., 1–16.

Bunnens, G. 2015. The re-emergence of Iron Age religious iconography in Roman Syria, in: M. Blömer et al. (edd.), Religious Identities in the Levant from Alexander to Muhammad. Continuity and Change, Turnhout, 107–128.

Butcher, K. 2005. Information, Legitimation, or Self-Legitimation? Popular and Elite Designs on the Coin Types of Syria, in: C. Howgego et al. (edd.), Coinage and Identity in the Roman Provinces, Oxford, 143–156.

Capdetrey, L. 2007. Le pouvoir séleucide. Territoire, administration, finances d'un royaume hellénistique (312–129 avant J.-C.). Paris.

Chaniotis, A. 2002. Foreign soldiers – native girls? Constructing and Crossing Boundaries in Hellenistic Cities with foreign Garrisons, in: A. Chaniotis and P. Ducrey (edd.), Army and Power in the Ancient World, Stuttgart, 99–113.

Chittenden, J. 1945. Hermes-Mercury, dynasts and emperors, in: The Numismatic Chronicle and Journal of the Royal Numismatic Society 5, 41–57.

Coşkun, A. 2015. Die Tetrarchie als hellenistisch-römisches Herrschaftsinstrument. Mit einer Untersuchung der Titulatur der Dynasten von Ituräa, in: E. Baltrusch and J. Wilker (edd.), Amicii – socii – clientes? Abhängige Herrschaft im Imperiums Romanum, Berlin, 161–197.

Diodorus Siculus, The Library of History, Fragments of books 33–40, with an English translation by F. R. Walton 1967.

Dowden, K. 2006. Zeus. London and New York.

Eckhardt, B. 2013. Ethnos und Herrschaft. Politische Figurationen jüdischer Identität von Antiochos III. bis Herodes I. Berlin and Boston.

Erickson, K. 2013. Seleucos I, Zeus and Alexander, in: L. Mitchell and C. Melville (edd.), Every inch a King. Comparative Studies on Kings and Kingship in the Ancient and Medieval World, Leiden, 109–128.

Gatier, P.-L. 2003. La principauté d'Abila de Lysanias dans l'Antiliban, in : Dossiers d'archéologie 2003, 120–127.

Gawlikowski, M. 2015, Bel of Palmyra, in: M. Blömer et al. (edd.), Religious Identities in the Levant from Alexander to Muhammad. Continuity and Change, Turnhout, 247–254.

Ghanimé-Marion, P. 2007, Qal'at el Hosn. Un site antique dans la montagne libanaise, in: BAAL 11, 103–141.

Grainger, J.D. 2015. The Fall of the Seleukid Empire 187–75 BC, Barnsley.

Herman, D. 2006. The coins of the Ituraeans, in: Israel Numismatic Research 1, 51–72.

Hill, G.F. 1899. Olba, Cennatis, Lalassis, in: Numismatic Chronicle and Journal of the Numismatic Society 19, 180–207.

Hvidberg-Hansen, F.O. 2007. 'Arşû and `Azîzû. A study of the West Semitic „Dioscuri" and the Gods of Dawn and Dusk. Copenhagen.

Kadman, K. 1961. The coins of Akko Ptolemais. Jerusalem.

Kaizer, T. 2008. Man and God at Palmyra: Sacrifice, *lectisternia* and Banquets, in: T. Kaizer (ed.), The Variety of Local Religious Life in the Near East in the Hellenistic and Roman Periods, Leiden, 179–192.

Kindler, A. 1990. The coins of the Ituraeans, in: Israel 5–6, 37–46.

Knauf, E.A. 1998. The Ituraeans: Another Beduin state, in: H. Sader and T. Scheffler and A. Neuwirth (edd.), Baalbek: Image and Monument 1889–1998, Beirut, 269–278.

Kosmin, P. 2014. The Land of the Elephant Kings. Space, Territory, and Ideology in the Seleucid Empire. Cambridge.

Kropp, A.J.M. 2013. Images and monuments of Near Eastern Dynasts. 100 BC–AD 100. Oxford.

Kulemann-Ossen, S. and M. Leicht and M. Heinz. 2007/2008. Kamid el-Loz. A reloading point in the long-distance trade during the Hellenistic period?, in: AHL 26/7, 170–179.

Lichtenberger, A. 2009. Tyros und Berytos. Zwei Fallbeispiele städtischer Identitäten in Phönikien, in: M. Blömer et al. (edd.), Lokale Identitäten im Römischen Nahen Osten. Kontext und Perspektiven, Stuttgart, 151–175.

Lorber, C.C. - P.P. Iossif 2009. The cult of Helios in the Seleucid East, in: Topoi 16, 19–42.

Mastrocinque, A. 2002. Zeus Kretagenès seleucidico. Da Seleucia a Praeneste (e in Guidea), in: Klio 84, 355–372.

Meadows, A. 2001. Money, Freedom, and Empire in the Hellenistic World, in: A. Meadows and K. Shipton (edd.), Money and its Uses in the ancient Greek World, Oxford, 55–61.

Meadows, A. 2014. The Spread of Coins in the Hellenistic World, in: P. Bernholz and R. Vaubel (edd.), Explaining Monetary and Financial Innovation. A Historical Analysis, Berlin, 169–198.

Merkelbach, R. 2001. Isis Regina – Zeus Sarapis, Die griechisch-ägyptische Religion nach den Quellen dargestellt. Munich and Leipzig.

Merlat, P. 1951. Observations sur les Castores dolichéniens, in: Syria 28, 229–249.

Mittag, P.F. 2006. Antiochos IV. Epiphanes. Eine politische Biographie. Berlin.

Mittag, P.F. 2016. Griechische Numismatik. Eine Einführung. Heidelberg.

Murray, W.M. 1991. The provenience and date: The evidence of the symbols, in: E. Linder and L. Casson and J.R. Steffy (edd.), The Athlit Ram, College Station, 54–56.

Myers, E.M. 2010. The Ituraeans and the Roman Near East. Reassessing the Sources. Cambridge.

Niehr, H. 2003. Ba'alšamem: Studien zu Herkunft, Geschichte und Rezeptionsgeschichte eines phönizischen Gottes. Leuven.

Niehr, H. 2014. Religion, in: H. Niehr (ed.), The Aramaeans in ancient Syria, Leiden,127–204.

Petrovic, I. 2007. Von den Toren des Hades zu den Hallen des Olymp. Artemiskult bei Theokrit und Kallimachos. Leiden and Boston.

Sartre, M. 2001. D'Alexandre à Zénobie. Histoire du Levant antique IVe siècle av. J-C. – IIIe siècle ap. J.-C. Paris.

Schottroff, W. 1982. Die Ituräer, in: ZDPV 98, 125–152.

Schwentzel, C.-G. 2009. La propagande des princes de Chalcis d'après les monnaies, in: ZDPV 125, 64–75.

Seyrig, H. 1970. Les dieux armés et les Arabes en Syrie, in: Syria 47, 77–111.

Starcky, J. 1971. Arca du Liban, in : Les Cahiers de l'Oronte 10, 103–117.

von Stuckrad, K. 2000. Das Ringen um die Astrologie. Jüdische und christliche Beiträge zum antiken Zeitverständnis. Berlin and New York.

Thalmann, J.-P. 2000. Tell Arqa, in: BAAL 4, 5–74.

Theuer, G. 2000. Der Mondgott in den Religionen Syrien-Palästinas. Unter besonderer Berücksichtigung von KTU 1.24. Fribourg.

Tscherikower, V. 1937. Palestine under the Ptolemies (A contribution to the study of the Zenon Papyri), in: Mizraim IV–V, 9–90.

Vollmer, D. 1991. Tetrarchie. Bemerkungen zum Gebrauch eines Antiken und Modernen Begriffes, in: Hermes 119, 436–441.

Walker, H. J. 2015. The Twin Horse Gods. The Dioscuroi in Mythologies of the Ancient World. London.

White, R. 2011.The Middle Ground: Indians, Empires, and Republics in the Great Lakes region, 1650-1815, (originally published 1991). Cambridge.

Will, E. 1947-48. Les Castores Dolichéniens, in: MUSJ 27, 21–36.

Wright, N.L. 2009/10. Non-Greek religious imagery on the coinage of Seleucid Syria, in: Mediterranean Archaeology 22/23, 193–206.

Wright, N.L. 2013. Ituraean Coinage in Context, in: The Numismatic Chronicle 173, 55–71.

Illustrations

Fig. 1: Bronze coin of Ptolemy, on the avers laureate head of Zeus right in dotted border; on the revers the Dioskuri within a laurel wreath, each holding a spear and facing each other, legend: PTOLEMAIOU TETRARXOU KAI ARXI IER; SNG Copenhagen 414. Image printed with permission of wildwinds.com.

Fig. 2: Bronze coin of Ptolemy, on the avers Artemis right with bow in dotted border; on the revers Nike walking in wreath and holding wreath and palm, monograms; Lindgren III, 1227 var. (monograms). Image printed with permission of wildwinds.com, ex Roland Müller Collection.

Fig. 3: Bronze coin of Ptolemy, on the avers laureate head of Zeus right in dotted border, countermark; on the revers eagle flying right, legend PTOLEMAIOU TETRARXOY; Lindgren I 2134A. Image printed with permission of wildwinds.com, ex CNG Auction 37 (2001).

Fig. 4: Bronze coin of Ptolemy, on the avers helmeted head of Athena right, countermark; on the revers the Dioskuri within a dotted border, each holding a spear and facing each other, monograms; Lindgren III 1232. Image printed with permission of wildwinds.com, ex Righetti Collection.

L'épigraphie du Hauran, reflet des mixités culturelles au Proche-Orient romain

Annie Sartre-Fauriat

L'histoire du Proche-Orient est longtemps restée à la marge des études scientifiques en raison de l'absence ou du faible nombre de textes documentant cette région, du moins si l'on prend en compte les provinces romaines de Syrie et surtout d'Arabie. Les choses ont commencé à changer avec les prospections épigraphiques systématiques qui ont permis de réunir à ce jour une documentation abondante et variée. Certes, le pourcentage est variable selon les zones, mais c'est sans doute dans la région la plus longtemps ignorée des études, le sud de la Syrie, généralement appelé le Hauran, que les textes épigraphiques ont été trouvés en abondance, permettant de nouvelles approches sur bien des sujets. Ce sont en effet plus de 4000 textes qui ont été réunis à ce jour, dont 1000 inédits depuis la reprise de la prospection dans cette région dans les années 1970. En 1982, paraissait le premier corpus consacré à *Bostra*, capitale de la province d'Arabie.[1] Après une trop longue période d'attente, les parutions se sont récemment accélérées avec le supplément de *Bostra* et la plaine de la Nuqrah en 2011,[2] deux volumes consacrés au plateau du Trachôn et ses bordures en 2014[3] et, en 2016, deux autres volumes réunissaient les textes de la plaine de la Batanée et du Jawlan oriental.[4] Au moins trois volumes encore devraient couvrir la zone du Jebel Druze, ils sont en cours de réalisation.[5]

De l'abondance et de la variété de ces textes, de nombreux sujets ont émergé, et c'est à quelques exemples que je m'attacherai afin de mettre en lumière le fait que l'épigraphie est aussi le moyen de rendre compte que le Hauran est bien au carrefour des influences exercées par la civilisation gréco-romaine, mais aussi un conservatoire des traditions régionales, comme un certain nombre d'autres régions de ce Proche-Orient.

Le premier enseignement fourni par l'épigraphie du Hauran est que l'écrasante majorité des textes qui y ont été retrouvés sont rédigés en grec et de façon beaucoup plus marginale en latin. Le latin reste en effet

---

[1] Sartre 1982a.

[2] Sartre 2011.

[3] Sartre-Fauriat et Sartre 2014a.

[4] Sartre-Fauriat et Sartre 2016.

[5] Ils auront pour référence IGLS XVI. Pour les inscriptions de cette région citées dans l'article, quand elles ne sont pas inédites, nous signalons aussi les précédents éditeurs.

118 Annie Sartre-Fauriat

essentiellement la langue de communication des soldats étrangers à la région et de l'autorité impériale. Le prouvent les textes provenant de *Bostra*, capitale de la province d'Arabie depuis 105–106, où cantonne la IIIe légion Cyrénaïque,[6] et ceux d'autres villages où des soldats sont en garnison ou de passage.[7] C'est là que l'on retrouve en général la plupart des inscriptions en latin sous la forme de dédicaces adressées par des soldats aux empereurs ou à leur famille, aux gouverneurs ou à des supérieurs (officiers), et aux dieux romains, parmi lesquels Jupiter est le mieux représenté. Lorsque des soldats ou des membres de leur famille sont morts sur place, leurs épitaphes sont en latin ainsi que le montrent celles retrouvées principalement à *Bostra*.[8] Quelques textes émanant du pouvoir central sont aussi en latin, comme des constructions de camps militaires, des ponts ou des fortins et aussi les milliaires.

L'ensemble de ces textes en latin représente moins de 200 inscriptions sur les 4000 actuellement recensées sur toute la région, soit 5% ; c'est-à-dire que le grec est majoritairement utilisé par l'ensemble de la population du Hauran pendant au moins six siècles et qu'il s'est substitué à l'araméen local dont seuls quelques exemples persistent encore au début du Ier siècle de notre ère, seul ou associé au grec dans des textes bilingues. Le phénomène d'hellénisation que traduit l'adoption de la langue grecque dans le Hauran est d'autant plus remarquable qu'il n'y a pas eu dans cette région d'installation de colons grecs après la conquête d'Alexandre et que l'autorité séleucide y est restée très discrète. Nous ignorons par quel canal le grec s'est diffusé aussi largement, y compris dans l'épigraphie privée que sont les inscriptions funéraires. On a fait l'hypothèse de l'influence des Hérodiens, en charge d'une partie de la région dès la fin du Ier siècle av. J.-C., sur les élites locales. Leur implication dans la construction et l'aménagement du grand sanctuaire de Siʿ a pu contribuer à introduire des habitudes grecques. On cite souvent à l'appui de cette hypothèse, l'architecture d'un grand tombeau à Suweida, ville proche du sanctuaire, qui fut certainement construit pour la femme d'un potentat local et qui s'inspire de modèles d'époque hellénistique dont on trouve des parallèles dans deux tombeaux de la vallée du Cédron à Jérusalem, construits au tournant de l'ère chrétienne. L'inscription qui figure sur le tombeau de Suweida associe

---

6   Sartre 1982a et 2011.

7   Par exemple *Phaina*-Mismiyyeh, *Saura*-Sur et *Saara*-Shaʿrah sur le Trachôn, *Airè*-Sanamein au nord de la Batanée, *Mothana*-Imtan dans le sud du djebel (cf. Sartre-Fauriat 2016, 67–81) ou à *Nemara* du Safa.

8   A *Bosora*-Busr al-Hariri (IGLS XV, n°242) Maiorinus, Préfet du prétoire d'Orient entre 344 et 346 ap. J.-C. qui y a été enterré constitue un cas à part, il était probablement originaire du village. La seule autre inscription funéraire de soldat en latin provient de *Airè*-Sanamein (IGLS XIV, n°565).

L'épigraphie du Hauran

l'araméen au grec et se place à une date précoce, la fin du Ier siècle av. ou le début du Ier ap. J.-C.[9]

Le grec s'est donc imposé de façon générale et la provincialisation par Rome n'a pas modifié les habitudes linguistiques, il reste la langue d'usage dans les inscriptions des cités et des villages jusqu'à la fin de l'Antiquité, même lorsqu'il s'agit pour les habitants de ces villages d'honorer des fonctionnaires romains dans l'exercice d'une fonction officielle en rapport avec une institution typiquement romaine. Un ensemble de textes provenant de *Airè*-Sanamein, village du nord de la Batanée, vient éclairer un aspect méconnu de la mise en place par Rome de structures d'administration qui montrent que le Hauran a connu un même type d'exploitation du sol que d'autres provinces de l'empire et que la prétendue marginalité ou singularité de la région n'était qu'un leurre. Il est en effet désormais incontestable qu'un domaine impérial a été installé en Batanée, dont on est assuré de l'existence au moins jusqu'au milieu du IVe siècle.

Les textes IGLS XIV, n°554 et 555 sont deux inscriptions honorifiques, gravées sur des consoles situées à l'intérieur du temple de la Tychè de Sanamein, achevé en 191 de notre ère sous le règne de Commode. Il y est question à chaque fois d'un « procurateur impérial » (ἐπίτροπος τοῦ Σεβαστοῦ), le même ou deux différents car le nom manque, que la « communauté » (que l'un des textes qualifie « des Airésiens », c'est-à-dire les habitants d'*Airè*) remercie d'avoir « rempli son office avec intégrité ». La présence d'un procurateur impérial dans ce village pourrait être fortuite, - bien que l'emplacement des inscriptions à l'intérieur du temple prouve l'importance du personnage honoré -, si nous n'avions un autre texte (IGLS XIV, n°555a) où c'est la Batanée personnifiée (ἡ Βατανέα) qui dresse une statue à un préfet du prétoire d'Orient sous Constance II, alors associé à Julien César, soit entre 355 et 360 ap. J.-C. Au même moment, un certain Flavius Maximus est « ducénaire du *saltus* » (δουκηνάριος τοῦ σάλτου). Ce fonctionnaire impérial de haut rang se désigne ainsi clairement en charge, encore au milieu du IVe siècle, du domaine impérial, ce que signifie sans ambiguïté le terme latin translittéré, *saltus*. Deux autres textes gravés en latin sur des autels, conservés aujourd'hui au musée de Dera, mais provenant aussi de Sanamein, viennent apporter un élément supplémentaire en faveur de l'existence de ce domaine. Sur le premier (IGLS XIV, n°561a), il est question d'un personnage au nom probable de Val(erius) Superianus,[10] dont la fonction est abrégée *PP*, qui fait une dédicace aux douze dieux pour les quinquennales de l'empereur Licinius, soit en 312 ap. J.-C. Cette fonction devait se compléter par une autre qu'il cumulait, mais mutilée

---

[9]   Cf. Sartre-Fauriat 2001, T.1, 196–198 et T. 2, 63–64.
[10]   La lecture du texte sur la pierre est très difficile.

dans le texte et qui aurait pu permettre de trancher entre deux propositions de restitution : *PP* par *p(rimi)p(ilus)*, ce qui a été souvent proposé sans certitude dans les autres cas connus (Kafr[11] et Ira IGLS XIII/2, n°9675) et *p(rae)p(osi-tus)*, restitution adoptée désormais, notamment en raison de cette abréviation sur les bornes de limites de villages en relation avec des recenseurs officiant au cours de la première tétrarchie. Dans ce dernier cas, cela renvoie à une fonction impériale et peut-être même à une fonction en lien avec la gestion du domaine impérial. Dans le texte IGLS XIV, n°561b, sans doute contemporain du premier en raison de l'écriture, la dédicace à deux empereurs est plus explicite, puisqu'elle est faite par un « affranchi » des empereurs, « adjoint d'un procurateur » (*adjutor procuratoris*), ce qui ne laisse aucun doute sur la présence de fonctionnaires impériaux chargés d'affaires financières. L'ensemble de ces textes, par la présence de fonctionnaires impériaux et la mention d'un *saltus*, vont dans le sens de la confirmation d'un domaine impérial de Batanée dont Sanamein était très certainement le centre administratif.

On ajoutera à ces textes, ceux qui témoignent d'une présence militaire constante dans ce village. Cela peut, certes, se justifier de multiples façons, mais on ne peut s'empêcher d'y voir un lien avec des services de l'administration impériale. En 191 de notre ère, un centurion de la 3e légion *Gallica* achève le Tychéion (IGLS XIV, n°548) ; trois soldats ont été enterrés sur place : un auxiliaire d'un *numerus* de cavaliers dalmates (IGLS XIV, n°565) ; un centurion d'une cohorte auxiliaire de Thraces (IGLS XIV, 567) ; un cavalier de la 3e légion *Gallica* (IGLS XIV, n°569) et, sur l'autel IGLS XIV, n°561a, il est apparemment question d'un soldat appartenant lui aussi à un *numerus* de Dalmates. On avait cru pendant un temps trouver dans un autre texte (IGLS XIV, n°565) la mention d'une *regio*. Une nouvelle lecture nous fait renoncer à cette interprétation.[12] Il n'y a pour l'instant en Batanée nulle trace de *regio*, dont pourtant l'existence est connue ailleurs : une *regio parhalia* sur la côte syrienne[13] et une *regio syriatica* mentionnée dans une inscription d'Ephèse.[14]

Pour cette partie de la Syrie devenue Arabie au tournant du IIIe siècle de notre ère, ce sont en tout cas les premières preuves épigraphiques du phénomène, qui viennent désormais confirmer un passage de Georges de Chypre

---

[11] Dussaud et Macler 1903, 652–653, n° 27 ; Littmann et Magie et Stuart 1921, n° 669 = IGLS XVI, n°414 (à paraître).

[12] Cf. à ce sujet Sartre 2001.

[13] Baudouin et Pottier 1879, 270, n°42.

[14] La *regio syriatica* mentionnée dans un cursus d'affranchi impérial à Ephèse n'est pas localisée avec précision (AE, 1982, 877). Cette *regio* n'est pas mentionnée dans l'inscription IGLS XIV, n°567, contrairement à ce qui est écrit dans Sartre 1999, 220, une relecture du texte a éliminé cette proposition.

qui, dans ses listes topographiques de l'éparchie d'Arabie, citait un *saltus Bataneos* en Syrie du Sud.[15]

Pour quelles raisons et quand la Batanée fut-elle érigée en domaine impérial ? Sans doute, l'opportunité en fut-elle saisie par le passage de la région sous l'administration directe de Rome à la fin du Ier siècle de notre ère (vers 90). La transformation en domaine impérial de propriétés confisquées, ou revenues dans l'administration impériale après une période de gestion par des princes ou rois clients, est bien connue en diverses provinces de l'Empire, en Occident comme en Orient (ex. forêts du Liban, baumiers de la mer Morte, palmeraie d'Archelaïs etc...). La Batanée était une région riche de possibilités agricoles, la Bible vante ce pays de Bashan, dont elle faisait partie, pour son abondante nourriture raffinée, la fleur du froment, son élevage d'ovins et de bovins.[16] Mais peut-être est-ce aussi en raison de la situation stratégique de la région, à la fois lieu de passage de nombreuses routes et pistes commerciales et en capacité de surveiller le plateau du Trachôn, longtemps repaire de brigands, raison pour laquelle d'ailleurs la région avait été donnée en administration à Hérode, ainsi que le raconte Flavius Josèphe.[17] Quelle était la superficie du domaine et son étendue ? Les limites en sont floues mais, une épitaphe trouvée à Kafr Nasij, village situé à une vingtaine de kilomètres de Sanamein, fait référence à un « préposé du *pagus* » (IGLS XIV, n°532). L'expression, translittérée en toutes lettres du latin (πρεπόσιτος πάγου), a suscité beaucoup d'interrogations en raison du sens multiple de la fonction de « préposé du *pagus* ». Cette fonction est en effet présente en Egypte à partir du IVe siècle où une réforme administrative a confié à ces personnages, en général plusieurs par villages, de lever l'impôt dans les circonscriptions rurales. Une lettre de Maximin Daia de 312 y fait d'ailleurs référence explicitement au sein d'une liste de magistrats.[18] On a peut-être ici, à défaut d'un complément d'information sur les domaines patrimoniaux, la preuve qu'une réforme que l'on attribuait à l'Egypte seule avait pu être aussi appliquée à l'Arabie, d'autant que le personnage porte un patronyme indigène, Maximos fils d'Annianos, extrêmement fréquent dans la région.[19] Dans une autre inscription d'un village de la plaine de *Bostra*, Taaleh (IGLS XIII/2, n°9825), la fonction de préposé du *pagus* apparaît également dans ce qui paraît être un cursus entre le titre de bouleute et deux autres magistratures non spécifiées. Cela pourrait signifier que le territoire de la cité de *Dionysias*-Suweida, auquel se rattache le village,

---

[15] Georges de Chypre Opuscule, 1076.

[16] Deuteronome, 32, 14; Jérémie, 50, 19; Ezéchiel, 39 ,18; Psaumes, 22, 13; Michée, 7, 14; Nahum, 1, 4.

[17] Flav. Jos. Antiquités, 17, 23–29.

[18] Eusèbe, Histoire Ecclésiastique 9, 1, 3–6.

[19] Le patronyme est attesté six autres fois en Batanée.

122 Annie Sartre-Fauriat

était peut-être, comme on le connaît en Occident, subdivisé en *pagi*. Mais, dans le cas de Kafr Nasij, on ne voit pas de quelle cité le village aurait pu dépendre dans cette région où il n'y en a pas et, en raison de sa proximité avec *Airè*-Sanamein, on ne peut exclure que la fonction soit elle aussi liée d'une manière ou d'une autre à une gestion financière au sein du domaine impérial.

Nous ne savons rien des modalités d'exploitation du domaine et notamment s'il l'était, à la manière de ceux de l'Afrique du Nord, sous la forme du colonat. Toutefois, l'épigraphie funéraire pourrait donner des indices en ce sens. On a remarqué en effet que les pratiques funéraires étaient très différentes entre la plaine de la Batanée à l'ouest du Hauran et la région de la montagne à l'est.[20] Dans cette dernière, les constructions de tombeaux monumentaux familiaux abondent, contrairement à la plaine où l'on en compte un très faible nombre, mais où, en revanche, les grandes nécropoles avec de petites stèles simples individuelles sont légion. Ne serait-ce pas le reflet d'une situation socio-économique différente? D'un côté dans la plaine, un faible nombre de grands propriétaires aisés, fermiers du ou des domaines, au milieu d'une population de colons dépendants, en opposition avec un monde de petits et moyens propriétaires indépendants dans la montagne?

Un autre constat va dans le sens de la présence d'un ou de plusieurs domaines impériaux en Batanée, celui du faible nombre de villages autonomes, pourvus d'institutions quasi civiques, comme c'est fréquemment le cas sur le plateau du Trachôn et dans la montagne, et l'absence de cités. C'est ainsi que Sanamein n'a livré aucun texte prouvant à ce jour son élévation au rang de cité, pas plus qu'à celui de *mètrokomia* que son importance dans la région aurait pu lui valoir, alors qu'on en connaît plusieurs, presque toutes situées dans ce secteur de la plaine : *Phaina*-Mismiyyeh (au nord), *Akraba*-Aqrabat à l'ouest, *Neila*-Inkhil au sud-ouest, Raïfa au sud,[21] ou *Saura*-Sur et *Zorava*-Ezra sur la bordure ouest du Trachôn (le seul exemple décentré est *Borechath-Sabaôn*-Breikeh sur la bordure sud du Trachôn). Cet échelon officiel dans la promotion des villages visait sans doute, comme il l'a été démontré par ailleurs,[22] à reconnaître leur importance stratégique, mais aussi à se substituer à l'absence de *poleis* auxquelles il aurait fallu concéder des terres sur le territoire impérial. Il serait étrange que *Airè*-Sanamein n'ait pas eu ce statut

---

[20] Sartre-Fauriat 2001, 20.

[21] Le site de Raïfa qui a livré l'inscription où il est question d'une *mètrokomia* n'est sans doute pas le siège de celle-ci, il devait être plus probablement situé dans le village dont le nom se terminait par *–roga* ou *–ropa* avant de devenir une cité sous le nom de *Néapolis*, que l'on localise aujourd'hui à Sheikh Meskin (cf. IGLS XIV, n° 393).

[22] Sartre 1999, 197–222.

L'épigraphie du Hauran

d'autant que, comme la plupart des autres, elle devint un évêché au moins avant 325, comme le prouve la présence de son évêque au concile de Nicée.[23]

Si l'épigraphie contribue à prouver que le Hauran est bien intégré culturellement et économiquement au monde gréco-romain, il arrive aussi qu'elle mette en évidence des particularités que la présence de Rome n'a pas fait disparaître. C'est le cas avec quatre textes en particulier dans lesquels on peut lire un terme difficile à expliquer, celui de Ἰατουραῖος qui, bien qu'en grec, renvoie à une réalité locale.

Trois de ces textes proviennent du village d'Atil (IGLS XVI, n°122-124[24]), situé sur la bordure occidentale du Jebel Druze, et le quatrième d'un village de la même région, mais plus au nord-est, Rdeimeh Sharqiyyeh (IGLS XVI, n°685). Les premiers (122–124) ont la particularité de concerner des bouleutes de la cité d'*Adraa* (actuelle Dera au sud de la Batanée), donc après le milieu du IIe siècle ap. J.-C.[25] : βουλευτοῦ Ἰατουραίου Ἀ[δρα]ηνοῦ qui, dans ce village éloigné de près de cinquante kilomètres de leur cité, font chacun une consécration d'atelier, τὸ ἐργαστήρ(ιον). Plusieurs questions se posent. Pourquoi ces trois bouleutes œuvrent-ils si loin de chez eux et hors du territoire civique par une action évergétique qui n'est même pas d'usage dans leur propre cité ?[26] Mais surtout, que signifie le terme Ἰατουραῖος, visiblement associé ici au nom de la cité ? Plusieurs hypothèses ont été émises, déjà par Ch. Clermont-Ganneau[27] suivi par R. Dussaud[28] qui voulaient y voir l'équivalent d'un ethnique apparenté à l'Iturée. Strabon[29] est pourtant formel là-dessus, avec d'autres auteurs (Luc,[30] Flavius Josèphe,[31] ou Dion Cassius[32]), qui situe l'Iturée beaucoup plus au nord-ouest dans la partie intérieure de la Phénicie, là où sévissait Ptolémée, fils de Ménaios, au moment de la conquête de la Syrie par Pompée. Par ailleurs l'Iturée, quand elle est citée, l'est sous la forme Ἰτουραία et non Ἰατουραία, tout comme ses habitants sont les Ἰτουραῖοι et non les Ἰατουραῖοι. Etant donné la séquence des mots dans l'inscription, l'épithète est clairement rattachée à *Adraènos*, lieu d'origine des bouleutes. A quoi cette épithète fait-elle référence ?

On aurait pu penser à un qualificatif d'*Adraa*, comme s'en donnent

---

[23] Sartre-Fauriat et Sartre 2014b, 471–486.
[24] Dunand 1932, 564, n° 78 et 77 (IGLS XVI, n°122 et 124) ; Brünnow et Domaszewski 1909, 202, n° 10 (IGLS XVI, n° 123).
[25] Cf. Sartre-Fauriat et Sartre 2014b, 471–486.
[26] Sur cette particularité du Hauran, entre autres, en Syrie, voir Sartre-Fauriat 2003, 517–538.
[27] Clermont-Ganneau 1901, 118–119.
[28] Dussaud, 1955, 177.
[29] Strabon, Géographie 16, 2, 10; 18, 20.
[30] Evangile selon saint Luc 3, 1.
[31] Flav. Josèphe Antiquités 13, 15, 392.
[32] Dion Cassius, Histoire Romaine, 49, 32.

d'autres cités en rapport avec le nom d'un empereur (*Traiana Bostra*), un district (*Scythopolis* de Koilè-Syrie), ou une particularité géographique. Ainsi *Adraa* aurait pu s'appeler « de Batanée », mais le terme est déjà associé à d'autres villages situés dans le nord de la plaine comme *Maaga* de Batanée ou *Neeila* en Batanée. Sur son monnayage en tout cas, elle a choisi d'associer plutôt son nom à la rivière qui la traverse, le *Hiéromax* aujourd'hui appelé Yarmuk, et fait graver : Ἀδραηνῶν Ἱερομύκης.[33] Il reste une hypothèse, celle de la désignation d'une tribu civique à partir d'un anthroponyme, comme cela se voit ailleurs (Palmyre, Suweida). On sait qu'*Adraa* est devenue cité au cours du IIe siècle de notre ère et, de ce fait, sa population a dû être divisée en tribus civiques dont les noms ont pu dériver d'anthroponymes. Dans son article de synthèse sur les Ituréens, Julien Aliquot proposait justement d'en faire un anthroponyme sémitique qu'il rapproche du nom *Iatouros* bien connu dans la région.[34] Malheureusement, une inscription de Rdeimeh Sharqqiyyeh (IGLS XVI, n°685) vient jeter le trouble. Le terme Ἰατουραῖος y est utilisé comme qualificatif d'un homme de la région (Nazalos, fils de Sithros) qui se déclare également issu « de la tribu des Sadènoi ». Il apparaît donc que ce terme, qui nous éloigne définitivement de l'Iturée, englobe une définition plus large, celui de toute une tribu dont on ne sait rien pour le moment, ce qui n'éclaircit pas le rapport entre cet homme et les bouleutes d'*Adraa*.

Le Hauran nous a déjà habitué à la permanence de ces tribus, tout particulièrement sur le Trachôn où leur présence dans l'épigraphie n'est attestée pas moins de neuf fois, dont cinq assorties du mot grec φυλή,[35] mais encore plus fréquemment dans le Jebel.[36] On ne reviendra pas sur l'ambiguïté du mot « tribu » qui peut désigner dans une cité l'appartenance à une tribu civique et, ailleurs, un groupe ou un clan indigène, mais il est clair que nous avons-là un exemple supplémentaire de ces permanences locales sous l'Empire romain qui montrent que, par-delà les siècles, les fusions culturelles ont aussi leurs limites.[37]

Ces deux exemples, pris dans des zones différentes du Hauran, ne sont que quelques-uns à témoigner, parmi bien d'autres, que l'épigraphie de cette région est un outil révélateur des mixités et des adaptations des institutions et des modes de vie communs au reste de l'Empire, et du maintien des particularismes locaux.

---

[33] Spijkerman 1978, 60–63, n° 6 et 11.

[34] Aliquot 1999-2000, 161–290.

[35] Cf. IGLS XV, n° 24–25.

[36] Cf. Sartre 1982b, 77–79.

[37] Sartre-Fauriat 2017, 181–190, où sont examinées les permanences dans les cultes du Trachôn et tout particulièrement celles de la dévotion au « dieu d'Untel ».

L'épigraphie du Hauran

Bibliographie

Sources

Ancien Testament, 2 vol., E. Dhorme (Ed.), Coll. La Pléiade, Gallimard, Paris, 1956 et 1959.

Georges de Chypre, in: Honigmann, Synecdemos d'Hiéroklès et l'Opuscule géographique de Georges de Chypre, textes, introduction, commentaire et cartes, Bruxelles, 1939.

Dion Cassius, Histoire Romaine, Livre 49, texte établi, traduit et annoté par M.-L. Freyburger et J.-M. Roddaz, Les Belles Lettres, Paris, 1994.

Eusèbe, Histoire Ecclésiastique, III, texte, traduction et notes de Gustave Bardy, Sources Chrétiennes 55, Paris, 1967.

Flavius Josèphe, Antiquités Judaïques, in Œuvres complètes, trad. Th. Reinach, Paris, 1926.

Strabon, Géographie, XVI, édit. et trad. H. L. Jones, Loeb Classical Library, Cambridge (Ma), 7e édit., 2000.

Ouvrages et articles

Aliquot, J. 1999–2000. Les Ituréens et la présence arabe au Liban, in: MUSJ 56, 161–290.

Baudouin, M. et E. Pottier. 1879. Collection de M. Péretié. Inscriptions, in: BCH 3, 257–271.

Brünnow, R.E. et A. von Domaszewski 1909. Die Provincia Arabia, III. Strasbourg.

Clermont-Ganneau, C. 1901. Inscriptions grecques du Hauran, in: RAO IV, 118–119.

Dunand, M. 1932. Nouvelles inscriptions du Djebel druze et du Hauran, in: Revue Biblique 41, 399–416 et 561–580.

Dussaud, R. 1955. La pénétration des Arabes avant l'Islam. Paris.

Dussaud, R. et F. Macler. 1903. Rapport sur une Mission scientifique dans les régions désertiques de la Syrie Moyenne. Paris.

Littmann, E. et D. Magie et D.R. Stuart. 1921. Publications of the Princeton University Archaeological Expeditions to Syria in 1904–5 and 1909, Division III A, Greek and Latin Inscriptions. Leyde.

Sartre, M. 1982a. Bostra, IGLS XIII/1. Paris.

Sartre, M. 1982b. Tribus et clans dans le Hauran, in: Syria 59, 77–79.

Sartre, M. 1999. Les metrokomiai de Syrie du Sud, in: Syria 76, 197–222.

Sartre, M. 2001. D'Alexandre à Zénobie. Histoire du Levant antique. IVe s. av. J.-C. – IIIe s. ap. J.-C. Paris.

Sartre, M. 2011. Bostra supplément et la plaine de la Nuqrah, IGLS XIII/2. Beyrouth.

Sartre-Fauriat, A. 2001. Des tombeaux et des morts. Monuments funéraires, société et culture en Syrie du Sud du Ier s.av. au VIIe siècle ap. J.-C., 2 tomes. Beyrouth.

Sartre-Fauriat, A. 2003. Les élites de la Syrie intérieure et leur image à l'époque romaine, in: Colloque international Les élites et leurs facettes, Clermont-Ferrand, 517–538.

Sartre-Fauriat, A. 2016. *Mothana*-Imtan : un village de garnison en Arabie, in: Syria, 93, 67–81.

Sartre-Fauriat, A. 2017. La vie religieuse sur le Trachôn à l'époque romaine. Les apports de l'épigraphie, in: R. Raja (Ed.), Contextualizing the Sacred in the Hellenistic and Roman Near East. Religious Identities in Local, Regional, and Imperial Settings, Leyde, 181–190.

Sartre-Fauriat, A. et M. Sartre 2014a. Le plateau du Trachôn et ses bordures, IGLS XV. Beyrouth.

Sartre-Fauriat, A. et M. Sartre 2014b. Les communautés civiques de Syrie du Sud dans l'Antiquité tardive, in : La città del Vicino Oriente nella tarda Antichità. Da Diocleziano alla conquista araba, Mediterraneano Antico. Economie Società Culture 17/2, 471–486.

Sartre-Fauriat, A. et M. Sartre. 2016. La Batanée et le Jawlan oriental, IGLS XIV. Beyrouth.

Spijkerman, A. 1978. The Coins of the Decapolis and the Provincia Arabia. Jérusalem.

L'épigraphie du Hauran

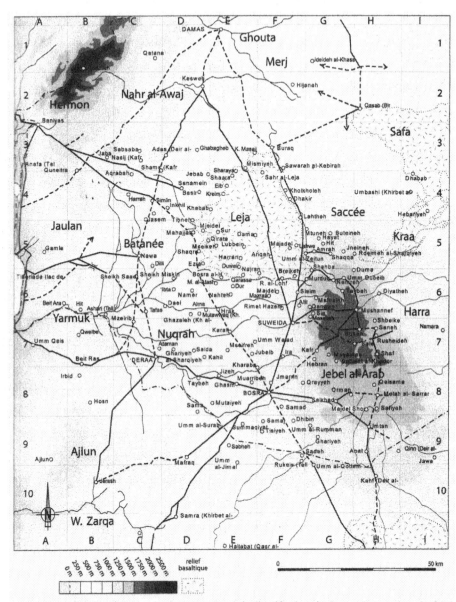

- Carte de la Syrie du Sud comportant les sites mentionnés dans la publication et le réseau routier connu (en traits pleins) ou restitué (en pointillés) (mission française en Syrie du Sud).

Managing the Middle Ground:
Priests in Palmyra and their iconographies[1]

Rubina Raja

1. Introduction

The oasis city Palmyra in antiquity also called Tadmor, has long been said to have been a melting pot, a meeting place between East and West, a place suspended between two mighty empires, Parthia and Rome, a city with a society that often is represented as if it almost exclusively aligned according to outside influences and needs and did not have a firmly rooted local culture.[2] We know of the site from sources going back to the second millennium BCE, but archaeologically the site only becomes truly graspable in the first century BCE and most archaeological and written evidence from the site stems from the first three centuries CE, when the site flourished due to the extensive trade relations it sustained.[3] Over the last decades, it has become clear, however, that Palmyra was not simply a place that was molded by outside influences and that only responded to reactions, but that Palmyrene society indeed put its own culture and traditions first and even had and further developed a strong local identity, which in several ways differed from that of other cities in the Roman period Near East.[4] This tribal based society, about which we know little in the period before the first century CE, seems to have been highly aware about the fact that it was part of a global world, where power structures could change rapidly and trust in one's own local resources and

---

[1] I would like to thank the Carlsberg Foundation for funding the Palmyra Portrait Project since 2012. Furthermore, I would like to thank the Getty Museum Scholars Programme for awarding me a Museum Scholar Fellowship within the framework of which I got to undertake further research on Palmyra in the summer of 2018. I am indebted to Timothy Potts, Jeffrey Spiers and not least Kenneth Lapatin, who invited me to lecture at the Getty Villa in 2016 on the Palmyrene funerary portraits and for their later invitation and support in realizing my stay at the Getty Villa. I also thank Julia Hoffman-Salz for inviting me to the conference "The Middle East as Middle Ground", which spurred intriguing discussions. Furthermore, I would like to thank the research assistants of the Palmyra Portrait Project, Dr. Olympia Bobou and Rikke Randeris Thomsen (MA), for the editorial support given for the realization of this article.

[2] For general literature on Palmyra see: Millar 1993, 319–336; Schmidt-Colinet 2005; Sommer 2005; Sartre-Fauriat and Sartre 2008; Sartre and Sartre-Fauriat 2016.

[3] For one source from the Mari Archive mentioning Palmyra see: Dossin 1952, 4, no. 23; Dossin 1954, 135, no. 2. Also see Dirven 1999, 18, note 77 for further references and a good summary of the discussion on the Semitic name of Palmyra, which was Tadmor.

[4] See Andrade's recent book on Syrian identity where an excellent chapter on Palmyra sets out the background for this discussion: Andrade 2013. Also see the recent book by Smith which deals with our evidence for the societal structure of Palmyra: Smith 2013.

network were things, which usually stayed stable and which one could rely on.[5] This, among other things, is reflected in the portrait tradition that was introduced in the city in the late first century BCE and continued until the late third century CE and which reflects an immense focus on the relations within extended families that made up the core of Palmyrene society and its power network.[6] The numerous priests of Palmyra, represented in the rich corpus of the funerary sculpture, are but one example, which clearly shows that local models acted as basis for local life and traditions and not influences from outside.[7] Therefore the representations of the priests will be the focus in this contribution. They will be addressed here to outline how the concept of Middle Ground may be used fruitfully, or perhaps not, in order to investigate local ways of acting and strategizing on a local level about how to situate a city and its society within what certainly was a globalized world at the time, when Palmyra truly flourished in the first three centuries CE, until the sack by the Roman emperor Aurelian and his troops put a stop to Palmyra's rise to fame.[8]

The concept of the Middle Ground has been used by a variety of scholars to describe situations in which meetings between people, their societies and their cultures have taken place. Such not always easy situations have led to the invention or coming into being of new situations and new positionings, which emerge out of the misunderstandings between cultures and their societies in first and new encounters between these, and are termed Middle Ground.[9] The concept has been used most widely in anthropology and sociology, however, it has been used in studies of ancient material as

---

[5] See Kaizer 2002, 43–51 for a summary on the discussion about the tribes of Palmyra and their significance. It has been extensively discussed how many tribes there were in Palmyra. Some have argued for twelve tribes, but according to Piersimoni we can count fourteen tribes (Piersimoni 1995a, 252–253; 1995b, II, 532–541).

[6] Kropp and Raja 2014. Also see Ingholt 1928, which was the first attempt of compiling a corpus of the rich funerary sculpture corpus from Palmyra. Furthermore, see the two publications by Sadurska and Bounni 1994; Sadurska 1995.

[7] See Raja 2017a; Raja 2017b; Raja 2017c for the most recent research on the priests of Palmyra.

[8] See Veyne 2015; Sartre and Sartre-Fauriat 2016. See the books cited above for differing views – to some extent extremely differing – on the city of Palmyra and its cultural background and setting within the Roman Empire.

[9] See for example White 1991 for one approach to and definition of Middle Ground. This is explained in more detail in the contribution by Lichtenberger in this volume as well as in the introduction to this volume by Hoffmann-Salz.

well.[10] While it is not unproblematic to apply concepts developed in the context of modern situations on ancient material, it is sometimes fruitful to explore new lines of enquiry or push borders in order to better understand the ways in which such ancient societies might have worked.

In this article the term of the Middle Ground will be explored within a Palmyrene context taking into consideration the fact that the city was a desert city, an oasis city whose wealth, but not subsistence, was based on the trade in which it was involved. While Palmyrene society could certainly have existed without the rich trade relations, it could not have thrived to the extent, which it did, without these.[11] Therefore there must also have been a Middle Ground to be consolidated within a Palmyrene societal context and not only with outside relations. Such Middle Ground will be explored here through the representations of the Palmyrene priests, largely stemming from the funerary sphere.[12] The priests have been chosen as a case study, since they make up a significant group of representations in Palmyrene visual culture and can be used to extrapolate societal patterns and structure of Palmyrene religious life and beyond.[13]

2. Palmyra as Middle Ground in the Syrian Desert?

Palmyra was no metropolis in antiquity. It was a city, whose society in the first three centuries CE built its wealth and importance on the trade relations, of which they often seem to have been primus motors and played a pivotal role for facilitating the trade and its movements.[14] Palmyra does, however, not seem to have produced anything noteworthy of export in itself. The city purely based, as far as we know, its growing wealth on the trade, in which it was involved, and which included caravan- and ship ownership as well as organization of the trade. The second century CE imperial tax tariff set up in

---

[10] See Lichtenberger in this volume, who also refers to the work of Christoph Ulf: Ulf 2009, as well as Ulf 2014.

[11] For Palmyrene trade relations see: Seland 2015a; Seland 2015b; Meyer and Seland and Anfinset (edd.) 2016; Seland 2016. These works have changed our understanding of the ways in which Palmyrene society engaged with and pushed the borders for ways of conducting trade in the first three centuries CE.

[12] The rich corpus of Palmyrene funerary sculpture has since 2012 been collected within the framework of the Palmyra Portrait Project. See the project's webpage for more information about the corpus and the publications, which have come out of the project since 2012. More than 3,600 portraits have until now been collected in the corpus, which makes this corpus the largest one consisting of portrait material stemming from one location in the Roman world. Webpage: http://projects.au.dk/palmyraportrait/

[13] Raja 2017c. See the above publication for an attempt at discussing family networks with the point of departure in the visual representations of the Palmyrene priests.

[14] See note 11.

the city tells us about the wealth of goods, which went through the site and about the fact that it also was here that camel caravans reloaded their stock on to mule caravans, which better could handle the terrain west of Palmyra.[15] With this trade-involvement and organization, an increase in military abilities also grew. We know that Palmyrene archers were famous in the Roman Empire for their skills and served in the Roman army.[16] They are even depicted on a relief on Trajan's column.[17] The society, which was based on either 12 or 14 tribes (extended families), as far as we know from the written evidence, developed from having been what in scholarship has been termed nomadic to sedentarized, but the process of this development has not yet been grasped through the evidence available to us.[18] Families in Palmyra seem to have been urban-based in the period of the first three centuries CE, but there is also much evidence stemming from around the city that large areas were irrigated and settlements were used at least periodically within the year, which indicate that agriculture and stock-raising would have taken place there.[19]

With the growing monumentalization of the urban landscape, the monumental tower tombs, for which the site is so known, were also introduced.[20] These up to six-story-high square buildings each founded by a family father came to house hundreds of portraits of deceased Palmyrenes and their family members. By the second century CE underground tombs, hypogea, were introduced, which also housed up to four hundred burials and were extended over generations.[21] It is in these tombs that we find most evidence for the Palmyrene extended families, their ties and their interrelations.[22]

---

[15] Shifman 2014 is a translation instigated by John Healey of the Russian original. It is the best discussion of the Palmyrene tax tariff, which indeed was meant for Palmyra alone and which does not discuss matters non-Palmyrene. The tax tariff does speak about goods from other places which came to Palmyra, but it also states that it is put up in order to regulate Palmyrene affairs, not affairs outside the city.

[16] Dirven 1999; Hartmann 2001; Hartmann 2008. See the above publications for discussions including aspects of the military units of Palmyra.

[17] Hannestad 1988, 160, fig. 97.

[18] See note 11. Also see Gawlikowski 2003 for a contribution on these discussions.

[19] Meyer 2013; Meyer and Seland and Anfinset 2016; Meyer 2016; Meyer 2017. See the work by Jørgen-Christian Meyer and his team for new insights into the landscape around Palmyra and its high versatility and the intense use of the land, which seems to have taken place to a much higher degree than hitherto thought.

[20] Henning 2013. Henning remains the most comprehensive study of the tower tombs of Palmyra.

[21] Gawlikowski 1970 for a contribution including the hypogea of Palmyra. Also see Raja 2016a for further references to publications on the tomb buildings of Palmyra.

[22] Raja 2016a. Furthermore, see contributions in Krag and Raja 2019a, including the introductory chapter by Krag and Raja 2019b. Also see Raja 2015a; Raja 2019a.

Priests in Palmyra and their iconography

The Palmyrene funerary portraits were produced from the first century CE until the sack of Palmyra in 273 CE. They depict Palmyrene men, women and children and numerous of them carry inscriptions giving us the names of the deceased and their family members, sometimes up to five generations back in time. The funerary sculpture and monuments were produced exclusively of the local limestone, which came from quarries situated around the city.[23] The limestone was of varying quality, but generally quite good and could be polished in some cases to resemble marble. However, it does not seem to have been a general desire to imitate marble in the sculpture as such. The funerary sculpture was in antiquity at least partly polychrome. Several busts today carry traces of pigment, in particular still red in the letters of the inscriptions accompanying the portraits. However, several pieces also carry color traces indicating that hair, facial features, headdresses, clothing and jewelry could be painted.[24] How the polychromy of the sculpture would have related to the polychromy in the rest of the graves, still remains to be investigated in details. Since most funerary contexts of the sculpture have been lost, this remains for the few in-situ and well-documented pieces, a much wished-for research endeavor.[25]

The inscriptions, which often accompanied the portraits, are fairly generic. They state first names of the deceased, his or her family relations, most often names of fathers, mothers, husbands, wives or children. However, in some cases grand- and great grand parents can be mentioned, as well as uncles and aunts, nieces and nephews. Together with the portraits the inscriptions would have shaped the history of the deceased depicted on the funerary monument and the inscription would further have individualized the person represented and situated him or her within the sphere of Palmyrene family-networks.[26]

The Palmyrene funerary portraits therefore make up a unique group of material for scholars of the ancient world to study, since they are the largest corpus of representations of individuals stemming from one place in the ancient world with a tight chronology and a well-established stylistic development. They therefore offer the opportunity of studying continuity and

---

[23] For recent publications on the quarries of Palmyra and further references see: Schmidt-Colinet 1990; Schmidt-Colinet and al-As'ad and al-As'ad 2013; Schmidt-Colinet 2017.

[24] Sargent and Therkildsen 2010, ibid., Raja and Sørensen 2015a. Furthermore, also see Raja and Sørensen 2015b, for references to the Ingholt diaries, which also include sketches of polychrome sarcophagi found in Palmyra during the excavations of Ingholt.

[25] All pieces with a known grave context have been collected within the Palmyra Portrait Project and an article on these is underway by the author.

[26] Among others see: Raja 2017c.

changes in portrait habit in detail and a backdrop upon which to discuss these as societal phenomena.

3. The representations of Palmyrene priests in the funerary sphere – local traditions in a globalized world

The Palmyrene priests make up a significant group within the funerary portraiture. 365 priest portraits have been collected until now, which amounts to approximately 10 percent of the complete corpus and to approximately 20 percent of all male representations.[27] On the so-called loculus reliefs, rectangular limestone slabs with more-than-bust reliefs depicting the deceased, the priests are most often shown alone (fig. 1).[28] Only in five cases are they depicted together with other individuals (fig. 2).[29] In the context of banqueting reliefs, they are most often represented together with one other individual, either a standing servant or a sitting wife (fig. 3). But in the sarcophagi scenes, they are depicted together with a wide variety of family members and most often more than one priest is depicted in the sarcophagi scenes underlining the family-based relations upon which the structure of Palmyrene priesthoods must have rested (fig. 4).[30] In other publications I have argued extensively and in detail for the ways in which the funerary representations of priests show that priesthood in Palmyra was not a profession as such, but rather is to be seen as a status symbol and an underlining of the membership of the utmost Palmyrene elite, which these men would have belonged to.[31]

Palmyrene priests were recognizable by their distinct priestly hats, round hats with flat tops, which seem to have been made of a sort of stiff textile or felt. The priests often wear decorated tunics covered by large cloaks, also sometimes decorated and fastened with big round decorated brooches. In their hands, they often carry the symbols of their trade, the libation pitcher and incense bowl. The priestly representations stand out from representations of priests from other places in the Near East through the distinct hats. These are unique for Palmyra.[32] The closest parallel are the hats, which date to a much earlier period, which the priests of the stelae found in Umm al-

---

[27] Raja 2017a; Raja 2017b; Raja 2017c; Raja 2017d.

[28] Raja 2016b; Raja 2019b.

[29] Raja 2017c; Raja 2019b.

[30] Raja 2019b for an overview of priests depicted together with other priests in sarcophagi scenes as well as considerations on the meaning of these scenes for the importance of the Palmyrene family.

[31] Raja 2017a.

[32] See for an article, which remains a standard work on the Palmyrene priests: Stucky 1973; Raja 2017b. Also see Raja 2017d.

Ahmad in Lebanon carry.[33] There does not seem to be any direct link between the two types of representations though. Priests from other parts of the region consistently wear conical hats.[34] The priestly hat therefore seems to be one trait which sets apart Palmyrene priests – iconographically speaking at least – from their fellow priests in the Roman Near East. It had slipped into scholarship that it was called a 'modius', a term introduced for the hat in the 1920s without any explanation, probably due to the round shape of hat, very remotely resembling the modius, measuring units, worn by among other deities, Serapis. This has recently been proven to be a term which should not be used for this item of clothing.[35]

The Palmyrene priests represented in the funerary sphere are our largest group of visual material from the Near East coming from one place. It allows us to study the representation of priesthood in one place and its development over almost three hundred years. However, it is striking to notice that over all these years there were only a few changes in the representations of these priests. This underlines the stable structure of Palmyrene society as being based on a tribal system consisting of extended families, who through a family father held power not only within the family but also outside and the family ties and family connections would have been determining for the importance which a given family held. Since the priests belonged to the elite of Palmyra, considering that 20 percent of the male funerary portraits depicts priests and that priesthood does not seem to have been a profession as such, but rather a role, which one held at certain points in time, it must be assumed that Palmyrene priests also held other societal roles, such as being actively engaged in the economic and political life of Palmyra. The insistence on the representation of Palmyrene priesthood in the graves over a period of almost three hundred years might underline an insistence on the continuity of the importance of this status symbol of religious life in general, but can also be seen as a way of creating a Middle Ground around which Palmyrene families could gather and around which they would have been able to connect across extended families. The image of priesthood and the actions carried out by priests became a media through which a Middle Ground, which could also have been an arena of competition, might have become a common ground.

---

[33] Stucky 1973.

[34] See for example Michael Blömer's work on priestly representation: Blömer 2014; Stucky 1973.

[35] See Raja 2018 for a study and overview of the historiography of the terminology used for the Palmyrene priestly hat. See Ingholt 1923 for the introduction of the terminology used since then for the Palmyrene priestly hat.

4. Priests in the public sphere

Palmyrene priestly representations stemming from the public sphere are not numerous.[36] This is due to the nature of the evidence, which has survived from the public sphere in Palmyra. Marble and bronze statues have mostly gone and limestone statues weathered. However, there are still representations depicting priests in the public sphere. These often come from the religious sphere, where sacrificial scenes are depicted, as the one on the altar in the Sanctuary of Nebu, on which a row of priests performing sacrifices are depicted.[37] Some statues also survive depicting priests in their full attire. These might have been set up on the streets of Palmyra or have been set up in sanctuaries. One relief found in the Sanctuary of Nebu depicts three generations of Palmyrene priests, showed with a seated grandfather in the middle with his son on the one side and his grandson on the other side, all depicted in the Palmyrene priestly attire. This relief, along with the scenes on the sarcophagi, underline the emphasis on the importance of Palmyrene priesthoods being kept and passed on and extended to son and grandsons within the Palmyrene families. In the public sphere the reliefs, although nowhere near as plentiful as the evidence from the funerary sphere, seem to underline the importance of interaction between several priests, with an emphasis on the sacrificial act. This is of course no surprise, but underlines that interaction within and among groups of priests was important. In the public religious life a Middle Ground can be observed through the sacrificial reliefs, which depict interaction within and across groups of priests.

5. The Palmyrene banqueting tesserae

The so-called banqueting tesserae from Palmyra is another group of underresearched material, which deserves more attention, when looking at the structure of religious life in Palmyra.[38] These small clay objects often held depictions of Palmyrene priests and inscriptions giving us the name of the priest(s) and/or the group, which he belonged to. The tesserae, which functioned as entrance tickets to religious banquets held in sanctuaries, were made in series.[39] More than 1200 different series of the tesserae exist.[40] One series

---

[36] See for example Yon 2002. Also see Stucky 1973.

[37] Bounni and Seigne and Saliby 1992, 104, figs. 93–95.

[38] du Mesnil du Buisson 1944; Ingholt and Starcky 1955; du Mesnil du Buisson 1962; Kaizer 2002. Furthermore, see Raja 2015b; Raja 2015c; Raja 2016c; Raja 2019c.

[39] al-As'ad and Briquel-Chatonnet and Yon 2005.

[40] Ingholt and Starcky 1955 was the first and until now only attempt at collecting a corpus of this material. More recent studies have been done by Kaizer 2002, al-As'ad and Briquel-Chatonnet and Yon 2005; Raja 2015b; Raja 2015c; Raja 2016c; Raja 2919c.

that was found in a complete state, buried in the Sanctuary of Nebu, held 125 tesserae.[41] Furthermore, the size of the banqueting hall in the Sanctuary of Bel is estimated to have been able to hold between 100 and 150 people. These facts tell us that there would have been limited space at these events and that the tesserae would have functioned as entrance cards to the event. However, it can be concluded that these items, which were found in large numbers in the sanctuaries of Palmyra and not least in the drains of the banqueting hall in the Sanctuary of Bel, seem to have lost importance when entrance to the banquet had been gained. They were simply often left behind and only served a purpose at a certain moment in time.[42] Whereas these objects have been interpreted as entrance tickets to banquets held in honor of dead priests, this in light of new research seems to have been unlikely. The tesserae, which hold intriguing iconography (fig. 5), are the richest source available to us on the religious life of Palmyra, since they, apart from giving information about the priests, also hold information about deities, religious symbols, dates of banquets, amounts of food and drink distributed as well as in general informing us about the iconography used in Palmyra within religious and cultic frameworks.[43]

Apart from telling us about one particular religious practice, namely the religious banquet, which was common in religious life across the Roman Empire, the tesserae also give insight into the structure of religious life in Palmyra. The iconography and the inscriptions on the tesserae give a wealth of information. What can be concluded from the inscriptions and the iconography on these tesserae is that the banquets were paid for by religious/cultic groups consisting of Palmyrene priests, since the tesserae, which worked as entrance tickets, often carried images of banqueting priests or priestly busts as well as inscriptions giving us the names of these. They never mention females and seldom show non-priestly male figures, and if they do, these are depicted together with priests.

The chronology of the tesserae is not firmly established. The small size of the tesserae, often measuring at the most 4 by 4 centimeters, makes it difficult, if not impossible, to detect any detailed stylistic developments. However, the tesserae were indeed very detailed in their iconographic repertoire, and not two identical series were issued. This underlines the importance that each set of entrance tickets had to be unique. What the reasons for this

---

[41] See note 39.

[42] Raja 2016c.

[43] See for example Kaizer and Raja 2019. Also see Abdul-Hak 1952; Stucky 1971; al-As'ad and Briquel-Chatonnet and Yon 2005 for specific studies of tesserae and tesserae series as well as further references.

was is not known. Did the Palmyrene priestly groups want to avoid falsifications? This seems to be an unlikely scenario, since we must assume that the religious scene in Palmyra would have been dominated by a tightly knit network of male priests who would have been aware of each other, and this would not have allowed for easy falsification of objects which would give access to religious events. So was it perhaps indeed rather a matter of a wish for individualization and for standing out that the tesserae were produced as unique series and used a highly varied iconographic language?[44] Did a group or an individual priest choose the combination of imagery on a given series of tesserae themselves and were they an expression of highly individualized choices combined with the often depicted banqueting priests? It seems to be a likely scenario. It might not be possible to come to a firm conclusion about this suggestion, but what the tesserae do indicate is that religious banquets were used as meeting places for a variety of religious groups. If they had been reserved for one group and its members only, then tickets might not have been necessary, since the individuals would have known each other. The banqueting tickets indicate that these events could have been used as places for interaction between a variety of religious groups, who may not all have belonged to the same extended families of Palmyra, and that these banquets therefore, among other things, served the purpose of being a meeting place – social and religious – perhaps even political and economic – where religious rituals and a ritual meal brought different groups with different interests together with a common purpose.[45] This sort of behavior and its expressions is one which can be thought of as creating a Middle Ground in a society, which also among the elite families must have been competitive.

6. Conclusion

So, while there is a lot we do not know about Palmyrene religious life and about the priests of Palmyra, the visual evidence does allow for some further interpretations. The funerary portraits, the portraits from the public sphere and the banqueting tesserae all give insight into different aspects of the shaping of religious life and the image of religious life in different situations. At the center of all three groups of material, however, stands the image of the Palmyrene priests. While the three groups are different in the expressions and meanings that they carry, they all carry the same representation, namely the portraits of Palmyrene priests. These portraits and their iconographic expressions did not change much over time. They were a stable factor within Palmyrene visual representation, whose language did change significantly

---

[44] Raja 2019c.
[45] Raja 2015c.

within other spheres over time.[46] Palmyrene priests, however, stayed the same. Their clothes, their hats, their decorative elements, their attributes. They can be said to have stood together through their similarities, and their differences were only noticed in the details. So as a coherent group they acted as a Middle Ground, at least within Palmyrene society, and may well have acted as such outside of Palmyrene society, since they most likely held other positions as well.

Palmyrene priests belonged to the elite. Therefore, they were also the ones in charge of the political and economic life. These elite male members of Palmyrene society were closely knitted together through religious groups as expressed by the tesserae, family relations as expressed in the funerary portraiture, and through generational links, and therefore they represented society as a tightly knit group making up 20 percent of the complete elite male population in Palmyra. In this way Palmyrene priests created a strong image both within Palmyra but also to the outsider of a well-founded traditional society, which adhered to local customs and ideas.

While earlier descriptions of Palmyra and Palmyrene society in some ways indicate that its society might in fact just have been a Middle Ground due to the location of the city and its situation between other empires, it indeed seems to be rather different when one looks at the evidence in detail. Palmyra much more seems to have been the place where Middle Ground in fact happened and was shaped. It is clear that Palmyrene society must be viewed as a society which operated on many different levels and interacted according to the societal spheres and framework within which certain groups or individuals were interacting. Certainly, interaction would have differed, and therefore, codes for such interaction, depending on whether an individual or a group was interacting in a domestic setting, in a funerary setting, in a religious setting, in a public setting, in a trade setting – within Palmyra or outside Palmyra – or depending on whether the individual was traveling or was at home, was alone or with other Palmyrenes and so on and so forth. The representations of the Palmyrene priests have been used here as a case study to try to show one way in which such codes can begin to be understood, in this case through the term of the Middle Ground.

---

[46] Kropp and Raja 2014; Krag and Raja 2019a; Krag 2018.

Bibliography

Abdul-Hak, S. 1952. L'Hypogée de Ta'ai a Palmyre, in: Annales Archéologiques Arabes Syriennes 2, 193–251.

al-As'ad, K. and F. Briquel-Chatonnet and J.-B. Yon. 2005. Sacred Banquets at Palmyra and the Functions of the Tesserae: Reflections on the Tokens Found in the Arşu Temple, in: E. Cussini (ed.), A journey to Palmyra: Collected Essays to Remember Delbert R. Hillers, Leiden, 1–10.

Andrade, N.J. 2013. Syrian Identity in the Greco-Roman World. New York and Cambridge.

Blömer, M. 2014. Steindenkmäler römischer Zeit aus Nordsyrien. Identität und kulturelle Tradition in Kyrrhestike und Kommagene. Bonn.

Bounni, A. and J. Seigne and N. Saliby. 1992. Le sanctuaire de Nabu à Palmyre. Beirut.

Dirven, L. 1999. The Palmyrenes of Dura-Europos. A Study of Religious Interaction in Roman Syria. Leiden.

du Mesnil du Buisson, R. 1944. Tessères et monnaies de Palmyre. Paris.

du Mesnil du Buisson, R. 1962. Les tessères et les monnaies de Palmyre. Paris.

Dossin, G. 1952. Correspondance de Iasmah-Addu. Paris.

Dossin, G. 1954. Répertoire analytique des tomes 1 à 5. Paris.

Freyberger, K.S. H. and A. Henning and H. von Hesberg (edd.). 2003. Kulturkonflikte im Vorderen Orient an der Wende vom Hellenismus zur römischen Kaiserzeit. Rhaden/Westf.

Gawlikowski, M. 1970. Monuments funéraires de Palmyre. Warsaw.

Gawlikowski, M. 2003. Palmyra: from a Tribal federation to a City, in: K.S.H. Freyberger and A. Henning and H. von Hesberg (edd.). Kulturkonflikte im Vorderen Orient an der Wende vom Hellenismus zur römischen Kaiserzeit, Rhaden/Westf., 7–10.

Hannestad, N. 1998. Roman Art and Imperial Policy. Aarhus.

Hartmann, U. 2001. Das palmyrenische Teilreich. Stuttgart.

Hartmann, U. 2008. Das palmyrenische Teilreich, in: K.-P. Johne (ed.). Die Zeit der Soldatenkaiser. Krise und Transformation des Römischen Reiches im 3. Jahrhundert (235–284), Berlin, 343–378.

Henning, A. 2013. Die Turmgräber von Palmyra. Eine lokale Bauform im kaiserzeitlichen Syrien als Ausdruck kultureller Identität. Rhaden/Westf.

Ingholt, H. 1923. Palmyrene reliefs: chronology and style, in: American Journal of Archaeology 27(1), 57–71.

Ingholt, H. 1928. Studier over Palmyrensk Skulptur. Copenhagen.

Ingholt, H. and J. Starcky. 1955. Recueil des tessères de Palmyre. Paris.

Kaizer, T. 2002. The Religious Life of Palmyra. A Study of the Social Patterns of Worship in the Roman Period. Stuttgart.

Kaizer, T. and R. Raja 2019 Divine symbolism on the tesserae from Palmyra: considerations about the so-called 'symbol of Bel' or 'Signe de la pluie', in: Syria 95, 297–325.

Krag, S. 2018. Funerary Representations of Palmyrene Women. From the First Century BC to the Third Century AD. Turnhout.

S. Krag and R. Raja 2019a (edd.), Families in Palmyra. Societal contexts, social roles and constellations of families in 1st-3rd centuries CE Palmyra. Copenhagen.

Krag, S. and R. Raja 2019b. Families in Palmyra – the evidence from the first three centuries CE, in: S. Krag and R. Raja (edd.), Families in Palmyra. Societal contexts, social roles and constellations of families in 1st-3rd centuries CE Palmyra, Copenhagen, 7–18.

Kropp, A.J.M. and R. Raja 2014. The Palmyra Portrait Project, in: Syria 91, 393–408.

Kropp, A.J.M. and R. Raja (edd.). 2016. The World of Palmyra. Copenhagen.

Millar, F. 1993. The Roman Near East 31 B.C.–A.D. 337. Cambridge.

Meyer, J.C. 2013. City and hinterland. Villages and estates north of Palmyra. New perspectives, in: Studia Palmyreńskie 12, 265–282.

Meyer, J.C. 2016. Palmyrena. Settlements, forts and nomadic networks, in: A. Kropp and R. Raja (edd.). The World of Palmyra, Copenhagen, 88–104.

Meyer, J.C. 2017. Palmyrena. Palmyra and the Surrounding Territory from the Roman to the Early Islamic Period. Oxford.

Meyer, J.C. and E.H. Seland and N. Anfinset (edd.). 2016. Palmyrena: City, Hinterland and Caravan Trade between Orient and Occident (Proceedings of the Conference held in Athens, December 1–3, 2012). Oxford.

Piersimoni, P. 1995a. Compiling a Palmyrene prosopography: methodological problems, in: Aram periodical 7, 252–260.

Piersimoni , P. 1995b. The Palmyrene Prosopography 2. Vols, unpublished PhD Thesis, University College London.

Raja, R. 2015a. Palmyrene Funerary Portrait in Context: Portrait Habit between Local Traditions and Imperial Trends, in: J. Fejfer and M. Moltesen and A. Rathje (edd.), Traditions: Transmission of Culture in the Ancient World, Chicago, 329–361.

Raja, R. 2015b. Staging "Private" Religion in Roman "Public" Palmyra. The Role of the Religious Dining Tickets, in: J. Rüpke and C. Ando (edd.), Public and private in Ancient Mediterranean Law and Religion. Historical and Comparative Studies, Berlin, 165–186.

Raja, R. 2015c. Cultic Dining and Religious Patterns in Palmyra. The Case of the Palmyrene Banqueting Tesserae, in: S. Faust and M. Seifert and L. Ziemer (edd.), Antike. Architektur. Geschichte. Festschrift für Inge Nielsen zum 65. Geburtstag, Aachen, 181–200.

Raja, R. 2016a. Powerful Images of the Deceased: Palmyrene Funerary Portrait Culture between Local, Greek and Roman Representations, in: D. Boschung and F. Queyrel (edd.) Bilder der Macht: Das griechische Porträt und seine Verwendung in der antiken Welt, Paderborn, 319–348.

Raja, R. 2016b. Representations of Priests in Palmyra. Methodological Considerations on the Meaning of the Representation of Priesthood in Roman Period Palmyra, in: Religion in the Roman Empire 2(1), 125–146.

Raja, R. 2016c. In and Out of Contexts: Explaining Religious Complexity through the Banqueting Tesserae from Palmyra, in: Religion in the Roman Empire 2(3), 340–371.

Raja, R. 2017a. To Be or Not To Be Depicted As a Priest in Palmyra. A Matter of Representational Spheres and Societal Values, in: T. Long and A.H. Sørensen (edd.). Positions and Professions: Palmyrenske Studier 2, Copenhagen, 115–130.

Raja, R. 2017b. You Can Leave Your Hat On. Priestly Representations from Palmyra – Between Visual Genre, Religious Importance and Social Status, in: R. L. Gordon and Petridou, G. and J. Rüpke (edd.). Beyond Priesthood, Religious Entrepreneurs and Innovators in the Imperial Era, Berlin, 417–442.

Raja, R. 2017c. Networking Beyond Death: Priests and Their Family Networks in Palmyra Explored Through the Funerary Sculpture, in: H.F. Teigen and E.H. Seland (edd.), Sinews of Empire: Networks in the Roman Near East and Beyond, Oxford, 121–136.

Raja, R. 2017d. Representations of the So-Called "Former Priests" in Palmyrene Funerary Art. A Methodological Contribution and Commentary, in: TOPOI 21(1), 51–81.

Raja, R. 2018. The matter of the Palmyrene "modius". Remarks on the history of research of the terminology of the palmyrene priestly hat, in: Religion in the Roman Empire 4:2, 237–259.

Raja, R. 2019a. Family Matters! Family Constellations in Palmyrene Funerary Sculpture, in: Acta Hyperborea 15, 245–270.

Raja, R. 2019b. It stays in the family. Palmyrene priestly representations and their constellations, in: S. Krag and R. Raja (edd.), Families in Palmyra. Societal contexts, social roles and constellations of families in 1st-3rd centuries CE Palmyra, Copenhagen, 95–156.

Raja, R. 2019c. Dining with the Gods and the Others. The Banqueting Tickets from Palmyra as Expressions of Religious Individualization, in: M. Fuchs and B.-C. Otto and R. Parson and J. Rüpke (edd.) Religious Individualization: Types and Cases. Historical and Crosscultural Explorations, Berlin and Boston, 243–256.

Raja, R. and A.H. Sørensen 2015a. The "Beauty of Palmyra" and Qasr Abjad (Palmyra): New Discoveries in the Archive of Harald Ingholt, in: Journal of Roman Archaeology 28(1), 439–450.

Raja, R. and A.H. Sørensen 2015b. Harald Ingholt and Palmyra, Aarhus.

Sadurska, A. 1995. La famille et son image dans l'art de Palmyre, in : F.E. König and S. Rebetez (ed.), Arculiana. Ioanni Boegli anno sexagesimo quinto feliciter peracto amici discipuli collegae socii dona dederunt AD XIIII Kalendas Decembris MDCCCCLXXXXV, Avenches, 583–589.

Sadurska, A. and A. Bounni 1994. Les Sculptures Funéraires de Palmyre. Rome.

Sargent, M.L. and R.H. Therkildsen 2010. The Technical Investigation of Sculptural Polychromy at the Ny Carlsberg Glyptotek 2009–2010 – An Outline. Copenhagen.

Sartre, M. and A. Sartre-Fauriat 2016. Palmyre.Vérités et légendes. Perrin.

Sartre-Fauriat, A. and M. Sartre 2008. Palmyre. La cité des caravanes. Paris

Schmidt-Colinet, A. 1990. Considerations sur les carriers de Palmyre en Syrie, in: M. Waelkens (ed.), Pierre éternelle du Nil au Rhin. Carrières et prefabrication, Bruxelles, 88–92.

Schmidt-Colinet, A. 2005. Palmyra. Kulturbegegnung im Grenzbereich. Mainz.

Schmidt-Colinet, A. 2017. Die antiken Steinbrüche von Palmyra. Ein Vorbericht, in: Mitteilungen der Deutschen Orient-Gesellschaft zu Berlin 149, 159–196.

Schmidt-Colinet, A. and K. al-As'ad and W. al-As'ad. 2013. Thirty years of Syro–German/Austrian archaeological research at Palmyra, in: Studia Palmyrénskie 12, 299–318.

Seland, E.H. 2015a. Palmyrene Long-Distance Trade: Land, River, and Maritime Routes in the First Three Centuries CE, in: M.A. Walter and J.P. Ito-Adler (edd.), The Silk Road: Interwoven History. Vol 1. Long-distance Trade, Culture, and Society, Cambridge, 101–131.

Seland, E.H. 2015b. Writ in water, lines in sand: Ancient trade routes, models and comparative evidence, in: Cogent Arts and Humanities 2.

Seland, E.H. 2016. Ships of the Desert and Ships of the Sea. Palmyra in the World Trade of the First Three Centuries CE. Wiesbaden.

Shifman, I.S. 2014. The Palmyrene Tax Tariff. Oxford.

Smith, A.M. 2013. Roman Palmyra. Identity, Community, and State Formation. Oxford.

Sommer, M. 2005. Roms orientalische Steppengrenze. Palmyra – Edessa – Dura-Europos – Hatra. Eine Kulturgeschichte von Pompeius bis Diocletian. Stuttgart.

Stucky, R.A. 1971. Figures apolliniennes grecques sur des tessères palmyréniennes, in: Syria 48, 135–141.

Stucky, R. A. 1973. Prêtres syriens I. Palmyre, in: Syria 50, 163–180.

Ulf, C. 2009. Rethinking Cultural Contacts, in: Ancient East and West 8, 81–132.

Ulf, C. 2014. Eine Typologie von kulturellen Kontaktzonen - oder: Rethinking Cultural Contacts auf dem Prüfstand, in: R. Rollinger and K. Schnegg (edd.), Kulturkontakte in antiken Welten: Vom Denkmodell zum Fallbeispiel, Leuven, 469–504.

Veyne, P. 2015. Palmyre. L'irremplaçable trésor. Paris.

White, R. 1991. The Middle Ground. Indians, Empires, and the Republics in the Great Lakes Region, 1650–1815. Cambridge.

Yon, J.-B. 2002. Les Notables de Palmyre. Beirut.

Illustrations

Fig. 1: Loculus relief with bust of priest wearing the priestly hat. Ny Carlsberg Glyptotek, Copenhagen, inv. IN 1033, 200–220 CE (Courtesy of Ny Carlsberg Glyptotek, photo by Palmyra Portrait Project).

Fig. 2: Loculus relief with two busts, one being of a priest. Last seen in Sotheby's auction catalogue, 150–170 CE (© Palmyra Portrait Project, Ingholt Archive at Ny Carlsberg Glyptotek, PS 252).

Fig. 3: Banqueting relief with a reclining priest. Ny Carlsberg Glyptotek, Copenhagen, inv. IN 1159 and IN 1160, 146/147 CE (Courtesy of Ny Carlsberg Glyptotek, photo by Palmyra Portrait Project).

Fig. 4: Sarcophagus from the grave of Yarḥaî, 237–255 CE. National Museum of Damascus (© Palmyra Portrait Project, Ingholt Archive at Ny Carlsberg Glyptotek, PS 890, 892).

Fig. 5: Banqueting tessera. Ny Carlsberg Glyptotek, Copenhagen, inv. IN 3198 (Courtesy of Ny Carlsberg Glyptotek, photo by Rubina Raja).

The Nabataean Ruler Cult and Ptolemaic Egypt

David F. Graf

The Nabataean kingdom is characteristically described as fiercely independent, resisting the imperialistic advances of the Hellenistic powers (Diod. II 48, 4–5). However, recent evidence suggests that in the early Hellenistic period the Nabataeans were not only under the shadow of the Ptolemaic kingdom in Egypt, but enjoyed cordial and friendly relations as their military allies in their struggle to control and govern Palestine. This exposure of the Nabataean kings to Ptolemaic statecraft and administrative policy also acquainted them with the Ptolemaic Ruler Cult. The purposes of this study is to suggest that the Nabataean dynasty adopted and adapted the Ptolemaic Ruler Cult in order to reinforce and enhance its status over its vast Arab kingdom and in its relations with the surrounding Hellenistic states.

It is well-known that the Ruler Cult was used by the Hellenistic kings to legitimize their rule and was influential on the smaller indigenous kingdoms throughout the Near East.[1] For the Nabataeans, it was the Ptolemaic kingdom that had an impact on its dynasty. The Ptolemies at an early stage in their rule of Egypt established a centrally organized dynastic cult, with the divinization of the ruling kings and queens, and a hierarchy of provincial priests.[2] The institution of the dynastic cult began as early as 272/1 BCE, when Ptolemy II Philadelphus and Arsinoe I became the *Theoi Adelphoi, i.e.* the ruling divine brother-king and sister-queen.[3] They were followed by Ptolemy III Euergetes and Berenike was *Theoi Eueregetai* in 243/2 BCE, Ptolemy IV Philopater and Arsinoe III as *Theoi Sotares* in 215/4 BCE, and later by *Königsspaar* rulers named *Theoi Philopatores* and *Theoi Epiphaneis*.[4] By the end of the second century BCE, there were even more cult titles, and more priests and priestesses supplementing the dynastic cult.[5] Of significance is Cleopatra III (142–101 BCE), with her son Ptolemy IX Soter (116–107 BCE), the *Theoi Philometores kai Soteres*, explicitly promoting their divinity as political propaganda[6], with the garrisons and soldiers the active adherents and promoters

---

[1] Chaniotis 2003; cf. Habicht 1970.

[2] Fraser 1972: I, 213–246; Winter 1978; Koenen 1993; Pfeiffer 2008; Thompson 2012, 117–128.

[3] Quaegebeur 1998a; Hölbl 2001, 92–98; cf. Hazzard 2000. Thedynastic festivals were a propoaganda mechanism for popularizing the cult: see Grabowski 2014, 21–41.

[4] Haubner 2011; Fraser 1972, I, 216–219; Thompson 2012, 124.

[5] Fraser 1972, I, 16–220.

[6] Quaegebeur 1978.

148   David F. Graf

of the dynastic cult.[7] The identification with deities culminates with Ptolemy XII Auletes and his daughter Cleopatra III identified as the *Neos Dionysos* and *Nea Isis*, respectively.[8] The royal ideology now represents the personification of the King as Osiris-Dionysos[9] and the Queen as Isis-Tyche.[10] These developments form the background for the emergence of the Ruler Cult in Nabataea.

1. The Nabataean Dynasty and the Ptolemaic Realm

The connections of the Nabataean dynasty with the Ptolemaic kingdom began as early as the rule of Ptolemy II Philaldelphus in the first half of the third century BCE, acquainting the Nabataean kings with the ruler cult at an early stage in the history of the dynasty. The first attested Nabataean king is now preserved in the Posidippus Papyrus and is contemporaneous with Ptolemy II Philadelphus, between 272 and 252 BCE, and who appears closely allied with the Ptolemaic dynasty in Egypt at the time, perhaps as military allies.[11] The document exposes gaps in our knowledge of the Nabataean dynasty in the early Hellenistic era, but some reasonable assumptions can be made about developments during this still fairly obscure period.

On the basis of these presumed intimate relations of the Nabataeans with the Ptolemaic empire, there is sufficient reason to suspect the Nabataean realm was influenced by Alexandrian politics and culture. The impact of Ptolemaic Egypt has already been traced along different lines, particularly its effects on Nabataean material culture visible from the beginning of the first century BCE. In regard to architecture, the "second Pompeian style" (of the first century BCE) has been detected in the architectural features in the facades of some tombs and assigned to Alexandrian influence.[12] In addition, other architectural features at Petra such as the obelisk, crows-step and elephant headed capitals have been attributed to Egyptian influence.[13] From the numismatic perspective, Nabataean issues displaying the busts of the kings and queens in jugate reflects Ptolemaic influence. The first appearance of the Nabataean queens in the public sphere is marked by the anonymous queen on the coins of Obodas II (30–9 BCE), and subsequent issues display the royal pair or *Königspaar* in jugate busts with close affinity to the Ptolemaic

---

[7]   Chaniotis 2003, 441; cf. Quaegebeur 1989.
[8]   OGIS 741 with Fraser 1972, 244 and n. 238, citing Plut. Ant. 54.
[9]   Thompson 2012: 108.
[10] Quaegebeur 1988; Hölbl 2001, 285–293.
[11] Graf 2006. For the Hellenization of the Nabataean army see Graf 1994.
[12] McKenzie 1990, 85–100, 124–126.
[13] Finlayson 2016, 83–101.

The Nabataean Ruler Cult

149

and Seleucid portraits of the kings and queens together on coins.[14] From the religious perspective, the adoption of the cult of Isis at Petra by the late first century BCE also demonstrates the influence of Ptolemaic Egypt on Nabataean culture, but it may even be earlier.[15] The onomasticon of the Fourth Century BCE Idumaean ostraca in Palestine has substantial Arab names, with several theophoric "servant names" with the Egyptian deity for Isis – see 'BD-'SY (A14: 3) and 'BD-'S (A215.1), and several for Osiris, 'BD-'WSYR' (EN 96. JA 86.A215.1 and more).[16] A Nabataean inscription also mentions the goddess Isis at Sīʿ in the Ḥaurān in the year 108/7 BCE.[17] At Petra, the signs of the adoption of the cult are later, attested first in a dedication to Isis at el-Mreriyye in Wadi es-Siyyagh in a relief of the goddess dated to 25 BCE.[18] The possible presence of Osiris in the relief at el-Mreriyye has led to the suggestion that the mysteries of Osiris were celebrated at Petra and that Isis herself had a small temple at the Nabataean capital.[19] The concentration of Isis statuettes at the Temple of Winged Lions at Petra shows the popularity of the cult.[20] There also are some twenty or more terracotta and stone figurines primarily from domestic contexts scattered throughout the civic center,[21] demonstrating the widespread popularity of the cult at Petra. A much later Greek inscription of 257 CE mentions a priest of Isis at Petra, who must have had precursors.[22] Nor is the presence of the Isis cult at Petra an isolated phenomenon in Arabia. But elsewhere, the evidence is later and fragmentary for the Isis Cult. At Gerasa of the Decapolis, statues of Sarapis and Isis were dedicated in 142/3 CE,[23] and a inscribed bust of Sarapis decorated with Isis crowns and headdresses is attested at Umm al-Jimāl in the second or third century CE. [24] In contrast, in Palestine the evidence is much earlier, consisting of an inscription and Isis-type pottery at Samaria-Sebaste of the late Hellenistic period.[25] There is also a dedication to Serapis and Dionysos at Nysa-

---

[14] Meshorer 1975, 33–34 and nos. 21–31, and now Barkay 2016b.

[15] Merklein and Wenning 1998; Healey 2001, 137-140; Vaelske 2013, 351–61.

[16] Porten and Yardeni 2014, 244, and add texts cited in Yardeni 2016: 652 for both names, including Eph'al and Naveh 1996, no. 96, 98 and 182. Note 'bdys also appears at Beersheeba: Navah 1979: nos. 37 and 45.

[17] Milik 2003, 269–74, correcting his date of 104/3 BCE.

[18] Milik and Starcky 1975, 120–124 = Bricault 2005, 513, no. 404/0501; cf. Janif 2004.

[19] Bricault 1992, 39 and 45.

[20] Roche 1987, 218.

[21] El-Khouri 2002, 11, 52–54.

[22] Milik and Starcky 1975, 123 = Bricault 2005, 514, no. 404/0502.

[23] Bricault 2005, 512, no, 404/0401.

[24] Weber 2006, 82, no. 61.

[25] Magness 2001, 158–165; Bricault 2005, 510, no. 403/0501; cf. Bricault 1999.

150 David F. Graf

Scythopolis of the Augustan era.[26] This evidence for Palestine and Arabia is just a reflection of the widespread popularity of Isis cult across the Mediterranean in the Hellenistic and Roman periods.[27] The substantial and extensive evidence of Isis at Petra and elsewhere is then not merely a local phenomenon,[28] but rather a phenomenon of large-scale proportions generated by Ptolemaic influence and the attraction of the Isis cult.

All of these elements of Egyptian influence provide a context for considering the adoption of the Ruler Cult in Nabataea. The Ruler Cult was not only prevalent in the cultural environment of the Hellenistic Near East, it was also an attractive political strategy for dynasts to bolster their status and increase their patronage. In the arguments that follow in support of the Nabataean adoption of the Ruler Cult in Ptolemaic guise, the progression is from the overtly explicit evidence for the Ruler Cult in Nabataea to arguments more implicit and plausible in nature.

2. Obodas the God

The only explicit literary evidence for the divinization of the Nabataean kings is a rather late tradition of the Byzantine era. According to the *Arabicus* of the historian Uranius, probably to be dated to the fourth century CE, [29] the Nabataean city of 'Avdat was "where King Obodas, whom they [i.e. the Nabataeans] deify, is buried." This tradition is preserved by the Byzantine grammarian Stephanus of Byzantium, in probably the sixth century CE.[30] The tradition receives verification by several Nabataean Aramaic texts stemming from 'Avdat in the Negev that mention "Obodas the God" [31] and another that asserts "as 'Obodas lives."[32] After the Roman annexation of Arabia, the tradition continues in Greek texts from 'Avdat that mention *Thea Oboda* and *Zeus Oboda*.[33] This evidence from Avdat-Obodas in the Negev is late, but there also is earlier evidence of the cult at Petra in the Nabataean heartland.

Less than a km south of the Main Theater in Petra, there is an important religious rock-cut triclinium complex at Jebel Numayr, where a century ago a statue was discovered that was dedicated to "'Obodas the god",

---

[26] Bricault 2005, 509, no. 403/0301.
[27] Bricault 2001; Map I, for the diffusion across the Mediterranean world; for the epigraphic evidence, see Bricault 2005, and for the numismatic evidence, Bricault 2008.
[28] *pace* Alpass 2010, 107.
[29] West 1974, 274.
[30] Stephanus of Byzantium, Ethnika = FgrH 675, F 4 = ed. Meineke 482, 15–17'.
[31] Negev 1986b, 56–60, for *'bdt 'lh*.
[32] RES 527, *ḥy 'bdt*.
[33] Negev 1981, nos. 3–7; cf. 1b and 11. For recent discussion, see Erickson-Gini 2014.

offered in behalf of King Aretas IV, queen Shaqilat, and other members of the royal family.[34] Recent excavations at the cultic complex discovered the fragments of a statue, ostensibly identified as the one offered to "Obodas the God."[35] In addition, over a hundred graffiti were found in the environs, some 40 of which seem to be associated with the open-air triclinium or chapel.[36] More importantly, subsequent excavations at the site have revealed beneath the religious complex associated with Aretas IV an even earlier open-air triclinium dating to the mid-second century BCE, based on early Nabataean pottery (Schmid Dekortype I), Hellenistic imports and ^{14}C tests.[37] The relationship of the various stages of the cultic center still needs to be established, but the unpublished graffiti may provide clues to possible continuity in the worship of "Obodas the God" at the site.

The worship of "Obodas the God" also extended elsewhere at Petra. At ed-Deir, on the heights above Petra, a Nabataean text indicates the presence of the members of a "symposium" (*marzēḥ*) who worshipped "Obodas the God."[38] More recently, evidence has emerged of the worship of Obodas in the settlement of al-Gaia (modern el-Jī or Wādī Mūsā) outside of inner Petra. A recent inscription on a bronze oil burner found in the Falāhat region in SW Wādī Mūsā preserves a temple dedication to "Obodas the God" (*ʿbdt ʾlh*) by a priest named *Zwyls* (perhaps Greek Zōilos, a personal name which appears several dozen times in the Greek world[39]) and, more importantly for us, his son ʿAbd-ʿObodat, dating to the reign of Rabbel II.[40] Another recent find from Wādī Mūsā is an inscribed bronze lamp of the first century CE, dedicated to "Obodas the God" (*ʿbdt ʾlh*) by a woman ʾAmat-Allah (a priestess?) and Taym-Dushara.[41] The noteworthy personal Basileophoric and Theophoric names of these dedicants suggest the worship of "Obodas the God" was an integral part of Nabataean religion, not a small peripheral sect or a family cult.

The problem is to identify which one of the Nabataean kings named ʿObodas' is designated by the expression "'Obodas the God." The preferred

---

[34] CIS II, 354 = Milik 1959a, 559–60; cf. Dijkstra 1995, 57–60.

[35] Nehmé 2002a, 247–50 and fig, 10–11 and 2002b, 452–55; Schwentzel 2006, 129; Kropp 2003b, 50; cf. Tholbecq et al. 2008; cf. for reservations see Wenning 2015, 44–46 and Al-Salameen and Falahat 2014, 299.

[36] Nehmé 2002a, 245; cf. 2002b.

[37] Tholbecq and Durand 2005 and 2013; cf. Nehmé 2012.

[38] Dalman 1912, 92–94, no. 73 = RES 1423.

[39] Wuthnow 1930, 51.

[40] Al-Salameen and Falahat 2014, 293–307.

[41] Al-Salameen and Shudaifat 2014, 43–45.

identification for the divinized king is Obodas I (ca. 96–84 BCE).[42] The possible short reign of a putative Obodas II (62–61 BCE), postulated only from questionable numismatic evidence, renders his existence questionable, and excludes this hypothetical king from consideration.[43] The depiction of Obodas III (30–9 BCE, probably better now designated as II) as uninterested in administrative and military affairs (Strab. 16, 4, 24 [781]), and "inactive and sluggish by nature" (Flav. Jos. ant. Jud. 16, 200), seems to exclude him as the possible defied king. Although Negev once earlier argued this later Obodas was the deified king, he later became more ambiguous, before finally proposing it was Obodas I.[44] This earlier Obodas remains the best option among the possible candidates.

But why was Obodas I divinized? The traditional explanation for Obodat I's divinization was to connect him with the defeat of the army of Antiochus XII Dionysos Epiphanes, which resulted in the death of the Seleucid ruler. According to Milik, this event "captured the imagination of the Nabataeans" and led to the divinization of Obodas I.[45] Several obstacles now seem to prohibit this explanation. Since Antiochus XII's coinage begins in 87/86 BCE at Damascus and ends in 83/82 BCE,[46] the climactic battle and his death must be assigned to 83/82 BCE.[47] But the association of the Nabataean king Obadas I with this victory is problematic. Josephus' account of the conflict only mentions the Nabataean victor is an anonymous "Arab king" (Flav. Jos. bell. Jud. 1,99–102; ant. Jud. 13, 387–91). Moreover, it now seems clear that Obadas' reign terminated before this event, and that another Nabataean king ruled at the time of Antiochus XII's defeat. On a statue from Qasr al-Bint at Petra, an inscription indicates it was dedicated to "Rabbel, King of the Nabataeans, [......]t, the king of the Nabataeans", in the 18th year of Aretas the king (CIS 349). The missing phrase can be restored as "son of Aretas" ([br ḥrt]t) or "son of Obodat ([br 'bd]t). Starcky dated it to Aretas III, [48], suggesting a dynastic sequence of Obodas [I], Rabbel [I],Aretas [III], which means a king named 'Rabbel' (I) must be squeezed in between Obodas I and Aretas III.

---

[42] As proposed by Starcky 1966, col. 906, and generally followed by later scholars, e.g. Bowersock 1983, 62, Negev 2003, 18*, and Barkay 2019, 14–15.

[43] For the numismatic evidence, see Huth 2010, 214–217, and for discussion Graf 1992, 971; *contra* Meshorer 1975, 16.

[44] Negev 2003, 18*, rejected his former proposal in 1981, 16, later regarded by him as uncertain (1986b).

[45] As cited in Starcky 1966, 906; cf. Bowersock 1983, 24–25.

[46] Houghton et al. 2008, 2471 and 2472A.

[47] As earlier suggested by Bellinger 1949, 77, but subsequently virtually ignored.

[48] Starcky 1966, col. 905.

The victorious anonymous king is then better identified with Rabbel I. A possible allusion to the event is in Uranius' *Arabika*, who lists under the Arab village Motho, the place "where Antigonus the Macedonian was killed by Rabbel, king of the Arabs."[49] But it is known that the Macedonian Antigonus, one of Alexander the Great's successors, died in the Battle of the Diadochoi at Ipsus (Phrygia) in 301 BCE (Plut. Demosthenes 29). This suggests that Uranius' text is corrupt, and it is attractive to emend the name 'Antigonus' in the text to 'Antiochus' and refer the incident to the Nabataean defeat of Antiochus XII in 83/82 BCE, in which the Seleucid ruler was killed. Josephus' anonymous "Arab king" (Flav. Jos. bell. Jud. 1, 99–102; ant. Jud. 13, 191) is then better identified with Rabbel I. Since the decisive conflict is located in the environs of Kana, identified as Khirbet Gazza at the entrance of Waldi al-Qina/Qena, just east of the southern end of the Dead Sea,[50] in proximity to modern Mauta in Moab, the location provides some support to the tradition. This site also agrees with Josephus' indication that the retreating Seleucid army "succumbed to starvation" at Kana (bell. Jud. 1, 101), where they "perished of hunger" (ant. Jud.13, 391). It also is possible that Rabbel I died himself from wounds suffered in the battle, for immediately afterward, the Nabataean king Aretas III is declared by the Damascenes the "King of Coele Syria" (Flav. Jos. bell. Jud. 1, 103) and began issuing coins at Damascus.[51]

If Obodas I is to be identified with 'Obodas the god', the only event that we can associate with such a development is the single fact that we know about his reign. According to Josephus, "Obodas, king of the Arabs", defeated the Hasmonean king Alexander Jannaeus in a battle at Gardara near the Golan in c. 95–93 BCE, just after the Judean king had conquered Moab and Galaaditis (Flav. Jos. bell. Jud. 90; ant. Jud. 13, 375). This significant victory provides for us the only basis for his deification and the cult of "Obodas the God," [52] but the circumstances remain obscure.[53] The problem remains why he was buried at 'Avdat. Avraham Negev was forced to hypothesize he must have been killed in an unrecorded battle in trying to reconquer the territory lost in the Negev after Alexander Janneaus' conquest of Gaza.[54] Admittedly, this is a scenario built on a series of assumptions, attributing his supposed recovery of the vital trade route between Petra and Gaza with an

---

[49]   FGrH 675 F 25 = Stephan of Byzantium.

[50]   Schmitt 1995, 202.

[51]   Newell 1939, 92 no. 144; Meshorer 1975, 14–16, 86–87, nos. 5–8.

[52]   Nehmé 2012.

[53]   See. Dijkstra 1995, 319–21.

[54]   Negev 2003, 18*.

unrecorded battle. Such conjecture and speculation must exist in the absence of any concrete evidence.

As a consequence, a more skeptical and pessimistic view of any apotheosis of a Nabataean king has been expressed.[55] Rather than a divinized king, it is proposed that "Obodas the God" represents a cult for a Nabataean deity of that name, centered at the Negev city, and the name was subsequently adopted by a series of Nabataean kings, none of whom were "deified."[56] As for the tradition preserved by the Arab historian Uranius, Wenning considers it an aetiological legend created to explain why the cult "Obodas the god" was associated with 'Avdat, a "political fiction" invented in late antiquity.[57] In the process, dubious myths and legends for which there is absolutely no evidence have replaced historical conjecture based on extensive parallels. The problem for this scenario is that the cult of Obodas is widespread at Petra, not limited to 'Avdat. In addition, this interpretation isolates the cult of "Obodas the God" from other evidence that suggests the existence of the Ruler Cult in Nabataea.

3. The Dynastic Statues at Petra

There are now numerous dedications of dynastic statues associated with the Nabataean temples and sanctuaries at Petra that suggest the existence of the royal cult in Nabataea. Most of these statues have been discovered in the vicinity of Qasr al-Bint and the adjacent temenos area. In Ptolemaic Egypt, such dynastic statues were placed in the sanctuaries of the local gods, popularly known as "temple-sharing gods," or what the Greeks called *synnaos theos*.[58] This practice began with Ptolemy II and Arsinoe II, and continued with the later Ptolemaic dynasts, and their extended family. The conglomeration of statues of Nabataean royalty in the precinct of Qasr al-Bint suggests the Nabataeans were replicating the Ptolemaic practice. This is first attested by a statue of Rabbel I, erected in the reign of Aretas III ca. 65 BCE found in the environs of Qasr al-Bint.[59] The second is the base for a statue of Aretas IV inserted into the southern temenos wall of Qasr al-Bint,[60] but clearly in a secondary context.[61] It is possible that it once was located in Qasr al-Bint.

---

[55] Wenning 2015, 55.

[56] Dijkstra 1995, 319–321; cf. Alpass 2013, 158.

[57] Wenning 1997, 191; cf. Alpass 2013, 158.

[58] Nock 1930; Smith 1988, 15–20.

[59] CIS II 349 with Schwentzel 2006, 126–127.

[60] Starcky and Strugnell 1966, 244–47 = Zayadine et al. 2003, 90, no. 1, and 225 no. 119; Schwentzel 2006, 127–128.

[61] Graf et al. 2007, 230–236.

The third is a statue of the princess Sha'udat, the daughter of King Malichos II, perhaps from the pronaos of Qasr al-Bint.[62] In addition, there is a marble plaque found near the Temenos Gate recording an offering to Malichos II,[63] which is perhaps to be associated with a gallery of statues at Qasr al-Bint. From what we can glean from these texts, the dynastic statues at Petra were dedications by the chiefs of clans or priests, not the monarchs themselves. Some fragmentary uninscribed statuary at Petra has been associated with the Nabataean kings and queens, but their interpretation remains speculative, as it is difficult to determine whether they represent divinities or divinized rulers.[64] Outside of Qasr al-Bint, the only addition at Petra is the statue of the divine Obodas erected at Jebel Numayr discussed earlier.[65] Elsewhere in Nabataea, there is a Greek-Nabataean bilingual inscription at Jerash (ancient Gerasa in the Decapolis) defining the sacred precinct that refers in the Aramaic section of the text to a statue erected perhaps to Aretas IV or Rabbel II (as it is dated to his reign of 70–106 CE), but the discernible "phrases are disconnected and uncertain".[66] As a consequence, this text is too fragmentary to contribute to the more explicit evidence accumulating at Petra.

Nevertheless, the presence of these royal statues in the Temple precinct at Petra suggests the Nabataean kings wished to portray themselves as the benefactors of their kingdom on the level of the divine order, similar to the *synnaos theos* Ptolemaic practice.[67] Unfortunately, none of the Nabataean royal statues survive. In the absence of any royal statuary or portraiture in stone, we must turn to the numismatic evidence for the depiction of the Nabataean kings.

4. The Iconographic Representation of the Nabataean Kings on Coins.

The iconographic representation of the Nabataean kings and queens on Nabataean coinage has been interpreted as reflecting Ptolemaic influence.[68] The kings are depicted as beardless youths with a royal headband, and long flowing hair in corkscrew locks or curls, precisely the hair-style of Dushara, the principle god of their dynasty.[69] (Fig. 1) This is exactly the late Hellenistic

---

[62] Zayadine et al. 2003, 91, no. 3 with 224 no. 116; Schwentzel 2006, 128.
[63] Zayadine et al. 2003, 90–91, no. 2,
[64] Schwentzel 2006, 131–40.
[65] See Schwentzel 2006, 128–131.
[66] H. Vincent and R. Savignac provided the Aramaic reading in C. B. Welles, The Inscriptions no. 1 in Kraeling 1938, 371–373.
[67] Schwentzer 2006, 127.
[68] Kropp 2013a, 241–43.
[69] Bowersock 1990, 31.

iconographic representation of Dionysos.[70] (Fig. 2) In addition, the "archaizing [Greek] corkscrew locks" of shoulder length with a flat diadem was became the common representation of Isis in Ptolemaic circles in the second century BCE and was adopted by their queens and others, including the kings.[71] (Fig. 3) For the adoption by Dushara, there is a medallion with a figure of Dionysiac character at the top of a stele under a cliff on the way to the High Place of Jabal al-Madbah at Petra is sometime assumed to be Dushara, but this is uncertain.[72] (Fig. 4) What makes the association of the kings with Dionysos clear is the Dionysiac diadem worn by the Nabataean kings, a simple 'white' headband with free-hanging ends that appears on the coins of Nabataean dynasts from Aretas III to Obodas II.[73] This type of diadem was the symbol associated with Dionysos' conquests in the East and became the royal symbol for the divinized kings of Asia.[74] (Fig. 5) The Nabataean dynasts are thus represented as adopting/adapting the divine imagery of the patron god of their dynasty for their own personal appearance and portraiture.[75] Dushara, as the dynastic god of the royal family is indicated in the expression "Dushara the god of our lord (the king)".[76] In similar fashion, the queens are represented as the Tyche (fortune deity) of the Nabataean realm, with a raised open palm, and a headdress decorated in the front with an Isis ornament. The same Isis iconographic elements are reflected in the representation of the goddess al-'Uzza.[77] The Isis headdress appears first with Queen Huldu in the reign of Aretas IV in 15 CE and later with Queen Shaqilat in 27 CE.[78] It continues with the later queens of Rabbel II, Gamilat and Hagiru.[79] (Fig. 6) The depictions suggest the numismatic images of Nabataean kings and

---

[70] Healey 2001, 100 and Zayadine 2003, 59; although considered inconclusive by Kropp 2011, 185–89.

[71] Smith 1988, 75 and 94, citing the Louvre Cleopatra (Cat. No. 56) and the Vienna Queen (Cat. No. 74), and for kings see Ptolemy V (204–180 BCE) in the guise of Isis: with diadem and corkscrew locks: Saltzmann 2013, 345, Abb 28 and Martin 2013, 410. On royal portraits and numismatic images, see Lorber 2011, 417–455.

[72] Healey 2001, 100 and Plate IVb.

[73] Schwentzel 2005, 152–153, and Barkay 20117c, 600–601.

[74] Smith 1988, 34–38, 44; cg. 1991, 65, and cf. Meyer 2013, 209–231, Haake 2013, 293–313, Dahmen 2013, 281–292, and Marin 2013, 395–423.

[75] Schwentzel 2005, 154; 2008, 290; 2010, 237–38; 2014, 152–153; cf. Kropp 2011, 188–189, and 2013b, 49, who admits there are Hellenistic Alexandrian elements in the royal Nabataean portraiture. For the diadem binding, see Schreiber 2013, 233–247.

[76] CIS 350.3–4, and RES 83, *'lh mr'n', 'god of our lord'*; Healey 2001, 97–98.

[77] Zayadine 1981, 117 and 1991, 283–306; cf. Schwentzel 2005, 162; Kropp 2013a, 242–43; Barkay 2019, 52.

[78] Hoover and Barclay 2010, 204 and Barkay 2019, 23–27, 48, cf. Kropp 2013a, 26.

[79] Schwentzel 2014, 156–58; Kropp 2013a, Barkay 2016b, 19 and 22.

queens have been infused with the divine symbols of Dionysos and Isis.[80] The influence of Ptolemaic royal portraiture in Nabataean coinage is rather explicit, but not unusual for the period. (Fig. 7)

In contrast, with the later Nabataean kings, there is a transition in royal symbolism marked by Aretas IV, who in 5 BCE replaces the diadem on coins with the laurel wreath, which becomes thereafter the royal insignia of the later Nabataean dynasty.(Fig. 6) But this should not be considered an innovation or infused with political significance – a strident attempt by Aretas IV to reject the diadem as a symbol of subservience to Rome, and replace it with the laurel wreath as an insignia of independence and defiance to Rome.[81] The laurel wreath appeared earlier on coins of Malichus I in 32/31 BCE and Obodas II in 21/20 BCE, perhaps commemorating some unknown event or some other purpose.[82] But Aretas IV was hardly a rebellious Nabataean king. In 6 BCE, he deferentially petitioned Augustus for his approval to his accession to the throne, even presenting the emperor with a precious golden wreath to gain recognition for his rule (Flav. Jos. ant. Jud. 16, 294–299 and 315–360). A few years later, at Herod's death in 4 BCE, Aretas IV, because of his "friendship with the Romans", provided a contingent from the Nabataean army to Quinctilius Varus, the Roman governor of Syria, to help quell the dissidence in Judaea (Flav. Jos. Ant. Jud. 17, 287 and 296). Decades later, during Germanicus' eastern expedition in 18 CE, at a banquet perhaps in Syria, Aretas IV presented to the young Roman prince and Agrippina "massive gold crowns," and lighter ones to the Syrian governor Piso and others (Tac. Ann. 2, 157). Nothing during his rule suggests anything but a compliant client-king, and the shoulder length 'Dionysiac' hair-style continues on with Aretas IV and his successors until the end of the dynasty.[83]

These depictions of Nabataean royal hair-style are similar to the Hellenistic royal style emerging in the late second century and first century BCE elsewhere in the Levant. Even the last Seleucid kings in the first century BCE

---

[80] *pace* Kaizer 2010, 119–120.

[81] *Contra* Kropp 2013c, 21–41. For Aretas IV in laureate, see Barkay 2017c, 600–1, who regards the laurel wreath as a "decorative element" for some celebration, not political symbol: 2016a, 186. Smith 1988, 43, considers its purpose as ambiguous and calls it a "bland option" to the diadem for non-divinizing dynasts, but without considering its appearance on coins of the later Nabataean kings. The use of laurel leaf and diadem he considers an unsatisfactory option, but Malichus I appears with BOTH laurel wreath and diadem in the same year: Barkay 2017c, 600.

[82] Barkay 2010, 42 and 2017c, 600 (Malichus I), 2016a, 185 and 2017c, 601 (Obodas II).

[83] Wenning 2003, 148 no. 32, observes that the Nabataean kings had varying hairstyles, but so did the Ptolemaic-Isis queens, see, for example, the Papyri Cleopatra in Smith 1988, Cat. no. 24. Kropp 2013a, 72, notes some Nabataean kings had shoulder length hair arranged in single braids, but this misses the point: all have shoulder length hair.

were portrayed as youths with long curling hair, reflecting a heroic divine-like idea.[84] Other examples of a divinizing king of the second century BCE are from Skythopolis in the Decapolis,[85] and perhaps some basalt heads from the Hauran of the first century BCE.[86] The coin image of Attembelos Soter Euergetes I (47–24 BCE) of Characene,[87] reinforces the portrayal of the contemporary Nabataean royal iconography on their coins as a divinized heroes with diadem and long corkscrew curls. A sculptured head in the Delos Museum has also been associated with Obodas II and Syllaeus' dedication,[88] but the badly defaced head seems more likely to represent Apollo, the god of the island.[89] Another statue with long-flowing corkscrew locks from Egypt now in the Louvre in Paris[90] has also been identified with a Nabataean king,[91] presumably Malichos I.[92] But its iconographic affinity with several other statues with similar masculine-like image and Isis locks, such as the Papyri Kleopatra[93] and the Vienna Kleopatra,[94] render dubious any certain association with Aretas III or some other early Nabataean king. It is more likely these statues are just the product of "a novel female royal style" that emerged in the mid-second century BCE associated with the Ptolemaic queens Cleopatra I, II and III, who "ruled in behalf of or through boy kings and weak kings."[95] As a result, any attempt to perceive these statues as representations of the Nabataean kings of the first century BCE seems adventurous both stylistically and chronologically.

The literary evidence for identifying Dushara with the Ptolemaic god Dionysos is a single text. Isidore of Charax, the author of the *Parthian Stations,* who was part of the entourage on Gaius Caesar's Eastern Expedition in the time of Augustus that included Juba of Mauretania, reputedly attested that "Dushara is the Nabataean Dionysus".[96] This fragment attributed to him is preserved by the 5th or 6th century CE lexicographer Hesychius, whose work was based primarily on Diogenianus' in the Hadrianic period, derived mainly

---

[84] Smith 1991, 24, with Fraser.

[85] Wenning 1983, 108–111= Smith 1991, fig. 264.

[86] Weber 2009, 84; Weber 2011.

[87] Smith 1988, 120 and pl. 78.7 and 1991, 225, fig. 280. For the ruler cult in Aracidd Parthia, see Dabrowa 2009 and Invernizza 2011. 417–455, for suggesting it was displayed throughout the royal court at Nisa.

[88] Schmidt 1999, 279–98.

[89] Schwentzel 2006, 134–35; Kropp 2013, 71.

[90] Ma 3546 = Smith 1988, 166–167, no. 56.

[91] Schmid 2013, 757–769.

[92] Schwentzel 2006, 135.

[93] Smith 1988, no. 24.

[94] Smith 1988, no. 74; cf. Schwentzel 2006, 136–137.

[95] Smith 1995, 208–209.

[96] FGrH 781 F5, with Roller 2004, 217–219.

The Nabataean Ruler Cult 159

from Pamphilius of the Julio-Claudian period, and Apion of the Augustan period, providing support for the alleged identification of the statement with Isidore of Charax.[97] There also is archaeological and epigraphic evidence for vineyards and wine-drinking in the Petra area dating to the Nabataean era, perhaps associated with Dionysos. At Baidha, 8 km north of Petra, excavations of a cultic rock-cut colonnaded cultic center exposed a triclinium, which appears to be associated with a Dionysian *thiasos* in the reign of Malichus I, based on the associated divine and zoological sculptures, and its location in a wine-growing region.[98] A nearby inscription of a *marzēaḥ* ("symposium") at Baidha[99] is now matched by similar attestations at Wadi Mūsā, the ancient al-Gaia.[100] Since the "god of al-Gaia" is identified in several Nabataean texts as "Dushara"[101], it may be assumed that the Nabataean supreme god Dushara was identified with Dionysos, the wine-drinking god of the Ptolemies.

From almost the beginning of Ptolemaic rule, the rulers identified with Dionysos. In the Grand Procession of Ptolemy II Philadelphus, Dionysos was recognized as the founder of the dynasty.[102] By the reign of Ptolemy IV Philopator (221–204 BCE), the Dionysiac cult was a fundamental aspect of Ptolemaic statecraft,[103] and in the later Ptolemaic dynasty, the kings not only associated themselves with Dionysos, but also appear convinced of their 'divine' character.[104] In similar fashion, the Ptolemaic queens identified themselves with Isis. Arsinoe II Philadelphos in the third Century BCE identified herself with a host of female deities, including Isis, Aphrodite and Hathor.[105] But by the reign of Cleopatra III (161–101 BCE), Isis is predominant.[106] The latter queen even represented herself as the "Sacred foal of Isis,

---

[97] Dickey 2007, 88–90, *pace* Tardieu 1990, 33–38, who assigns the fragment to a 5th century CE source, followed meticulously by Patrich 2005, on the misguided assumption that the Arabs did not drink wine. But see Maraqten 1993 for wine-drinking in pre-Islamic Arabia, including Nabataea. There are numerous Nabataean wine presses in the Baidha district north of Petra and dozens more in adjacent regions: see Knodell et al. 2017, 651; Al-Salameen 2005, 115–127; and Graf 2020.

[98] Bikai et al. 2008.

[99] Zayadine 1976.

[100] Al-Salameen and Falahat 2012, 37–5.

[101] Wenning 2015, 55.

[102] FrGH 627 F2 = Athenaios 196–202; commentary in Rice 1983 and cf. Kahill 1996, 79–80.

[103] Tondriau 1946, 169; cf. 1947, 1950; Van Nuffelen 1999, 183, 188; Pfeiffer 2008, 41; Wellensorf 2008, 33–38.

[104] Van Nuffelen 1999, 176.

[105] Müller 2009, 280–299; Caneva 2012, 12; cf. Quaegebeur 1978.

[106] Van Nuffelen 1999, 179.

the Great Mother of the gods," a clear attestation the Ptolemaic queen identified herself with Isis.[107] By the first century BCE, the ruling king and queen were now thoroughly divinized, the *Königspaar*,[108] and incorporated into the Egyptian cult "during their lifetime".[109] This culminates with Antony and Cleopatra, identifying themselves as the *Neos Dionysos* and the *Nea Isis.*[110] It is precisely this time that the Nabataean dynasts begin portraying themselves as Dionysos and Isis.

The subject of divinized rulers perhaps requires some clarification. If there is a distinction between mortals and immortals, there also is a sharp difference between divinized rulers and the gods. In the case of the Ptolemaic dynasts, they were never incorporated into the Egyptian pantheon nor the objects of sacrifices. Rather, they are depicted as presenting offerings themselves to the Egyptian gods.[111] Still they had a distinctively different status than mere mortals that was conferred on them by their subjects based on their status as rulers, and the merit of their benefactions and protection of the state. The bifurcation between mortals and immortals was breached by rulers achieving this unusual ideal status primarily by nomenclature and iconography.[112] By contrast, in Rome, the emperor was not considered *deus* ('god') in his lifetime, but became *divus* after his death, when 'heavenly honors' were conferred to him by the Senate.[113] However, in the Greek East, the emperor was commonly referred to as *theos*, assimilated to a Zeus, Helios or Dionysos, and the recipient of *isotheoi timai*, "honors equivalent to the gods, on par with divinity, worthy of a god."[114] The ruler was still clearly less than the gods, but of higher status than mere mortals, in essence "god-like". Whether the Nabataean kings and queens, represented as being assimilated to Dionysos or Isis, regarded themselves as similarly "god-like" is difficult to determine. As A. D. Nock observed, "it is not easy to draw a definite line between comparison and identification" but that a ruler could be the reincarnation of a particular deity was not foreign to ancient ideology.[115] In the case of the Nabataean dynasts, there is epigraphic and iconographic evidence that this was the case.

---

[107] Fraser 1972, 221, and no. 249; cf. Colin 1994, 272–283, and Plantzos 2011, 395.
[108] Colin 1994, 293.
[109] Quaegebuhr 1989, 107.
[110] Fraser 1972, I, 245–246; Quaegebeur 1998, 53; cf. Roller 2010, 114–117.
[111] Thompson 2012, 126; cf. Koenen 1993.
[112] Smith 1988, 39.
[113] Price 1984, 83; Gradel 2002.
[114] Montanari 2015, 986.
[115] Nock 1928, 32–35.

5. The Royal Title and Epithets of the Nabataean Kings

Anotherexpression of the Nabataean royal cult is the titles and epithets employed by the Nabataean kings on their coins and in inscriptions that were similar to those used by the Hellenistic divinized dynasts. The first title of Aretas III on his Damascene issues was *philhellenos* in Greek, probably to portray himself as successor to the Seleucid kings at Damascus,[116] so not of great import for any claim to divine status. But later kings utilize epithets in Aramaic inscriptions that are similar to those used by other Hellenistic rulers. Aretas IV is ascribed with regularity as the one who "loves or cares for his people" (*rḥm ʿmh*), beginning at the inception of his reign (CIS II 197), essentially equivalent to Greek *philopatris* ("lover of his fatherland"), as appears on the coins of Archelaos of Cappadocia (36 BC–CE 17), implying the "protector" of his realm.[117] Later, Rabbel II is proclaimed as the one "who has given life and saves his people" (*dy ʾḥyy wšyzb ʿmh*), beginning in 85/6 CE.[118] The comparable Greek term would be *Sōtēr* ("savior") or *Euergetēs* ("benefactor"), or perhaps both,[119] reflecting an "external divine rescue", ostensibly associated with Dionysos' eastern conquests,[120] and a ruler who brought peace and order out of chaos.[121] What prompted or provoked the use of these epithets by the Nabataean kings, expressing god-like qualities, remains unknown. In the few known instances elsewhere, the epithets were promoted by the people (App. Syr. 45 and 69) or the army (Lucian, Zeuxis 11), not the monarchs themselves.[122] The rulers typically were promoted to divinity for specific achievements or actions in behalf of their kingdom. The circumstances and agents in the case of the epithets for the Nabataean dynasts remain obscure, but they may relate to their gaining royal status, as each emerged to the throne in their minority.[123] In the case of Rabbel II, his quelling of a rebellion may have led to his epithet.[124] It is interesting that *philhellene, sōtēr* and *euergetēs* are associated regularly with the Ptolemies and Seleucids, the Pontic dynasts, the Parthians, and the kings of Characene and Bactria.[125] For example, Attambelos I of Characene (47–24 BCE) is proclaimed *Basileus Soter and Euergetes*

---

[116] Bowersock 1983, 25–6.
[117] De Callatay and Lorber 2011, 452; *pace* Kropp 2013c, 34.
[118] Meshorer 1975, 71, 75–76.
[119] Nock 1951, 127–148, Marshak 2015, 35 no. 11 and 231–238.
[120] Smith 1988, 50.
[121] Nock 1951, 137.
[122] Bickerman 1938, 237.
[123] Schwentzel 2013,191–192.
[124] Winnett 1973, 54–57; Bowersock 1983, 156.
[125] De Callatay and Lober 2011, 450/1 and 455.

on his coins.[126] In contrast, *philorōmaios* is never used by the Nabataeans at all, as one might expect of a client-kingdom of Rome. All of the epithets, *philopatris, sōtēr* and *euergetēs,* could be interpreted as suggesting aspects of a "divinized" ruler. The epithets became common in the Augustan era and early imperial period to express the well-being of a ruler's province or a city,[127] so they are entirely appropriate for a Nabataean dynast governing the vast regions of his vast kingdom.

In spite of the clear evidence of Ptolemaic influence, there has been reticence to follow these "divine" elements to their logical conclusion. Schwentzel considers the Nabataean dynasty only adapted ("revue et corrigé") the Hellenistic model, according to their "interests propres," without any suggestion of a royal cult[128] and Kropp suggests "the cultic overtones are mere accompaniment."[129] From their perspective, the divine elements are merely regarded as "sound and fury, signifying nothing," empty symbols devoid of any content. In response, it may be suggested that it is unlikely mere iconographic propaganda and nomenclature would be successful in legitimizing, unifying and consolidating the Nabataean realm if it did not incorporate the same values as the Hellenistic royal ideology. The Nabataean kings were clearly portraying themselves like other Hellenistic kings.

The influence of the Ptolemaic Ruler Cult may even be reflected in in the Seleucid realm, although the evidence is more fragmentary.[130] By 205 BCE, Antiochus III was the grand master, promoter and organizer of the dynastic cult in the Seleucid realm,[131] later marked in 193 BCE by the launching of the empire-wide cult of his queen Laodike, associated with that of the king and the *progonoi* of the dynastic cult of the Seleucid dynasty.[132] His successors followed suit, as is reflected in the list of divinized Seleucid kings of the second century BCE from Teos (OGIS 246), which extends from Antiochus III to Demetrius II Nicator (145–140 and 129–125 BCE), including even Ptolemy VI Philometor, the only Ptolemy ever crowned as a king in the Seleucid Empire.[133] But the development of a Seleucid royal cult perhaps appears even earlier than 205 BCE. An inscription from Lydia, dating to 228/9 CE, attests the cult of 'Zeus Seleukios', as the patron of the Seleucid

---

[126] Smith 1988, 120.

[127] Nock 1951, 138–143.

[128] Schwentzel 2005, 164

[129] Kropp 2005, 164

[130] Bickerman 1938, 236–57; Van Nuffelen 2004, 300; Sartre 2006, 177–188; Kosmin 2014; Erickson 2018.

[131] Bickerman 1938, 247–48, 255; Van Nuffelen 2004, 279–285.

[132] Robert 1967, 281–97; Kosmin 2014, 136–37 and 328 no. 103.

[133] Piejko 1982, 129–31.

The Nabataean confrontation with the Seleucid Ruler Cult becomes clear in the first century BCE, when the Seleucid king Antiochus XII adopted the Ptolemaic practice. This is reflected by his coinage, which introduces the epithet *Dionysos* in 83/82 BCE as part of his titular: *Antiochos Dionysos Epiphanes Philopator Kallinikos,* which appears both on the silver and bronze issues of his reign.[136] The inclusion of the Ptolemaic title "Dionysus" (OGIS I, 258–260) may just express that he is the son of Antiochus VIII and Cleopatra Tryphaina, but it also may reflect the regaining of Damascus with Ptolemaic support.[137] The other epithets of his titular are also important: "Epiphanes" refers to the Seleucid Ruler Cult, a title associated with at least nine Seleucid kings.[138] The dynastic title "Philopator" and the political-military name "Kallinikos" follow. These epithets of his coinage provide some insight into the political and ideological climate of the period. Such reverberations of Ptolemaic propaganda in this highly politically-charged atmosphere of the time illustrate what may have developed even earlier among the Nabataeans, the allies of the Ptolemies now for several centuries. It is reasonable to believe that these contacts would have influenced the Nabataean kings to divinize their dynasty and adopt Ptolemaic epithets used in the ruler cult.

6. The Basileophoric Names in Nabataean Inscriptions.

One of the unusual features of Nabataean onomastics is the appearance of so many basileophoric names, essentially "Servant names" combined with the names of the Nabataean kings, rather than a theophoric element. Already in 1888, Clermont-Ganneau, with his uncanny instinct, observed that this suggested the Nabataean kings were divinized.[139] At the time, not all the known Nabatean royal names appeared in such "pseudo-theophoric" names, but the phenomenon is now well-documented, inclusive of all the known Nabataean dynastic names. In addition to *ʿbd-ʿbdtm,* the name *ʾbḥrtt* appears

---

[134] Nock 1928, 42; Bikerman 1938, 255.
[135] P. Dura 25 dated to 180 CE, with comments of Kosmin 2014. 342 no. 174.
[136] Houghton et al. 2008, no. 2481–2483.
[137] Ehling 2008, 246.
[138] Kosmin 2014, 24 and 177–78.
[139] Clermont-Ganneau 1888, 39–47, 142; for a listing of the "servant names" see Milik 1959b, 148–149.

at least 10 times,[140] *'bd-mlkw* 8 times,[141] and *'bd-rb'l* six times.[142] Starcky, supporting Clermont-Ganneau's pioneering observation, suggested these "theophoric anthroponyms" indicated that not only were the Nabataean kings divinized, but also the queens, as signified by the servant names *'bd-šqlt* and *'bd-ḥld*.[143] Since many of these names were adopted by administrative and military officials, as well as cultic personnel, the royal Nabataean court seemed to be the nexus of the practice.[144]

More recently, reservations have been expressed about interpreting these basileophoric Nabataean "servant" names as evidence for the divinization of the Nabataean kings.[145] In addition, Healey not only considers it dubious that the "servant names" imply the divinization of the Nabataean kings, but also categorically rejects that any of the Nabataean queens were ever divinized.[146] Neither makes reference to Clermont-Ganneau's study of the basileophoric names as evidence for the divinization of the Nabataean kings and queens, proposed on less evidence that it is now currently available. It should also be observed that the phenomenon of the "servant names" in Nabataean Aramaic inscriptions is distinctive and exceptional among the various Semitic languages. For example, although attested frequently in Phoenician and Punic inscriptions, they are exclusively theophoric.[147] The explanation for the frequent appearance of basileophoric names in Nabataean in contrast to their rarity or absence in other Aramaic dialects and other Semitic languages has been attributed to foreign influence, namely the Arabic character of the Nabataean onomasticon.[148] But it is more compelling to consider the "pseudo-theophoric" or basileophoric names in Nabataean Aramaic as the product of the adoption of the Ruler Cult by the Nabataean kings, influenced by the divinized rulers in Ptolemaic Egypt.

Furthermore, as is well known, these practices were adopted by the Roman emperors, beginning with the establishment of the imperial cult under Augustus, across the Mediterranean world, including Egypt[149], Syria-Palestine and Arabia.[150] These divine honors were extended even to the Roman

---

[140]   Negev 1991, no. 802; add Graf 1994, 294.

[141]   Negev 1991, no. 808; add Graf 2014, 352.

[142]   Negev 1991, no. 824.

[143]   Starcky 1966, col. 1015.

[144]   Graf 1994, 292–96; cf. Strootman 2014, 111–135.

[145]   Dijkstra 1995, 321 no. 7.

[146]   Healey 2001, 150.

[147]   See Benz 1972, 148–164, for the theophoric names *'bd-'šmn* 150–5, and *'bd-mlqrt* 155–161.

[148]   Silverman 1981, 363.

[149]   Dörner 2014, 153–276.

[150]   See Fritz Graf 2008, 760–63, for documentation.

The Nabataean Ruler Cult   165

"queens," beginning with the worship of the "empress" Livia, the *Diva Augusta;* after the veto of the senate after her death in 29 CE (Suet. Tib. 51), the Emperor Claudius instituted them by decree in 42 CE, precisely on January 17, the day of her marriage to Octavian.[151] In the East, earlier recognition of Livias was given by Herod Antipas, who fortified Bethramphtha in the Peraea and renamed it Livias-Julias (Flav. Jos. ant. Jud. 18, 27) and the renaming of Bethsaida in Galilee Julia, after the emperor's daughter (ant. Jud. 18, 17), joining the imperial cities of Caesarea Maritima and Sebaste created for Augustus. It has even been surmised that Livia appeared in the guise of Roma in the *Augusteum* at Casarea, Sebaste, and Banias.[152] Finally, Marcus Agrippa, the administrator of the eastern empire after 18 BCE, was recognized as *euergetēs kai sōtēr* at Athens (ID 1593), and the *Theoi Sōtēr* in Larissa in Thessaly and Mytilene on Lesbos, celebrated in a festival on Kos (*Sylloge*[3] 1065), and a month named after him on Cyprus, all during his lifetime and before12 BCE.[153] His relations with Herod and his visit to his realm in 15 CE (Flav. Jos. ant. Jud. 16, 12–26; cf. 157) may have produced similar expressions in Palestine, but the evidence is lacking. Whatever the case, the Nabataeans could not have been oblivious to Herod's promotion of the imperial cult within his realm.

Just how powerful and penetrating the Ruler Cult was in the Near East during the early Roman imperial era is indicated by another custom similar to that of the basileophoric names: individuals, usually members of the elite, occasionally designated a ruler as their "own god."[154] For example, with Mark Antony at Alexandria in 34 BCE (OGIS 195: τὸν ἑαυτοῦ θεὸν καὶ εὐεργέτην), or for Tiberius on Cyprus (OGIS 283 line 10: τῶι ἀτοῦ θεῶι), or Nero on Cyprus in 60/61 CE (ISalamis XIII no. 135: τῷ ἰδίῳ θεῷ καὶ σωτῆρι), or King Sauromates I of Hermonassa on the Black Sea c. 93–124 CE (IOSPE II 358: [τὸ]ν ἴδι[ον θεὸν? καὶ σω]τῆρα), or Marcus Aurelius (IGR IV 685: τὸν ἴδιον θεὸν [καὶ] εὐεργέτην)); or King Sauromates II; Hermonassa and Phanagoreia, ca. 174–210 CE (IOSPE II 357 and SEG LVI 931: τὸν ἴδιον θεὸν καὶ δεσπότην). The same usage is attested also for gods, but less often: In Kos, it was used by a priest, who dedicated a statue "of his own goddess" (IG XII.4.621, second century), and in Egypt for an anonymous god, possibly Pan (Bernand 1984: no. 98, τῷ ἰδίῳ θεῷ μεγίστῳ, Imperial period). The emotional weight of this phrase becomes clear when we see how it was used by the parents of a child who died at the age of four, when they affectionately call him θεὸς ἴδιος ἐπήκοος (IGUR 1702, "their own god, who listens to

---

[151] Suet. Claudius 11, 2; Cass. Dio 60, 5 [41] with Levick 1990, 47, citing ILS 4995 and coins.
[152] Bernett 2007; cf. Marshak 2015, 212–17.
[153] Habicht 2005, 242–246.
[154] Kindly brought to my attention by Angelos Chantiotis.

them", θεῷ ἰδίῳ ἐπηκόῳ, Rome, third century CE). Such expressions denote – through "religious" devotion – loyalty. To name a child after a king, instead of using a theophoric name, indicates a similar display of affection and loyalty to the dynast or to the Ruler Cult. In similar fashion, the baseileophoric Nabataean names are particularly common among administrative and military officials, as were the *philo-basileistes* names among Ptolemaic officials. The Nabataean servant-names can then be seen expressions of loyalty to the royal dynasty and indicators of the absorption of the Ruler Cult by inhabitants of the Nabataean realm.[155]

When all of this evidence is taken into consideration, the arguments for the Nabataean dynasty developing along the lines of a Hellenistic and Ptolemaic model are substantial and compelling. As we know from 'Avdat and Petra, the worship of "Obodas the god", ostensibly the cult of a Nabataean dynast, can now be traced back to the first century BCE. The evidence for the divinization of the later Nabataean kings appears first in the late Hellenistic period and early Roman imperial era when Nabataean material culture first becomes visible. The reception of statues to the king and royal family at and in the precincts of the Qasr al-Bint Temple replicates the standard Ptolemaic practice of *synnaos theos*. The statues are not extant, but the numismatic iconography of the kings and queens provides illustrations of how the kings and queens represented themselves in the kingdom. They are depicted on coins in the characteristic Hellenistic style of Dionysos and Isis, implying the adoption of the Ptolemaic Ruler Cult in Nabataea. These conclusions are reinforced by the epithets of the kings which portray them as divine benefactors and protectors of the state. In the onomasticon of the Nabataean hierarchy, in particular, the phenomenon of transforming theophoric type names into basileophoric names as expressions of loyalty to the divine monarchs may be interpreted as signs of allegiance and devotion to the divine Nabataean monarchs. In sum, the existence of the Ruler Cult in Nabataea based on the Ptolemaic model represents the most compelling explanation for understanding the above phenomena.

---

[155] Graf 1994, 291–293.

Bibliography

Abbreviations of Greek Inscriptions are according to B. H. McLean, An Introduction to Greek Epigraphy of the Hellenistic and Roman Periods (Ann Arbor, 2002).

Alpass, P. 2010. The Basileion of Isis and the religious art of Nabataean Petra, in: Syria 87, 93–113.

Alpass, P. 2013. The Religious Life of Nabataea. Leiden.

Al-Salameen, Z. 2005. Nabataean Wine Presses from Baydha, in: ARAM 17, 113–127.

Al-Salameen, Z. and H. Falahat 2012. Two New Nabataean Inscriptions from Wādī Mūsā, with Discussion of Gaia and the Marzēaḥ, in: Journal of Semitic Studies 57, 37–51.

Al-Salameen, Z. and H. Falaht 2014. An Inscribed Nabataean Bronze Object dedicated to Obodas the God from Wādī Mūsā, Southern Jordan, in: Palestine Exploration Quarterly 146, 293–307.

Al-Salameen, Z. and Y. Shudaifat 2014. A new Nabataean inscribed bronze lamp, in: Arabian Archaeology and Epigraphy 25, 43–49.

Barclay, R. 2010. The Coinage of the Nabataean King Malichus I (59/58-30 BCE), in: Israel Numismatic Journal 17, 39–47.

Barkay, R. 2016a. The Coinage of the Nabataean King Obodas II (c. 30–9 BC), in: Numismatic Chronicle 176, 83–109.

Barclay, R. 2016b. The Nabataean Queens as Reflected on Coin, in: Israel Numismatic Journal 19, 13–32.

Barkay, R. 2017a. The Coinage of the Nabataean Usurper Syllaeus (9–6 BC), in: Numismatic Chronicle 177, 67–81.

Barkay, R. 2017b. New Sela'in of Aretas IV, King of the Nabateans, in: Israel Numismatic Research 12, 99–112.

Barkay, R. 2017c. Portraits of the Nabataean Kings as Depicted on their Coins, XV International Numismatic Congress Taormina 2015 Proceedings, Roma- Messina, 600–603.

Barkay, R. 2019. Coinage of the Jordanian Journal for History and Archaeology, Nabataeans. Qedem 58. Jerusalem.

Bellinger, A.R. 1949. The End of the Seleucids, in: Transactions of the Connecticut Academy of Arts and Sciences 38, 55–102.

Benz, L. 1972. Personal Names in the Phoenician and Punic Inscriptions. Rome.

Bernett, M. 2007. Der Kaiserkult in Judäa unter den Herodiern und Römern: Untersuchungen zur politischen und religiösen Geschichte Judäas von 30 v. bis 66 n. Chr. Tübingen.

Bernand, A. 1984. Les portes du désert. Recueil des inscriptions grecques d'Antinooupolis, Tentyris, Koptos, Apollonopolis Parva et Apollonopolis Magna. Paris.

Bickerman, E.J. 1938. Institutions des Séleucides. Paris.

168 David F. Graf

Bikai, P. and C. Kanellopoulos and S. Saudener 2008. Beidha in Jordan: A Dionysian Hall in a Nabataean Landscape, in: American Journal of Archaeology 112, 465–507.

Bowersock, G.W. 1983. Roman Arabia. London.

Bowersock, G.W. 1990. The Cult and Representation of Dushares in Roman Arabia, in: F. Zayadine (ed.), Petra and the Caravan Cities, Amman, 31–36.

Bricault, L. 1992. Isis Dolente, in : Bulletin de Institut française d'archéologique orientale 92, 37–49.

Bricault, L. 1999. Sarapis et Isis: Sauveurs de Ptolémé IV à Raphia, in: Chronique d'Égypte 74, fasc. 148, 334–43.

Bricault, L. 2001. Atlas de la diffusion des cultes isiaques (IVe siecle av. J-C.–IV siecle apr. J.-C.), Memoires de l'Academie des Inscriptions et Belles-Lettres 23. Paris.

Bricault, L. 2005. Recueil des inscriptions concernant les cultes isiaques, Mémoires de l'Académie des inscriptions et belles-lettres, nouvelle série 31. Paris.

Bricault, L. 2008. Sylloge nummorum religionis isiacae et sarapiacae (SNRIS), Mémoires de l'Académie des Inscriptions et Belles-Lettres 38. Paris.

Caneva, S.G. 2012. Queens and Ruler Cults in Early Hellenism: Festivals, Administration, and Ideology, in: Kernos 25, 75–101.

Cantineau, J. 1930. Le Nabatéen, I. Paris.

Cantineau, J. 1932. Le Nabatéen. Paris.

Carney, E. 2000. The Initiation of Cult for Royal Macedonian Women, in: Classical Philology 95, 21–43.

Chaniotis, A. 2003. The Divinity of Hellenistic Rulers, in: A. Erskine (Ed.), A Companion to the Hellenistic World, Malden (Ma.), 431–445.

Clermont-Ganneau, C. 1888. Les noms royaux nabatéens employés comme noms divins, in : Recueil d'archéologie orientale I: 39–47 = Revue Archéologique (Troisième Série) 5 (1885), 170–178.

Colin, F. 1994. L'Isis "dynastique" et la mère des dieux phrygienne: essai d'analyse d'un processus culturelle, in : Zeitschrift für Papyrologie und Epigraphik 102, 271–295.

Collombert, P. 2008. La stèle de Saïs'et l'instauration du culte d'Arsinoé II dans la *chora*, in : Ancient Society 38, 83–99.

Dalman, G. 1912. Neue Petra-Forschungen und der heilige Felsen von Jerusalem. Leipzig.

De Callataÿ, F. and C.C. Lorber. 2011. The pattern of royal epithets on Hellenistic coinages, in: P. Iossif et al. (edd.), More than men, less than gods: studies on royal cult and imperial worship, Leuven, 417–455.

Dahmen, K. 2012. Alexander und das Diadem: die archäologische und numismatische Perspektive, in: A. Lichtenberger (ed.), Das Diadem der hellenistischen Herrscher: Übernahme, Transformation oder Neuschöpfung eines Herrschaftszeichens?, Bonn, 281–292.

Dickey, E. 2006. Ancient Greek Scholarship. Oxford.

Dijkstra, K. 1995. Life and loyalty: a study in the socio-religious culture of Syria and Mesopotamia in the Graeco-Roman period based on epigraphical evidence. Leiden.

Dörner, N. 2014. Feste und Opfer für den Gott Caesar: Kommunikationsprozesse im Rahmen des Kaiserkultes im römischen Ägypten der julisch-claudischen Zeit. 30 v.Chr. – 68 n.Chr. Rahden (Westf.).

Ehling, K. 2008. Untersuchungen zur Geschichte der späten Seleukiden (164–53 v. Chr.). Stuttgart.

El-Khouri, L. 2002. The Nabataean Terracotta Figurines. Oxford.

Eph'al, I. and J. Naveh 1996. Aramaic Ostraca of the Fourth Century from Idumaea. Jerusalem.

Erickson, K., 2018. Another century of gods? A re-evaluation of Seleukid ruler cult, in: Classical quarterly 68, 97–111.

Erickson-Gini, T. 2014. Oboda and the Nabateans, in: Srata: Bulletin of the Anglo-Israel Archaeological Society, 32, 81–108.

Finlayson, C. 2016. The Obelisk, the Crow-Step, and the Elephant in Nabataean Contexts, in: N. Khairy (ed.), Studies in Nabataean Culture II, Amman, 75–104.

Fraser, P.M. 1972. Ptolemaic Alexandria, 3 vols. Oxford.

Grabowski, T. 2014. The Cult of the Ptolemies in the Aegean in the 3rd Century BC, in: Electrum 21, 21–411.

Gradel, I. 2002. Emperor Worship and Roman Religion. Oxford.

Graf, D.F. 1992. Nabataeans, in: Anchor Bible Dictionary IV, 970–973.

Graf, D.F. 1994. The Nabataean Army and the *Cohortes Ulpiae Petraeorum*, in: E. Dąbrowa (ed.), The Roman and Byzantine Army in the East, Krákow, 265–311.

Graf, D.F. 2006. The Nabataeans in the Early Hellenistic Period: The Testimony of Posidippus of Pella, in: Topoi: Orient-Occident 14, 47–68.

Graf, D.F. and S.G. Schmidt and E. Ronza and S.E. Sidebotham 2007. The Hellenistic Petra Project: Excavations in the Qasr al-Bint Temenos Area: Preliminary Report of the Second Season, 2005, in: Annual of the Department of Antiquities in Jordan 51, 223–238.

Graf, D.F. 2008. s.v. Ruler Cult, in: Brill's New Pauly 12, 760–763.

Haake, M. 2012. Diadem und "basileus": Überlegungen zu einer Insignie und einem Titel in hellenistischer Zeit, in: A. Lichtenberger (ed.), Das Diadem der hellenistischen Herrscher: Übernahme, Transformation oder Neuschöpfung eines Herrschaftszeichens?, Bonn, 293–313.

Habicht, C. 1970. Gottmenschentum und griechische Städte. Munich.

Habicht, C. 2005. Marcus Agrippa Theos Soter, in: Hypeboreas 11/2, 242–246.

Harding, G.L. 1971. An Index and Concordance of Pre-Islamic Arabian Names and Inscriptions. Toronto.

Hazzard, R.A. 2000. Imagination of a Monarchy: Studies in Ptolemaic Propaganda. Toronto.

170 David F. Graf

Hauben, H. 2011. Ptolémée III et Bérénice II, divinités cosmiques, in: P. Iossif et al. (edd.), More than men, less than gods: studies on royal cult and imperial worship, Leuven, 357–388.

Healey, J. 2001. The Religion of the Nabataeans: A Conspectus. Leiden.

Hölbl, G. 2001. A History of the Ptolemaic Empire. London and New York.

Hoftijzer, J. and K. Jongeling 1995. Dictionary of the North-West Semitic Inscriptions. Leiden.

Hoover, O. and R. Barkay 2010. Important Additions to the Corpus of Nabataean Coins since 1990, in: M. Huth and P. G. van Alfen (edd.), Coinage of the Caravan Kingdoms: Studies in Ancient Arabian Monetization, New York, 197–212.

Houghton, A. and C. Lorber and O.D. Hoover 2008. Seleucid Coins: A Comprehensive Catalogue, part 2, Seleucus IV through Antiochus XIII, 2 vols. New York.

Huth, M. 2010. Some Nabataean Questions Reconsidered, in: M. Huth and P. G. van Alfen (edd.), Coinage of the Caravan Kingdoms: Studies in Ancient Arabian Monetization, New York, 213–226.

Invernizza, I. 2011. Royal Cult in Arsacid Parthia, in: P. Iossif et al. (edd.), More than men, less than gods: studies on royal cult and imperial worship, Leuven, 417–455.

Janif, M. 2004. L'écrit et le "figuré" dans le domaine relioeux des Nabatéenns: Le sanctuaire rupestre du Sadd al-Mreriyyeh à Pétra, in: Syria 81, 119–130.

Kahil, L. 1996. Cults in Hellenistic Alexandria, in: J. Walsh and T. F. Reese (edd.), Alexandria and Alexandrianism, Malibu, 75–84.

Kaizer, T. 2010. Kings and Gods: Some thoughts on religious patterns in Oriental principalities, in: T, Kaizer and M. Facella (edd.), Kingdoms and Principalities in the Roman Near East, Orient et Occidens 19, Stuttgart, 113–124.

Kosmin, P.J. 2014. The Land of the Elephants: Space, Territory and Ideology in the Seleucid Empire. Cambridge.

Koenen, L. 1993. The Ptolemaic king as a religious figure, in: A. Bulloch et al. (edd.), Images and ideologies: Self-definition in the Hellenistic World, Berkeley, 25–115.

Kraeling, C. 1938. Gerasa, City of the Decapolis. New Haven (Conn.)

Kropp, A.J.M. 2011. Nabataean Dushārā (Dusares) – an Overlooked Cuirassed God, in: Palestine Exploration Quarterly 143, 176–197.

Kropp, A.J.M. 2013a. Images and Monuments of Near Eastern Dynasts, 100 BC – AD 100. Oxford.

Kropp, A.J.M. 2013b. Kings in Cuirass - Some Overlooked Full-Length Portraits of Herodian and Nabataean Dynasts, in: Levant 45, 45–56.

Kropp, A.J.M. 2013c. Kings without Diadems – How the Laurel Wreath Became the Insignia of Nabataean Kings, in: Archäologischer Anzeiger 2, 21–41.

Knodell, A.R. et al. 2017. The Brown University Petra Project: Landscape Archaeology in the Northern Hinterland of Petra, Jordan, in: American Journal of Archaeology 121, 621–83.

Levick, B. 1990. Claudius. London.

Lichtenberger, A. (ed.) 2012. Das Diadem der hellenistischen Herrscher: Übernahme, Transformation oder Neuschöpfung eines Herrschaftszeichens?. Bonn.

Littmann, E. 1945–49. Neues zur altnordarabischen Dialektkunde, in: Zeitschrift der Deutschen Morgenländischen Gesellschaft 99, 168–180.

Lorber, C. C' 2011. Theos Augiochos: The Aegeis in Ptolemaic Portrraits of Divine Rulers, in: P. Iossif et al. (edd.), More than men, less than gods: studies on royal cult and imperial worship, Leuven, 417–455.

Lozano, F. 2011. The Creation of Imperial Gods: Not only Imposition versus Spentaneity, in: P. Iossif et al. (edd.), More than men, less than gods: studies on royal cult and imperial worship, Leuven, 475–515.

Magness, J. 2001. The Cults of Isis and Kore at Samaria-Sebaste in the Hellenistic and Roman Periods, in: Harvard Theological Review 94, 157–177.

Maraqten, M. 1993. Wine-Drinking and Wine Prohibition in Arabia before Islam, in: Proceedings of the Seminar for Arabian Studies 23, 95–115.

Marshak, A.K. 2015. The Many Faces of Herod the Great. Grand Rapids (Ma.)

Martin, K. 2012. Königin und Göttin: Zur Präsenz des Diadems auf Königinnen-Münzen, in: A. Lichtenberger (ed.), Das Diadem der hellenistischen Herrscher: Übernahme, Transformation oder Neuschöpfung eines Herrschaftszeichens?, Bonn, 395–423.

McKenzie, J. 1990. TheArchitecture of Petra. Oxford.

Merklein, H. and R. Wenning 1998. Ein Verehrungsplatz der Isis in Petra neu untersucht, in: Zeitschrift des Deutschen Palästina-Vereins 114, 162–178.

Meshorer, Y. 1975. Nabataean Coins, in : Qedem 3.

Meyer, K.-M. 2013. Die Binder des Dionysios als Vorbild für das Königsdiadem?, in: A. Lichtenberger (ed.), Das Diadem der hellenistischen Herrscher: Übernahme, Transformation oder Neuschöpfung eines Herrschaftszeichens?, Bonn, 293–313.

Milik, J.T. 1959a. Notes d'épigraphie et topographie palestinniennes, in: Revue Biblique 66, 550–75.

Milik, J.T. 1959b. Notes d'épigraphie et de topographie jordaniennes, in: Liber Annuus 10, 147–84.

Milik, J.T. 2003. Une bilingue araméo-grecque de 105/104 avant J.-C., in: J. Dentzer-Feydy et al. (edd.), Hauran II, Beirut, 269–274.

Milik, J.T. and J. Starcky 1975. Inscriptions récemment découvertes à Pétra, in: Annual of the Department of Antiquities in Jordan 20, 111–30.

Montanari, F. 2015. The Brill Dictionary of Ancient Greek. Leiden.

Müller, H. 2000. Der hellenistische Archiereus, in: Chiron 30, 519–642.

Müller, S. 2009. Das hellenistische Königspaar in der medialen Repräsentation: Ptolemaios II. und Arsinoe II. Berlin and Boston.

Naveh, J. 1979. The Aramaic Ostraca from Tel Beer-Sheba (Seasons 1971–1976), in: Tel Aviv 6, 182–198.

Negev, A. 1981. The Greek Inscriptions from the Negev, in: Studium Biblicum Franciscanum.

Negev, A. 1986a. Nabataean Archaeology Today. New York.

Negev, A. 1986b. Obodas the God, in: Israel Exploration Journal 36, 56–60.

Negev, A. 1991. Personal names in the Nabataean Realm. Jerusalem.

Negev, A. 2003. Obodas the God in a Nabataean-Arabic Inscription from the Vicinity of Oboda and a Review of Other Nabataean Inscriptions, in: R. Rosenthal-Heginbottom (ed.), The Nabataeans in the Negev, Haifa, 7*–20*.

Nehmé, L. 2002a. La chapelle d'Obodas à Pétra, Rapport preliminaries sur la champagne 2001, in : Annual of the Department of Antiquities in Jordan 46, 243–56.

Nehmé, L. 2002b. Petra, The Obodas Chapel, in: American Journal of Archaeology 106, 452–455.

Nehmé, L. 2012. Le dieu Obodas chez les Nabatéens: hypothèes anciennes et découvertes récentes, in: I. Sachet and C. Robin (edd.), Dieux et déesses d'Arabie. Images et représentations, Paris, 181–224.

Newell, E.T. 1939. Late Seleucid Mints in Ake-Ptolemais and Damascus. New York.

Nock, A.D. 1928. Notes on Ruler-Cult, I-IV, in: Journal of Hellenic Studies 48, 21–43.

Nock, A.D. 1930. Σύνναος Θεός, in: Harvard Studies in Classical Philology 41, 1–62 = A. D. Nock. 1972. Essays on Religion and the Ancient World I, Oxford, 202–51.

Nock, A.D. 1951. Soter and Euergetes, in: S.L. Johnson (ed.), The Joy of Study: Papers on New Testament and related subjects Presented to Honor Frederick Clifton Grant, New York, 127-148 = A. D. Nock. 1972. Essays on Religion and the Ancient World II, Oxford, 720–735.

Patrich, J. 2005. Was Dionysos, the Wine God, venerated by the Nabataeans, in: ARAM 17, 95–113.

Pfeiffer, S. 2008. Herrscher- und Dynastiekulte im Ptolemäerreich: Systematik und Einordnung der Kultformen. Munich.

Piejko, F. 1982. Ptolemies in a List of Deified Seleucids from Teos, OGIS 246, in: Zeitschrift für Papyrologie und Epigraphik 49, 129–131.

Plantzos, D. 2011. The iconography of assimilation: Isis and royal imagery on Ptolemaic seal impressions, in: P. Iossif et al. (ed.), More than men, less than gods: studies on royal cult and imperial worship, Leuven, 389–415.

Porten, B. and A. Yardeni 2014. Textbook of Aramaic Ostraca from Idumaea, 1. Winona Lake (Ind.)

Price, S.F.R. 1984. Gods and Emperors: The Greek Language of the Roman Imperial Cult, in: Journal of Hellenic Studies 104, 79–95.

Quaegebeur, J. 1978. Reines ptolémaïques et traditions égyptiennes, in: H. von Maehler and V.M. Strocka (edd.), Das ptolemäische Ägypten, Mainz, 245–62.

Quaegebeur, J. 1989. The Egyptian Clergy and the Cult of the Ptolemaic Dynasty, in: Ancient Society 20, 93–116.

Quaegebeur, J. 1998a. Documents égyptiens anciens et nouveaux relatifs à Arsinoé Philadelpia, in: H. Melaerts (ed.), Le culte du souverain dans l'Égypte ptolémaïque au IIIe siècle avant notre ère, Leuven, 73–108.

Quaegebeur, J. 1998b. Cleopatra VII and the cults of the Ptolemaic queens, in: R.S. Bianchi et al. (edd.), Cleopatra's Egypt: Age of the Ptolemies, New York, 41–54.

RES = Répertoire d'épigraphie sémitique, Paris.

Rice, E.E. 1983. The grand procession of Ptolemy Philadelphus. Oxford.

Robert, L. 1967. Encore une inscription grecque de l'Iran, in : Comptes rendus l'Académie des inscriptions et belles-lettres 111, 281–297.

Roche, M.-J. 1987. Le cultes d'Isis et l'influence égyptienne à Pétra, in: Syria 64, 217–222.

Roller, D.W. 2004. The World of Juba II and Kleopatra Selene: royal scholarship on Rome's African frontier. Abingdon.

Roller, D.W. 2010. Cleopatra: A Biography. Oxford.

Salzmann, D. 2013. Anmerkungen zur Typologie des hellenistischen Königsdiadems und zu anderen herrscherlichen Kopfbinden, in: A. Lichtenberger (ed.), Das Diadem der hellenistischen Herrscher: Übernahme, Transformation oder Neuschöpfung eines Herrschaftszeichens?, Bonn 337–385.

Sartre, M. 2006. Religion und Herrschaft: Das Seleukidenreich, in: Saeculum, 57, 163–190.

Schreiber, T. 2013, Die funktionale Binde, in: A. Lichtenberger (ed.), Das Diadem der hellenistischen Herrscher: Übernahme, Transformation oder Neuschöpfung eines Herrschaftszeichens?, Bonn, 233–247.

Schwentzel, C.-G. 2005. Les thèmes du monnayage royal nabatéen et le modèle monarchique hellénistique, in: Syria 82,149–60.

Schwentzel, C.-G. 2006. Statues royales nabatéennes, in: Res Antiquae 3, 123–137.

Schwentzel, C.-G. 2008. La double représentation du dieu Dousares: bilinguisme figurative ou syncrétisme?, in: Metis n.s. 6, 149–66.

Schwentzel, C.-G. 2010. Arétas IV 'roi des Nabatéens' d'après monnaies, in: Numismatica e antichità classiche 39, 233–49.

Schwentzel, C.-G. 2013. Juifs et Nabatéens. Les monarchies ethniques du Proche-Orient hellénistique et romain. Rennes.

Schwentzel, C.-G. 2014. La reine Huldu et coiffe isiaque, Isis et le pouvoir royal à Pétra (Ier s. av. J.-C.-Ier s. ap. J.-C.), in: L. Bricault and M. J. Versluys (edd.), Power, Politics and the Cults of Isis, Leiden, 147–62.

Schmid, S.G. 1999. Un roi nabatéen à Délos, in: Annual of the Department of Antiquities in Jordan 43, 279–298.

Schmid, S.G. 2013. Early Nabataean Royal Portraiture, in: Studies in the History and Archaeology of Jordan 11, 757–769.

Schmitt, S.G. 1995. Siedlungen Palästinas in griechisch-römischer Zeit: Ostjordanland, Negeb und im Westjordanland (in Auswahl). Wiesbaden.

Silverman, M. 1981. Servant (ʿebed) Names in Aramaic and Other Semitic Languages, in: Journal of the American Oriental Society 101, 361–366.

Smith, R.R.R. 1988. Hellenistic Royal Portraits. Oxford.

Smith, R.R.R. 1991. Hellenistic Sculpture: a Handbook. London.

174 David F. Graf

Smith, R.R.R. 1996. Ptolemaic Portraits: Alexandrian types, Egyptian version, in: J. Walsh and T. F. Reese (edd), Alexandria and Alexandrianism, Malibu, 203–21.

Starcky, J. 1966. Pétra et la Nabatène, in : Dictionnaire de la Bible, Supplément 7: cols. 886–1017.

Starcky, J. and J. Strugnell 1966. Petra: deux nouvelles inscriptions nabatéenes, in: Revue Biblique 73, 236–243.

Strootman, R. 2014. Courts and Elites in the Hellenistic Empire. Edinburgh.

Tardieu, M. 1990. Les Paysage Reliques. Routes et haltes syriennes d'Isidore à Simplicius. Leuven.

Thompson, D.J. 2012. Memphis under the Ptolemies, Second edition. Princeton.

Tholbecq, L and C. Dunand. 2005. A Nabataean Rock-Cut Sanctuary in Petra. Preliminary Report on Three Excavation Seasons at the "Obodas Chapel", Jabal Numayr (2002–2004), in: Annual of the Department of Antiquities of Jordan 49, 299–311.

Tholbecq, L. and C. Durand and C. Bouchaud 2008. Nabataean Rock-Cut Sanctuary in Petra: Second Preliminary Report on the 'Obodas Chapel' Excavation Project, Jabal Numayr (2005–2007), in: Annual of the Department of Antiquities in Jordan 52, 235–254.

Tholbecq, L. and C. Durand 2013. „A late second century BC Nabataean occupation at Jabal Numayr: the earliest phase of the 'Obodas Chapel' sanctuary", in: M. Mouton and S.G. Schmid (Edd.), Men on the Rocks: The Formation of Nabataean Petra, Berlin, 205–222.

Tondriau, J. 1946. Les thiases dionysiaques royaux de la cour ptolémaïque, in: Chronique d'Égypte 21, 149–171.

Tondriau, J. 1948. Rois lagides compares ou identifies à des divinités, in: Chronique d'Égypte 23, 127–146.

Tondriau, J. 1950. La dynastie ptolémaïque et la religion dionisiaque, in: Chronique d'Égypte 25, 283–316.

Vaelske, V. 2013. Isis in Petra: Chronological and Topographical Aspects, in: M. Mouton and S.G. Schmid (edd.), Men on the Rocks: The Formation of Nabataean Petra, Berlin, 351–361.

Van Nuffelen, P. 1999. Le culte des souverains hellénistiques: le gui de la religion grecque, in: Ancient Society 29, 175–189.

Van Nuffelen, P. 2004. Le culte royal de l'empire des Séleucides: une réinterprétation, in: Historia 53, 278–301.

Weber, T. 2006. Sculptures from Roman Syria in the Syrian National Museum at Damascus. Worms.

Weber, T. 2009. Die Skulpturen aus Sahr und die Statuendenkmäler der römischen Kaiserzeit in südsyrischen Heiligtümern, in: J.-M. Dentzer and T.M. Weber (Edd.), Hauran. 4, Sahr al-Ledja: recherches syro-européennes 1998–2008 = syrisch-europäische Forschungen 1998-2008, II, 1–263.

Weber, T. 2011. Arabia in exotischem Gewand, in: Antike Welt, 6/11, 11–16.

Wellendorf, H. 2008. Ptolemy's political tool: Religion, in: Studia Antiqua 6, 33–38.

Wenning, R. 1983. Hellenistische Skulpturen in Israel, in: Boreas 6, 105–118.

Wenning, R. 1997. Bemerkungen zur Gesellschaft und Religion der Nabatäer, in: R. Albertz (ed.), Religion und Gesellschaft. Studien zu ihrer Wechselbeziehung in der Kultur des Antiken Vorderen Orients, Münster, 177–201.

Wenning, R. 2003. Hellenistische Denkmaler aus Petra: Überlegungen zum Hellenisierungsprozess der Nabatäer, in: G. Zimmer (ed.), Neue Forschungen zur hellenistischen Plastik: Festschrift für George Delrop, Eichstätt, 141–164.

Wenning, R. 2015. Obodas Theos: Der statuarische Befund eines nabatäischen Gottes, in: Zeitschrift des Deutschen Palästina-Vereins 131, 44–58.

Wenning, R. and H. Merklein 1997. Die Götter in der Welt der Nabatäer, in: T.M. Weber and R. Wenning (edd.), Petra. Antike Felsstadt zwischen arabischer Tradition und griechischer Norm, Mainz, 105–110.

West, J.M.I. 1974. Uranius, in: Harvard Studies in Classical Philolog 78, 282–84.

Winnett, F.V. 1973. The revolt of Damasī: Safaitic and Nabataean Evidence, in: Bulletin of the American Schools of Oriental Research 211, 54–57.

Winter, E. 1978. Der Herrscherkult in den ägyptischen Ptolemäertempeln, in: H. von Maehler and V.M. Strocka (edd.), Das ptolemäische Ägypten, Mainz, 147–160.

Wuthnow, H. 1930. Die semitischen Menschennamem in griechischen Inschriften und Papyri des Vorderen Orients. Leipzig.

Yardeni, A. 2016. The Jeselsohn Collection of Aramaic Ostraca from Idumaea. Jerusalem.

Zayadine, F. 1981. L'iconographie d'Al-`Uzza-Aphrodite, in: L. Kahil and Chr. Augé (edd.), Mythologie gréco-romaine. Mythologies périphériques. Études d'iconographie, Paris, 113–118.

Zayadine, F. 1986. A Symposiarch from Petra, in: L. Geraty and L. Herr (edd.), The Archaeology of Jordan and Other Studies Presented to Siegfried H. Horn, Berrien Springs (Mich.) 465–474.

Zayadine, F. 1990. The pantheon of the Nabataean inscriptions in Egypt and the Sinai, in: Aram 2, 151–174.

Zayadine, F. 1991. L'iconographie d'Isis à Petra, in : Mélanges de l'École française de Rome, 103, 283–306.

Zayadine, F. and F. Larche and J. Dentzer-Feydy 2003. Le Qasr al-Bint de Pétra: l'architecture, le décor, la chronologie et les dieux. Paris.

Figures and Illustrations

Fig. 1. Depiction of Obodas II on coin, 9–6 BCE. Hellenistic Petra Project III, 2007, No. 1, Obv. (photo S.E. Sidebotham).

Fig. 2. Dionysos. Marble statue from cella of the Temple of Isis (Photo by D. F. Graf with permission of the Ministero dei Beni e delle Attività Culturali e del Turismo - Museo Archeologico Nazionale di Napoli).

Fig. 3. Isis. Marble statue from the porticus of the temple of Isis (Photo by D. F. Graf with permission of the Ministero dei Beni e delle Attività Culturali e del Turismo - Museo Archeologico Nazionale di Napoli).

Fig. 4. Dionysiac figure (Dushara?) from path to the High Place of Jabal al-Madbah at Petra.

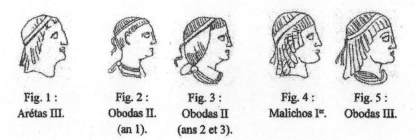

Fig. 5. The Nabataean Kings of the First Century BCE (from Schwentzel 2005, 152).

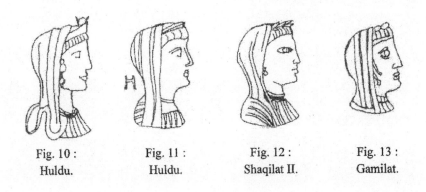

Fig. 6. The Nabataean Queens (from Schwentzel 2005, 155).

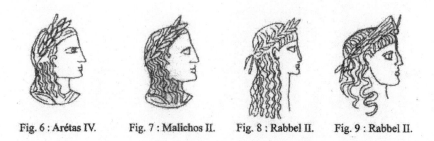

Fig. 7. The Nabataeans Kings of the first Century CE (from Schwentzel 2005, 153).

The Gymnasium of Jerusalem – a Middle Ground?

Benedikt Eckhardt

1. Cultural Interaction and its Discontents

The most famous example for the introduction of a gymnasium into a Middle Eastern city is undoubtedly the Hellenistic reform of Jerusalem in 175 BCE. The events are described in a short but precise report in the second book of Maccabees:

> When Seleucus (IV) died and Antiochus (IV), who was called Epiphanes, succeeded to the kingdom, Jason the brother of Onias (III) obtained the high priesthood by corruption, promising the king at an interview three hundred sixty talents of silver and from another source of revenue eighty talents. In addition to this he promised to pay one hundred fifty more, if permission were given to establish by his authority a gymnasium and a body of youth for it and to draw up the list of the 'Antiochenes' amongst those in Hierosolyma. When the king assented and he came to office, he at once shifted his compatriots over to the Greek way of life.[1]

The report goes on to brand activities in the gymnasium as "an extreme of Hellenization", a word attested here for the first time, and puts it into direct opposition to the "lawful way of living", elsewhere called *Ioudaismos*.[2] 2 Maccabees thus posits a radical clash of cultures in Jerusalemite society, deliberately caused by Jason for personal reasons.

On reading this report, written approximately half a century after the events, the idea that the gymnasium could ever have served as a "Middle Ground" does not impose itself.[3] Our author does not see it as a "place in

---

[1]   2 Macc 4, 7–10: Μεταλλάξαντος δὲ τὸν βίον Σελεύκου καὶ παραλαβόντος τὴν βασιλείαν Ἀντιόχου τοῦ προσαγορευθέντος Ἐπιφανοῦς ὑπενόθευσεν Ἰάσων ὁ ἀδελφὸς Ονιου τὴν ἀρχιερωσύνην ἐπαγγειλάμενος τῷ βασιλεῖ δι' ἐντεύξεως ἀργυρίου τάλαντα ἑξήκοντα πρὸς τοῖς τριακοσίοις καὶ προσόδου τινὸς ἄλλης τάλαντα ὀγδοήκοντα. πρὸς δὲ τούτοις ὑπισχνεῖτο καὶ ἕτερα διαγράφειν πεντήκοντα πρὸς τοῖς ἑκατόν, ἐὰν ἐπιχωρηθῇ διὰ τῆς ἐξουσίας αὐτοῦ γυμνάσιον καὶ ἐφηβεῖον αὐτῷ συστήσασθαι καὶ τοὺς ἐν Ιεροσολύμοις Ἀντιοχεῖς ἀναγράψαι. ἐπινεύσαντος δὲ τοῦ βασιλέως καὶ τῆς ἀρχῆς κρατήσας εὐθέως πρὸς τὸν Ἑλληνικὸν χαρακτῆρα τοὺς ὁμοφύλους μετέστησε. Translation by J. Schaper (*New English Translation of the Septuagint*). The parallel account in 1 Macc 1, 11–15 is devoid of details and can be ignored here.

[2]   2 Macc 4, 13: ἦν δ' οὕτως ἀκμή τις Ἑλληνισμοῦ; 4,11: τὰς μὲν νομίμους καταλύων πολιτείας παρανόμους ἐθισμοὺς ἐκαίνιζεν. For Ἰουδαϊσμός, see 2,21; 8,1; 14,38.

[3]   For the concepts of Middle Ground and cultural brokerage, see the introduction to this volume.

between" anything; it is a decidedly Greek institution incompatible with local customs, but nevertheless superimposed on them by a power-hungry individual. Later events may seem to corroborate this initial impression: seven years later, a civil war between Jason and his successor Menelaus provoked a reaction by Antiochus that included military occupation, the rededication of the sanctuary to Zeus Olympius, and the introduction of Dionysiac processions in Jerusalem.[4] There seems to be little room here for attempts to persuade others or for the emergence of shared practices, the hallmarks of cultural interaction.

However, the perspective of our text is obviously polemical, and influenced by subsequent events, most notably the Maccabaean revolt and the emergence of a new high priestly dynasty that was keen to brand its predecessors as enemies of the people. Most scholars would now agree that there was no direct connection between Jason's project and the oppression of 168 BCE,[5] and even 2 Maccabees does not suggest that anyone *at the time* thought that erecting a gymnasium was a bad idea. Its introduction may indeed have been acknowledged as a successful act of cultural brokerage: Jason made use of a Greek institution to forge a closer connection with the king that should have been advantageous to the Judaeans, while at the same time modifying that institution in a way that adapted it to local customs. There was apparently no worship of Heracles or the king himself in this particular gymnasium (our text would not have failed to mention such abominations), and when representatives of the "Antiochenes" were sent to Tyre to participate in the games in honour of Heracles-Melqart, they specified that the gift they brought was not to be used to finance sacrifices.[6] At least until the events of 168, it was quite possible to have the best of both worlds.

That the gymnasium could serve as a place of cultural interaction rather than oppression seems obvious enough: it was here that people who had originally been non-Greeks encountered Greek culture, and it is a fair guess that the latter might itself undergo changes and local reinterpretations in the process.[7] Those who were more proficient in these matters – people with

---

[4] 2 Macc 5–7. Several new interpretations have been offered recently, most importantly by Honigman 2014 and Bernhardt 2017.

[5] This had been argued by Bickerman 1937. For an overview over recent debates, see Eckhardt 2018.

[6] 2 Macc 4, 18–20. The text claims that Jason had actually given them the money for a sacrifice which they then refused, but this is easily explained as an attempt to make Jason look as bad as possible; see Engels 2014, 63–64. For a similar assessment of the nondisruptive character of the gymnasium, see Gruen 1993, 258–59; the literary strategy of our report is analyzed by Honigman 2014, 199–217.

[7] Accessibility is obviously relevant here. If Greekness (ethnic or acquired) was a precondition of entry, as is usually assumed, cultural interaction inside the gymnasium would be

The Gymnasium of Jerusalem

Greek names like Kephalon of Uruk, or Jason of Jerusalem – may then be imagined as "cultural brokers", acting as guides to the possibilities the respective other culture had to offer. There would always be people like the author of 2 Maccabees who were not interested in such offers and even found them preposterous, but this in itself does not disprove (and perhaps even strengthens) the notion that attempts at cultural brokerage were indeed made. Another aspect of the situation is more problematic in light of the concepts employed here. Where there is a clear hierarchy of cultural signifiers, strategies of adaptation and brokerage only make sense for the party that is deemed inferior. The gymnasium might then perhaps be seen as an institution that facilitated assimilation, but not as a Middle Ground that genuinely had its own rules. As there is no question that Greek culture was deemed superior by authorities in the Seleucid kingdom, a Greek civic institution could never be equated with true cultural Middle Grounds like the Roman-Persian frontier.

And yet, despite this objection, Jason's use of the gymnasium as a means of gaining authority in Jerusalem at least points to the role of this institution in mediating contact with the king. It is worth investigating this role more closely, and an adapted version of the "Middle Ground" may well prove useful here, if two slightly less obvious aspects of the situation are taken into account.

First, the gymnasium as an institution was more "Greek" than both kings and (most) subjects in the Seleucid empire. It was an idealized and symbolically charged space, not just a natural part of either party's "culture". There were clear cultural expectations connected to it, but these were expectations that both sides, kings and subjects, frequently had to adapt to. As both sides could also use them to their own advantage, the gymnasium could become a Middle Ground in political negotiations. Second, due to its peculiar characteristics, the gymnasium could develop tendencies of quasi-autonomous self-regulation. This could in turn foster the emergence of formal or informal communities within a given city, and those communities might then approach both kings and cities on their own terms. There were obvious limits to this process due to the civic framework into which gymnasia were normally embedded. But where such tendencies emerged, they must have contributed to turning a potential focal point of cultural interaction into a Middle Ground for political negotiations.

The aim of this article is to explore the implications of seeing the gymnasium not only as the quintessential epitome of Greek culture, but as a potential Middle Ground where kings and subjects of the Seleucid empire could negotiate their relationship. This also involves looking at the possibility that "cultural brokers" exploited the dual, cultural and political capacity of the

---

limited; cf. the remarks by Groß-Albenhausen 2004. It is unclear how widespread such conditions were in the Seleucid empire; they certainly did not apply in Jerusalem.

182   Benedikt Eckhardt

gymnasium in times of crisis and change. Jason's actions can thus be put in context. He remains our main case study, but to fully make sense of his project and perhaps explain his failure as well, we need to systematically think about possible configurations of "the gymnasium as Middle Ground". This will allow us to integrate our information about Jerusalem into a picture that takes into account local traditions and political developments.

2. Three Models for the Gymnasium as Middle Ground

The following discussion presents three possible constellations in which the gymnasium can be conceived of as a Middle Ground, the uniting element being that they all have to do, in one way or another, with the creation of new cities. The first model is based on two cases of post-war restoration. This is a quite specific context, but it can serve to elucidate both the basic expectations of Seleucid kings and the basic mechanisms of brokerage. The second is based on the elevation of a military settlement to city status, whereas the third model integrates evidence for the creation of Greek cities (or merely Greek communities within cities?) in places with a long tradition of non-Greek civic government.

a.   Sardis and Limyra.

Having served as the capital of Achaeus' usurpation, Sardis was taken by Antiochus III in 213 BCE, following a two-year siege of the citadel.[8] The city and its inhabitants now had to be reintegrated into the Seleucid kingdom, a process that can partially be reconstructed on the basis of royal letters preserved in inscriptions. These do not mention the fate of Achaeus and those who had supported him. Instead, they focus on reconstitution and reconciliation. Both the city's infrastructure and the relationship of trust between king and subjects had suffered during the war, and both needed to be rebuilt. The letters are only partially preserved, but it is clear that the gymnasium had an important role to play in the process.

The earliest letter of Antiochus III (March 213) not only deals with tax reductions, but also notes that the king has ordered "that the gymnasium which you used formerly be restored to you".[9] Perhaps it had been used as a temporary military base. Another letter written in the summer of the same year marks the transition from restoration to active improvement of the Sardians' situation: the "young men" (νέοι) will receive, "as replacement for what you received previously", 200 *metretai* of oil for anointing themselves in the

---

[8]   On the usurpation of Achaeus, see Chrubasik 2016, 101–122.

[9]   SEG 39,1283 (= Ma 2005, 285 no. 1), ll. 6–7: καὶ τὸ γυμνάσιον ὧι πρότερον ἐχρῆσθε | συντετάχαμεν ἀποκαταστῆσαι ὑμῖν (transl. J. Ma).

The Gymnasium of Jerusalem   183

gymnasium, and a special fund is set aside to guarantee that sum in future years.[10] Already before Antiochus' conquest, the gymnasium had clearly been an important civic institution, the treatment of which could be read as an indicator of the city's relations to the Seleucid ruler. The origins of the gymnasium are unknown, but it is unlikely to predate the transformation of the city under Antiochos I.[11] When Sardis was reconstituted as a Seleucid city, all parties agreed that there should be a recognizable focus on this particular institution.

In all likelihood, this was not an exceptional case. A fragmentary inscription from Limyra seems to presuppose a similar situation after the Seleucid conquest of 197 BCE.[12] It is impossible to be certain about the Seleucid (?) protagonist writing the letter, but a number of similar features emerge from the mutilated text. Again, we see matters relating to the gymnasium being treated as matters of direct relevance to the relationship between city and empire. Again, specific people are in the spotlight. In Sardis, the νέοι – organized young men between 20 and 30 years old, with the social and economic status necessary to devote time to gymnasial activities – were singled out as recipients of royal euergetism; in Limyra, the gymnasium established (recently?) by a certain Phanokrates and its current gymnasiarchs are explicitly mentioned in a context that remains elusive.[13] Again, a stage where the gymnasium was inhabited by soldiers seems to be overcome through diplomatic exchange.[14]

The gymnasium may be seen as a Middle Ground in the sense that it provided a space where very different parties entangled in asymmetric hierarchies could communicate on the basis of shared, but to some degree artificial cultural assumptions. If that is so, can we point to "cultural brokers" who initiated that communication? The role of the νέοι and the gymnasiarchs may well be worth a closer look. The symbolic position of the gymnasium at the heart of a Hellenistic city, particularly in the East, has often been pointed out, and it obviously gives us one reason why kings had an interest in a durable association with this particular institution.[15] But in this context, it is easy to

---

[10] SEG 39,1285 (= Ma 2005, 287–88 no. 3), ll. 3-6: τοῖς τε γὰρ νέοις ἀποτετάχαμεν εἰς ἐλαιοχρίστιον | ἀνθ' ὧν πρότερον ἐλαμβάνετε κατ' ἐνιαυτὸν ἐλαίου μετρητὰς | διακοσίους καὶ εἰς τοῦτο τὸ πλῆθος συνετάξαμεν ἀποτάξαι | προσόδους ἀφ' ὧν ἐξ ὑποκειμένου λήψεσθε εὐτάκτως.

[11] See Kosmin 2019, 78–79.

[12] SEG 61,1236 (= Wörrle 2011).

[13] Ll. 17-21: [- - - περὶ] τοῦ γυμνασίου δὲ οὗ ἀνέθηκεν Φανοκράτης εἰρήκαμεν | [- - ca. 32 - - στρ]ατιωτῶν ἵνα μήτε δίσκοι μήτε γυμνασίαρχοι δισσοὶ | [- - ca. 36 - -] αὐτῶι χρᾶσθαι εἰς ἃ ἂν προαιρῆσθε καὶ τὰ λοιπὰ δε- | [- - ca. 27 - - ἀεί τι τῶν ὑ]μῖν χρησίμων σ[υγ]κατασκευῶμεν τῆι πόλει πε- | [πεισμένοι ὅτι - - -].

[14] See the commentary by Wörrle 2011, 409–10.

[15] On memorialization of kings in gymnasia, see now Mania 2017, 77–82.

overlook the significant degree of autonomy gymnasia – and age classes like the νέοι – could have in Greek cities.[16] In many places, the νέοι were independently organized and had their own finances. They could support their cities in times of trouble, but they could also cause trouble themselves.[17] Their military capacity, their economic potential and the fact that they were undeniably the future of the citizenry all contributed to making them a partially independent factor in the political landscape. These were the people a king had to have on his side. The special role of gymnasiarchs could be tied to this very context. In some cases, the νέοι could vote for their own gymnasiarchs, and even where this was not (or no longer) possible, the supervision of the young men, including the ephebes, was a very significant responsibility.[18] It is no coincidence that the gymnasiarchy was affected by trends towards "aristocratization" early on, although it was only in the Roman period that it regularly became a lifelong responsibility.[19] The high costs associated with providing for oil made offers by wealthy donors particularly attractive, and the reasons for aristocrats to take on such positions may well have gone beyond a mere desire to shine. There was real influence to be wielded here.

The inscriptions mention organized young men and gymnasiarchs at important points in the process of re-integrating a city into the Seleucid empire. These institutions could develop their own agenda, but they could also support the city and the king in their attempts to negotiate a workable relationship. Jason's proposal as reported by 2 Maccabees emphasized the importance of organizing the youth by explicitly mentioning the *ephebeion*.[20] Some common assumptions thus certainly connect his project with the gymnasia of Sardis and Limyra. However, in those cities, the precondition for the

---

[16] On the νέοι, see Dreyer 2004; Kennell 2013; van Bremen 2013.

[17] E.g. the νέοι of Kolophon pressured the city to honour their gymnasiarch (SEG 55,1251 with van Bremen 2013, 49–50), while those at Methymna offered financial support in a difficult situation (IG XII Suppl. 116 with Migeotte 2013, 117).

[18] E.g. the gymnasium of Beroia in Macedonia was turned from an autonomous entity to a civic institution in the second century BCE; the long gymnasiarchic law (I. Beroia 1) includes very detailed regulation of responsibilities and obligations. On the different constellations, see with further examples Gauthier 1995, 7–8 (gymnasia) and Kennell 2013, 225–26 (νέοι). For an instructive case from Teos, see the new inscription published by Adak and Stauner 2018.

[19] See on the developments Schuler 2004, esp. 189; Curty 2015, 293–299 (pointing out that private expenses incurred by gymnasiarchs were still exceptional for most of the Hellenistic period, see also 342–349 on Schuler); on developments in the imperial era see Scholz 2015.

[20] I follow Schaper (in the translation cited at the beginning of this article) and others in the understanding of ἐφηβεῖον as an organization of ephebes, not a building (although the latter meaning is the one recorded by Vitruvius and often assumed in translations and scholarship, e.g. Sartre 2009, 244). The verb συστήσασθαι, used for both γύμνασιον and ἐφηβεῖον, is typically used for foundations of groups or festivals; when it comes to the actual building of the gymnasium, 2 Macc uses καθίδρυσεν (4, 12).

middling role of the gymnasium and its organization of young men was that neither had to be built from scratch. Sardis and Limyra were "new cities" in the sense that the Seleucid conquest called for a redefinition of their status and a rebuilding of trust, but the institutions that mattered in the process could be treated as traditional.[21] It is therefore not surprising that recent research has favoured a different case study as a model for developments in Jerusalem.

b. Toriaion

Ever since its publication in 1997, the decree of Eumenes II granting city status to what may have been a Seleucid military settlement in Phrygia Paroreios dominates debates on the creation of new cities in the Hellenistic period.[22] Eumenes had reacted to a request brought forward by the settlers themselves, at some point in the 180s BCE. He gave them the right to have a gymnasium and a council and to use their own laws, although he reserved for himself the right to evaluate those laws and replace them with better ones. The aim of the whole procedure is explicitly said to be the creation of "one civic body" (ἓν πολίτευμα), encompassing both the settlers and the epichoric population living with them.[23]

There are many things one could find important when a new city emerges. It is all the more interesting that the elements we already know are strongly emphasized in the first letter. The gymnasium is at the core of the whole process, mentioned on a par with πολιτεία and νόμοι.[24] The νέοι are again mentioned explicitly: the erection of the gymnasium and the distribution of oil to the "young men" are among the areas where Eumenes seems to doubt the competence of the new city dwellers, and offers help regarding the paperwork.[25] Clearly, these institutions were of particular importance to the royal administration. Much emphasis has been placed on the symbolic dimension involved, and on the importance of the gymnasium for "Greekness" and the conception of the "Polis". But Greekness is not mentioned at all in the

---

[21] As with Sardis, the gymnasium in Limyra is not explicitly attested before the document cited above, i.e. the moment of Seleucid conquest. On what is now known about Ptolemaic Limyra, see recently Seyer 2019.

[22] Jonnes and Ricl 1997; on the location, see Thonemann 2008, 43–53.

[23] SEG 47,1745, ll. 26–27: συνχωρῶ καὶ ὑμῖν καὶ τοῖς μεθ᾽ ὑμῶν συνοι|κοῦσιν ἐγχωρίοις εἰς ἓν πολίτευμα συνταχ[θ]ῆναι.

[24] Ll. 9–11: ἐπιχωρηθῆναι ὑμῖν πολιτείαν | τε καὶ νόμους ἰδίους καὶ γυμνάσιον καὶ ὅσα τούτοις ἐστὶ | ἀκόλουθα.

[25] Ll. 31–34: καὶ δώσομεν τοὺς ἐπιτηδείους (sc. νόμους) καὶ βουλὴν καὶ ἀρχ[ὰς] | καθιστάναι καὶ δῆμον νέμειν εἰς φυλὰς καταμερισθέντα, | καὶ γυμνάσιον ποιησαμένους τοῖς νέοις τιθ[έ]ναι ἄλειμ|μα.

letters, and neither is the term πόλις, the significance of which has been over-estimated.[26] What we do find is a lengthy and fairly unusual explanation of the difference between real and imaginary authority, with Eumenes asserting his own position as the sole legitimate source of the grant bestowed upon the settlers.[27] This is about future political relations, and the gymnasium and its νέοι seem to have a role to play in them.

Nothing can be said about the "brokers" involved in this process. We also do not know if things would have gone the same way in the Seleucid empire, and how common this sort of procedure was.[28] The special situation of Attalid Asia Minor after Apameia may have determined both the form of the request and the royal reply to a significant degree. Important parallels to Jason's request have to be noted nonetheless. In both cases, locals approached the respective kings who granted their requests, and in both cases, the terms used to express this affirmation are ἐπιχωρέω and ἐπινεύω.[29] There are differences as well, to be discussed below, but it is easy to see how Toriaion could become the primary model for explaining events in Jerusalem.

However, yet again conditions were not quite comparable to those encountered by Jason and Antiochus IV. Jerusalem was not a recently founded military settlement, but had been a city for centuries, acknowledged as such by Antiochus III.[30] Local authority was based on traditional structures of legitimacy, and those structures were intimately tied to a central sanctuary. Any re-foundation based on a gymnasium thus had to take factors into account that did not play any role in Toriaion, and at best a marginal one in Sardis or Limyra. There is thus room for a third model based on a different case study, one that presents both major problems and striking parallels.

c. Babylon and beyond

Like Jerusalem, Babylon was controlled by a priestly aristocracy for centuries; as in Jerusalem, power derived from association with a central sanctuary, the Esagil. As in Jerusalem, Greek political structures were introduced to the city under a Seleucid king, perhaps Antiochus IV. A text of 163 BCE describes the community associated with these structures as "the Greeks, as they are called, the p[olitai], who in the past at the command of king Antiochus [had

---

[26] Mileta 2009, 81–82 tries to explain the absence of the term; against such attempts, see Eckhardt 2014, 204.

[27] Ll. 17–24; see on this passage and possible implications for the dating Savalli-Lestrade 2018.

[28] Skepticism was already expressed by Schuler 1999, 132: "Für andere Gebiete, insbesondere die östlichen Satrapien des seleukidischen Reichs, dürfte Tyriaion nur von begrenzter Aussagekraft sein".

[29] See Ameling 2003, 107–8; Bringmann 2004, 324–25; Kennell 2005, 16–17.

[30] Flav. Jos. ant. Jud. 12, 138: παραγενομένος δ' εἰς τὴν πόλιν.

The Gymnasium of Jerusalem 187

entered] Baby[lon] and who anoint with oil just like the *pol*[*itai*] who are in Seleucia, the royal city, on the Tigris and the King's Canal".[31] Yet again, the gymnasium has a decisive role in determining the political identity of a community. Its use connects the "citizens" of Babylon with those elsewhere – a welcome confirmation of the relevance of shared cultural expectations, tied to a specific institution. A later inscription shows that the gymnasium of Babylon did indeed lead to the development of the full organizational apparatus, with gymnasiarchs, ephebes and "young men".[32]

Another parallel connects Babylon even closer to events in Jerusalem. In 168 BCE, the year of Antiochus' cultic measures in the temple of Jahwe, changes were carried out in Babylon as well: "a certain Babylonian, a jeweller, a brother of the *šatammu* of Esagila, who in his stead p[erformed?] the duties of *šatammu*, was entrusted with the office of *zazakku*, by a message of the king".[33] The implications of this change are not entirely clear, but it certainly seems that the brother of the leading cultic administrator rose to a newly created position, now surpassing his brother in authority.[34] This is more than a little reminiscent of Jason ousting his brother Onias in 175 BCE.[35] In both cases, the new appointment was made against traditional expectations, based not on rules of succession but on royal fiat. In both cases, the introduction of a Greek citizen body tied to the gymnasium and a reconfiguration of temple hierarchies occur at about the same time. And in both cases, royal interference in matters that had hitherto been locally and autonomously administered must have entailed a significant potential for conflicts.

The implications of these similarities depend, at least in part, on our reconstruction of the situation at Babylon.[36] One model to explain the evidence for the *politai* is "ethnic segregation" or "apartheid": according to this view, Greeks and Babylonians lived in communities that were completely shut off from each other in both political and administrative terms.[37] Both had their own institutions, and both had their own dealings with the king, although he privileged the Greeks. The choice of terminology may not be the most fortunate one. It is plausible to assume that most "Greeks" were not actually Greek, and as we do not know how permeable the boundaries between the two communities were, there is little reason to evoke the systemic

---

31   BCHP 14; transl. R. van der Spek. OGIS 253 (166 BCE) calls Antiochus IV κτίστης τῆς πόλεως, but it cannot be proven to come from Babylon. For arguments in favour of Antiochus III see Clancier and Monerie 2014, 211-212; Garslin-Thomé 2017, 227–229.

32   SEG 7,39 (111/10 BCE). On the Greek citizen communities under the Parthians see Ramsey 2019.

33   AD 2, –168 A, r. 12'-13'; transl. P. Clancier.

34   Clancier 2017, 74-75; see also Capdetrey 2007, 326; Boiy and Mittag 2011, 117–18.

35   Also noted by Honigman 2014, 357; Graslin-Thomé 2014, 79–82.

36   The confused miscellany by Geller and Potts 2015 does not offer anything in this regard.

37   Van der Spek 2009.

racism connected to a term like "apartheid".[38] However, the recent attempt to do away with the distinction altogether and see *politai* as a general term for the whole "Polis of Babylon" pushes things too far.[39] When the texts record conflicts between the *politai* and "the people of the land who are in Babylon",[40] the easiest explanation remains that these were two different forms of organization with different interests. We certainly do not need to imagine a permanent conflict, let alone an all-encompassing segregation; in fact, we may assume that the *politai* – as a status group officially recognized by the king – acted as primary brokers of royal benevolence for all the inhabitants of Babylon. But Babylon as a whole did not become a Greek city. The relevant privileges were mediated through – and primarily addressed to – an elitist, politically and legally independent organization defined by its activity in the gymnasium.

If this remains the most plausible solution for Babylon, we may look for similar phenomena in the Southern Levant. The "Antiochenes in Jerusalem" have always been compared to the "Seleukeians in Gaza" known from coins, but the crucial question is what this means. Were the Seleukeians a πολίτευμα in the Ptolemaic sense of a legally independent association, perhaps with a military background, or had Gaza as a whole been re-founded as Seleukeia?[41] The example of Toriaion suggests the latter, but the evidence from Babylon may justify a return to the former view. Similar questions arise elsewhere, e.g. in Gadara, where a late Hellenistic inscription on the city wall may refer to the "Seleukeians in the midst of Gadara".[42] Perhaps the old assumption that "Antioch in Jerusalem" and "Seleukeia in Gadara" were separate communities inside a larger city has more to recommend itself than the success of the Toriaion-paradigm would suggest. In fact, even that text, which has certainly changed the debate with regard to Jerusalem,[43] shows that two options were conceivable. While the πολίτευμα (in the sense of "citizenry") explicitly encompasses all the inhabitants, the emphasis that it should be "one" πολίτευμα suggests that there could also have been more than one.[44]

---

[38] On the Greekness of the Babylonian "Greeks", see Van der Spek 2009, 112–13; Boiy and Mittag 2011, 123–24.

[39] Clancier 2017. Cf. Clancier and Monerie 2014, 211–220.

[40] BCHP 14.

[41] For the coins, see Hoover 2010, 139–141 (no. 583–587, 592). For the two views, contrast Bickerman 1937, 61–62 (πολίτευμα) with Bickerman 1938, 234–35 (πόλις); the latter view is now the usual one, to be found, e.g., in Cohen 2006, 286–88; but contrast Engels 2014, 53. On the Ptolemaic πολιτεύματα, see Kayser 2013; Kruse 2015.

[42] SEG 58,1756: (Ἔτους) ηκσ' Φιλώτας | καὶ Σελε[υκέ]ων | τῶν ἐν μέσ[η/ῳ Γαδ(αρα)] | ἡ πόλι[ς].

[43] In addition to the works cited in n. 29, see Schwartz 2008, 530–31; Eckhardt 2013, 47–50; Bernhardt 2017, 130–31.

[44] Also noted by Gauthier, BE 1999, 681.

The Gymnasium of Jerusalem 189

It is clear that cultural brokerage using the gymnasium as Middle Ground would have to be imagined differently in each of the three models discussed here. In the first model, the protagonists operate from within a well-established civic institution, strengthening both their own and their city's position by acting as guarantors of present and, crucially, future loyalty towards the king. In the second model, the gymnasium and its users are primary representatives of the newly created city as such; it is established on the basis of royal authority in the first place, and the authority of brokers could rely on having secured the king's permission. In the third model, the protagonists operate from within an elitist community that stands in opposition to traditional institutions; they may act as brokers for others, but this is not their purpose and they do not have to do so. In each case, the basic expectations connected to the gymnasium, its users and its hierarchies were the same. But the communicative channels thus created, and the ensuing relationships between kings and cities, could vastly differ.

3. An Honest Broker in Jerusalem?

We can now try to situate Jason's gymnasium in this matrix. To begin with, we should recall again the verbal correspondences with the decree from Toriaion, and the structural similarity of the petition-and-response pattern. The latter connects Jerusalem to Toriaion, but not to Babylon, where settlers were apparently brought in from elsewhere upon the king's request. The transactional dimension of Jason's request is not paralleled in Toriaion or elsewhere. It is a plausible assumption that the high priest of Jerusalem acted as a tax farmer, and Ptolemaic parallels for Jason's payment to the king have been adduced.[45] But none of them can make sense of the fact that 2 Maccabees explicitly mentions two payments, one for the office and another for the right to build the gymnasium and enlist the "Antiochenes". No other tax farmer seems to have founded a city. It has also been suggested that Jason paid the king to free the new city from the obligation to worship him, but even if there was such an obligation, its relationship to the status of a city is not at all clear.[46] While this problem thus cannot be solved on the basis of our present evidence, we are on safer ground when it comes to the *ephebeion*.

---

[45] Monson 2016.

[46] See Bernhardt 2017, 142–44 for the suggestion. The introduction (or not) of a civic cult in honour of Antiochus would have been left to the city anyway, and the dynastic cult was organized by satrapal high priests, regardless of the status of individual cities (see Capdetrey 2007, 322–27). The dynastic renaming of a city would certainly justify the expectation that the new founding figure would be worshipped, but there is no evidence for this being an enforceable obligation.

The importance of institutionalized education of the young in the communication with kings is a feature we know well from the first two models discussed above. 2 Maccabees stresses this aspect a second time when it notes that Jason brought even the strongest of the ephebes "under the *petasos*".[47]

So far, combined information taken from models one and two is sufficient to elucidate the events, but there remains the vexed question of the "Antiochenes in Jerusalem". After much earlier debate, it is now common to understand the phrase τοὺς ἐν Ιεροσολύμοις Ἀντιοχεῖς ἀναγράψαι as referring to the transformation of Jerusalem as a whole into a Greek city. According to this view, Jason registered "those who lived in Jerusalem as Antiochenes", not "the Antiochenes among those living in Jerusalem".[48] But we have seen above that the idea of distinct organizational entities operating alongside each other cannot easily be dismissed: this is not only what seems to characterize the case of Babylon, but it can also be aligned with the general tendency of the gymnasium to create a distinct and somewhat autonomous social space with its own hierarchies. If this was the case in cities with a long tradition of civic enfranchisement, it might all the more have been the case where city (Antioch) and gymnasium came into being at the same time.

The most important alternative to the Toriaion-paradigm does indeed presuppose separate entities: according to John Ma, the Antiochenes of Jerusalem were constituted as an independent "Polis" alongside the "Ethnos" of the Judaeans.[49] The gymnasium would have been the centre of the "Polis", while the temple remained the core institution of the "Ethnos". This conforms well with the third model described above, but there are significant problems with this view.[50] Its formulation depends on the Aristotelian dichotomy between *polis* and *ethnos*, a concept that was never used as an administrative principle in the Hellenistic world.[51] It does not take into account the different foundation stories (a request by locals in the case of Jerusalem, a settlement of foreigners ordered by the king in the case of Babylon), and it cannot explain how Jason could be founder of the "Polis" and high priest of the "Ethnos" at the same time. It may thus be tempting to dismiss this reconstruction and go back to our models one and two, with a special focus on

---

[47] 2 Macc 4, 11: τοὺς κρατίστους τῶν ἐφήβων ὑποτάσσων ὑπὸ πέτασον ἤγαγεν.

[48] See for many Kennell 2005, 15. 2 Macc 4,19 does not decide the issue: ἀπέστειλεν Ἰάσων ὁ μιαρὸς θεωροὺς ὡς ἀπὸ Ιεροσολύμων Ἀντιοχεῖς ὄντας παρακομίζοντας ἀργυρίου δραχμὰς τριακοσίας εἰς τὴν τοῦ Ἡρακλέους θυσίαν. Jerusalem's official festival observers were Antiochenes, but Jason would of course have chosen θεωροί from among the Antiochenes if those were a specific group, which to me seems the slightly more natural reading of this passage.

[49] Ma 2012, 76–79.

[50] For criticism, see Eckhardt 2013, 51–52 n. 59; Doran 2016, 182–85; Bernhardt 2017, 130.

[51] Eckhardt 2014.

The Gymnasium of Jerusalem

Toriaion. However, archaeological and numismatic evidence has been adduced to show that a similar separation of a Greek and an indigenous community characterized the elevation of Gerasa to Antioch on the Chrysarhoas under Antiochus IV.[52] The argument remains speculative, but if we combine it with our reassessment of "Seleukeians" elsewhere, there is good reason to revisit the possible implications of organizational separation for our understanding of events in Jerusalem.

It has always been acknowledged that Jason's control over the list of Antiochenes gave him significant power. Whatever structure we envisage for "Antioch in Jerusalem", you do not ask for the right to draw up a list of citizens if you intend to include everyone. The criteria for inclusion in the list are not given in 2 Maccabees. Wealth may have been one factor, and one that would not necessarily clash with common expectations surrounding gymnasium and *ephebeia*.[53] But as Jason had just come to power in an unprecedented way, and against traditional rules of succession, it is plausible to assume that he also had wealthy enemies who would not be included in the list.[54] When traditional structures of authority are replaced by new ones that are based only on an external factor (the approval of the king), there are bound to be losers.

The parallel from Babylon mentioned above is instructive here despite some differences. There, the successful brother did not become *šatammu* himself, but was appointed to a new, superior position that was apparently revived solely for this purpose.[55] Still, the process is sufficiently similar, and in connection with the introduction of the *politai* around the same time, a pattern seems to emerge that connects Babylon and Jerusalem. It is not exactly true that Antiochus followed a strategy of appointing *homines novi* to high cultic offices in order to replace elite families who might work against him.[56]

---

[52] Lichtenberger 2017 (also on Hippos and Gadara).

[53] The elitist character of the Athenian *ephebeia* is particularly visible in the Roman period, but Perrin-Saminadayar 2013 points to Hellenistic roots. Hin 2007 cautions against taking Athens as a model and overestimating the aristocratic character of the Hellenistic *ephebeia*, but acknowledges that the institution would necessarily replicate the social stratification of a given city. The ephebarchic law of Amphipolis, now published by Lazaridou 2015, has long been believed (based on rumors about the text's content) to support the case for an aristocratic *ephebeia*, and has indeed been understood by its editor to exclude those from the *ephebeia* whose parents did not have possessions worth at least 30 minae (ll. 14–18). But this view has been shown to be problematic by Rousset 2017, 70–73: before the financial assessment, there is an assembly of "all the ephebes" in the palaestra (l. 8); the following regulations seem to put special obligations regarding attendance on the rich ephebes, without excluding the others.

[54] I find it difficult to believe that Onias III was happy to pass the office on to his brother, as argued by Bernhardt 2017, 138.

[55] On the office of *zazakku*, see Clancier and Monerie 2014, 212–213.

[56] As argued by Gorre and Honigman 2013.

In both cases, the new administrator of the sanctuary came from the same family as his predecessor. Neither was the introduction of strict political (let alone ethnic) segregation a precondition for these developments. Jason remained responsible for both the gymnasium and the temple. However, both cases have in common that the creation of a new political elite (the "Greeks") and royal interference with traditional temple hierarchies are connected in time, and at least for Jerusalem we can show that both processes were actually initiated by the same "cultural broker".

At the core of all this were the gymnasium and its users. The institution brought an element of Greek culture to Jerusalem, and we have to assume that Jason and his supporters expected to be able to convert their "Greekness" into prestige.[57] Nothing suggests that this calculation was wrong, and no resistance against the gymnasium or "Hellenization" is on record. The wider population of Jerusalem is necessarily involved in this reasoning, but it is not needed anywhere else in this reconstruction. It comes into view only as a diffuse source of affirmation, without being directly involved in the transformation of the city. It is therefore possible to see Jason and his clique as an elitist club, possibly even a private association in origin,[58] that came to monopolize communication with the king through clever use of the Middle Ground. For his adherents and those whose names were recorded in the list of Antiochenes, Jason must indeed have appeared as a powerful cultural broker who employed the gymnasium as a Middle Ground par excellence, creating a fusion of Greek culture and local sensibilities.

But what about the others? If Jason was a "cultural broker", he offered his services selectively. For the supporters of Onias III at least, he would merely be seen as an illegitimate high priest. 2 Maccabees actually contrasts Jason with another diplomat, Johannes, who had gained royal privileges for Jerusalem at an earlier date. These were privileges for the whole population, and 2 Maccabees claims that Jason's reform somehow undid this laudable success.[59] According to this view, Johannes was an honest broker, whereas

---

[57] Along the lines indicated by Chrubasik 2017.

[58] Engels 2014, 52 discards this idea because of the high sums of money involved, but the payment might mark the transition from a private club to the formally recognized citizenry of the new Antiochia. Bernhardt 2017, 139 points out that the Antiochenes might have been a loyalty club prior to this recognition, analogous to the Ptolemaic *basilistai*. As the latter were soldiers (see Fischer-Bovet 2014, 287–290), the value of the parallel is somewhat doubtful, although Kennell 2005 stresses the potential role of Jerusalem's gymnasium in military education. One may add to this that although *basilistai* are not known from Seleucid contexts, the εὐε[ργ]εσιασταί and the Κεραυνιασταί mentioned in the canal inscription from Antioch of 73/74 CE (SEG 35,1483, l. A 47 and B 27–28) might go back to similar clubs, particularly if we relate the Κεραυνιασταί not to Zeus Ceraunus (as does Feissel 1985), but to Seleucus III Ceraunus; see Eckhardt 2019, 16–17.

[59] 2 Macc 4, 11: καὶ τὰ κείμενα τοῖς Ιουδαίοις φιλάνθρωπα βασιλικὰ διὰ Ιωάννου τοῦ πατρὸς Εὐπολέμου τοῦ ποιησαμένου τὴν πρεσβείαν ὑπὲρ φιλίας καὶ συμμαχίας πρὸς τοὺς

The Gymnasium of Jerusalem   193

Jason was a fraud who only thought about his own position. Perhaps we may see in this evaluation of Jason's reform a confirmation of the suspicion voiced above: brokers could have their own agendas, and the autonomous structures often associated with gymnasia could serve to reinforce them.

4. Failure

Internal resistance does not seem to have been the reason for Jason's failure to keep his position for more than three years, but we have to confess that we do not know much. The king replaced him with a certain Menelaus, thus demonstrating clearly that from his perspective, appointments no longer needed to take local rules into account. According to Judaean tradition, the high priesthood should have been unavailable for political disputes; as succession rules were clear, there were no debates to be had, no decisions to be made. But a gymnasiarch was replaceable, and so was a cultural broker. Jason's actions thus had one consequence he cannot have foreseen: the high priesthood became associated with the Middle Ground, where everything was subject to constant re-negotiation.[60]

His replacement by Menelaus in 172 BCE triggered the conflicts that would end in open civil war, leading to the military and cultic measures of 168 and to the Maccabaean revolt. While these events had nothing to do with cultural conflicts, they can certainly be seen as the result of failed cultural brokerage.

Ῥωμαίους παρώσας καὶ τὰς μὲν νομίμους καταλύων πολιτείας παρανόμους ἐθισμοὺς ἐκαίνιζεν. The reference may be to the negotiations that had preceded the "Charta" of Antiochus III (200 BCE); in any case, Jason's gymnasium did not abolish any privileges or local customs.

[60] The caveat here is that we do not know anything about Menelaus' position vis-à-vis the gymnasium (the claim in Flav. Jos. ant. Jud. 12, 241 that he was actually the initiator of the whole project has no value). It is plausible to assume that Antiochus saw the high priest as the natural gymnasiarch of Jerusalem, but we cannot prove this.

Bibliography

Adak, M. und K. Stauner. 2018. Die Neoi und das Temenos des Dionysas. Eine hellenistische Prachturkunde aus Teos, in: Philia 4, 1–25.

Ameling, W. 2003. Jerusalem als hellenistische Polis: 2 Makk 4,9–12 und eine neue Inschrift, in: BZ N.F. 47, 105–111.

Bernhardt, J.C. 2017. Die Jüdische Revolution. Untersuchungen zu Ursachen, Verlauf und Folgen der hasmonäischen Erhebung. Berlin und Boston.

Bickerman, E. 1937. Der Gott der Makkabäer. Untersuchungen über Sinn und Ursprung der makkabäischen Erhebung. Berlin.

Bickerman, E. 1938. Institutions des Séleucides. Paris.

Boiy, T. and P.F. Mittag. 2011. Die lokalen Eliten in Babylonien, in: B. Dreyer and P. F. Mittag (edd.), Lokale Eliten und hellenistische Könige. Zwischen Kooperation und Konfrontation, Berlin, 105–131.

Bringmann, K. 2004. Gymnasion und griechische Bildung im Nahen Osten, in: D. Kah and P. Scholz (edd.), Das hellenistische Gymnasion, Berlin and Boston, 323–333.

Capdetrey, L. 2007. Le pouvoir séleucide. Territoire, administration, finances d'un royaume hellénistique (312–129 avant J.-C.). Paris.

Chrubasik, B. 2016. Kings and Usurpers in the Seleukid Empire. The Men Who Would Be King. Oxford.

Chrubasik, B. 2017. From Pre-Makkabaean Judaea to Hekatomnid Karia and Back Again. The Question of Hellenization, in: B. Chrubasik and D. King (edd.), Hellenism and the Local Communities of the Eastern Mediterranean. 400 BCE–250 CE, Oxford, 83–109.

Clancier, P. 2017. The Polis of Babylon. An Historiographical Approach, in: B. Chrubasik and D. King (edd.), Hellenism and the Local Communities of the Eastern Mediterranean. 400 BCE–250 CE, Oxford, 53–81.

Cohen, G. M. 2006. The Hellenistic Settlements in Syria, the Red Sea Basin, and North Africa. Berkeley.

Clancier, P. und J. Monerie. 2014. Les sanctuaires babyloniens à l'époque hellénistique. Évolution d'un relais du pouvoir, in: Topoi 19, 181–237.

Curty, O. 2015. Gymnasiarchika. Recueil et analyse des inscriptions de l'époque hellénistique en l'honneur des gymnasiarques. Paris.

Doran, R. 2016. Resistance and Revolt. The Case of the Maccabees, in: J.J. Collins and J.G. Manning (edd.), Revolt and Resistance in the Ancient Classical World and the Near East. In the Crucible of Empire, Leiden, 175–188.

Dreyer, B. 2004. Die Neoi im hellenistischen Gymnasion, in: D. Kah and P. Scholz (edd.), Das hellenistische Gymnasion, Berlin and Boston, 211–236.

Eckhardt, B. 2013. Ethnos und Herrschaft. Politische Figurationen judäischer Identität von Antiochos III. bis Herodes I. Berlin and Boston.

Eckhardt, B. 2014. Vom Volk zur Stadt? Ethnos und Polis im hellenistischen Orient, in: JSJ 45, 199–228.

Eckhardt, B. 2018. Die "hellenistische Krise" und der Makkabäeraufstand in der neueren Diskussion, in: TLZ 143, 983–998.

Eckhardt, B. 2019. Some Aspects of the History of Private Associations in the Ancient Levant, in: AncSoc 49, 1–39.

Engels, D. 2014. 'Da richteten sie in Jerusalem ein Gymnasion her, wie es auch die Heiden hatten'. Das Gymnasion von Jerusalem und der Aufstand der Makkabäer: Sport, Religion und Politik, in: Electrum 21, 43–71.

Feissel, D. 1985. Deux listes de quartiers d'Antioche astreints au creusement d'un canal (73-74 après J.-C.), in: Syria 62, 77–103.

Fischer-Bovet, C. 2014. Army and Society in Ptolemaic Egypt. Cambridge.

Geller, M.J. and Potts, D.T. 2015. The Gymnasium at Babylon and Jerusalem, in: M.J. Geller (ed.), The Archaeology and Material Culture of the Babylonian Talmud, Leiden, 387–395.

Gauthier, P. 1995. Notes sur le rôle du gymnase dans les cités hellénistiques, in: M. Wörrle and P. Zanker (edd.), Stadtbild und Bürgerbild im Hellenismus, München, 1–11.

Gorre, G. and S. Honigman. 2013. Kings, Taxes and High Priests: Comparing the Ptolemaic and Seleukid Policies, in: S. Bussi (ed.), Egitto. Dai Faraoni agli Arabi, Pisa, 105–119.

Graslin-Thomé, L. 2014. De Jérusalem à Babylone. Les relations entre le temple de Jérusalem et les souverains achéménides et hellénistiques à la lumière des sources mésopotamiennes, in: Topoi 19, 57–100.

Graslin-Thomé, L. 2017. La règne d'Antiochos III vu depuis Babylone: Antiochos III dans les sources Cuneiforms, in: C. Feyel and L. Graslin-Thomé (edd.), Antiochos III et l'Orient, Nancy, 211–242.

Groß-Albenhausen, K. 2004. Bedeutung und Funktion der Gymnasien für die Hellenisierung des Ostens, in: D. Kah and P. Scholz (edd.), Das hellenistische Gymnasion, Berlin and Boston, 313–322.

Gruen, E. S. 1993. Hellenism and Persecution: Antiochus IV and the Jews, in: P. Green (ed.), Hellenistic History and Culture, Berkeley at al., 238–264.

Hin, S. 2007. Class and Society in the Cities of the Greek East: Education during the Ephebeia, in: AncSoc 37, 141–166.

Honigman, S. 2014. Tales of High Priests and Taxes. The Books of the Maccabees and the Judean Rebellion against Antiochos IV. Berkeley.

Hoover, O. 2010. Handbook of Coins of the Southern Levant. Phoenicia, Southern Koile Syria (including Judaea), and Arabia. Fifth to First Centuries BC. Lancaster.

Jonnes, L. and Ricl, M. 1997. A New Royal Inscription from Phrygia Paroreios: Eumenes II Grants Tyriaion the Status of a Polis, in: EA 29, 1–30.

Kayser, F. 2013. Les communautés ethniques du type politeuma dans l'Égypte hellénistique, in: F. Delrieux and O. Mariaud (edd.), Communautés nouvelles dans l'Antiquité grecque. Mouvements, integrations et representations, Chambéry, 121–153.

Kennell, N.M. 2005. New Light on 2 Maccabees 4:7–15, in: JJS 56, 10–24.

Kennell, N.M. 2013. Who Were the Neoi?, in: P. Martzavou and N. Papazarkadas (edd.), Epigraphical Approaches to the Post-Classical Polis. Fourth Century BC to Second Century CE., Oxford, 217–232.

Kosmin, P.J. 2019. Remaking a City: Sardis in the Long Third Century, in: A. M. Berlin and P. J. Kosmin (edd.), Spear-Won Land. Sardis from the King's Peace to the Peace of Apamea, Madison, 75–90.

Kruse, T. 2015. Ethnic Koina and Politeumata in Ptolemaic Egypt, in: V. Gabrielsen and C.A. Thomsen (edd.), Private Associations and the Public Sphere, Copenhagen, 270–300.

Lazaridou, K. D. 2015. Ἐφηβαρχικὸς νόμος ἀπὸ τὴν Ἀμφίπολη, in: AEph. 154, 1–45.

Lichtenberger, A. 2017. Die Jerusalemer Religionsreform im Kontext. Antiochos IV., Antiochia und Zeus Olympios, in: F. Avemarie and P. Bukovec and S. Krauter and M. Tilly (edd.), Die Makkabäer, Tübingen, 1–20.

Ma, J. 2005. Antiochos III and the Cities of Western Asia Minor. 2nd ed. Oxford.

Ma, J. 2012. Relire les *Institutions des Séleucides* de Bickerman, in: S. Benoist (ed.), Rome, a City and Its Empire in Perspective. The Impact of the Roman World through Fergus Millar's Research, Bonn, 59–84.

Mania, U. 2017. Gymnasia: From a Space to an Institution of Remembrance, in: E. Mortensen and B. Poulsen (edd.), Cityscapes and Monuments of Western Asia Minor. Memories and Identities, Oxford, 77–88.

Migeotte, L. 2013. Les souscriptions dans les associations privées, in: P. Fröhlich and P. Hamon (edd.), Groupes et associations dans les cités grecques (IIIe siècle av. J.-C. – IIe siècle apr. J.-C.), Geneva, 113–127.

Mileta, C. 2009. Überlegungen zum Charakter und zur Entwicklung der Neuen Poleis im hellenistischen Kleinasien, in: A. Matthaei and M. Zimmermann (edd.), Stadtbilder im Hellenismus, Berlin, 70–89.

Monson, A. 2016. The Jewish High Priesthood for Sale: Farming out Temples in the Hellenistic Near East, in: JJS 67, 15–35.

Perrin-Saminadayar, E. 2013. Stratégies collectives, familiales et individuelles en œuvre au sein de l'éphébie attique: l'instrumentalisation d'une institution publique (IIIe s. av. J.-C.-IIe s. apr. J.-C.), in: P. Fröhlich and P. Hamon (edd.), Groupes et associations dans les cités grecques (IIIe siècle av. J.-C. – IIe siècle apr. J.-C.), Geneva, 159–175.

Ramsey, G. 2019. Generals and Cities in Late-Seleukid and Early-Parthian Babylonia, in: A. Coşkun and D. Engels (edd.), Rome and the Seleukid East, Brussels, 435–456.

Rousset, D. 2017. Considérations sur la loi éphébarchique d'Amphipolis, in: REA 119, 49–84.

Sartre, M. 2009. Histoires grecques. Snapshots from Antiquity. Cambridge M.A. and London.

Savalli-Lestrade, I. 2018. Nouvelles considérations sur le dossier épigraphique de Toriaion, in : ZPE 205, 165–177.

Scholz, P. 2015. Städtische Honoratiorenherrschaft und Gymnasiarchie in der Kaiserzeit, in P. Scholz and D. Wiegandt (edd.), Das kaiserzeitliche Gymnasion, Berlin, 79–96.

Schuler, C. 1999. Kolonisten und Einheimische in einer attalidischen Polisgründung, in: ZPE 128, 124–132.

Schuler, C. 2004. Die Gymnasiarchie in hellenistischer Zeit, in: D. Kah and P. Scholz (edd.), Das hellenistische Gymnasion, Berlin, 163–92.

Schwartz, D. R. 2008. 2 Maccabees. Berlin.

Seyer, M. 2019. Some Aspects of the Urbanistic Development in Limyra in the Hellenistic and Early Roman Periods, in: RA 67, 375–389.

Thonemann, P. 2008. Cistophoric Geography: Toriaion and Kormasa, in: NC 168, 43–60.

Van Bremen, R. 2013. Neoi in Hellenistic Cities: Age Class, Institution, Association?, in: P. Fröhlich and P. Hamon (edd.), Groupes et associations dans les cités grecques (IIIe siècle av. J.-C. – IIe siècle apr. J.-C.), Chambéry, 31–58.

Van der Spek, R. 2009. Multi-Ethnicity and Ethnic Segregation in Hellenistic Babylon, in: T. Derks and N. Roymans (edd.), Ethnic Constructs in Antiquity. The Role of Power and Tradition, Amsterdam, 101–115.

Wörrle, M. 2011. Epigraphische Forschungen zur Geschichte Lykiens X: Limyra in seleukidischer Hand, in: Chiron 41, 377–415.

The Origins and Function of Hellenistic Patterns in the Hasmonean Kingship

Edward Dąbrowa

There is no doubt that the Hasmonean kingship contained elements of a Hellenistic monarchy. Yet there is disagreement among scholars regarding their significance and functions. This lack of consensus is largely caused by the difficulties caused by the very classification of the power model created by the rulers of Judaea, since all the male rulers from the Hasmonean family held both religious and secular power. Synonymous with the former was the function of high priest, and with the latter was the use of first the title of ethnarch and later king. Where scholars disagree is the issue of which of these two components of their rule was dominant. Those who favour the view whereby the secular aspect was in the ascendancy refer to this pattern of government as the Royal Priesthood. Their counterparts who point to a greater significance of religious aspects in the governmental system created by the Hasmoneans, on the other hand, call it the Priestly Monarchy.[1] A characteristic that the two models have in common is the presence of elements of Hellenistic origin. We are therefore justified in asking what function these elements fulfilled in the Hasmonean kingship. First, however, we should consider which of the Hellenistic patterns was adopted by the rulers of Judaea, as well as when and in which circumstances this took place.

From a formal point of view, the introduction of a monarchical system of government in Judaea came in 104 BCE, when Aristobulus I adopted the royal title (βασιλεὺς). However, this event should be treated as an act that concluded the long period of formation of this governmental model. The sources leave no doubt that the scope of the authority of Aristobulus's I predecessors – Jonathan, Simon, and John Hyrcanus – was so large that, regardless of the titles they used, their rules were monocratic. This is why we use the concept of the Hasmonean kingship to refer to the model of rule in the entire period of their rule over Judaea.

This matter is the chronological framework of our reflections. There is no doubt that they must focus on the period when the Hasmoneans rule became stronger, since only then were they able to take full advantage of the means for strengthening their leadership and creating their own image. This formula certainly did not include the period of the uprising battles under the leadership of Mattathias and Judah Maccabee, whose main objective was to

---

[1] On the discussion of the nature of Hasmonean rule, see Goodblatt 1994; Rooke 1998; 2000; van der Kooij 2007, 263; Regev 2013, 171–173.

defend Jewish religious tradition, rather than to free Judaea from the suzerainty of the Seleucids. The nature of this struggle also meant that any attempts to refer to the Hellenistic governmental models were out of the question. This also applies to the initial period of the activity of Jonathan, who became the leader of the Hasmonean faction after Judah Maccabee's death. A complete change in the nature of his leadership took place only with the rivalry for the throne of Syria between Demetrius I and Alexander Balas. At this point, in exchange for backing Alexander in 152 BCE, Jonathan received from him a nomination for the position of high priest of the Jerusalem Temple (1 Macc 10, 20; Flav. Jos. ant. Jud. 13, 45). This act was tantamount to official recognition of his leadership in Judaea. This extremely important moment marks the beginning of the period of interest to us; its end came in 63 BCE, with Judaea's loss of independence.[2]

Owing to its political dimension, it seems natural to pinpoint Jonathan's nomination as the starting point for the discussion on the origin and function of the Hellenistic models in the Hasmonean kingship. In spite of the religious nature of this position, Jonathan became not only the religious leader of the Jews, but also a political ally of the king of Syria. The position of high priest lost its purely religious character as early as the rule of Antiochus IV. On account of the tough financial position resulting from the need to pay a contribution imposed on Antiochus III for the lost war in 190–188 BCE against Rome as well as the significant expenditure involved in rebuilding the state's power, Antiochus IV agreed to entrust Jason with the position of high priest of the Jerusalem Temple – although Onias was incumbent – in return for a promised sizable payment to the royal treasury (2 Macc. 4, 7–10). When Jason failed to fulfil his obligations, Antiochus IV had no scruples in awarding the position to Menelaus, also in return for the promise of payment (2 Macc 4, 24–25). Upon taking up the role, Menelaus turned out to be more of a ruthless official of the king than a priest. His successor, Alcimus (2 Macc 14, 3-14), also served the Syrian king with similar zeal. This radical transformation in the manner of exercising the function of high priest, sanctified by Jewish tradition, meant that from Antiochus IV onwards, the high priests, named by the rulers of Syria, in fact became royal officials with a wide range of political power, which they used for carrying out the political and administrative tasks imposed on them.

With the nomination of Jonathan, however, came honours which none of his predecessors were permitted (1 Macc 10, 20; Flav. Jos. ant. Jud. 13, 45). Alexander Balas included him in the lowest-ranking circle of "royal

---

[2]   Owing to the exceptional circumstances of Antigonus Mattathias' assumption of power, we will omit the brief period of his rule here.

Origins and Function of Hellenistic Patters in Hasmonean Kingship   201

friends".[3] In so doing, he also bestowed upon him the purple robes that were an external attribute of belonging to this group,[4] as well as a gold crown, the symbol of the high priest's power in the Jerusalem Temple.[5]

Alexander Balas soon showed further signs of favour to Jonathan. After his victory over Demetrius I, the Syrian king decided to marry the daughter of Ptolemy VI, Cleopatra. The wedding ceremony was to take place in Ptolemais, and to be attended by both kings (1 Macc 10, 48–58). Jonathan was also invited to participate (1 Macc 10, 59; Flav. Jos. ant. Jud. 13, 83). In the course of the ceremony, Alexander once again publicly bestowed the purple robes upon him, and he took an honorary place at the king's side (1 Macc 10, 62–63; Flav. Jos. ant. Jud. 13, 84–85). Further important honours granted to Jonathan during his stay in Ptolemais were his inclusion among the "first friends of the king", which put him considerably higher in the hierarchy of ranks of royal friends, as well as according him with military and administrative power in Judaea.[6] Certainly, Alexander Balas also used his authority to support Jonathan in the struggle with his political opponents (cf. 1 Macc 10, 61, 63–64). In his dealings with Alexander Balas and Ptolemy VI, Jonathan acted in accordance with the protocol of the Hellenistic courts. He arrived at the next meeting with Ptolemy with the pomp befitting his position, and bestowed his royal hosts and the members of the accompanying retinues valuable gifts reflecting their rank (1 Macc 10, 60). For his military services in the victorious campaign against Apollonius, a general fighting under the banner of Demetrius II, the latest pretender to the throne of Syria, Alexander Balas awarded him with the highest court honour, membership in the group of royal kinsmen (συγγενής) as well as award of Ekron (1 Macc 10, 89; Flav. Jos. ant. Jud. 13, 102). The attribute of belonging to the ruler's nearest circles was the privilege of wearing a golden buckle.[7]

The victory that Demetrius II soon earned over Alexander Balas neither affected Jonathan's position in Judaea nor had a negative influence on his relations with the new ruler of Syria. The power that Jonathan had at the

---

[3]   It is likely that there was a hierarchy of four ranks of "royal friends" in the Seleucid court, three of which are attested in sources; cf. Bikerman 1938, 40–42. For more on the role and duties of *philoi*, see Bikerman 1938, 46–50; Savalli-Lestrade 1998; Dąbrowa 2010a, 126, note 45 (more bibliographical references).

[4]   Bikerman 1938, 42.

[5]   Bikerman 1938, 44.

[6]   καὶ ἐδόξασν αὐτὸν ὁ βασιλεὺς καὶ ἔγραψεν αὐτὸν τῶν πρώτων φίλων καὶ ἔθετο αὐτὸν στρατηγὸν καὶ μεριδάρχην: 1 Macc 10: 65. Based on this source, it is hard to assess the nature of this nomination. However, the context of the events it describes suggests that their objective was Alexander Balas' formal recognition of Jonathan's military and political leadership in Judaea. The nominations also put Jonathan among the ranks of the Syrian king's official allies.

[7]   Bikerman 1938, 42–44.

time dissuaded Demetrius II from opposing him, although the Judaean leader's political opponents were urging him to engage in such a confrontation and Jonathan himself created a pretext for this because, exploiting the confusion that the change in ruler on the Syrian throne brought, he attempted to remove the Syrian garrison from Jerusalem by force. However, Demetrius II was concerned with his own problems, and therefore preferred to establish mutual relations on the basis of an accord. This was his aim in summoning Jonathan for the meeting in Ptolemais (1 Macc 11, 20–22; Flav. Jos. ant. Jud. 13, 123). The latter arrived with a retinue and generous gifts with which he won the favour of the king and his court (1 Macc 11, 23–24). As a result, Demetrius gave him a guarantee of support in fighting his political opponents, agreed to his becoming the high priest, awarded him a place among the "first royal friends"[8], and confirmed all the honours that Alexander Balas had bestowed upon Jonathan (1 Macc 11, 26–27; Flav. Jos. ant. Jud. 13, 124–125). In spite of these gestures of friendship from both parties and Jonathan's provision of military support to the Syrian king in his struggle with internal opposition, their mutual relations were not the best. When the young Antiochus VI was placed on the throne of Syria by Tryphon, a rebel general of Demetrius II, Jonathan had no hesitation in taking the new ruler's side.

This decision brought him significant political benefits and honours. Antiochus VI confirmed his function as high priest, incorporated him among his circle of "friends" and bestowed valuable presents upon him. He also permitted him to drink from gold cups and wear the purple robes and a golden buckle (1 Macc 11, 57–58; Flav. Jos. ant. Jud. 13, 145–146). Owing to the nature of these privileges, available only for the "royal kinsmen", we can assume that Jonathan was again included in the highest rank of dignitaries.[9]

The history of Jonathan's career portrays him as a skilful and effective politician who quickly managed to adopt the behaviours typical of members of Hellenistic courts to ensure himself a strong position in relations with them. At the same time, his role in the Hellenistic "theatre of power" meant that the symbols of power that Jews had previously associated mostly with a civilisation hostile to them were transferred to Judaea in a natural fashion.

Simon, who took his brother's place, soon entered into relations with Demetrius II, expecting him to acknowledge his rule over Judaea without reservations given his own difficult situation owing to the struggle with Tryphon. His calculations were correct, and Demetrius indeed confirmed his status as high priest and ruler of Judaea and included him among his "friends"

---

[8] Jonathan did not keep the rank of "royal kinsman" that he had previously acquired, as upon coming to the throne, each of the rulers of Syria was not fettered by his predecessor's decisions regarding the people with whom they collaborated, and was able to choose as he saw fit; cf. Bikerman 1938, 41.

[9] Cf. Bikerman 1938, 43–44.

Origins and Function of Hellenistic Patters in Hasmonean Kingship   203

(1 Macc 13, 36). Demetrius II's declaration had far-reaching political consequences. Simon's supporters recognised it as the beginning of the era of Judaea's independence, and introduced a practice of dating documents according to a calendar corresponding to the years of his rule (1 Macc 13, 41–42; Flav. Jos. ant. Jud. 13, 213–214). This practice was only previously employed in Judaea by the chancellery of the Seleucids to refer to the rulers of Syria. Shortly thereafter, Jerusalem was the site of a major gathering of supporters of the Hasmoneans representing various groups of inhabitants of Judaea. The resolutions of this assembly formed the basis of the political system of the Jewish state. They specified the scope of Simon's rule (and that of his successors) and determined its insignias. Simon was accorded the exclusive right to wear purple robes and a golden buckle (1 Macc 14, 44), and one cannot fail to notice that this privilege corresponded precisely with the honours to which dignitaries belonging to the "kinsmen" of Syrian rulers were entitled. It is also worth noting a particular detail in the resolutions of the "great assembly": the decision to engrave its contents on bronze plaques. These were then to be placed on public view within the Jerusalem Temple (1 Macc 14, 48). This is a well-known practice from the Hellenistic world.[10]

A new element was added to the insignias of power assigned to the Judaean ruler only in the rule of Aristobulus I, when he adopted the royal title.[11] His new status was marked by a diadem (Flav. Jos. bell. Jud. 1, 70; ant. Jud. 13, 301; 20, 241), a symbol of royal power characteristic of Hellenistic rulers.[12] Here we should stress that the kings of Judaea drew from Hellenistic tradition not only external symbols of power, but also its personal character.[13]

As a result of the Hasmoneans' coming to power in Judaea, a court emerged around them that was necessary for effective government. We have no sources indicting its structure and how it functioned during the rule of Jonathan and Simon, although there is no doubt that it *did* exist, at least in Simon's time (1 Macc 15, 32–36). Based on what we know about the royal courts of Aristobulus I, however, we can state that they were largely modelled on Hellenistic courts.[14] Imitation of the practices known from Hellenistic monarchies is also visible in military affairs. Such a practice imported to Judaea was the custom of its rulers, starting from John Hyrcanus, maintaining

---

[10] Gruen 1998, 35; van Henten 2001; Krentz 2001.

[11] According to Strabo's account (16,2,40), the first of the Hasmoneans to adopt the title of king was Alexander Jannaeus. However, scholars unanimously question its credibility: Gruen 1998, 25 and note 105.

[12] Regarding the origin of the diadem and the associated ideological contents, see Ritter 1965; Schwentzel 2012, 183–184; Haake 2012; Haake 2014.

[13] Cf. Dąbrowa 2010a, 114–115; Regev 2013, 131–133.

[14] Cf. Dąbrowa 2010a, 126–129. For more on the subject of the various aspects of the organisation, functions and working of the Hellenistic royal courts, see Regev 2013, 135–136; Strootman 2014.

204   Edward Dąbrowa

units of mercenaries recruited among the peoples inhabiting Asia Minor and
the Balkans.[15]

A number of symbols of Hellenistic lineage can also be observed in
the Hasmoneans' minting. However, the character as well as the iconography
of this minting permit interpretations that go beyond the Hellenistic canon.[16]
The rulers of Judaea minted low-denomination coins from bronze, which also
indicates that they were intended for circulation within their state borders.[17]
The images used on the coins were therefore meant for addressing contents
solely to the rulers' own subjects. To this end, the Hasmoneans used symbols
known from Hellenistic iconography, but assigned new meanings to them to
respond to the needs of their own propaganda programme.[18] To express
these contents, they employed not only borrowed symbols, but also a unique
symbolic language. The legends on most of the coins they minted were in
Hebrew (only a few issues had legends in Aramaic), but the writing used resembled Paleo-Hebrew script. Imitation of this was an intentional reference
to biblical tradition.[19] A particular characteristic of these legends that set them
apart from those of the Hellenistic rulers was the fact that the vast majority
of them referred to the function of religious leaders held by the Hasmoneans.
Their political leadership was reflected only on the coins minted by Alexander
Jannaeus.[20] These can be divided into three groups, each of them with obverses in Greek. On the coins of one group, on the obverse the ruler's name

---

[15] Cf. Flav. Jos. ant. Jud. 13, 374; 377–378; Dąbrowa 2010a, 160–162.
[16] Cf. Kanael 1963, 44–45; Hoover 1994, 41-55; Jacobson 2000, 73–80; Kindler 2000, 317–
      323; Meshorer 2001, 33–37; Hoover 2003, 29–37; Schwentzel 2007, 138–148; Lichten-
      berger 2013, 71–74; Regev 2013, 199–214; Schwentzel 2014, 121–122; Lykke 2015, 43–
      47, 51.
[17] Cf. Meshorer 2001, 32–33; Schwentzel 2014, 119–120. Of marginal significance in the
      Hasmoneans' minting were coins struck from lead, with a legend bearing the name of
      Alexander Janneus and his royal title on the obverse in Greek and on the reverse in Ara-
      maic; cf. Hendin 1994–99, 63–64; Meshorer 2001, 211 (Group M); Fontanille 2007, 91–
      92, no. 2. On the obverse of these coins is an image of an upturned anchor. The reasons
      for this issue are unknown. Most finds of them come from the area of Transjordan, which
      might suggest that this was the location of the mint where they were struck: Meshorer
      2001, 47–48.
[18] Regev 2013, 199–201; Lichtenberger 2013, 72–74; Schwentzel 2014, 121–127; Lykke
      2015, 51–52. There is a lack of agreement among scholars not only on the origin of the
      individual symbols used in Hasmonean minting, but also their meaning; cf. Hoover 1994;
      Kindler 2000; Hoover 2003; Main 2006. The reason for this is the debate over whether
      the Hasmonean state was of the Hellenistic or national type. Choosing one of these op-
      tions determines the way in which we interpret the images on the coins of the Judean
      rulers. Besides, political meanings are also ascribed to certain iconographic elements,
      which could explain the reasons for their use in the minting of the rulers of Judaea.
[19] Cf. Meshorer 2001, 48–49. See also Hanson 1964, 26–42; Lykke 2015, 47–50.
[20] The unique character of these issues makes them the subject of interest of many research-
      ers seeking to explain the reasons for this: Schwentzel 2014, 129.

is accompanied by a royal title (ΑΛΕΞΑΝΔΡΟΥ ΒΑΣΙΛΕΩΣ) as well as an image of an upturned anchor, while the reverse features a Hebrew legend, also with the royal title, and an image of a star and diadem.[21] All these iconographic elements are also present on the second type of coins. The two types are distinguished by their weight as well as the fact that on the obverse of the second type, the Greek legend, with the royal title and king's name, is accompanied by the number 25 (ΒΑΣΙΛΕΩΣ ΑΛΕΞΑΝΔΡΟΥ/ ΛΚΕ), while on the reverse is a legend in Aramaic (MLK' 'LKSNDRWS ŠNT KH), also with the number 25, corresponding to the years of Alexander Jannaeus' rule.[22] The third group of coins bears the legend ΑΛΕΞΑΝΔΡΟΥ ΒΑΣΙΛΕΩΣ on the obverse, encircling an image of an upturned anchor inside a diadem, and on the reverse it has an image of a lily flower with the Hebrew inscription YHWNTN HMLK.[23] Although the iconography of these types of coins is distinguished by the presence of obvious Hellenistic influences, as in the case of symbolism of coins from other Hasmonean issues, its contents are mostly addressed to their own subjects.[24] The final group of coins on which the name and royal title of Alexander Jannaeus appear have a legend only in Hebrew, while the symbols represented on them are Jewish in their contents.[25]

While pointing out the presence of various Hellenistic elements in the Hasmonean kingship and in the organisation of their state, we should note that not all the characteristics and elements of the style of rule of the monarchs of the Hellenistic world are reflected in the actions of the rulers of Judaea. Striking is the lack of any actions from their side that would suggest support for Greek culture[26] or a friendly attitude towards the Greek cities under their rule.[27] There are also no traces of their having conducted a broader urbanisation programme.[28] Among the elements present in their political actions that can be regarded as invoking practices known from the Hellenistic world, we can count the Hasmoneans' efforts to form an official

---

[21] Meshorer 2001, 209–201 (Group K). Cf. Kindler 2000, 320; Schwentzel 2007, 143; Schwentzel 2012, 184–186.

[22] Meshorer 2001, 210 (Group L); cf. Kindler 2000, 321. This is the only known type of dated coin minted during Hasmonean rule. The date on this coin allows us to state that it was minted in 78 BCE.

[23] Meshorer 2001, 211 (Group N).

[24] Meshorer 2001, 37–38; Schwentzel 2007, 143–145; Regev 2013, 211–214.

[25] Meshorer 2001, 211 (Group O).

[26] Certain unspecified pro-Greek sympathies can be suspected only of Aristobulus I, perhaps for this reason known as Philhellene (Flav. Jos. ant. Jud. 13, 318). But the lack of any sources on this subject prevents us from determining in what way and regard these sympathies were manifested.

[27] Cf. Gruen 1998, 26. Based on archaeological finds in various sites, however, we can assert that hostility towards Greeks did not mean that the Hasmoneans entirely destroyed the cities they lived in; cf. Safrai 2000.

[28] Cf. Dąbrowa 2020, 284–293.

historical source legitimising their position as the family chosen by God to lead the Jews,[29] as well as the naming of the fortresses they built after family members.[30] Bearing in mind all the practices of the Hasmoneans referring to Hellenistic traditions and models, we can conclude that the list of them, when compared to other Hellenised states of the Middle East, is too modest to regard the model of kingship they created as being close to the canon of the typical Hellenistic monarchy.[31] This conclusion require the question as to the reasons for which the Hasmoneans adopted Hellenistic patterns and the objectives they were to serve.

To find the answers to these questions, we should examine the way in which the Hasmoneans presented their religious and secular power. What should be discussed first are the issues regarding their function as high priests of the Jerusalem Temple. Undoubtedly, scholars pay most attention to the dispute provoked by the Pharisees during John Hyrcanus' rule regarding the Hasmoneans' right to this position on account of their origin. They questioned the purity of Hyrcanus' origin because his mother was said to have been a hostage in the hands of the Seleucids. Although there was little cause to suggest that this accusation was baseless, it also appeared in the context of the conflict of the Pharisees with Alexander Jannaeus.[32] The scale of this conflict meant that scholars have not devoted sufficient attention to other aspects of the Judaean rulers' holding of the function of high priest, and only a few issues have been of interest to them. Significant progress in research has only come in recent years. This can be seen in the studies of Eyal Regev, which provided us with a complete picture of Hasmonean religious leadership. Regev's analysis of written sources and archaeological and numismatic data enabled him to portray them against the wide background of their religious and social policy as well as through propaganda contents. His findings irrefutably prove that in the kingship model created by the Hasmoneans, the religious aspect of their rule considerably outweighed the political dimension.[33]

Regev's conclusions depict the Hasmoneans as rulers who, contrary to their critics' allegations, treated the duties of high priest extremely seriously.

---

[29] The largest contribution to painting this picture was made by the First Book of Maccabees. The pro-Hasmonean sympathies of its anonymous author leave no doubt. Scholars are increasingly of the opinion that 2 Macc also has pro-Hasmonean undertones; cf. Dąbrowa 2010a, 139–146; Honigman 2014.

[30] Cf. Dąbrowa 2010a, 136.

[31] Cf. Regev 2013, 129–141. Owing to the nature of this article, the present author omitted to present the full catalogue of those symbols, models and practices to which the Hellenistic lineage is assigned and whose presence is discerned in Judaea under Hasmonean rule; see Mendels 1997, 55–79; Gruen 1998, 1–40; Rajak 2001b, 61–79.

[32] Cf. Friedlaender 1913/14, 443–448; Rabin 1956, 3–11; Geller 1979, 202–211; Regev 2013, 155–160, 215–217.

[33] Regev 2013, 103–128.

They built their authority as religious leaders upon actions designed to ensure that the Jerusalem Temple maintained its status as the most important sanctuary of Judaism. Among the acts that supported this was the destruction of the Samaritan temple on the Mt. Gerizim, ordered by John Hyrcanus.[34] His successors also spared no expense in developing Jerusalem and its sanctuary.[35] In their dynastic propaganda, the Hasmoneans liked to promote the image of the family as having been entrusted by God with the mission of defending the religion of their ancestors and its shrine. The significance of the Temple in the Hasmoneans' religious policy is confirmed by 2 Maccabees, whose ideological message scholars often – wrongly – contrast with 1 Maccabees.[36]

Although various controversies and criticisms were aimed at the Hasmoneans by their opponents regarding their holding of the function of high priest, there is no doubt that they took advantage of the power it gave them. They were able to unite religious life in their state by pursuing a policy of forced Judaisation of the non-Jewish sections of the population[37], carry out significant reforms strengthening the economic position of the priesthood, and even introduce to religious life new elements of religious customs and ritual.[38]

One way in which the Hasmoneans created their own image of their religious leaders was their minting. From when John Hyrcanus became the first of the Hasmoneans to issue his own coins, they recorded the fact that the dynasty held the function of high priest. This was testified both by images

---

[34] The destruction of the temple on Mount Gerizim was carried out by Antiochus, John Hyrcanus' son: Flav. Jos. bell. Jud. 1, 63; ant. Jud. 13, 255–256. Cf. Dąbrowa 2006, 115–118; 2010b, 10.

[35] As high priest, Simon was also awarded a full range of administrative power over the Temple and its personnel by a resolution of the "great assembly" (1 Macc 14, 42). Cf. also Galor/Bloedhorn 2013, 65, 69–71; Regev 2013, 84–93; Bieberstein 2017, 104–115.

[36] Cf. Honigman 2014.

[37] Cf. Dąbrowa 2006, 113–118; 2010a, 75–78 (with further bibliograhical references); 2010b; Regev 2013, 273–278. Sources show that Simon, John Hyrcanus, Aristobulus I and Alexander Jannaeus enforced compulsory Judaisation in various ways and with differing intensity. This policy was particularly intensive with regard to the inhabitants of the lands which the Hasmoneans conquered. There is no doubt that its objective was the religious unification of the state; cf. Dąbrowa 2010b, 8–12. A separate matter is the fact that the Hasmoneans also carried out compulsory Judaisation of the Greeks, as mentioned, in reference to the Greek inhabitants of Pella, by Josephus (ant. Jud. 13,397). According to some scholars, there is no other unequivocal evidence that the rulers of Judaea actually enforced this practice; cf. Gruen 1998, 27 and note 118; Schwartz 2011, 339–359.

[38] During the Hasmonean rule, the obligation to pay the so-called half-shekel tax was probably introduced, and the custom of pilgrimage to Jerusalem become popular: Regev 2013, 73–82, 280–281. Their religious policy also resulted in the propagation among followers of Judaism of the practice of ritual cleansing, which involved construction of a large number of ritual baths (*miqwa'ot*). There is archaeological confirmation of their presence in both private homes and the palace complex built by the Hasmoneans near Jericho.

containing religious contents[39] and by legends in Hebrew or Aramaic. The same formula was followed by the coins of all subsequent rulers of Judaea, whose names were invariably accompanied by the title of high priest. Furthermore, monetary legends also referred to the fact that they presided over the body named *heber ha-yehudim*.[40] The lack of any other information on this assembly means that we are unable to determine its composition and role in the Hasmonean state. Some scholars suggest that it was an organ that represented only a certain part of society, whereas others think it represented the whole of it.[41]

To exercise his religious duties, the high priest was required to wear liturgical robes, which he could use only within the walls of the Jerusalem Temple (cf. Flav. Jos. ant. Jud. 18,91). Religious tradition stretching back to biblical times clearly demonstrated the appearance of these garments (Exodus 28: 2–39; Flav. Jos. bell. Jud. 5,231–236; ant. Jud. 3,159–178; cf. 3,184–187; 215–218). The Hasmoneans' emphasis of their attachment to biblical tradition decidedly excludes the possibility that they would have dared to enrich their liturgical robes with any of the Greek symbols of power, the use of which Simon and his successors gained the exclusive right to based on the resolution of the "great assembly". This suggests that the Hasmoneans appeared in the purple garments decorated with golden buckles, either wearing a diadem or not, only when outside the walls of the Temple, i.e. when functioning as secular leaders. These attributes then served to display their status as ruler. Use of these symbols was necessary in all situations that required their status to be made evident, such as in contacts with the kings of Syria and their emissaries, and during public appearances before their subjects, travels around the country, and military campaigns.

On the basis of these remarks, we can conclude that the Hasmoneans' use of Hellenistic models did not result from their acculturation, but was an imitation dictated by pragmatic concerns. Contacts with the Greek world forced them to make use of the same language of symbols and behaviours that applied there. This was necessary right up to the time when Judaea gained its independence, as it made the Hasmoneans' contacts with their political

---

[39] An image of an expressly religious significance is that depicting a crown of laurel leaves on the obverses of coins with a legend inside containing the title of high priest alongside the name. The Hasmoneans' reference to this symbol clearly serves as a reminder that, together with his nomination for the position of high priest, Jonathan received a golden crown: Meshorer 2001, 35–36; Regev 2013, 201–203.

[40] Leadership of this body is only stated clearly on the coins of John Hyrcanus: Meshorer 2001, 207–209 (Group H, I, J). On the coins of Alexander Jannaeus and Aristobulus (I or II), its name appears next to theirs.

[41] For more on scholars' positions regarding the nature of this body, see Kanael 1963, 44; Sperber 1965, 85–91; Jeselsohn 1980, 13–17; Goodblatt 1998, 8-13; Dąbrowa 2010a, 110; Regev 2013, 186–199; Schwentzel 2014, 127–128.

suzerains, i.e. the rulers of Syria, considerably easier. According Jonathan and Simon honorary court titles and other honours strengthened their position not only in their own country but also beyond its borders, as it allowed them to be incorporated in the structures of the Hellenistic world, without the need to abandon their cultural and religious identity. This also permitted them to reinforce their political leadership over Judaea and to give it the shape sanctioned by the resolutions of the "great assembly". These resolutions lent a new character to the patterns and symbols borrowed from the Hellenistic world. They became part of the Jewish political symbolism, which no longer gave rise to any negative associations, despite its alien origin, and could be used by the successors of Jonathan and Simon without any fear of being exploited in propaganda and self-presentation as well as political practice.[42]

The Hasmoneans' adoption of Hellenistic symbols of monocratic power permitted them to keep the two areas of rule which they exercised – secular and religious – distinctly separate. The symbols of their religious rule was their authority over the Jerusalem Temple and the high priest's liturgical robes, and those of their secular rule were the behaviours, models and symbols adopted from the Hellenistic canon. Their use of these by the individual rulers of Judaea varied considerably over time. The scale of these practices depended upon various factors, which certainly included their personal attitude towards the culture of the Greek world, the intensity of external contacts and the establishment of the monarchy. As kings, the Hasmoneans felt a considerably larger need to demonstrate their position and power than they had when their main position had been high priest. By using ready-made and distinct Hellenistic patterns, they were able to attain this objective more easily.

---

[42] Cf. 1 Macc 13, 27–30; Flav. Jos. ant. Jud. 13, 211–212. For more on this subject: Gruen 1998, 34; Dąbrowa 2010a, 134–146.

Bibliography

Baslez, M.-F. and O. Munnich (edd.) 2014. La Mémoire des persécutions. Autour des livres des Maccabées. Paris and Louvain.

Bieberstein, K. 2017. A Brief History of Jerusalem. From the Earliest Settlement to the Destruction of the City in AD 70. Wiesbaden.

Bikerman, E. 1938. Institutions des Séleucides. Paris.

Day, J. (ed.) 1998. King and Messiah in Israel and the Ancient Near East. Proceedings of the Oxford Old Testament Seminar. Sheffield.

Dąbrowa, E. 2006. Religion and Politics under the Hasmoneans, in: R. Rollinger and B. Truschnegg (edd.), Altertum und Mittelmeerraum: Die antike Welt diesseits und jenseits der Levante. Festschrift für Peter W. Haider zum 60. Geburtstag, Stuttgart, 113–120.

Dąbrowa, E. 2010a. The Hasmoneans and their State. A Study in History, Ideology, and the Institutions. Kraków.

Dąbrowa, E. 2010b. The Hasmoneans and the Religious Homogeneity of their State, in: Scripta Judaica Cracoviensia 8, 7–14.

Dąbrowa, E. 2020. The Hasmoneans' Attitude towards Cities, in: R. Oetjen (ed.), New Perspectives in Seleucid History, Archaeology and Numismatics. Studies in Honor of Getzel M. Cohen, Berlin and Boston, 284–295.

Ehling, E. and G. Weber 2014. Hellenistische Königreiche. Darmstadt.

Fontanille, J.-P. 2007. Two Unrecorded Hasmonean Coins, in: Israel Numismatic Research 2, 89–92.

Friedlaender, I. 1913/14. The Rupture between Alexander Jannai and the Pharisees, in: Jewish Quarterly Review 4, 443–448.

Galor, K. and H. Bloedhorn 2013. The Archaeology of Jerusalem. From the Origins to the Ottomans. New Haven.

Geller, M. J. 1979. Alexander Jannaeus and the Pharisee Rift, in: Journal of Jewish Studies 30, 202–211.

Goodblatt, D. 1994. The Monarchic Principle. Studies in Jewish Self-Government in Antiquity. Tübingen.

Goodblatt, D. 1998. From Judaeans to Israel: Names of Jewish States in Antiquity, in: Journal for the Study of Judaism 29, 1–36.

Gruen, E.S. 1998. Heritage and Hellenism. The Reinvention of Jewish Tradition. Berkeley et al.

Haake, M. 2012. Diadem und *Basileus*. Überlegungen zu einer Insignie und einen Titel in hellenistischer Zeit, in: A. Lichtenberger et al. (edd.), Das Diadem der hellenistischen Herrscher. Übernahme, Transformation oder Neuschöpfung eines Herrschaftszeichens? Kolloquium vom 30.-31. Januar 2009 in Münster, Bonn, 293–313.

Haake, M. 2014. Das Diadem – königliches Symbol in hellenistischer Zeit, in: E. Ehling and G. Weber (edd.), Hellenistische Königreiche, Darmstadt, 24–28.

Hanson, R.S. 1964. Paleo-Hebrew Scripts in the Hasmonean Age, in: Bulletin of the American Schools of Oriental Research 175, 26–42.

Hendin, D. 1994/99. Four New Jewish Lead Coins or Tokens, in: INJ 13, 63–65.

Honigman, S. 2014. Tales of High Priests and Taxes. The Books of the Maccabees and the Judaean Rebellion against Antiochus IV. Berkeley.

Hoover, O.D. 1994. Striking a Pose: Seleucid Types and Machtpolitik on the Coins of John Hyrcanus I, in: The Picus. The Annual Journal of the Classical and Medieval Numismatic Society 3, 41–57.

Hoover, O.D. 2003. The Seleucid Coinage of John Hyrcanus I: the Transformation of a Dynastic Symbol in Hellenistic Judaea, in: American Journal of Numismatics 15, 29–39.

Jacobson, D.M. 2000. The Anchor on the Coins of Judaea, in: Bulletin of the Anglo-Israel Archaeological Society 18, 73–81.

Jeselsohn, D. 1980. Hever Yehudim – A New Coin, in: PEQ 112, 11–17.

Kanael, B. 1963. Ancient Jewish Coins and their Historical Importance, in: Biblical Archaeologist 26(2), 38–62.

Kindler, A. 2000. The Hellenistic Influence on the Hasmonean Coins, in: B. Kluge and B. Weisser (edd.), XII. Internationaler Numismatischer Kongress, Berlin 1997: Akten – Proceedings – Actes, vol. 1, Berlin, 316–323.

Krentz, E. 2001. The Honorary Decree for Simon the Maccabee, in: J.J. Collins and G. E. Sterling (edd.) 2001. Hellenism in the Land of Israel, Notre Dame (Ind.), 146–153.

Lichtenberger, A. et al. (ed.) 2012. Das Diadem der hellenistischen Herrscher. Übernahme, Transformation oder Neuschöpfung eines Herrschaftszeichens? Kolloquium vom 30.-31. Januar 2009 in Münster. Bonn.

Lichtenberger, A. 2013. Anker, Füllhorn, Palmzweig. Motivbeziehungen zwischen 'jüdischen' und 'paganen' Münzen, in: A. Lykke (ed.), Macht des Geldes – Macht der Bilder. Kolloquium zur Ikonographie auf Münzen im ostmediterranen Raum in hellenistisch – römischer Zeit, Wiesbaden, 69–91.

Lykke, A. 2015. Reign and Religion in Palestine. The Use of Sacred Iconography in Jewish Coinage. Wiesbaden.

Main, E. 2006. Des mercenaires « rhodiens » dans la Judée hasmonéenne? Étude du motif floral des monnaies de Jean Hyrcan et Alexandre Jannée, in: Revue des Études Juives 165, 123–146.

Mendels, D. 1997. The Rise and Fall of Jewish Nationalism. Jewish and Christian Ethnicity in Ancient Palestine, 2nd ed. Grand Rapids (Mich.)

Meshorer, Y. 2001. A Treasury of Jewish Coins: From the Persian Period to Bar Kokhba. Jerusalem.

Rabin, C. 1956. Alexander Jannaeus and the Pharisees, in: Journal of Jewish Studies 7, 3–11.

Rajak, T. 2001a. The Jewish Dialogue with Greece and Rome. Studies in Cultural and Social Interaction. Leiden.

Rajak, T. 2001b. The Hasmoneans and the Uses of Hellenism, in: T. Rajak, The Jewish Dialogue with Greece and Rome. Studies in Cultural and Social Interaction, 61–80.

Regev, E. 2013. The Hasmoneans. Ideology, Archaeology, Identity. Göttingen.

Ritter, H.W. 1965. Diadem und Königsherrschaft. Untersuchungen zu Zeremonien und Rechtsgrundlagen des Herrschaftsantritts bei den Persern, bei Alexander dem Grossen und im Hellenismus. München.

Rollinger, R. and B. Truschnegg (edd.) 2006. Altertum und Mittelmeerraum: Die antike Welt diesseits und jenseits der Levante. Festschrift für Peter W. Haider zum 60. Geburtstag. Stuttgart.

Rooke, D.W. 1998. Kingship as Priesthood: the Relationship between the High Priesthood and the Monarchy, in: J. Day (ed.), King and Messiah in Israel and the Ancient Near East. Proceedings of the Oxford Old Testament Seminar, Sheffield, 187–207.

Rooke, D.W. 2000. Zadok's Heirs. The Role and Development of the High Priesthood in Ancient Israel. Oxford.

Safrai, Z. 2000. The Gentile Cities of Judaea: Between the Hasmonean Occupation and the Roman Liberation, in: G. Galil and M. Weinfeld (edd.), Studies in Historical Geography and Biblical Historiography presented to Zecharia Kallai, Leiden, 63–90.

Santinelli-Foltz, E. and C.-G. Schwentzel (edd.) 2012. La puissance royale. Image et pouvoir de l'Antiquité au Moyen Âge. Rennes.

Savalli-Lestrade, I. 1998. Les philoi royaux dans l'Asie hellénistique. Geneva.

Schwartz, D.R. 2011. Yannai and Pella, Josephus and Circumcision, in: Dead Sea Discoveries 18, 339–359.

Schwentzel, C.-G. 2007. La monarchie hasmonéenne d'après le témoignage des monnaies: État juif ou État hellénistique?, in: Res Antiquae 4, 135–148.

Schwentzel, C.-G. 2012. Le *diadèma* et l'aigle : problèmes liés à deux images du pouvoir monarchique en Judée (IIe – Ier siècles av. J.-C.), in: E. Santinelli-Foltz and C.-G. Schwentzel (edd.), La puissance royale. Image et pouvoir de l'Antiquité au Moyen Âge, Rennes, 183–193.

Schwentzel, Chr.-G. 2014. Les choix identitaires des Hasmonéens d'après leurs images monétaires, in : M.F. Baslez and O. Munnich (edd.), La Mémoire des persécutions. Autour des livres des Maccabées, Paris and Louvain, 119–132.

Sperber, D. 1965. A Note on Hasmonean Coin-Legends. Heber and Rosh Heber, in: PEQ 97, 85–93.

Strootman, R. 2014. Courts and Elites in the Hellenistic Empires. The Near East after the Achaemenids, c. 330 to 30 BCE. Edinburg.

Van der Kooij, A. 2007. The Greek Bible and Jewish Concepts of Royal Priesthood and Priestly Monarchy, in: T. Rajak et al. (edd.) Jewish Perspectives on Hellenistic Rulers, Berkeley. 255–264.

Van Henten, J.W. 2001. The Honorary Decree for Simon the Maccabee (1 Macc 14: 25–49) in its Hellenistic Context, in: J.J. Collins and G.E. Sterling (edd.) 2001. Hellenism in the Land of Israel, Notre Dame (Ind.), 116–145.

Lukian and the Hellenistic Legacy

Sabine Müller

Lukian of Samosata might offer an individual example of finding a place in the Middle Ground as cultural accommodation.[1] Born in the capital of the Roman province of Kommagene, according to his own self-ironic comments a "Syrian" or "barbarian" in the sense of being no native speaker of Greek,[2] Lukian studied Greek cultural heritage to such an extent that he became one of the most erudite ancient writers able to point out the shortcomings of contemporary native speakers of Greek regarding their treatment of the Greek Classical and Hellenistic literary legacy that played a most crucial role in the Second Sophistic.[3] Exemplarily, while ridiculing contemporary Atticists using an artificial language by avoiding all vocabulary not attested by Greek classical authors,[4] simultaneously, Lukian demonstrates his own mastery in writing in "an elegant approximation to the classical language."[5]

Lukian's main theme is the relationship of truth and truthfulness with lie and hypocrisy.[6] Systematically vanishing behind various – significantly unheroic – masks,[7] Lukian, the enigmatic distant observer, ridicules stock characters of pseudo-authorities in different social sectors,[8] addressing contemporary issues. One key theme regarding his pseudo-intellectuals is their failure to embody the lessons of *paideia* properly to use the Greek literary heritage for their own and their recipients' moral improvement. It is important to note

---

[1]   On the concept of the Middle Ground see White 1991, 50–53.

[2]   Luk. Bis Acc. 14, 25; 27, 34; Pisc. 19; Ind. 19. Cf. Porod 2013, 10; Hopkinson 2008, 1 (Aramaic as his native language); Swain 2007, 30–34; Karavas 2005, 13; Swain 1996, 299, 302 (Syriac as his native language); Bracht Branham 1989, 32; Jones 1986, 7.

[3]   Cf. Zweimüller 2008, 107; Galli 2007, 10–14; Conolly 2001, 341–342, 349; v. Möllendorff 2000, 3; Schmitz 1997, 44–67, 83–90, 101–109; Anderson 1993, 101–114; Jones 1986, 149.

[4]   Cf. Hopkinson 2008, 6

[5]   Hopkinson 2008, 4. According to Macleod 1974, Lukian's vocabulary chiefly derives from Platon – who plays a central role in his work (cf. Berdozzo 2011, 191, 202–203; Schlapbach 2010, 274; Bracht Branham 1989, 67–80; see also his special treatment in Luk. *VH* II 17) –, Aristophanes and Menander. Lukian also knows how to imitate Thukydides' style or Herodotos' Ionic dialect: Hist. Conscr. 1; 34; 38; 39, 42; 54; 57; Dom. 20. Hopkinson 2008, 6 calls Lukian an atticist writer who also uses *koine* elements.

[6]   Cf. Müller 2014b, 152; Porod 2013, 94; Müller 2013b, 27–29, 35; Berdozzo 2011, 194–195; Petsalis-Diomidis 2010, 55–56, 65; Schlapbach 2010, 253; Zweimüller 2008, 44–45, 130, 138; Gunderson 2007, 479, 482–483; Koulakiotis 2006, 184; Swain 2007, 23; Rütten 1997, 35–37.

[7]   Cf. Baumbach and von Möllendorff 2017, 13; Sidwell 2009, 117; Karavas 2005, 13; Swain 1996, 311–314; Bracht Branham 1989, 32.

[8]   Cf. Swain 2007, 23.

214   Sabine Müller

that, as such, Lukian is not critical of the Greek classical authors or historical
political actors at whose expense he jokes. Rather, he ridicules the phenomenon that instead of critically studying the works from the past, learning from
their knowledge *and* errors, his pseudo-intellectuals treat them as factors for
legitimization of their own claims using them as undisputable testimonies of
the sheer truth while often indulging in pure name-dropping.[9]

Due to the Macedonian rise to hegemony in the 4th century BCE,
Macedonians became part of the Greek collective memory. This paper aims
at exploring which political actors from Argead and Hellenistic times and in
which contexts and for which purpose are mentioned by Lukian. It will be
argued that they appear as correctives to failings of their reception and perception in Lukian's time.

Not surprisingly, the most prominent Macedonians in his work are
the most famous Macedonians in the Second Sophistic in general: Philip II
and Alexander III.[10] As Lukian ridicules the pretentions of contemporary intellectuals using the past to glorify their present status, the marginality of the
other Argeads in his oeuvre mirrors their insignificance as points of reference
in his time.[11] Instructively, Lukian's treatment of Philip in *How to write History*

---

[9]   Cf. Müller 2013a, 188–189; Gilhuly 2007, 67–68; Georgiadou and Larmour 1998, 2–3;
        Rütten 1997, 42–44, 133; Bracht Branham 1989, 4. Exemplarily, by locating Herodotos at
        the Island of the Damned as a punishment for his lies in his *True Stories* (II 31), a sarcastic
        parody of travel-writing in particular and of forms of historiographical verification in gen-
        eral, Lukian does not make fun of Herodotos himself but of those contemporary authors
        who accept everything in his *Histories* as true citing him in order to verify their own claims.
        Cf. Müller 2013a, 181; Georgiadiou and Larmour 1998, 21, 28; Anderson 1976, 68–69,
        72–78.
[10]   Alexander III: only the name: Peregrin. 25; Par. 35–36; Herm. 4; as *persona agens*: Dom. 1;
        Hist. Conscr. 12; 38; 40; VH II 9; Laps. 8–9; Pr. Im. 9; Hdt. Siv. Aet. 5–6; DM 12–14;
        Calumn. 17–18; Ind. 21; Gall. 25; Rh. Pr. 5; Alex. 1; 6; 7; 16; 41; Nav. 28; Philipp II: only
        as a patronym: Nav. 28; Alex. 1; VH II 9; DM 13.1; Nav. 28; in connection with the Attic
        orators: Par. 42; J. Trag. 14; Somn. 12; Ph. Pr. 10; as a *persona agens*: Hist. Conscr. 3; 38;
        Fug. 25; Nec. 17; DM 14; Ind. 21. Cf. Asirvatham 2020; Müller 2020. On Alexander's
        iconic status in Lukian's time: Burliga 2013, 79; Billault 2010, 633–634; Koulakiotis 2006,
        179; Whitmarsh 2005, 66–68.
[11]   Other Argeads: Perdikkas II: (and his anonymous stepmother): Hist. Conscr. 35;
        Archelaos: Par. 35; Hist. Conscr. 1; Amyntas III: DM 14.1; Perdikkas III (?): Ind. 21 (un-
        certain); Olympias: Alex. 7; DM 13.1. Macedonians associated with the Argeads (including
        the Successors): Antipatros: Nav. 33; Laps. 8; Ptolemy: Hist. Conscr. 62 (indirectly as one
        of the Theoi Soteres); Prom. Es 4–5; DM 13.1; DM 13.1; Gall. 25; Calumn. 2–4 (?); Nav.
        28; Laps. 10; Hephaistion: Hdt. Siv. Aet. 5; Calumn. 17–18; DM 14.4; Laps. 8; Pr. Im. 27;
        Kleitos: DM 13.6; DM 14.4; Hist. Conscr. 38; Lysimachos: Icar. 15; Hist Conscr. 1; Se-
        leukos: Gall. 25; Laps. 10; Salt. 58–59; Perdikkas, son of Orontes: Gall. 25; Calumn. 18;
        DM 13.2; Demetrios Poliorketes: Pr. Im. 20; Kassander: Ind. 21. Greeks associated with
        Macedonians: Euripides: Nec. 1; Peregrin. 2; 3; 12; Hist. Conscr. 1; Par. 35; Ind. 19; 27;
        Merc. Cond. 41; Aristotle: DM 12.3; DM 13.4; DM 13.5; Par. 43; Salt. 4; Merc. Cond. 24;
        Eun. 4; 9; Theopompos: Hist. Conscr. 59; Pseudol. 29; Anaxarchos von Abdera: Par. 35–

Lukian and the Hellenistic Legacy 215

shows how he uses him as a corrective and warner against uncritical credulity in his historiographical reception: One point of reference in this alleged manual of ancient historiography – in fact an ironic accumulation of contradictions –[12] is erroneous. The mistake occurs when Lukian recommends that a good historiographer must not be concerned that Philip got his eye shot out by Aster from Amphipolis, the archer in Olynthos.[13] However, the good historiographer will have known that Philip lost his eye during the siege of Methone[14] and the fictitious avenger of Greek freedom, symbolically called Aster, "star" (hinting at a higher force),[15] first visible in Douris' moralistic work,[16] reportedly came from Olynthos, not Amphipolis.[17] Surely voluntarily, Lukian integrates an error about Philip's career in a treatise that pretends to be a manual for historiographers while in fact mirroring shortcomings of contemporary historiography. In this sense, this reference to Philip points at the lack of historical accuracy in contradiction to claims of complete veracity.

Philip's relationship with the Attic orators in Lukian reflects the specific interests of Second Sophistic authors who held the speeches from this "Golden Age" of Greek oratory in honor.[18] Particularly Demosthenes,

---

6; Kallisthenes: DM 13.6; Aristoboulos: Hist. Conscr. 12; Onesikritos: Hist. Conscr. 40; Peregrin. 25; Eumenes of Kardia: Laps. 8. Hellenistic protagonists: Pyrrhos: Ind. 21; Laps. 11; Agathokles Lysimachou: Icar. 15; Antiochos I: Laps. 9; Zeuxis 8–11; Hist. Concr. 35; Salt. 58–59; Icar. 15; Stratonike: Hist. Conscr. 35; Pr. Im. 5–6; Salt. 58; Icar. 15; [Luk.] Syr. D. 17-26; Ptolemy II: Icar. 15; Nav. 28 (?); Ptolemy IV/XII: Calumn. 2-4; 16; Kleopatra VII: Apol. 5; Salt. 37; Alexander I. Balas: Ind. 20; Andriskos (Philip VI): Ind. 20; Sostratos of Knidos: Hist. Conscr. 62. On the insignificance of other Argeads in Second Sophistic literature see Asirvatham 2017, Asirvatham 2020, Müller 2020.

12 These are the most obvious contradictions: advice to tell only the truth (Hist. Conscr. 7) vs. historical errors (Hist. Conscr. 3; 38); no use of poetical language (Hist. Conscr. 8; 22; 46) vs. poetical battle descriptions (Hist. Conscr. 4; 45; 57); advice to tell only useful and true things (Hist. Conscr. 9) vs. reporting amusing and fictitious things (Hist. Conscr. 13; 59-60); no praise (Hist. Conscr. 10; 13; 47) vs. praise (Hist. Conscr. 59–60); advice not to use historiography in favor of one's own advantage (Hist. Conscr. 13) vs. writing about history to become famous (Hist. Conscr. 62); being critical of imitators of classical authors such as Herodotos and Thukydides (Hist. Conscr. 14–19; 26) vs. imitation of passages by Herodotos and Thukydides (Hist. Conscr. 1; 34; 38; 39, 42; 54; 57); no use of mythological comparisons (Hist. Conscr. 19) vs. mythological comparisons (Hist. Conscr. 49); advice to be selective (Hist. Conscr. 20; 27–28; 32) vs. dwelling on trivial matters (Hist. Conscr. 56).

13 Luk. Hist. Conscr. 38.

14 Diod. 16, 4, 5; Just. 7, 6, 14; Theopomp. BNJ 115 F 52.

15 Cf. Pownall 2013, 33–34; Landucci Gattinoni 1997, 90–93.

16 Douris BNJ 76, F 36.

17 [Plut]. Mor. 307 D–F.

18 References to Attic orators: Demosthenes: Merc. Cond. 25; Par. 42; 56; Somn. 12; Ind. 4; Bis Acc. 31; Rh. Pr. 9; 10; 17; 21; J. Trag. 14-15; Aischines: Par. 42; 56; Rh. Pr. 10; Ind. 27 (reference to his speech against Timarchos); Somn. 12; Isokrates: Par. 42; Rh. Pr. 17; Hypereides: Par. 42; 56; Demades: Par. 42; Lykourgos: Par. 42.

famous as Philip's Athenian antagonist, was read as a model of style by Second Sophistic teachers of rhetoric.[19] Mockingly, in *Zeus Rants*, Lukian shows that not even Zeus could measure up to these high standards: When Hermes advises him to deliver one of Demosthenes' speeches against Philip, with only little modification, for this was the *dernier cri* regarding oratory,[20] Zeus duly starts with a speech modelled on the *First Olynthiac* but fails after a few sentences, admitting that his Demosthenes is running short.[21] Probably, Lukian mocks the arrogant self-praise of contemporary orators pretending to be superior to others. In *The Parasite*, mockingly raising parasitic living to the level of a *techne*, Lukian shows his knowledge of Demosthenes' most famous speeches by citing the latter's unflattering polemics against Philip as a scoundrel from Macedonia where one could not even buy a decent slave.[22] However, instead of glorifying the Attic orators, Lukian ridicules these famous role models as corrupted cowards and bigmouths: Demosthenes is accused of having fled from the battlefield of Chaironeia echoing Aischines' reproaches.[23] Aischines and Demades are said to have collaborated with Philokrates betraying Athens to Philip out of fear.[24] Hypereides and Lykourgos are depicted as frightened bigmouths rallying against Philip only in the *ekklesia* or by resolutions written at the safe shelter of their home.[25] Tychiades, one of Lukian's masks, dryly comments: "But they were orators cultivating the delivery of speeches, not virtue."[26] The Attic orators would have been deeply shocked at this remark: According to their own self-images, they were prototypes of the perfect Athenian citizen embodying all civic virtues.[27] However, Lukian certainly did not intend to criticize the Attic orators but ridicule their uncritical glorification based on the admiration of their style by his contemporaries. Therefore, he shows the Attic orators as fallible human beings involved in political structures and events, no iconic superhuman creatures. By stressing that records of their misdeeds were preserved, referring to the

---

[19] Luk. Rh. Pr. 9–10; Cf. Hopkinson 2008, 4.

[20] Luk. J. Trag. 14. In Ind. 27, Lukian also hints at the importance when the protagonist, the ignorant book collector, is asked whether he has read the orators, in particular Aischines' speech *Against Timarchos*.

[21] Luk. J. Trag. 15. Cf. Dem. 1.1. There are other references to speeches by Demosthenes, cf. Luk. Bis Acc. 26 (Dem. 3.1; 18.1); Luk. Merc. Cond. 5 (Dem. 3.33).

[22] Luk. Par. 42: Φίλιππος γὰρ ὁ Μακεδὼν ὄλεθρος, ὅθεν οὐδὲ ἀνδράποδον πρίαιτό τίς ποτε; Dem. 9.31: ὀλέθρου Μακεδόνος, ὅθεν οὐδ᾽ ἀνδράποδον σπουδαῖον οὐδὲν ἦν πρότερον πρίασθαι.

[23] Luk. Par. 42. Cf. Aischin. 3.244; 253.

[24] Luk. Par. 42. In Somn. 12, Lukian refers again to the accusation that Aischines was bribed by Philip.

[25] Luk. Par. 42.

[26] Luk. Par. 43: ἀλλ᾽ οὗτοι μὲν ῥήτορες καὶ λόγους λέγειν ἠσκηκότες, ἀρετὴν δὲ οὔ.

[27] Cf. Aischin. 1, 1–2; 2, 1–4; Dem. 18, 72; 18, 88–89; 18, 247.

forensic speeches against them,[28] he brings them back into their socio-political context.

By depicting Philip II in Hades, on the one hand, Lukian challenges predominant ideas of life after death as propagated by contemporary cults or philosophical schools, pointing at the hopelessness of metaphysical certainty.[29] Thus, he creates a scene of inversion in the underworld: "When I saw Philip of Macedonia, I could not help laughing. He was shown to me while he was sitting in a corner cobbling worn-out sandals for pay!"[30] A different depiction of Philip in Hades mirrors another key aspect of his reception: his fatherhood. Usually, in his literary afterlife, Philip plays a minor role as a supporter of his son's achievements.[31] In his *Dialogues of the Dead*, Lukian restores Philip's authority over Alexander:[32] A clearly dominant Philip waits for his son to arrive in Hades to give him a severe telling-off. Scolding Alexander like a naughty child, Philip voices the traditional accusations against him such as being a megalomaniac tyrant, priding himself with his victories over weak enemies and riding roughshod over Macedonian *nomoi*. Firmly, Philip points at the superiority of his own deeds as compared to his son's conquests:

> τίνων δὲ ἐκράτησας σύ γε ἀξιομάχων ἀνδρῶν, ὃς δειλοῖς ἀεὶ ξυνηνέχθης τοξάρια καὶ πελτάρια καὶ γέρρα οἰσύϊνα προβεβλημένοις; Ἑλλήνων κρατεῖν ἔργον ἦν, Βοιωτῶν καὶ Φωκέων καὶ Ἀθηναίων, καὶ τὸ Ἀρκάδων ὁπλιτικὸν καὶ τὴν Θετταλὴν ἵππον καὶ τοὺς Ἠλείων ἀκοντιστὰς καὶ τὸ Μαντινέων πελταστικὸν ἢ Θρᾷκας ἢ Ἰλλυριοὺς ἢ καὶ Παίονας χειρώσασθαι, ταῦτα μεγάλα ...

> What enemies did you conquer that were worth fighting? Your adversaries were always cowards, and armed with nothing better than bows and bucklers and wicker shields. But conquering Greeks, conquering Boeotians, Phocians, and Athenians was a real task, and subduing Arcadian heavy troops, Thessalian horse, javelin men of Elis, and light troops of Mantinea, or Thracians, Illyrians or Paeonians was a great achievement.[33]

Due to Philip's forceful and fierce appearance, Lukian's Alexander is forced to accept his subordination to him while adopting the role of a meek, disturbed child trying in vain to defend himself, desperately aiming at his father's approval. However, a seriously upset Philip finishes his curtain-lecture by

---

[28] Luk. Par. 56.

[29] Luk. DM 1.1.

[30] Luk. Nec. 17: Φίλιππον γοῦν τὸν Μακεδόνα ἐγὼ θεασάμενος οὐδὲ κρατεῖν ἐμαυτοῦ δυνατὸς ἦν ἐδείχθη δέ μοι ἐν γωνίᾳ τινὶ μισθοῦ ἀκούμενος τὰ σαθρὰ τῶν ὑποδημάτων.

[31] Cf. Asirvatham 2010, 196–197, 201.

[32] Luk. DM 14.

[33] Luk. DM 14.2. Trans. M.D. Macleod.

admonishing his son to be ashamed of himself.[34] By depicting two iconic warriors and conquerors as an angry father telling off his naughty son who weepily vies for his paternal affection, again, Lukian deconstructs their artificial status showing them as fallible human beings ridiculing their over-exaggerated images in contemporary literature.

Another central concern of Lukian is the criticism of flattery, a traditional theme in ancient literature. However, again, Lukian contradicts conventions and disappoints expectations. In *How to write history*, he reverses the predominant image of Alexander as a victim of his flatterers by depicting him as being critical of his own hagiographic treatment: He characterizes Onesikritos' literary praises as opportunistic and throws Aristoboulos' writings into the river telling him that he deserved the same treatment for his blatant flattery.[35] Lukian's ironical exaggerations are not authentic episodes but serve as examples of certain shortcomings of contemporary historiography: It will surely be no coincidence that Aristoboulos was named by Arrian as one of his two main sources for his *Anabasis Alexandrou* and characterized as most trustworthy.[36]

Also, Demetrios Poliorketes is referred to by Lukian as an object of over-exaggerated flattery. Interestingly, he does not refer to Demochares' or Douris' criticism of the Athenians who bestowed far-reaching honors on him, or to the hostile image of Demetrios as a shameless guest of the Athenian Parthenon.[37] Disappointing general expectations, Lukian tells a trivial story about one of Demetrios' *kolakes* concerned with a traditional theme: flatterers reacting to their sick or wounded monarch trying to please him by emphasizing the uniqueness of their disease or imitating his suffering:[38] Kynaithos praised Demetrios who had caught a cold, saying that he cleared his throat melodiously.[39] While a key element of such moral episodes is the monarch's reaction,[40] casting light on his state of mind, Lukian again disappoints any expectations by leaving it open.

In *A Slip of the Tongue in Greeting*, Lukian uses a historical Macedonian setting in order to joke about contemporary (hyper)atticists being extremely sensitive and prescriptive concerning questions of diction while using an

---

34 Cf. Müller 2013a, 182–184.
35 Luk. Hist. Conscr. 40; 12. Cf. Porod 2013, 95, 125, 127; Wirth 1964, 239. On the conventional images of Alexander as a victim of flattery: Plut. Mor. 60 C; 65 C–F; 180 E; 737 A; Plut. Alex. 23, 4; 28, 2; 49, 6; 52, 4; Arr. An. 4, 8.2–4; 4, 9, 9; Athen. 6.249 D–E; 6.250 F; 12.538 F (about the *Alexandrokolakes*).
36 Arr. An. Pr. 1, 1. Cf. Koulakiotis 2006, 184.
37 Athen. 6.253 B–E. Cf. Plut. Demetr. 10, 4; 23; Diod. 20, 46, 2.
38 Cf. Athen. 6.250 F–251 D; Plut. Alex. 28, 2; Plut. Mor. 180 D–E.
39 Luk. Pr. Im. 20.
40 Cf. f.e. Plut. Alex. 28, 2; Athen. 6.251 C–D.

Lukian and the Hellenistic Legacy

219

idiom far removed from everyday speech.[41] By apologizing for an unsuitable greeting, mockingly characterized as a great and shameful misfortune, Lukian points at a historical example of such a slip of the tongue:

> ὅτε Ἀλέξανδρος τὴν ἐν Ἰσσῷ μάχην ἀγωνιεῖσθαι ἔμελλεν, ὡς Εὐμένης ὁ Καρδιανὸς ἐν τῇ πρὸς Ἀντίπατρον ἐπιστολῇ λέγει, ἕωθεν εἰσελθὼν εἰς τὴν σκηνὴν αὐτοῦ ὁ Ἡφαιστίων, εἴτ' ἐπιλαθόμενος εἴτ' ἐκταραχθεὶς ὥσπερ ἐγὼ εἴτε καὶ θεοῦ τινος τοῦτο καταναγκάσαντος, ταὐτὸν ἐμοὶ ἔφη, Ὑγίαινε, βασιλεῦ, καιρὸς ἤδη παρατάττεσθαι. ταραχθέντων δὲ τῶν παρόντων πρὸς τὸ παράδοξον τῆς προσαγορεύσεως καὶ τοῦ Ἡφαιστίωνος ὀλίγου δεῖν ὑπ' αἰδοῦς ἐκθανόντος.

> Right before the battle of Issos, as Eumenes wrote in a letter to Antipatros, Hephaistion entered early Alexander's tent. He either blundered or was confused just like I was or was forced by some god and when he said like I did: 'Health to you, king, it is the right moment to set the battle-line.' All the others around were irritated by the contradictory address and Hephaistion nearly died for shame.[42]

The absurd, ironic episode, uniquely attested by Lukian, is to be regarded as a symbolic fiction illustrating how historical persons were used by contemporary intellectuals to cover up their own shortcomings. Lukian's mask (mis)uses Hephaistion to explain why he could happen to say *hygiainein* instead of *chairein* in the morning. The shocked reaction of Alexander's *entourage* shows that these are Second Sophistic hyperatticists only superficially disguised as Macedonians of the 4th century BC: Instead of focusing on their strategy right before the important battle, they waste time caring about the correct usage of Greek language and being upset about one of the generals' linguistic confusion. Probably, Lukian additionally ridicules the traditional Greek images of the Macedonians as rude, uncouth outsiders and lowbrows from the North with a strange dialect.[43] This cliché does not even apply to Lukian's Hephaistion: While being guilty of the slip of the tongue, he is quick to notice it and duly feel ashamed about it. Therefore, no hope is lost and Alexander graciously forgives him his linguistic incorrectness. On a second level, Lukian may also make fun of the tendency of contemporary historiographers to trust in the historicity of alleged letters from famous persons and to use such doubtful material as proof of their own trustworthiness and efforts to do research. Exemplarily, Plutarch quotes several of these suspicious

---

[41] Cf. Hopkinson 2008, 5. This is a common theme in Lukian, cf. his *The Consonants at Law*, *Lexiphanes* and *The Mistaken Critic*.

[42] Luk. Laps. 8.

[43] Cf. Strattis, PCG 638, F 29 (28 K.) (ap. Athen. 7.323 B). Cf. Plut. Alex. 51, 4; Eum. 14, 5; Mor. 292 E; Pyrrh. 2, 1; 11, 4; Curt. 6, 9, 34–36; Strab. 7, 7, 8; Paus. 4, 29, 3; Liv. 31, 29, 15.

letters in his *Life of Alexander* without ever doubting their authenticity.[44] Additionally, Lukian may be joking when he says that Eumenes told this unflattering story about Hephaistion. An erudite reader would have known about the reports that Eumenes was hostile to Hephaistion.[45] Perhaps, Lukian's tale implies that Eumenes – as Philip's and Alexander's *archigrammateus* duly interested in how to speak well –[46] maliciously slandered Hephaistion,[47] hence another warning to be cautious in accepting stories from the past at face value.

In *On the Hall*, Lukian jokes about falsely chosen historical *exempla* unveiling the lack of knowledge of pseudo-intellectuals. Again, Alexander as a frequent point of reference plays a central role as a corrective. A speaker talks about his wish to perform in a beautiful, sumptuously decorated hall aiming at forming part of this beauty by adding his words. As usual in Lukian's time, the speaker starts his oration by referring to a widely known historical example: Alexander's fatal desire to take a bath in the icy river Kydnos ending up with him nearly drowning and falling seriously ill.[48] Regarding this outcome of the plunge, the speaker's choice of the *exemplum* foreshadows his own "drowning." While Alexander was seduced by the sparkling stream, the speaker is blinded by the beautiful adornment of the hall, driven by impulse instead of reason and consideration and likely to shipwreck as an orator.[49] Another example of a wrong choice of an *exemplum* is the *ekphrasis* in Lukian's *Herodotos or Aëtion*. The speaker intends to win the hearts of all the Macedonians at once with his description of a painting by Aëtion showing Alexander's visit to Roxane's bridal chamber.[50] Again, Lukian shows a speaker driven by vanity and blindness who unmasks himself as ignorant and will shipwreck with his speech. A Macedonian audience would probably have been not amused at all: While it was a good idea to speak about the Macedonians' most successful warrior king, it was unwise not to choose a description

---

[44] Plut. Alex. 41, 3–4; 47, 1–2; 55, 4–5. While Plutarch (Alex. 41, 3) admits that he is astonished that Alexander had so much time to write such a lot of letters, this does not lead to any doubts about their authenticity on his side. It is suggested that most of these letters were invented and circulated in collections in Hellenistic times: Pearson 1954/55, 443–454.

[45] Plut. Alex. 47, 5-6: Plut. Eum. 2, 1–5; Arr. An. 7, 13, 1; 7, 14, 9. Cf. Reames-Zimmerman 1998, 109–110.

[46] Athen. 10–434 B; Plut. Eum. 1, 2; Arr. An. 5, 24, 6–7.

[47] Comparably, one of Lukian's masks is slandered by someone who ridiculed his language in *The Mistaken Critic*.

[48] Luk. Dom. 1.

[49] Cf. Müller 2018b; Goldhill 2001, 160; Thomas 2007, 229–230; Newby 2002, 127.

[50] Luk. Hdt. siv. Aet. 4–6. Ironically, Lukian compares himself to Herodotos who allegedly tried the same in Greece by reading his *Histories* to the masses in Olympia as "the shortcut to glory" (Hdt. 3. Trans. K. Kilburn). The satire is manifest: According to Lukian, Herodotos chose the *opisthodon*, the backside of the temple for his ambitious plan – where in fact nobody could see him. This anecdote is regarded as fictitious: Erbse 1955, 102–103.

of Alexander victorious in battle but an event highly unpopular with the Macedonians: Alexander's marriage to a barbarian no-name whose father and allies he failed to defeat in battle.[51] Furthermore, Lukian makes clear that the reluctant bridegroom has to be dragged with force towards his bride by one of the *erotes*, away from his beautiful male company,[52] Hephaistion holding a torch and a pretty youth who according to Lukian might be Hymenaios, the god of marriage. Usually, when Lukian pretends to be unsure, this is a literary device serving to draw his audience's attention to an ironic joke. In this case it applies also to this passage, for usually, Hymenaios is depicted with a torch. Thus, the lovely *meirakion* on whom the person with the torch leans, may in fact be Hephaistion, hence raising the suspicious question why Hymenaios seems to link *him* and Alexander rather than Alexander and Roxane. Thereby, Lukian hints at the rumours brought up in Roman literary tradition that Hephaistion was Alexander's lover.[53] In all likelihood, this was not the predominant image of Alexander in the Macedonian collective memory.

A third example of a badly chosen metaphor is provided by Lukian's unique story of Ptolemy's Baktrian camel. Lukian, hidden behind one of his masks, reacts modestly when being praised for his invention of a new genre, the blending of dialogue and comedy. He argues that he does not want to end up like Ptolemy who brought a completely black Baktrian camel as a novelty to Egypt, assembled the Egyptians in the theatre and tried to amaze them by the sight of the camel adorned with gold, purple cloth, and Persian gems. The spectators were frightened and Ptolemy realized that the Egyptians did not like any novelties but appreciated only the beauty of form and line. Thus, Lukian voices his fear that his work might be like this black camel in Egypt.[54] The comparison has its flaws: First, Lukian parallels an intellectual product consisting of two important literary genres to an irrational animal. Even worse, the animal comes from a land perceived as wild and uncivilized.[55] Second, his comparison raises the question which element of his new genre is to be equated with the Persian treasuries associated with decadence. Third, he offends his erudite Roman readers by likening them to Ptolemy's Egyptians

---

[51] Curt. 8, 4, 25–30; 10, 6, 13–14; Just. 13, 2, 5–6. Cf. Atkinson 2009, 182; Baynham 1998, 152; Heckel 2006, 238, 242; Bosworth 1995, 132.

[52] Cf. Stewart 2003, 41.

[53] Curt. 7, 9, 19; Just. 12, 12, 11–12; Epiktet. 2, 22, 17; Ael. VH 7, 8; 12, 7; Diogenes Sinopensis Epist. 24, 1 (Hercher). Not explicitly: Arr. An. 1, 12, 6; 7, 14, 4. Lukian is aware of these rumours: DM 14, 4; Calumn. 17. He may satirize Aëtion's actual painting showing the wedding of Ninos und Semiramis (Plin. NH 35, 78). Cf. Müller 2011, 439–440. Probably, also an old woman carrying the torch formed part of it. Thus, perhaps Lukian mocks the romanticized perception of Alexander and Hephaistion in his days as presented by Arrian.

[54] Luk. Prom. Es 4.

[55] Cf. Curt. 5, 10, 3; 8, 1, 35–36; 8, 2, 15–18.

who were "barbarians" in Roman eyes. According to Roman ideology, "barbarians", lacking *ratio*, appreciated only mere outer beauty and wealth while being unable to understand art and artfulness intellectually.[56] On another level, Lukian ridicules also his own mask hinting that he was striving for the wrong aims: fame, attention and praise instead of moral improvement.[57]

One of Lukian's central concerns are historiographers trying to increase their symbolic capital by writing about iconic figures from the past, thereby often sacrificing the "historical truth" in favour of an idealized portrait of their protagonists while simultaneously claiming the contrary. A major example is Arrian who in his "second preface" of his *Anabasis Alexandrou* compares himself to Homer commemorating Achilles' deeds and emphasizes his devotion to *paideia* that made him the only one qualified to write the true history of Alexander.[58] When Lukian wrote *Alexander or the False Prophet* about the success of a wicked fraud posing as an oracle founder,[59] the otherwise not attested protagonist of the indeed existing cult seems to carry the name Alexander for a reason: In his introduction, Lukian literally echoes Arrian's self-representation claiming that he and Arrian both wrote biographies of criminals:

καὶ Ἀρριανὸς γὰρ ὁ τοῦ Ἐπικτήτου μαθητής, ἀνὴρ Ῥωμαίων ἐν τοῖς πρώτοις καὶ παιδείᾳ παρ' ὅλον τὸν βίον συγγενόμενος, ὅμοιόν τι παθὼν ἀπολογήσαιτ' ἂν καὶ ὑπὲρ ἡμῶν Τιλλορόβου γοῦν τοῦ λῃστοῦ κἀκεῖνος βίον ἀναγράψαι ἠξίωσεν. ἡμεῖς δὲ πολὺ ὠμοτέρου λῃστοῦ μνήμην ποιησόμεθα, ὅσῳ μὴ ἐν ὕλαις καὶ ἐν ὄρεσιν, ἀλλ' ἐν πόλεσιν οὗτος ἐλῄστευεν, οὐ Μυσίαν μόνην οὐδὲ τὴν Ἴδην κατατρέχων οὐδὲ ὀλίγα τῆς Ἀσίας μέρη τὰ ἐρημότερα λεηλατῶν.

Arrian, the disciple of Epiktetos, a Roman of the highest distinction, and a life-long devotee of letters, laid himself open to the same charge, and so can plead our cause as well as his own; he thought fit, you know, to record the life of Tilloboros, the brigand. In our case, however, we shall commemorate a far more savage brigand, since our hero plied his trade not in forests and mountains, but in cities, and instead of infesting just Mysia and Mount Ida and harrying a few of the more deserted districts of Asia, he filled the whole Roman Empire, I may say, with his brigandage.[60]

---

[56] Cf. Goldhill 2001, 160–162; Thomas 2007, 230. Ridiculed by Luk. Dom. 5–6.

[57] This is a common theme in Lukian, cf. Hafner 2017, 360.

[58] Arr. An. 1.12.1-5. Cf. Burliga 2013, 106; Koulakiotis 2006, 179; Moles 1985, 165, 167: As Arrian's wording evokes the genealogic boast of the Homeric hero, he claimed 'heroic' status: "Great deeds can only be proper commemorated by great literature".

[59] Cf. Müller 2015; Petsalis-Diomidis 2010, 43–66; Gunderson 2007, 479–510; Swain 2007, 41–43; Jones 1986, 133–148.

[60] Luk. Alex. 2. Trans. A.M. Harmon. This is Lukian's only explicit reference to Arrian. On Lukian's relationship to Arrian see Müller 2018a.

Lukian and the Hellenistic Legacy

Significantly, Arrian's alleged biography of a robber is not attested elsewhere – surely not coincidentally: Arrian who defined himself through his subject would hardly ever have chosen a minor brigand as his protagonist.[61] In consequence, Lukian's reference was certainly no respectful gesture after Arrian's death[62] but a sardonic allusion to Arrian's *Anabasis*.[63] The image of the robber is in accordance with Alexander's reception as a brigand by Roman writers.[64] The name Tilloboros/Tilliboros which is attested epigraphically,[65] may have been associated with a brigand known in his times and therefore chosen by Lukian as a characteristically criminal name.

Another example of showing off with one's fake *paideia* is the protagonist of Lukian's *Ignorant Book-Collector* who believes himself to be wise. In order to make him realize that this is an illusion, he is told a story about Pyrrhos of Epeiros who was so spoilt by his *kolakes* that he erroneously believed to be Alexander's spitting image. He was cured when he met an old woman in Larisa:

> ὁ μὲν γὰρ Πύρρος ἐπιδείξας αὐτῇ εἰκόνα Φιλίππου καὶ Περδίκκου καὶ Ἀλεξάνδρου καὶ Κασσάνδρου καὶ ἄλλων βασιλέων ἤρετο τίνι ὅμοιος εἴη, πάνυ πεπεισμένος ἐπὶ τὸν Ἀλέξανδρον ἥξειν αὐτήν, ἡ δὲ πολὺν χρόνον ἐπισχοῦσα, ' Βατραχίωνι,' ἔφη, 'τῷ μαγείρῳ:' καὶ γὰρ ἦν τις ἐν τῇ Λαρίσῃ Βατραχίων μάγειρος τῷ Πύρρῳ ὅμοιος.

> Pyrrhos showed her *eikones* of Philip, Perdikkas, Alexander, Kassander and other kings, and asked her whom he resembled, quite certain that she would fix upon Alexander. But, after delaying a good while, she said: Batrachion, the cook: and as a matter of fact, there was in Larisa a cook called Batrachion who resembled Pyrrhos.[66]

Of course, looking like a "little frog" (*Batrachion*) was not flattering.[67] However, the episode, uniquely attested by Lukian, is to be seen as symbolic. Apart from the improbability that a ruler carried around his collection of royal portraits in order to interview the "people on the streets" whom he resembled, there is an element of inversion implicit: In classical Greek literature, Thessalians were characterized as extremely decadent and dissolute, thus often

---

[61] Cf. Moles 1985, 167.

[62] As suggested by Carlsen 2014, 211; Porod 2013, 20; Burliga 2013, 82-83; Anderson 1980, 122; Bosworth 1980, 37.

[63] Cf. Müller 2013a, 185–187; Koulakiotis 2006, 177, 184–185; Whitmarsh 2005, 68, n. 43; Macleod 1987, 258; Tonnet 1988, 73, 83; Wirth 1964, 233. Contra Burliga 2013, 81; Billault 2010, 629; Victor 1997, 133; Swain 1996, 326, n. 101.

[64] Sen. De ben. 1, 13, 3; Ep. 94, 62; Luk. Phars. 10, 20–21; Luk. Navig. 28. Cf. Koulakiotis 2006, 177; von Möllendorff 2006, 322.

[65] PIR² T 210. Cf. Victor 1997, 133; Stadter 1980, 162.

[66] Luk. Ind. 21. Trans. A.M. Harmon.

[67] Cf. von Möllendorff 2006, 324, n. 21.

associated with the Macedonian court and parasitic lifestyle.[68] Hence, a woman from Thessalian Larisa posing as a representative of *parrhesia* and truthfulness is an ironic joke. As often, while pretending to correct shortcomings, self-ironically, Lukian deconstructs the alleged wisdom of his mask.

Another aspect involving Macedonian protagonists as correctives concerns the grievance of partisanship. In *On Slander*, Lukian complains about the malicious effects of *diabole* –[69] ironically, a well-known device of the Attic orators.[70] Sarcastically, Lukian mentions as an example that after Hephaistion's death, Alexander gave orders to honor him as a god and punish any objection by death.[71] While criticizing slanderers, Lukian himself slanders Alexander by telling such a tale: Hephaistion received cultic honors as a hero, not as a god, and there is no information about any death penalty.[72] Even worse, Lukian adds the unique claim that Alexander's *kolakes* told him about dreams of Hephaistion, and ascribed visitations, cures, and prophecies to him, whereas Alexander prided himself with being not only the son of a god but also able to make new gods. Besides slandering Alexander as a megalomanic psychopath, Lukian may refer to a passage in Arrian's *Periplous Ponti Euxini*. The last part of this boastful literary letter to Hadrian is devoted to the island of Leuke, which Arrian himself did not visit. It does not prevent him from claiming that stories about the locally honored Achilles and Patroklos appearing to sailors in their dreams attested by second- or third-hand witnesses are trustworthy.[73] Probably, Arrian intended to please Hadrian by associating him with Achilles and his then recently deceased favorite, Antinoos, with Patroklos.[74] Lukian will also have known that in his *Anabasis*, Arrian associated Alexander with Achilles and depicted Hephaistion as Alexander's own personal Patroklos.[75] Again, Lukian's story offers no authentic information about Alexander's court but it concerns issues regarding *kolakeia* and partisanship in the literature of Lukian's time.

To sum up, Lukian uses Macedonian protagonists from the Argead and Hellenistic past as indicators or correctives of contemporary

---

[68] Athen. 4.167 B; 6.260 B–C; Plut. Demetr. 27, 2; Arr. An. 7, 25, 1. Cf. Pownall 2009.

[69] Luk. Calumn. 20–21.

[70] Cf. f.e. Aischin. 1,116 (Timarchos' sexual *hybris*); 2,22; 2,78; 2,180; 3,172–173 (Demosthenes' 'barbarian' roots); 3.156; 3.210 (Demosthenes' corruption by Persian gold); 3.152; 3,247; 3,253 (Demosthenes' cowardice); Dem. 19, 196–198 (Aischines' brutality); Din. 1, 41 (Demosthenes as a robber and traitor).

[71] Luk. Calumn. 17.

[72] Arr. An. 7, 23, 6; Hyp. 6, 20 (polemic). Diod. 17, 115, 6 is mistaken. Cf. Palagia 2000, 168.

[73] Arr. Per. 21, 1–3.

[74] Cf. Bosworth 1993, 249.

[75] Arr. An. 1, 12, 7; 7, 14, 4. Cf. Müller 2014a, 131–132; Stadter 1980, 38–39. By indicating that Alexander was the Macedonian Achilles, Arrian implies that he was his Homer: Bosworth 1972, 167.

shortcomings regarding *paideia*, historiography, and rhetoric. He often tells unique episodes that are not authentic but symbolical, pointing at failures of intellectuals in his time. In cases in which he refers to historical events attested by other sources, he either puts them in a different context or reverses predominant ideas about the protagonists in the collective memory. Additionally, by depicting different images of them in his whole oeuvre dependent on the context, Lukian points at the problems and shortcomings of their reception by contemporary intellectuals. Thus, the Macedonians become warners against the texts written and words spoken about themselves. By pointing out shortcomings of the educational sector in his time, Lukian could be seen as an embodiment of the Middle East as Middle Ground.

Bibliography

Anderson, G. 1976. Studies in Lucian's Comic Fiction. Leiden.

Anderson, G. 1980. Arrian's *Anabasis Alexandri* and Lucian's *Historia*, in: Historia 29, 119–124.

Anderson, G. 1993. The Second Sophistic. London.

Asirvatham, S. 2010. His Son's Father? Philip II in the Second Sophistic, in: E.D. Carney and D. Ogden (edd.), Philip II and Alexander the Great. Father and Son, Lives and Afterlives, Oxford, 193–204.

Asirvatham, S. 2017. The Argeads in the Second Sophistic, in: S. Müller and T. Howe and H. Bowden and R. Rollinger (edd.), The History of the Argeads – New Perspectives, Wiesbaden, 281–294.

Asirvatham, S. 2020. Second Sophistic, in: W. Heckel and J. Heinrichs and S. Müller and F. Pownall (edd.), Lexicon of Argead Makedonia, Berlin, 467– 468.

Atkinson, J.E. 2009. A Commentary on Q. Curtius Rufus' *Historiae Alexandri Magni*. Book 10. Oxford.

Bartlett, A. (ed.). 2009. A Lucian for Our Times. Cambridge.

Baumbach M. and P. von Möllendorff. 2017. Ein literarischer Prometheus. Lukian aus Samosata und die Zweite Sophistik. Heidelberg.

Baynham, E. 1998. Alexander the Great. The Unique History of Quintus Curtius. Ann Arbor.

Berdozzo, F. 2011. Götter, Mythen und Philosophie: Lukian und die paganen Göttervorstellungen. Berlin.

Billault, A. 2010. Une biographie singulière: *Alexandre ou le faux prophète* de Lucien, in: Revue des Études Grecques 123, 623–639.

Bosworth, A.B. 1972. Arrian's Literary Development, in: Classical Quarterly 22, 163–185.

Bosworth, A.B. 1980. A Historical Commentary on Arrian's *History of Alexander*, I. Oxford.

Bosworth, A.B. 1993. Arrian and Rome: The Minor Works, in: Aufstieg und Niedergang der Römischen Welt II 34.1, 226–275.

Bosworth, A.B. 1995. A Historical Commentary on Arrian's *History of Alexander*, II. Oxford.

Bosworth, A.B. and E. Baynham (edd.). 2000. Alexander the Great in Fact and Fiction. Oxford.

Bracht Branham, R. 1988. Unruly Eloquence: Lucian and the Comedy of Traditions. Cambridge (Mass.) and London.

Burliga, B. 2013. Arrian's *Anabasis*. An Intellectual and Cultural Story. Gdánsk.

Carlsen, J. 2014. Greek History in a Roman Context: Arrian's *Anabasis of Alexander*, in: J. Majbom Madsen and R.D. Rees (edd.). Roman Rule in Greek and Latin Writing. Double Vision, Leiden and Boston, 210–223.

Carney, E.D. and D. Ogden (edd.). 2010. Philip II and Alexander the Great. Father and Son, Lives and Afterlives. Oxford.

Conolly, J. 2001. Problems of the Past in Imperial Greek Education, in: Y. Lee Too (ed.), Education in Greek and Roman Antiquity, Leiden and Boston, 339–372.

Cordovana, O.D. and M. Galli (edd.) 2007. Arte e memoria culturale nell'èta della Seconda Sofistica. Catania.

Erbse, H. 1955. Vier Bemerkungen zu Herodot, in: Rheinisches Museum für Philologie 98, 99–120.

Galli, M. 2007. Processi della memoria nell'èta della Seconda Sofistica, in: O.D. Cordovana and M. Galli (edd.), Arte e memoria culturale nell'èta della Seconda Sofistica, Catania, 8–14.

Georgiadou, A. and D.H.J. Larmour. 1998. Lucian's Science Fiction Novel True Histories. Interpretation and Commentary. Leiden.

Gilhuly, K. 2007. Bronze for Gold: Subjectivity in Lucian's *Dialogues of the Courtesans*, in: American Journal of Philology 128, 59–94.

Goldhill, S. 2001. The Erotic Eye: Visual Stimulation and Cultural Conflict, in: S. Goldhill (ed.), Being Greek under Rome – Cultural Identity, the Second Sophistic and the Development of Empire, Cambridge, 154–194.

Gunderson, E. 2007. Men of Learning: The Cult of *paideia* in Lucian's *Alexander*, in: T.C. Penner and C. Vander Stichele (edd.), Mapping Gender in Ancient Religious Discourses, Leiden, 479–510.

Hafner, M. 2017. Lukians Schrift "Das traurige Los der Gelehrten." Einführung und Kommentar zu *De Mercede Conductis Potentium Familiaribus*, lib. 36. Stuttgart.

Hall, J. 1981. Lucian's Satire. New York.

Heckel, W. 2006. Who's Who in the Age of Alexander the Great. Oxford.

Heckel, W. and J. Heinrichs and S. Müller and F. Pownall (edd.) 2020. Lexicon of Argead Makedonia. Berlin.

Hopkinson, N. 2008. Lucian. A Selection. Cambridge.

Jones, C.P. 1986. Culture and Society in Lucian. Cambridge (Mass.) and London.

Karavas, O. 2005. Lucien et la tragédie. Berlin.

Koulakiotis, E. 2006. Genese und Metamorphosen des Alexandermythos im Spiegel der griechischen nicht-historiographischen Überlieferung bis zum 3. Jahrhundert n. Chr. Konstanz.

Landucci Gattinoni, F. 1997. Duride di Samo. Rom.

Macleod, M.D. 1974. Luciani Opera, II. Leiden and Boston.

Macleod, M.D. 1987. Lucian's Relationship to Arrian, in: Philologus 131, 257–264.

Majbom Madsen, J. and R.D. Rees (edd.). 2014. Roman Rule in Greek and Latin Writing. Double Vision. Leiden and Boston.

von Möllendorff, P. 2000. Auf der Suche nach der verlogenen Wahrheit: Lukians *Wahre Geschichten*. Tübingen.

von Möllendorff, P. 2006. Lukian. Gegen den ungebildeten Büchernarren. Düsseldorf and Zurich.

Moles, J.L. 1985. The Interpretation of the 'Second Preface' in Arrian's *Anabasis*, in: Journal of Hellenic Studies 105, 162–168.

Müller, S. 2010. Philip II, in: J. Roisman and I. Worthington (edd.), A Companion to Ancient Macedonia, Oxford and Malden, 166–185.

Müller, S. 2011. In Abhängigkeit von Alexander? Hephaistion bei den Alexanderhistoriographen, in: Gymnasium 118, 429–456.

Müller, S. 2013a. Trügerische Bilder? Lukians Umgang mit Tyrannen- und Orienttopoi in seinen Hadesszenen, in: Gymnasium 120, 169–192.

Müller, S. 2013b. Die Schule(n) der Lügen: Lukian über schlechte Vorbilder und ihre Konsequenzen, in: C. Hoffstadt and S. Müller (Edd.) 2013. Von Lehrerkritik bis Lehrermord, Bochum and Freiburg, 25–37.

Müller, S. 2014a. Alexander, Makedonien und Persien. Berlin.

Müller, S. 2014b. 'Denn wer weiß schon, was nach dem Leben kommt?' Lukian zu Tod und Jenseits, in: C. Hoffstadt and M. Möller and S. Müller and M. Nagenborg and F. Peschke (edd.), Zwischen Vorsorge und Schicksal. Über die Beherrschbarkeit des Körpers in der Medizin, Bochum and Freiburg, 151–166.

Müller, S. 2015. Making Money with Sacredness: The Case of Lucian's Alexander of Abonuteichos, Global Humanities 2: Religion and Poverty, 35–51.

Müller, S. 2018a. Icons, Images, Interpretations: Arrian, Lukian, their Relationship, and Alexander at the Kydnos, in: Karanos 1, 67–86.

Müller, S. 2018b. Wie man vor Publikum untergeht – Rezeptionsblüten und rhetorisches Kentern in Lukians *De Domo*, in: K. Ruffing and K. Droß-Krüße (edd.), *Emas non quod opus est, sed quod necesse est*, Wiesbaden, 413–428.

Müller, S. 2020. Lucian of Samosata, in: W. Heckel and J. Heinrichs and S. Müller and F. Pownall (edd.), Lexicon of Argead Makedonia, Berlin, 316–317.

Müller, S. and T. Howe and H. Bowden and R. Rollinger (edd.). 2017. The History of the Argeads – New Perspectives. Wiesbaden.

Newby, Z. 2002. Testing the Boundaries of Ekphrasis: Lucian on the Hall, in: Ramus 31, 126–135.

Palagia, O. 2000. Hephaestion's Pyre and the Royal Hunt of Alexander, in: A. B. Bosworth and E. Baynham (edd.). Alexander the Great in Fact and Fiction, Oxford, 167–206.

Pearson, L. 1954/55. The Diary and Letters of Alexander the Great, in: Historia 3, 429–454.

Penner, T.C. and C. Vander Stichele (edd.) 2007. Mapping Gender in Ancient Religious Discourses. Leiden.

Petsalis-Diomidis, A. 2010. Truly Beyond Borders: Aelius Aristides and the Cult of Asklepios. Oxford.

Porod, R. 2013. Lukians Schrift *Wie man Geschichte schreiben soll*. Kommentar und Interpretation. Wien.

Pownall, F. 2009. The Decadence of the Thessalians: A Topos in the Greek Intellectual Tradition from Critias to the Time of Alexander, in: P. Wheatley and R. Hannah (edd.), Alexander and his Successors. Essays from the Antipodes, Claremont, 237–260.

Pownall, F. 2013. Duris of Samos, in: Brill's New Jacoby Online.

Reames-Zimmerman, J. 1998. Hephaistion Amyntoros: Éminence Grise at the Court of Alexander the Great. PhD. Pennsylvania.

Roisman, J. and I. Worthington (edd.). 2010. A Companion to Ancient Macedonia. Oxford and Malden.

Rütten, U. 1997. Phantasie und Lachkultur. Lukians wahre Geschichten. Tübingen.

Schlapbach, K. 2010. The *logoi* of Philosophers in Lucian of Samosata, in:

Classical Antiquity 29, 250–177.

Schmitz, T. 1997. Macht und Politik. Zur sozialen und politischen Funktion der zweiten Sophistik in der griechischen Welt der Kaiserzeit. München.

Sidwell, K. 2009. The Dead Philosopher's Society, in: A. Bartlett (ed.), A Lucian for Our Times, Cambridge, 109–118.

Stadter, P.A. 1980. Arrian of Nicomedia. Chapel Hill.

Swain, S. 1996. Hellenism and Empire. Language, Classicism, and Power in the Greek world A.D. 50–250. Oxford.

Swain, S. 2007. The Three Faces of Lucian, in: C. Ligota and L. Panizza (edd.). 2007. Lucian of Samosata Vivus et Redivivus, London and Turin, 17–44.

Tonnet, H. 1988. Recherches sur Arrien, I. Amsterdam.

Thomas, E. 2007. Monumentality and the Roman Empire. Architecture in the Antonine Age. Oxford.

Victor, U. 1997. Lukian von Samosata. *Alexandros oder der Lügenprophet*. Leiden.

Wheatley, P. and R. Hannah (edd.). 2009. Alexander and his Successors. Essays from the Antipodes. Claremont.

White, R. 1991. The Middle Ground. Indians, Empires, and Republics in the Great Lakes Region, 1650–1815. Cambridge.

Wirth, G. 1964. Anmerkungen zur Arrian-Biographie: Appian – Arrian – Lukian, in: Historia 13, 209–245.

Whitmarsh, T. 2005. The Second Sophistic. Oxford.

Worthington, I. 2008. Philip II of Macedon. Oxford.

Zweimüller, S. 2008. Lukian, *Rhetorum praeceptor*. Einleitung, Text und Kommentar. Göttingen.

Hellenisierung, Sinisierung, Arabisierung: Komparatistische Überlegungen

David Engels

1. Hellenismus und Hellenisierung

Die Komplexität und Aufspaltung der Debatte um den Begriff der „Hellenisierung" hat einen solchen Grad erreicht, dass nur der Blick von außen durch den Vergleich mit anderen, analog gelagerten Prozessen noch eine echte Klärung zu ermöglichen scheint, wie in vorliegendem Beitrag angerissen werden soll.

„Hellenismus", einstmals ein zentraler Schlüssel zum Verständnis der klassischen Antike, ist heute in Folge einer nahezu endlosen Debatte zu einem konzeptuell kaum noch nutzbringenden Begriff geworden. Wo noch das 19. Jh. in naiv-teleologischer Weise die Beglückung eines barbarischen Orients mit dem Geschenk griechischer Freiheit und Geistigkeit erblickte, da scheinen uns heute vielmals Intensität, Entwicklung und Zielsetzung von Hellenisierungsprozessen in solchem Maße komplex und fragwürdig, dass meist von einer monolithischen Nutzung des Begriffes selbst abgesehen wird und man mit Klaus Bringmann eher von „Hellenismen" als von „Hellenismus" zu sprechen geneigt ist,[1] da die zeit- wie ortsgebundenen Unterschiede so fundamental voneinander abweichen können, dass es schwierig fällt, ein ausgewähltes Phänomen im hellenistischen Baktrien des 3. Jh.s gewinnbringend mit seinem Analogon im hellenistischen Karthago des 2. oder dem hellenistischen Athen des 1. Jh.s zu vergleichen. Wenn es nun auch freilich stimmt, dass eine bloße Nebeneinanderstellung verschiedenster konkret fassbarer Phänomene (z.B. Kultpraktiken, literarische Texte, Kunstformen oder politische Institutionen) oft nur wenig Sinn machen mag, so dürfte man doch wenigstens hoffen, zumindest den Prozess, der zu ihrer Entstehung führte, unter einem einheitlichen Gesichtspunkt betrachten zu können, hinter den „Hellenismen" also zumindest eine halbwegs einheitlich analysierbare „Hellenisierung" vorauszusetzen, also jenen Prozess, der ab dem späten 4. Jh. zur breiträumigen, wenn auch sehr uneinheitlichen und vielfach gebrochenen Übertragung politischer, wirtschaftlicher, sprachlicher, künstlerischer oder kultischer Kulturformen vom engeren griechischen Bereich auf den mittelmeerischen und vorderasiatischen Raum geführt hat.

Doch auch die Analyse einer solchen prozessualen Meta-Ebene ist alles andere als einfach. Denn was bedeutet denn nun eigentlich

---

[1] Bringmann 1995, 152: „Hellenismen statt Hellenismus: Die Bezeichnung Hellenismus täuscht eine Einheitlichkeit vor, die es nicht gab, und verdeckt die mannigfachen Facetten der historischen Erscheinungen."

232 David Engels

„Hellenisierung": die dauerhafte Sicherung einer oberflächlichen militärischen Kontrolle oder eine langfristige ethnische Assimilation? Die fruchtbare Zusammenarbeit mit autonomen lokalen Eliten oder eine großflächige politische Annexion mitsamt rücksichtsloser Einsetzung eigenen Verwaltungspersonals und politischer Praktiken? Die mehr oder weniger desinteressierte Garantie dauerhafter Religionstoleranz oder eine gezielte missionarische Bekehrung? Und vor allem: die Schaffung eines alexandrinisch-humanistischen Kosmopolitismus oder eine gewaltsame Gräzisierung rückständiger Barbaren? Freilich sind diese Dichotomien, wenn sie teils auch noch die ältere Forschung prägten,[2] bewusst holzschnittartig formuliert, da sich mit einigen Ausnahmen die Realität wie üblich im mittleren Spannungsfeld dieser Extreme bewegt, welches natürlich auch noch gemäß komplexer Kriterien wie der Frage nach den regionalen Gegebenheiten, den bereits vorgefundenen Tendenzen und Dynamiken, den Interessen und Verhaltensweisen der handelnden Akteure und schließlich ihrer Intentionen durchdekliniert werden muss.

Wie diese allzu kurze Aufzählung deutlich macht, erstreckt sich das Problem einer zufriedenstellenden Definition von Hellenisierung auf nahezu alle Bereiche des politischen, religiösen und kulturellen Lebens der letzten drei Jahrhunderte v.Chr. und liegt offensichtlich nicht nur in unserem eigenen, defizienten Verständnis der Faktengeschichte dieser Zeit begründet, sondern vielmehr in der Vielfalt und Vieldeutigkeit, welche bereits in der Antike selbst die jeweiligen Phänomene charakterisierte. Müssen wir deshalb aber nun gleich das gesamte Konzept der „Hellenisierung" verwerfen und, einmal mehr in der gegenwärtigen Geschichtswissenschaft, einen umfassenden historischen Terminus opfern und durch eine bloße Addition von „Einzelfällen" ersetzen, die nur in ihrem jeweiligen Kontext, nicht aber in ihrer Gesamtheit zu begreifen wären?

Ganz sicher nicht, und es ist daher auch kein Wunder, dass sich in der neuen Forschung zum Prozess der Hellenisierung neue, erheblich differenziertere Betrachtungsmuster ergeben haben, um dem komplexen Phänomen der Hellenisierung gerecht zu werden (bzw. dieses überhaupt auf seine Existenz als einheitliches Phänomen hin zu prüfen); eine Frage, die in der neueren Forschung oft mit der Analyse des Seleukidenreichs als des kulturell wohl heterogensten hellenistischen Staatswesens verbunden wird. Während etwa Rostovtzeff[3] unter „Hellenisierung" im Wesentlichen die Ausdehnung einer angeblich typisch griechischen Form bürgerlichen Wirtschaftens und Verwaltens verstand, welches das einzige Band gewesen sei, um ansonsten völlig unverbunden nebeneinanderstehende regionale Gegebenheiten zusammenzuzwingen, verlagerte sich seit der epochalen Studie von Sherwin-White

---

[2] Zu einer allgemeinen Übersicht über die ältere Forschungsgeschichte bis in die 1980er s. Bichler 1982; s. allg. auch Schmitt und Vogt 2005.

[3] Rostovtzeff 1941.

und Kuhrt[4] der Fokus des Interesses auf die seleukidische Schaffung eines imperialen Raums in bewusster Kontinuität zu den vorderorientalischen Großreichen, ihren Eliten und ihrer inneren, auch verwaltungstechnischen und wirtschaftlichen Logik, welche nur behutsam an die neuen Gegebenheiten angepasst worden seien.[5] Und während für frühere Generationen wie Droysen[6] „Hellenisierung" in der dialektischen Öffnung des „barbarischen" Traditionalismus für griechisches Verstandesdenken lag, zeigte sich seit Momigliano,[7] dass dieser Prozess mindestens zweiseitig war, da eben auch die griechische Welt nur allzu bereit war, fremde „Weisheit" zu übernehmen, wenn auch in einer vielfach gebrochenen und fehlverstandenen Weise, wie kürzlich auch eindringlich von Stevens[8] untersucht wurde. Gleichzeitig galt es auch, die inhärenten Systemzwänge einer jeden Schaffung überregionaler Kultur- und Politikräume zu erforschen, die Notwendigkeiten also von den Akteuren gewissermaßen auf die Geographie und die innere Logik weitgespannter Netze des Austauschs von Ideen und Gütern zu verlagern, wie sich nicht nur in Hordens und Purcells Studie zur Makroökonomie und -kultur des Mittelmeerraums abzeichnete[9], sondern auch in der neueren Debatte um die Übertragung des Konzepts der Globalisierung auf die alte Welt, für die kürzlich Pitts und Versluys plädiert haben.[10] Dass es bei diesen Hellenisierungs-Prozessen aber nicht lediglich um einen bloßen „Kompromiss" zwischen zwei kulturellen Extrempositionen ging, sondern den Versuch, auf Grundlage der jeweiligen Gegebenheiten gänzlich neuartige Konzepte zu schaffen, wurde in den letzten Jahren eindrücklich von Kosmin nahegelegt, der auf dem Feld der Erforschung des neuen seleukidischen Raum- wie Zeitgefühls die epochale Bedeutung jenes Prozesses nachgewiesen hat.[11]

2. Die komparatistische Herangehensweise als nächste Stufe im Rahmen der Hellenisierungsdebatte

Wie bereits anhand dieses kurzen Überblicks über jüngere Forschungstendenzen deutlich wird,[12] zeigt sich die zunehmende Tendenz, Hellenisierungsprozesse nicht mehr im streng abgezirkelten Raum der klassischen Altertumswissenschaften zu untersuchen, sondern sowohl im breiteren überregionalen

---

[4]   Sherwin-White und Kuhrt 1993.

[5]   Als vertiefende Studie dieser Forschungsrichtung mit Fokus auf dem iranischen Raum vgl. Engels 2017b.

[6]   S. allg. zu Droysens Geschichtsbild Wagner 1991.

[7]   Momigliano 1971.

[8]   Stevens 2019.

[9]   Horden und Purcell 2000.

[10]   Pitt und Versluys 2015; dazu auch Engels 2015.

[11]   Kosmin 2014 und 2018.

[12]   Eine umfassendere Übersicht über neuere Veröffentlichungen bis 2017 findet sich auch in Engels 2017c.

234 David Engels

Zusammenhang als auch unter Zugrundelegung abstrakter Konzepte mit globaler, also auch auf andere Zivilisationen anwendbarer Tragweite. Dies entspricht einer erstmals nach längerem Hiatus wiederaufgenommenen und gegenwärtig vor allem im Bereich der Imperiums-Forschung[13] und des Vergleichs Rom-China fruchtbar gemachten Tendenz,[14] auf die komparatistische Methode als einer vielversprechenden Möglichkeit zu verweisen,[15] durch Erweiterung unseres historischen Horizontes zu einem tieferen morphologischen Verständnis der allgemeinen wie der besonderen Eigenheiten des jeweils im Zentrum der Betrachtung stehenden Phänomens zu gelangen. Tatsächlich mag sich in diesem wie in vielen anderen Fällen durch eine ausschließliche Verengung unseres Blickwinkels allein auf die klassische Antike oft eine gewisse Verzweiflung einstellen, da die Fülle der Zeugnisse bzw. der Herangehensweisen generelle Tendenzen meist nur schwer als solche erkennbar werden lässt. Der Blick auf andere Kulturräume aber ermöglicht es oft, gerade im Detail das Charakteristische und im scheinbar Offensichtlichen das Akzidentelle zu erkennen und den Blick für allgemeinere historische Muster und Mechanismen zu schärfen.

Ganz konkret bedeutet dies die Vermutung, dass viele der augenscheinlichen inneren konzeptionellen Widersprüche komplexer Begriffe wie etwa der „Hellenisierung" keineswegs in einem unzulänglichen Verständnis des Phänomens an sich beruhen und somit eine Ablehnung der Hellenisierung als eines spezifischen historischen Vorganges mit sich bringen sollten, sondern sie ganz im Gegenteil im Inneren untrennbar zusammengehören und erst als Ganzes das „Typische" des Prozesses ausmachen, da sich analoge Situationen mit vergleichbaren Problemen auch in anderen Epochen der Menschheitsgeschichte wiederfinden.

Es ist daher sicher kein Zufall, dass viele neuere Studien zur Antike[16] auf eine Begrifflichkeit rekurrieren, die im Zusammenhang neuzeitlicher, meist post-kolonialer Untersuchungen entwickelt wurden, wie etwa „Middle Ground",[17] „Creolization",[18] „Hybridisierung"[19], „Bricolage"[20] oder „Acculturation",[21] welche sich alle bemühen, tragfähige Modelle zwischen den

---

[13]   Mackenzie 2004, Hurlet 2004, Burbank und Cooper 2010, Gehler und Rollinger 2014.

[14]   Mutschler und Mittag 2008, Scheidel 2009, Auyang 2014, Denecke 2014, Scheidel 2015.

[15]   Vgl. zum theoretischen Hintergrund meine eigenen Vorstudien: Engels 2013, 2017b (485–515), 2017b, 2018 a–b, im Druck a–c.

[16]   Vgl. hierzu die Ausführungen in der Einleitung zu diesem Band.

[17]   S. allg. zum Konzept White 1991; auf die Antike übertragen bei Bonnet 2015.

[18]   S. allg. zum Konzept Baron und Cara 2011, auf die Antike übertragen bei Webster 2001.

[19]   S. allg. zum Konzept Heidemann und de Toro 2006; auf die Antike angewandt bei Fludernik 2004.

[20]   S. allg. zum Konzept Lévi-Strauss 1966; auf die Antike angewandt bei Briant 1994.

[21]   S. allg. zum Konzept Berry und Segall und Kagitcibasi 1997; auf die antike übertragen bei Funck (Hg.) 1996, hier v.a. die mit Hans-Joachim Gehrke verfasste Einleitung „Akkulturation und politische Ordnung im Hellenismus".

Extremen von Assimilation auf der einen und monadenhaften Nebeneinanders auf der anderen Seite zu konzeptualisieren, wohl wissend, dass ein solches Mittelfeld, das in vielerlei Hinsicht auf „cultural brokers"[22] angewiesen ist, welche allein vermögen, kreativ zwischen den Partnern zu vermitteln, zutiefst von der jeweiligen politischen Machtsituation abhängig war und sich jederzeit in Richtung eines der Extreme hin entwickeln konnte, solange der entsprechende Prozess sich nicht stabilisiert und zur Genese einer neuen Form kultureller Identität oder doch zumindest breit geteilter Schnittmenge verstetigt hat.[23]

Aufgrund des begrenzten Raums können wir diese Problematik natürlich nur in aller Kürze anreißen und anhand einiger ausgewählter Vergleichsgrößen illustrieren, wobei wir als der Hellenisierung potentiell analoge Dynamiken die Sinisierung Ostasiens im 4. und 3. Jh. v.Chr. und die Arabisierung des Nahen Ostens im 7. und 8. Jh. n.Chr. in den Blick nehmen wollen.[24] Es würde zu weit gehen, im Rahmen dieser Untersuchung mehr als skizzenhaft zu erwähnen, dass die Begriffe „Sinisierung" und „Arabisierung" wohl mindestens ebenso komplex und vielfältig sind wie „Hellenisierung"; und wenn auch der jeweilige Sitz im Leben jener Prozesse ein gänzlich anderer ist, so sind die Übereinstimmungen in der Debatte doch auffällig. Mit „Sinisierung" (manchmal auch „Sinifizierung")[25] ist der Prozess gemeint, mit dem sich die im 2. und vor allem 1. vorchristlichen Jahrtausend ausgehandelten Grundlagen der Hochkultur der Huang-Ho-Ebene nicht nur bis zu dem heutigen Siedlungsgebiet der sogenannten Han-Chinesen verbreitert, sondern kulturell auch weite Teile Ost- und Südostasiens geprägt haben. Dabei ist es bereits interessant, die chinesische Begrifflichkeit zu erwähnen, denn mit *huà* (化) ist zunächst einmal bloß die Idee einer moralisch-zivilisatorischen „Transformation", einer „Kultivierung" gemeint, was auf den Gedanken verweist, dass es sich bei diesem Prozess nicht so sehr um die Assimilation an eine Ethnie unter anderen handelt, sondern vielmehr um den Übergang von einem barbarischen, gleichsam vor- oder außerhistorischen Zustand auf die Ebene „echter" Zivilisation.[26] Bezeichnenderweise erscheint der heute gebräuchlichere Sinisierungs-Begriff des *hànhuà* (漢化), der „Transformation zum Han-

---

[22] Connell Szasz 2001, 22–23.

[23] White 1991, xxxi.

[24] Die übergeordneten, programmatischen Gründe für diese spezifische Auswahl finden sich anderswo ausführlicher erläutert: Vgl. Engels 2018c.

[25] So umfangreich die Literatur zu Sinisierungsprozessen im kaiserzeitlichen China ist, so schwierig ist die Lage aus Gründen der Quellenarmut und der schwierigen sprachlichen Interpretation vorkaiserzeitlicher Ideogramme für das 1. Jahrtausend v.Chr. Einführung bei Chin 2012 und Chin 2014 und zentrale Fallstudie bei Sage 1992.

[26] S.u. für eine ausführlicher Diskussion des chinesischen Bilds von Barbarei und Zivilisation.

236 David Engels

Chinesentum", erst seit dem 19. Jh.[27] und verrät dadurch bereits die spezifische Zuspitzung des vorher un-ethnisch verwendeten Terminus wie auch wesentliche Unterschiede zum Konzept der Hellenisierung wie auch der Arabisierung: Erstere war überaus sprachgebunden, während im chinesischen Kontext angesichts der Vielzahl von Dialekten die gesprochene Sprache eine geringere Bedeutung hatte als die allseits gebräuchlichen und auch unabhängig vom sprachlichen Substrat operativen Schriftzeichen selber; letztere allerdings ist lange Zeit weitgehend gleichbedeutend gewesen mit der Übernahme der islamischen Religion als des wesentlichen, wenn auch nicht einzigen Referenzpunkts arabischer Sprache und Zivilisation.

Dies bezeichnet daher auch bereits die Eigenheit der „Arabisierung" (*taʿrīb*) (تعريب): Wenn sich die arabische Sprache auch bereits vor dem Wirken des Propheten über weite Teile des Nahen Ostens verbreitet hatte, war es doch erst die im 7. Jh. einsetzende politisch-religiöse Expansion des Islam, welche das sich heute bietende Bild nachdrücklich prägte. Hierbei ist zu betonen, dass die (von den islamischen Akteuren selbst lange nicht gewünschte[28]) „Arabisierung" fremder Individuen und Völker von diesen selbst unter religiösen Vorzeichen gesehen wurde, also nicht als Eintritt in einen wesentlich ethnisch-sprachlich oder rituell-zivilisatorisch gefassten Kreis geschichtlicher Superiorität, sondern vielmehr als Erfüllung eines gottgegebenen teleologischen Heilsversprechens. Erst in späterer Zeit, zunächst mit der Zersplitterung des Kalifats, dann mit der osmanischen Expansion, kam es zu einer Stärkung von auch kulturellen Partikularinteressen, welche dann zu einer Ent-Arabisierung führten, wie wir sie vor allem im modernen Iran und der Türkei feststellen können, so dass Islamisierung und Arabisierung zunehmend an Überlappung verloren.

Die inhaltlichen Unterschiede zwischen diesen drei Kulturen sind also beträchtlich, doch betreffen sie nicht, so jedenfalls eine der Annahmen dieses Aufsatzes, die strukturellen Entwicklungen, welche die formale Entfaltung jener Gesellschaften kennzeichnete. So ist bereits als gemeinsamer Ausgangspunkt festzuhalten, dass wir in Ostasien und der Levante zum jeweiligen Zeitraum ganz wie in der frühen hellenistischen Welt eine augenscheinlich analoge Kombination aus demographischem Druck, innenpolitischer Rivalität und expansiver Ideologie als vergleichbare Ausgangssituation finden, aus der sich dann breiträumige militärische Unternehmungen mit der Folge einer langfristigen sprachlichen, religiösen, politischen, wirtschaftlichen und institutionellen Anpassung der neuen Territorien an die neuen Hegemone mitsamt einer entsprechenden, nicht zu unterschätzenden kulturellen Rückkoppelung auf deren eigene Identität ergaben; eine Parallele, welche in der

---

[27] Chin 2017, 486.

[28] Zum schwierigen Umgang des frühen Islams mit Konvertiten s.u.

Forschung sowohl für die chinesische[29] als auch für die arabische Welt[30] hier und da bereits angedeutet wurde, ohne breiter ausgeführt zu werden.[31]

Wir werden daher im Folgenden versuchen zu zeigen, dass trotz jener nur oberflächlich skizzierten charakteristischen Eigenheiten zentrale Probleme des Hellenisierungsbegriffs sich eben auch beim Phänomen der Sinisierung und der Arabisierung wiederfinden. Ziel ist es dabei aber keineswegs, die oben kurz angerissenen methodologischen Sachverhalte in der einen oder anderen Weise zu „klären" und den Ausschlag für ein einziges wie auch immer geartetes Erklärungsmodell zu bieten. Viel wichtiger scheint es, den Begriff der „Hellenisierung" als eines gerade aufgrund seiner übermäßigen Komplexität trotzdem in sich stimmigen Terminus zu „retten" und somit der Tendenz einer Missdeutung jenes historischen Phänomens als eines letztlich beliebigen chronologischen Ausschnitts aus einer ebenso beliebigen geographischen Region entgegenzuwirken. Anders ausgedrückt: Gerade die Tatsache, dass wir in völlig anderen Kulturkreisen zu gänzlich anderen Zeiten ähnlich gelagerte Phänomene explosiver politischer Expansion und schwerwiegender langfristiger kultureller Transformation kennen, zeigt, dass der Prozess der Hellenisierung wie auch seine Manifestation im Hellenismus als ein spezifischer und autonomer Abschnitt weiterhin im Rahmen der Altertumswissenschaften seinen Platz hat und mehr ausmacht als nur die Summe seiner Bestandteile. Der Schwerpunkt der Untersuchung soll dabei nicht in der Akkulturation der ursprünglich initiativ wirkenden Akteure (das griechisch-

---

[29] Zu den Parallelen zwischen der Hellenisierung des Ostens und der Sinisierung Sìchuāns vgl. Sage 1992, 134: "Colonists sent to reside in Shu numbered in the tens of thousands, perhaps hundreds of thousands during the century of Qin control. The statistic is comparable to, and may exceed, the contemporary Hellenization of Egypt and the Persian lands in the wake of Alexander's conquests." Vgl. auch die zahlreichen Publikationen von Lloyd (z.B. Lloyd und Zhao 2017) zum Vergleich verschiedener Epochen der griechischen und hellenistischen Geschichte mit dem vor- und frühkaiserzeitlichen China.

[30] Was die Analogien mit der Arabisierung des Nahen Ostens betrifft, vgl. Reitemeyer 1912, 5: „Wenn man die Städtegründungen der Araber mit denen anderer Völker vergleicht, dann erinnern ihre Städte, welche als Heerlager gegründet wurden, am meisten an die Militärkolonien der Römer und auch an die von Alexander erbauten Städte, die zum Teil in denselben Ländern gegründet wurden wie die der Araber. Alle diese Städte sollten dazu beitragen, dem Sieger den Besitz des eroberten Landes zu sichern. Zwischen den Städten Alexanders und denen der arabischen Halifen besteht auch insofern eine Ähnlichkeit, als für die Gründung von beiden der Wille des Herrschers maßgebend war. Während aber die Städte Alexanders von Anfang an dazu bestimmt waren, die hellenistische Kultur und Bildung zu verbreiten, und auch die römischen Kolonien die unterworfenen Völker mit der Kultur Roms bekannt machten, mussten sich die Araber in ihren Städten zuerst selbst eine höhere Kultur mit Hilfe der besiegten Völker aneignen. Nachdem dies geschehen war, haben auch die Städte der Araber kulturfördernd gewirkt." Man denke in diesem Kontext auch an die universalhistorischen komparatistischen Vergleiche bei Geschichtsphilosophen wie Spengler und Toynbee, auf die hier nicht weiter eingegangen werden kann.

[31] S. auch Pollock 2013, 59.

makedonische Heer, die Reiche der Huang-Ho-Ebene oder die arabisch-islamischen Stämme) in ihrem neuen Habitat liegen, sondern im Gegenteil vielmehr auf der Überprägung der lokalen Gesellschaften durch Übernahme we-
sentlicher Züge der neuen Kultur im Spannungsfeld zwischen Ablehnung
und Anpassung, und zwar auf den Feldern der militärisch-kolonisatorischen
Durchdringung, der politisch-gesellschaftlichen Ordnung, der Religion und
der allen diesen Entwicklungen zugrundliegenden Vorstellungen von Barbarei und Zivilisation.[32]

3. Von der Kontrolle zur Assimilation

Erste Analogien zeigen sich bereits, wenn man die ganz konkrete Keimzelle
jener Prozesse von Hellenisierung, Sinisierung und Arabisierung betrachtet,
nämlich die militärisch-kolonisatorische Durchdringung der erworbenen Gebiete im Spannungsfeld zwischen der oberflächlichen Kontrolle einer ansonsten kaum angetasteten fremden Gesellschaft und ihrer weitgehenden Anpassung, teils gar Assimilation an die von außen kommende Herrschaftselite.

So hat die Forschung der letzten Jahrzehnte im Falle der vom Seleukidenreich betriebenen Kolonisation des hellenistischen Ostens deutlich gemacht, dass es hierbei kaum um den Versuch einer richtiggehenden ethnischen oder selbst kulturellen Transformation des alten Achaimenidenreiches
durch griechisch-makedonische Siedler ging, wie in der älteren Forschung
häufig hervorgehoben.[33] Vielmehr wird zum einen klar, dass es sich bei den
meisten dieser doch zahlenmäßig recht begrenzten Siedlungen um militärische und verwaltungstechnische Stützpunkte handelte, welche wesentlich die
Kontrolle über zentrale strategische Räume und Kommunikationslinien sichern[34] und oft nicht nur die Loyalität der unterworfenen Bewohner, sondern
auch die der Kolonisten selber garantieren sollten, deren Treue selbst oft genug zweifelhafter Art war, wie die Aufstände in Baktrien[35] oder der Umgang
Seleukos' mit den Kolonisten des Antigonos nahelegen,[36] wobei hier sicherlich auch der Konflikt zwischen Griechen und Makedonen zum Tragen kam.
Zum anderen zeigt sich an der Tempel- und Palastarchitektur[37] wie auch an

---

32 Späteren Studien mag es vorbehalten sein, ausführlicher auf die wirtschaftlichen, sprachlichen, monarchischen, charismatischen, kunsthistorischen oder militärischen Fragen ein-
zugehen, welche den Umfang dieser Studie deutlich sprengen würden.

33 Zu einem allg. Forschungsüberblick s. Brodersen 2001.

34 S. allg. Tcherikover 1927, Cohen 1978, Briant 1978, Billows 1995, Cohen 2006, Cohen
2013. Vgl. eine Neubewertung bei Engels 2017b.

35 Zum seleukidischen Baktrien vgl. Tarn 1951; Wolski 1982; Masson 1982; Bopearachchi
1994; Coloru 2009, Wenghofer 2018.

36 Man denke hier etwa an die Auflösung von Antigoneia sowie die Umbenennung von Pella
in Apameia; allg. hierzu die entsprechenden Kapitel in Kosmin 2014, Engels 2017b und
Engels und Grigolin 2018.

37 Allg. hierzu Held 2002, 2005, 2008 und 2014.

der Aufteilung der Kolonien in ethnische Viertel,[38] dass viele jener Siedlungen schnell einen multiethnischen Charakter aufwiesen und daher wohl nicht als fremde Brückenköpfe zu verstehen sind, sondern vielmehr als beispielhafte Vorbilder für Konzepte des künftigen Zusammenlebens der verschiedenen Reichsvölker unter den neuen politischen Gegebenheiten griechisch-makedonischer Herrschaft.[39] Auf die pragmatisch gesicherte politische und militärische Durchdringung folgte dann aber rasch auch die kulturelle Ausstrahlung des neuen Modells. Diese beruhte zwar vor allem auf dem Einfluss der dominierenden, hier also griechisch-makedonischen Gruppe, deren allgemeine Verhaltensmuster den kulturellen Rahmen bestimmten, war aber gleichzeitig auch für vielerlei synkretistische Tendenzen offen, die sich sowohl aus dem proportionalen Verhältnis der verschiedenen Bevölkerungsgruppen als auch aus den materiellen regionalen Gegebenheiten ergaben. Hierbei waren es vor allem lokale Eliten wie etwa die babylonische und jerusalemitische Priesterschaft oder Klienteldynastien wie die Frataraka, denen eine bedeutende Rolle als Vermittler zwischen den beiden einander begegnenden Welten zukam. So wurden Unterägypten, Syrien, Mesopotamien und Baktrien zwar zu Herzländern einer immer bedeutenderen Ausstrahlung griechisch-makedonischer Kultur, empfingen aber auch eine typische regionale Prägung, welche zunehmend zur Ablösung der relativ einheitlichen frühhellenistischen Siedlungskultur durch lokale Varianten führte.

Die seleukidische „Hellenisierung" durch Garnisonen und Kolonien, wenn auch ursprünglich offensichtlich zentral geplant, enthielt also von Anfang an die Öffnung gegenüber dem lokalen Element als konstitutivem Bestandteil langfristiger griechisch-makedonischer Machtsicherung und entwickelte zudem bald ein Eigenleben, das sich eben nicht nur auf der Ebene der unterworfenen Bevölkerung, sondern auch der neuen Herrschaftselite durch verschiedenste Arten von Synkretismen niederschlug.

Eine ganz ähnliche Entwicklung finden wir im später sinisierten bzw. arabisierten Bereich. Auch in Ostasien sollte die Ausdehnung der an der Peripherie der damaligen chinesischen Kultur liegenden Reiche in der Zeit der „Kämpfenden Staaten" sich meist durch die Anlage von ländlichen militärischen

---

[38]   Zu den Iranern in Antiocheia vgl. Feissel 1985 (SEG 35.1483 = AÉ 1986, 694); zu den Juden s. Flav. Jos. ant. Jud. 12, 119–120; zu den Arabern in Damaskus s. 2 Kor 11,32; zur multiethnischen Gliederung von Alexandreia Polyb. 34, 14, 1–6.

[39]   Zur multiethnischen Natur der seleukidischen Kolonien s. Engels 2017b, 157212. Inwieweit (und wo) die Aufteilung in kulturell geschiedene Viertel durchgängig beibehalten wurde oder rasch einer größeren Durchmischung wich, kann kaum noch eruiert werden, zumal Hinweise auf die Eigenverwaltung einiger dieser Gruppen (etwa die Nabatäer in den levantinischen Städten oder die hellenistischen/hellenisierten Gemeinden in Babylon oder Jerusalem) nicht zwingend eine räumliche Separierung bedeuten müssen, so dass man zwar von einer logistisch bedingten relativen, nicht aber ausschließlichen Konzentration ausgehen sollte.

240 David Engels

Kolonien (unter den Hàn als 屯田, túntián bezeichnet) in den neuunterworfenen „barbarischen" Gebieten vollziehen,[40] wie etwa die Durchdringung der Staaten Shǔ (蜀) und Bā (巴) in Sìchuān[41] durch die Qín seit 316 oder die systematische Südausdehnung des Reichs von Chǔ zeigen,[42] bei denen die Umsiedlung von Soldaten, Kriegsgefangenen und Armen sowohl innenpolitische Probleme im jeweiligen Heimatland meistern als auch politische Loyalität durch Ansiedlung mitten in einem fremden Gebiet sichern sollte. Die Anlage bzw. Umgestaltung von vorhandenen Städten wie etwa das nach dem Vorbild von Xiányáng befestigte Chéngdū[43] wie auch die stark befestigten Siedlungen Pi und Línqióng in Shǔ und Jiāngzhōu in Bā sollten nicht nur Vorbilder für die Sinisierung liefern, sondern auch den neuen multiethnischen und politischen Charakter des Reichs kennzeichnen, wie etwa die innere Mauer zeigt, welche Chéngdū in eine chinesische Verwaltungs- und eine autochthone Wohnstadt trennte.[44] Gleichzeitig zeigt das differenzierte Vorgehen gegenüber den verschiedenen Adelsfamilien von Shǔ und Bā, welche in unterschiedlichem Maße in die Reichshierarchie übernommen wurden, den bewussten Versuch der Konstruktion einer Schicht kultureller und politischer Vermittler, die sich als überaus tragfähig erweisen sollte. So wurden die peripheren Reiche der Zeit der „Kämpfenden Staaten", die wie Makedonien aufgrund ihrer Randlage von einer zentralen Perspektive aus als kulturelle Außenseiter betrachtet wurden, zum Träger der allmählichen Sinisierung der südlichen Hoch- und nördlichen Tieflande, schufen aber mit ihren kolonisatorischen Unternehmungen neue regionale Synkretismen und unterlagen oft sogar selbst den Einflüssen der neuerworbenen Gebiete, wie besonders das Beispiel Chǔs zeigt, das viele Elemente der autochthonen Yuè-Kultur wie etwa eine schamanistische Bildsprache und eine originelle musikalische Tonsprache aufnahm.[45]

Auch im Bereich der klassischen chinesischen „Kämpfenden Staaten" war Sinisierung durch politische Expansion und ethnische Kolonisation also ein komplexer Prozess: Zum einen wurde von Anfang an die Möglichkeit eingeplant, die städtischen Zentren der neuerworbenen Territorien als Inklusionsräume zu gestalten (was freilich keineswegs eine hierarchische Staffelung der verschiedenen Ethnien ausschloss und freiwillige kulturelle Anpassung an die neue Herrschaftsschicht durch sozialen Aufstieg belohnte); zum anderen zeigte sich, dass gerade in jenen Königreichen, in denen der Übergang zwischen stark und schwach sinisierten Zonen auch geographisch fließend war,

---

[40] Vgl. zu den frühen chinesischen Militärkolonien Keightley 1969, Lau 1999.

[41] Zu Sìchuān vgl. Bagley 1990, Zheng 1945, Zheng 1947, Zheng 1957, Treistman 1974, Sage 1992.

[42] Zur Geschichte des Reichs Chǔ vgl. Peters 1983, Lawton 1991, Cook und Major 1999.

[43] Allg. zur Geschichte von Chéngdū vgl. Faurot 1992

[44] Vgl. Sage 1992, 126ff.

[45] Zu den Yuè-Einflüssen auf die Chǔs-Kultur s. Waley 1955, Hawkes 1985, So 2000.

Hellenisierung, Sinisierung, Arabisierung   241

die politisch dominante Gesellschaft durchaus Elemente der unterworfenen Gruppen übernehmen und es zur Herausbildung gewisser Mischformen kommen konnte.

Ebenso wie die Diadochen in Siedlungen wie Alexandreia, Antigoneia, Seleukeia-Tigris oder Ai-Khanoum Veteranen, Kolonisten und zunehmend auch freie oder an Klerouchien gebundene Einheimische zu neuartigen städtischen Gemeinden vereinten, die als militärische wie wirtschaftliche und politische Zentren ganzer Großregionen fungieren sollten, errichteten die frühen islamischen Herrscher mit Basra, Kufa, Wasit, Dabik, Fustat und Kairuan Heerlager (amṣar أمصار , sg. miṣr), welche zunächst als Rekrutierungsgrund arabischer Veteranen und zentrale Kontrollpunkte neuunterworfener Großgebiete fungierten und oft genug auch unter dem Gesichtspunkt innenpolitischer Zwistigkeiten und Feindschaften zwischen den in verschiedenen Vierteln (Ḥiṭaṭ) wohnenden arabischen Clans angelegt worden waren.[46] Zwar sollten diese Städte im Prinzip rein muslimischen Charakter tragen, wie die Gründungsgeschichte Basras zeigt,[47] im Falle Kufas wissen wir allerdings von der Beteiligung zahlreicher lokaler Baumeister und sogar der Versuchung des Gouverneurs, sich einen Palast nach örtlichem Vorbild anlegen zu lassen.[48] Durch den raschen Zuzug nicht nur weiterer Araber,[49] sondern auch der Umwohner, die sich teils islamisierten und in das arabische Klientelsystem begaben, teils in eigens umgrenzten Vierteln wohnten,[50] wurden sie dann aber rasch zu Siedlungen mit einem jeweils eigenen kulturellen Charakter, wie bereits durch die doppelte Etymologie Basras deutlich wird, das zum einen arabisch als „die Überwachende“ (baṣrah), zum anderen persisch als „Wegkreuzung“ (bas-rah) verstanden wurde.[51] Dies ermöglichte zum einen rasches Wachstum und die Entwicklung von Modellstädten, die als Vorbild für das kulturelle Miteinander auch in das Umland hinein wirken konnten, und zum anderen eine willkommene Stärkung der Schlagkraft der muslimischen Heere. Gerade die freiwillige Kooperation lokaler Notablenfamilien wird hier als wichtige Vermittlung zwischen den nur rudimentären Kompetenzen der neuen arabischen Oberherren bei der Verwaltung des gewaltigen Reichs wie auch der Anwendung der komplexen örtlichen Rechtssysteme gewirkt haben. In nur wenigen Jahrzehnten lösten diese Kolonien die älteren Metropolen in

---

[46]   Allgemein zum Konzept des Misr s. Reitemeyer, 1912, Hakim 1979, Djait 1986, Abu-Lughod 1987, a-Sayyad 1991, Hillenbrand 1999.

[47]   Zur Gründung Basras vgl. Pellat 1953 und Donner 1984; die Gründungsgeschichte läßt sich bei nahezu allen wichtigen Chronisten nachlesen (aṭ-Ṭabarī, al-Balāḏūrī, al-Yaʿqūbī).

[48]   Zur Gründung Kufas vgl. allg. Massignon 1935, Djait 1986. Auch diese Beschreibung ist weit verbreitet; die bekannteste Version ist wohl bei aṭ-Ṭabarī zu lesen.

[49]   Zur Ansiedlung arabischer Minderheiten s. Lapidus 1981, Morony 1981.

[50]   Zu den Minderheiten im Islam s. Biegel 1972, Franz 1978, Diesenberger und Corradini und Reimitz 2003.

[51]   Zur Etymologie Basras vgl. de Lafayette 2017, 259f.

ihrer Bedeutung ab und entwickelten eine enorme kulturelle Strahl- und Assimilationskraft. Und wenn auch der Iraq, Syrien, Ägypten oder der Maghreb trotz der ursprünglichen Präsenz identischer arabischer Clans und der raschen Arabisierung und Islamisierung zunehmend eigenständige regionale Kulturen hervorbrachten, geschah dies doch unter den neuen kulturellen Rahmenbedingungen.

Die heterogene Natur der arabischen Expansion war in diesem Fall also bereits in der Stammesstruktur der Eroberer angelegt, welche sich in der Folge als wichtiger Motor der innenpolitischen Entwicklung herausstellen und auch die Modalitäten der Selbst-Arabisierung der unterworfenen Bevölkerung bestimmen sollte. Sicherlich auch deshalb war das arabische Reich ebenfalls von Anfang an auf die Notwendigkeit multiethnischen Zusammenlebens ausgerichtet und vermochte es, die unweigerlich sich ergebenden Spannungen geschickt zur Festigung der Macht im Inneren und Ausdehnung nach außen einzusetzen.

4. Von der Autonomie zur Integration

Eine ähnliche Dynamik findet sich im Bereich der Entwicklung der politischen und gesellschaftlichen Strukturen im hellenistischen Osten, steht doch am einen Ende das Konzept der lockeren königlichen Oberherrschaft über nur schwach urbanisierte Gebiete bzw. solche, deren Städte einem griechischen Auge kaum als autonome, unter breitem Einschluss der Bürgerschaft verwaltete Körperschaften erscheinen mussten, am anderen das der Transformation in einen Zusammenschluss einzelner griechischer *poleis*.

„Hellenisierung", das scheint zumindest in der Anfangsphase nicht viel mehr als die fast bruchlose Übernahme achaimenidischer und pharaonischer Traditionen durch die Seleukiden und Lagiden zu bedeuten, bei denen der neue makedonische Herrscher und sein Hof letztlich nur den Austausch der regierenden Dynastie zu symbolisieren scheinen, von denen die lokalen Eliten, örtlichen Autonomien und jahrhundertealten Sonderregelungen nur wenig tangiert wurden,[52] wie am Beispiel des babylonischen Königtums der Seleukiden,[53] des Fortlebens orientalischer Hoflegenden[54] oder der Herrschaft der Frataraka über die hellenistische Persis[55] deutlich wird. Erst allmählich sollte sich zeigen, dass sich im Hintergrund dieses Prozesses eine unmerkliche politische Transformation angebahnt hatte, bei der durch Landverteilungen wie Städtegründungen das Modell der griechischen *polis* bis an den

---

[52] Zum komplexen Thema der Kontinuität zwischen Achaimeniden und Seleukiden s. Bikerman 1966, Briant 1990, Tuplin 2008, Engels 2017b.

[53] Zum seleukidischen Babylon s. Sherwin-White 1983, Oelsner 1986, Kuhrt 1996, Scharrer 1999, Boiy 2004, Strootman 2013, Stevens 2014.

[54] Vgl. hierzu etwa die Apama- und Stratonike-Legenden; Engels und Erickson 2016.

[55] Zu den Frataraka vgl. Wiesehöfer 1994, Plischke 2014, Engels 2017b, 247–306.

Hindukusch exportiert worden war und zumindest Kleinasien, Syrien und Teile des Zweistromlands mit einer Kette von Siedlungen überzogen hatte, die alle über Institutionen wie Demokratie, Volksversammlung, *boule*, Gymnasium und Theater verfügten.[56] Die Attraktivität des Bürgerrechts, das sicherlich an den Erwerb der griechischen Sprache und die Teilnahme an das Griechentum konstituierenden Praktiken wie etwa dem Gymnasiumsbesuch gebunden war,[57] dürfte anfangs den autochthonen Bevölkerungsgruppen nur wenig deutlich gewesen sein; die zunehmende Bedeutung der *polis* in Wirtschaft und Politik lieferte aber einen zunehmenden Anreiz zur Einpassung in dieses neue Gefüge, so dass es zu einer gewissen „Politisierung" der alten Eliten kam, wie wir dies etwa für die zweisprachige Verwaltungsspitze Babylons und Uruks[58] oder für die hellenisierungswillige Jerusalemer Priesterschaft[59] nachweisen können, und die Dichotomie zwischen Griechen und Einheimischen von derjenigen zwischen hellenistischer Stadt- und aramäischer Landbevölkerung abgelöst wurde, wie sie uns vor allem im großsyrischen Raum entgegentritt.[60] Und während es noch zu Beginn des 1. Jh.s so scheinen mochte, als ob jene Transformation in eine griechisch inspirierte Städtelandschaft langfristig zur Schwächung der Zentralgewalt führen musste, zeigt doch die an die Krise des Seleukidenreichs anschließende Bereitschaft vieler levantinischer *poleis*, sich freiwillig Monarchen wie zunächst Tigranes II. und dann dem römischen Imperium anzuschließen,[61] dass im globalen Kontext des späten Hellenismus städtische Autonomie nur unter der Rahmenbedingung einer überregionalen Schutzmacht denkbar war.

Was also anfangs nur als Verlegenheitslösung zur besseren Ansiedlung griechisch-makedonischer Veteranen, Siedler und Verwaltungsbeamten gedacht war, entwickelte sich zu einer Blaupause für die Umwandlung des gesamten Herrschaftsgebiets, schuf somit aber auch eine eigene Dynamik, welche aus dem Zweckbündnis zwischen dem König und einigen vereinzelten *poleis* schließlich ein nahezu flächendeckendes Organisationsprinzip schuf, welches auch die Dynastie überlebte, die an ihrem Ursprung stand.

Auch diese institutionelle Entwicklung, bei der die Frage nach der Planung oder Unfreiwilligkeit des Prozesses kaum zu beantworten ist, findet eine bezeichnende Parallele in anderen Gesellschaften. So bemühte sich die

---

[56] Zu den Institutionen v.a. der seleukidischen Kolonien vgl. neben der oben zitierten Literatur auch Musti 1966, Rey-Coquais 1991, Capdetrey 2007, Engels 2007b, 409–455.

[57] Zur schwierigen Frage der Verbindung von Bürgerrecht und Gymnasionsbesuch s. Mehl 1992, von Hesberg 1995, Kah und Scholz 2004 sowie Engels 2017b, 347–382.

[58] Zur zweisprachigen Elite Babyloniens vgl. Sarkisian 1976, Sherwin-White 1983, Sartre 2007.

[59] Zum seleukidischen Jerusalem s. Hengel 1996, Collins 1999, Schipper 2006, Mazzucchi 2009, Engels 2017b, 347–382.

[60] Hierzu etwa Andrade 2013.

[61] Hierzu ausführlich Engels 2017, 409–448.

Kolonialverwaltung der chinesischen „Kämpfenden Staaten" zunächst um einen größtmöglichen Respekt vor den autonomen Strukturen der ethnisch und kulturell oft vielfältig zersplitterten neueroberten Gebiete,[62] wie im Umgang der Qín mit den Reichen Shǔ und Bā in Sìchuān deutlich wird,[63] wenn wir unseren Hauptquellen, Sīmǎ Qiān und dem *Huáyáng Guó Zhì* (Aufzeichnungen zum Land südl. des Bergs Guó) glauben, wurde doch etwa das alte Herrscherhaus, die Kaiming-Dynastie (開明), im Range einer von einem Qín-Gouverneur kontrollierten Markgrafschaft (hóu)[64] weiter an der Machtausübung beteiligt und erst schrittweise in der Folge mehrerer, meist von der Qín-Verwaltung selbst ausgehender Aufstände abgesetzt,[65] während in Bā der herrschende Clan mit Heiratsbündnissen und Privilegien gewonnen, in den Qín-Adel aufgenommen und offensichtlich von Landneuverteilungen und Kolonisten weitgehend ausgenommen wurde,[66] da man dieses Grenzgebiet zum Nachbarstaat Shǔ keineswegs durch allzu große Assimilationsbestrebungen verschrecken wollte. Im Rahmen der zahlreichen militärischen und demographischen Verwerfungen der „Kämpfenden Staaten" wie auch der zunehmenden Vorbildwirkung chinesischer Agrar- und Verwaltungstechnik kam es dann zu einer allmählichen Anpassung des Sìchuān-Beckens an die nordchinesischen Verhältnisse, welche durch die Reichseinigung durch Qín mitsamt ihrer zahlreichen Reformen beschleunigt wurde, so dass der in Sìchuān hergestellte koloniale Kompromiß zwischen Qín, Shǔ, Bā und Chǔ geradezu Vorbildcharakter trug und nicht von ungefähr zur politischen Basis des Hàn Gāozǔ und somit zur Keimzelle der Hàn-Dynastie wurde.[67]

Die graduelle, lokal unterschiedlich gehandhabte, aber stetig auf größtmögliche Anpassung zielende Eingliederung Sìchuāns in das straffe Institutionengeflecht des Qín-Staates war somit nicht nur ein Mittel zur punktuellen Stärkung des Qín-Königreichs im Kampf gegen seine Nachbarn, sondern verwandelte es auch von einer regional und ethnisch recht klar definierten Macht in einen überregional ausgerichteten Akteur und lieferte somit die Blaupause zur gesamten Reichseinigung.

Auch die Arabisierung des Nahen Ostens folgte einer ähnlichen Entwicklung. Am Anfang stand hier ebenfalls eine eher oberflächliche Präsenz, als die Araber von den jährlichen Razzien zur Besetzung übergingen und ein eigenes imperiales Denken[68] sowie eine lose Provinzverwaltung (mit dem ǧund als mittlerer Verwaltungsebene in Syrien) zur Sammlung der zunächst recht

---

[62] Hierzu einführend Treistman 1968.
[63] Zur Frühzeit der Reiche Shǔ und Bā vgl. Kleeman 1998.
[64] Zur chinesischen Aristokratie vgl. Engels 2016.
[65] Zu den frühen Aufständen in Sichuan vgl. Sage 147–156.
[66] Zur Integration des lokalen Adels vgl. Sage 1992, 130–141.
[67] Zur Bedeutung Sìchuān als Basis des späteren Hàn-Reichs vgl. Sage 1992, 157–167.
[68] Allg. zum islamischen politischen Denken vgl. Watt 1980.

attraktiven Boden- und Kopfsteuer errichteten,[69] die sich weiterhin der lokalen Behörden bediente,[70] so dass etwa in Syrien Griechisch noch 50 Jahre Verwaltungssprache blieb und das Persische im Osten nie ganz zurückgedrängt wurde, und erst unter ʿAbd al-Malik (685–705) ansatzweise arabisiert werden konnte.[71] Unter frühislamischer Herrschaft genossen die nicht-islamischen Bevölkerungsgruppen auch im Rahmen der auf ʿUmar II[72] (717–720) zurückgeführten, sicherlich aber noch älteren Bestimmungen weitgehende innere Autonomie bei der Rechtsprechung und sonstigen Selbstverwaltung, sofern die Interessen des islamischen Staates nicht tangiert wurden, und konnten de facto, wenn auch nicht de jure, in hohe Staatsämter aufsteigen, solange sich nicht geeignetes arabisch-islamisches Personal fand. Freilich bewirkten die steuerlichen und rechtlichen Privilegien der muslimischen Bevölkerung einen großen Anreiz zur Bekehrung,[73] die aufgrund des Übersetzungsverbots des Qurʾāns auch auf den Erwerb der arabischen Sprache hinauslief, welche ohnehin große Nähe zum Aramäischen aufwies, das von vielen Bewohnern des Fruchtbaren Halbmonds gesprochen wurde, so dass die ersten Jahrzehnte islamischer Herrschaft paradoxerweise eher vom Versuch geprägt waren, Arabisierung und Islamisierung zu bremsen als zu fördern, bis es dann unter den Abbasiden zum Durchbruch der neuen Ordnung kam.[74]

Die zunehmende Bedeutung neu-bekehrter lokaler Eliten bewirkte dann allerdings eine rasche Professionalisierung der arabischen Verwaltung, wobei nach dem Einfluss der byzantinischen Administrationspraxis vor allem die alte iranische Beamtenschicht als tragende Reichselite hervortreten sollte. Dies führte nicht nur zu einer Optimierung des arabischen Imperiums, sondern auch zu einer allmählichen Loslösung von seinen ursprünglichen, ethnisch begrenzten Grundlagen, so dass es rasch zur Herausbildung halbwegs autonomer Wesirs- und schließlich Sultans-Dynastien kam, unter denen dann zwar lokale Tendenzen wiederauflebten, welche aber unwiderruflich auf dem islamischen Gesellschafts- und Kulturkonsens errichtet waren.

5. Toleranz und Bekehrung

Ein weiterer wichtiger Aspekt beim Versuch, die inneren Widersprüche des Konzepts der Hellenisierung zu erfassen, ist die Dialektik zwischen

---

[69] Zum Steuerwesen im Islam s. Poliak 1940, Shemesh 1967, Cooper 1976, Coşgel et al. 2009.

[70] Zur Verwaltungskontinuität vgl. etwa Crone 1987.

[71] Allg. zur frühislamischen Verwaltung vgl. Løkkegaard 1950, Lambton 1953, Morimoto 1981.

[72] Allg. zum Pakt von ʿUmar vergleiche etwa Tritton 1930; Barakat Ahmad 1980, Scheiner 2004.

[73] Allg. zu Steuer und Bekehrung vgl. Dennett 1950.

[74] Zu Bekehrungswille und -verbot s. Arnold 1896, Lapidus 1972, Bulliet 1979, Levtzion 1979, Donner 1981.

Bestrebungen religiöser Toleranz auf der einen und Vereinheitlichungsversuchen auf der anderen Seite, wobei es auch hier in keinem Fall zu einer bewussten und erzwungenen Assimilation lokaler Bevölkerungen an die religiösen Vorstellungen der herrschenden Elite gekommen ist, sondern vielmehr eine Dynamik geschaffen wurde, welche eine graduelle Anpassung als gesellschaftlich gewinnbringend und kulturell attraktiv erscheinen ließ, bis schließlich eine unumkehrbare Entwicklung in Gang gesetzt wurde, welche dann auch Episoden forcierter Über- und Umprägung mit sich brachte.

Diese Spannung tritt uns einmal mehr vor allem am Beispiel des Seleukidenreichs stark vor Augen. Nachdem der Alexanderzug in einer ersten Zeit als gesamtgriechischer „Rachefeldzug" zur Wiedergutmachung der Zerstörung griechischer Heiligtümer durch die Perser deklariert worden war, scheint es trotz der meist eher religions- (bzw. kult-)indifferenten Grundhaltung griechisch-makedonischer Politik zu einem gewissen Konflikt mit dem Zoroastrianismus gekommen zu sein,[75] der sich nicht nur in der Zerstörung von Persepolis und den späteren Vorwürfen sassanidischer Quellen spiegelt, Alexander habe das religiöse Wissen der Mazdäer vernichtet,[76] sondern auch in den Auseinandersetzungen mit den Einheimischen um zoroastrische Bestattungs- bzw. Leichenaussetzungssitten, wie sie für Baktrien literarisch belegt sind.[77] Auf diese erste Phase folgte dann aber rasch eine unter dem Zeichen der *interpretatio Graeca* stehende Periode kultischer Toleranz und Kompatibilität, wie wir sie durch die Gründung orientalischer Heiligtümer in seleukidischen Kolonien wie Ai Khanoum[78] oder die beeindruckenden Zeugnisse griechisch-iranischen Synkretismus' aus dem Oxos-Heiligtum exemplifiziert finden;[79] auch der Mithraskult, erstmals im Kontext der östlichen Expeditionen des Pompeius erwähnt, mag sich diesem intellektuellen Umfeld verdanken, und es ist klar, dass jene Synkretismen eben nicht nur die lokalen Kulte, sondern auch die griechischen prägten, wie sich schön an der Übernahme nicht-griechischer Bauformen in griechische Tempelanlagen zeigen lässt.[80] Trotzdem stellte sich zunehmend die Frage nach den Grenzen der Toleranz, bedenkt man den in seiner Ausdehnung und Bedeutung immer noch umstrittenen seleukidischen Herrscherkult,[81] der, wie vermutet wurde, zu einer Ausschließung der orthodoxen zoroastrischen Elite von wichtigen

---

[75] Hierzu immer noch Eddy 1961, Boyce und Grenet 1991; zur Stellung Alexanders in der iranischen Tradition s. Stoneman und Erickson und Netton 2012, Van den Berg 2013.

[76] Zur Zerstörung zoroastrischer Bücher durch Alexander s. z.B. das Buch Arda Viraf.

[77] Zum Konflikt um die baktrischen Bestattungssitten vgl. Porph., Abst. 4.21.22–27 und hierzu Grenet 1984, 73–75 sowie Engels 2017b, 227–237.

[78] Allg. zu Ai Khanoum vgl. etwa Bernard 1973, Leriche 1974, Francfort 1984, Grenet 1991, Rapin 1992.

[79] Zum Oxos-Heiligtum s. etwa Litvinskij 1985, Bernard 1987.

[80] S. hierzu die Studien von Held 2005, 2008, 2014.

[81] Zum seleukidischen Herrscherkult vgl. Millward 1973, Funck 1991, Debord 2003, Van Nuffelen 2004.

Staatsämtern geführt haben könnte,[82] und vor allem das Religionsedikt Antiochos' IV.,[83] mit dem die jüdische Religion als Element identitärer Selbstabgrenzung und autonomistischer Bestrebungen ausgeschaltet werden und zumindest in jüdischer Wahrnehmung reichsweit eine gewisse religiöse Vereinheitlichung gesichert werden sollte (eine Entwicklung, welche ja dann mit dem Disput um den römischen Staats- und Kaiserkult eine gewisse Fortsetzung fand).

Somit wird klar, dass die religiöse Gemengelage des seleukidischen Staates vor allem durch die Kontinuität älterer Kulte geprägt war, welche teils von griechischen Charakterzügen überlagert wurden, während neugeschaffene griechische Kultstätten oder -formen ihrerseits lokale Eigenheiten eingliederten. Diese Annäherung, bestärkt durch die kultische Anbindung der eigenen wie fremden Eliten an den Staat mittels des Königskultes, führte dann zu einer zunehmenden Schrumpfung der kulturellen Distanzen und machte gelegentlich auch Versuche forcierter Vereinheitlichung möglich, wo dies politisch opportun schien.

Die religiöse Dynamik im Ostasien der „Kämpfenden Staaten" ist erheblich weniger gut bekannt,[84] was zum einen an der schwierigen Quellenlage, zum anderen aber auch an den ganz anderen religiösen Rahmenbedingungen liegt. Trotzdem ist nicht zu übersehen, dass seit der Zeit der Östlichen Zhou die Übernahme des komplexen chinesischen Ritualismus, der sich aufgrund der allgegenwärtigen Bedeutung des Ahnenkults auf alle Gebiete des öffentlichen Lebens erstreckte, als Gradmesser für den zivilisatorischen Status angesehen wurde,[85] so dass es besonders im Kontakt zu den nördlichen Nomadenstämmen, deren Religion in einer recht direkten Verehrung der Naturkräfte lag, zu bedeutenden Kontrasten kam.[86] Andererseits konnte es dort, wo der Kontakt mit Völkern oder Untertanen, welche noch nicht von der Kultur der Huang-Ho-Ebene geprägt waren, auch zu einer Umformung des eigenen Ritualismus kommen, wie besonders am Beispiel der späten Chŭ deutlich wird, deren Ritus nicht nur stark daoistisch geprägt war und sich dem Konfuzianismus weitgehend entzog, sondern auch unter den Einfluss schamanistischer Vorstellungen geriet, wie unser reicher archäologischer Bestand nahelegt.[87] Allerdings wurde auch in China von den chinesischen Denkern nach Konfuzius

---

[82] Zur möglichen Ausschließung der zoroastrischen Elite vom seleukidischen Herrscherkult vgl. Panaino 2003.

[83] Zum Religionsedikt Antiochos' IV. vgl. die entsprechenden Bringmann 1980, E.S. Gruen 1993, Keel und Staub 2000, Mittag 2006, Aperghis 2011, Gorre und Honigman 2014.

[84] Zur religiösen Struktur der "Kämpfenden Staaten" vgl. Ching 1993; Lagerwey 2004; Lagerwey und Kalinowski 2008; Nadeau 2012.

[85] Zum Ritualismus als Gradmesser für Zivilisation vgl. die Rede des Mou Fu, Herzog von Zhai, bei Sima Qian 4 (p. 255 Chavannes).

[86] Allg. Barfield 1989.

[87] Hierzu Major 1999.

248 David Engels

bald hervorgehoben,[88] dass der wahre Glauben nicht im Ritus, sondern in der gelebten Frömmigkeit liege, die sich eben auch bei den Barbaren finde, während umgekehrt in der legalistischen Philosophie eine systematische Anpassung der Riten an die Staatsraison gefordert wurde.[89] Das Qín-Reich, gestützt auf die jahrzehntelange Vorarbeit der anderen „Kämpfenden Staaten" bei der Sinisierung der peripheren, „barbarischen" Völker, führte dann durch eine Mischung von Zwang und Zensur zu einer zumindest oberflächlichen weitgehenden Vereinheitlichung der religiösen Riten im gesamten ostasiatischen Raum,[90] und nach der Festigung des Hàn-Kaiserreichs kam es schließlich, v.a. unter Hàn Wǔdì, zur gewaltsamen Verbindlichkeit eines konfuzianisch interpretierten Ritualismus, der nunmehr als weitgehend unhintergehbar betrachtet und auch im Inneren durch wesentlich personalpolitisch motivierte Hexenprozesse (wūgǔ) streng durchgesetzt wurde und den Nährboden für die spätere buddhistische Opposition lieferte.[91]

Auch im chinesischen Raum ist die Ausdehnung des „klassischen" Ritualismus der Großen Ebene im Zeitalter der Kämpfenden Staaten nicht etwa als religiöser Imperialismus zu sehen, sondern vielmehr als Teil einer politisch gestützten kulturellen Expansion, welche zusammen mit einer Reihe anderer Techniken und Verhaltensmuster auch ritualistische Vorstellungen transportierte, welche von der örtlichen Bevölkerung als neuer Vektor zum Ausdruck eigener Überzeugungen genutzt wurde, während dort, wo das Bevölkerungsgleichgewicht massiv zuungunsten der herrschenden Elite ausschlug, auch deren eigenen Kultformen durch lokale Vorstellungen überlagert werden konnten. Durch diese Loslösung des Kults vom eigentlichen lokalen Substrat kam es allmählich zur Herausbildung sozusagen transportabler Formen von Religion, welche dann gezielt im Zusammenhang des Kampfes um Machterhaltung eingesetzt werden konnten, während umgekehrt die Macht selbst sich auch über die Garantie jenes reichsweiten Ritualismus definieren konnte.

Es ist vor allem im arabischen Bereich, dass wir eine der hellenistischen Situation recht ähnliche Entwicklung nachweisen können. Auch hier stand im Anfang zwar eine Kombination aus Beutesuche, territorialer Expansion und religiösem Sendungsbewusstsein, doch stellte sich nach anfänglichen Konflikten schnell eine realistische Vorgehensweise ein, die im Wesentlichen in einer Tolerierung anderer monotheistischer Religionen bestand und selbst im

---

[88]   S. auch die Rede des You Yu bei Sīmǎ Qiān 5 (p. 41 Chavannes). Zum geistigen Kontext s. auch Pines 2009.

[89]   Man vergleiche hier die Anweisungen im *Shāng jūn shū* 1,6. Zum intellektuellen Kontext s. Fu 1996.

[90]   Zur Politik des Qín Shǐhuángdì s. Twitchett und Loewe 1986, Kern 2000, Loewe 2006, Lewis 2007, Portal 2007, Pines et al. 2014, Engels 2017 und Engels im Druck a, b und c.

[91]   Zu den Hexenprozessen dieser Zeit vgl. Cai 2014; zum Kontext Shryock 1966.

Falle dualistischer Strömungen wie dem Manichäismus zunächst eine gewisse Großzügigkeit an den Tage legte, zumal die weitgehende Reduktion des Islams auf die arabischen Stämme eine maximale Konzentration von Macht wie staatlicher Rentenzahlung ermöglichte.[92] Arabisierung und Islamisierung waren dabei in Anbetracht der jeweiligen Selbstdefinition größtenteils deckungsgleich, wie bereits eingangs erläutert,[93] und so kam es aufgrund der sozialen wie steuerlichen und machtpolitischen Attraktivität des Islams rasch zu einer ungeahnten Selbstarabisierung und zahlenmäßigen Vermehrung der Neubekehrten, die zwar nach einer Übergangsphase, in welcher diese sich gleichzeitig in das arabische Klientelwesen (walā') ein- und somit sozial unterzuordnen hatten,[94] zu einem verhältnismäßigen Rückgang der arabischen Eliten führte, die Stabilität des neuen Systems aber verstärkte, da selbst regionalistische Strömungen sich wesentlich durch die Zugehörigkeit zur islamischen Gesellschaftsordnung zu legitimieren suchten. Im Gegenzug ist (entgegen der späteren Selbstdarstellung der islamischen Religionsgeschichtsschreibung) unverkennbar, dass zumindest in der Anfangsphase des Islams erhebliche Versuche unternommen wurden, die Darstellung des eigenen Glaubens möglichst kompatibel mit den örtlichen Religionen zu gestalten, so dass die Unterschiede manchmal auf beeindruckende Weise verschwimmen, wie nicht nur die Architektur, sondern auch die textuelle Ausstattung des Felsendoms zeigen.[95] Als dann die Macht des Islams insoweit gefestigt war, dass nicht mehr denkbar war, das ursprüngliche christliche oder zoroastrische Gesellschaftsbild zu restituieren, und als die Bemühung der Mu'taziliten, den Islam an die Vorgaben griechischen Rationalismus anzupassen, als abgeschlossen gelten konnten,[96] kam es zu einem systematischen Versuch gezielter Zurückdrängung der nicht-islamischen Minderheiten, unter denen zuerst der staatlich verfolgte Manichäismus zu leiden hatte,[97] dann, durch Verschärfung der bereits im „Pakt des 'Umar" angelegten Diskriminationsmaßnahmen, auch die Buchreligionen, wenn auch in regional wie zeitlich sehr unterschiedlichen Größenordnungen.[98]

---

[92] Allg. zur Toleranz im Islam vgl. Pareth 1970, Noth 1978, Khoury 1980, Sina 1991, Abou al-Fadl 2002, Engels 2013.

[93] Allg. zum arabisch-islamischen Selbstverständnis Hodgson 1974, Marranci 2008.

[94] Zum arabischen Klientelwesen s. Roberts 1925, Levy 1957, Juda 1983, Crone 2009.

[95] Man denke hier nur an die zahlreichen neuesten Publikationen der Saarbrücker Schule, welche (jenseits jeder Einschätzung der Tragweite ihrer revisionistischen Thesen zur Schriftentstehung) zeigen, in welchem Grade jene Inschriften auch christologisch anschlussfähig gelten mochten.

[96] S. allg. zur Einführung Adang et al. 2007.

[97] Zur Verfolgung der Manichäer s. Guidi 1927, Colpe 1954, Giorgi 1989, Browder 1992, Chokr 1993.

[98] Allg. zur Stellung der Christen im Islam vgl. Fattal 1958, Barakat 1980, Lewis 1980, Bosworth 1982, Chokr 1993, Cahen 1999, Goddard 2000, Hoyland 2004.

250 David Engels

Wenn auch die massiven Unterschiede zwischen der Rolle von Religion als Teil der Selbstdefinition im Kontext hellenistischer, sinisierter und arabisierter Gesellschaften kaum geringzuschätzen sind, ist doch auffällig, dass auch und gerade im islamischen Raum, den man in jeglicher Beziehung als „religiös par excellence" betrachten kann, zwar das kulturelle Selbstverständnis und der politische Kitt der arabischen Eroberer genuin religiös waren, das Ziel der Eroberung aber keineswegs eine forcierte Massenbekehrung war, sieht man natürlich von der Verfolgung der nicht-monotheistischen Religionen als außerhalb des abrahamitischen Grundkonsenses stehend ab: Erst die Verfestigung der neuen Hierarchie mitsamt ihrer breitem lebensweltlichen Annäherung ermöglichte dann den episodischen Versuch einer forcierten Vereinheitlichung.

6. Zivilisation und Barbarei

Und somit erklärt sich dann auch der allmähliche Wandel der Definition kultureller Identität, wie wir ihn nicht nur im Bereich der hellenistischen, sondern auch der chinesischen und arabischen Gesellschaft feststellen, und der ganz im Spannungsfeld zwischen einem ethnischen und einem universalistischen Verständnis von „Zivilisation" angesiedelt ist.

Wo wir im griechisch-makedonischen Bereich in einer ersten Phase einer rein ethnischen Definition von „Identität" begegnen, die sich, wie bei Herodot exemplifiziert,[99] durch die Gemeinsamkeit von Sprache, Blut und Kult ergibt, wurden diese Komponenten im Laufe der Perserkriege zunehmend mit politischen Aspekten angereichert, die sich aus der ideologischen Aufheizung des Kriegs mit dem Achaimenidenreich ergeben hatten. Barbar[100] war nun nicht mehr, wer sich einer nicht-griechischen Sprache bediente, sondern, denkt man an Aristoteles,[101] auch jeder, der nicht an der Freiheit des polis-Bürgers teilhatte, die weniger als eine historisch akzidentelle Entwicklung Griechenlands denn vielmehr als eine natürliche Eigenschaft des griechischen Menschen gesehen wurde. Dies öffnete den Weg für die allmähliche Gleichsetzung zwischen Griechentum und freier Bildung, wie wir sie bei Isokrates finden,[102] und stellte die Ausgangsposition für die geistige Verarbeitung der Eroberung des Ostens dar. Der überraschende Sieg Alexanders und die Minderheitssituation der griechisch-makedonischen Elite bewirkten hier freilich einen Wiederaufschwung einer rein ethnisch-patriotischen Definition von Griechentum und somit politischer Führungsschicht, bedenkt man den Widerstand der makedonischen Soldaten und Eliten angesichts der

---

[99] Vgl. Hdt. 8, 144; hierzu Dihle 1994 und Hall 2002.
[100] Zu Barbaren- und Hellenentum s. allg. Jüthner 1923, Dauge 1982, Hall 1989, Georges 1994.
[101] Arist. Pol. 1252b8.
[102] Hierzu etwa Isocr. Pan. 4,50.

alexandrinischen Fusionspläne.[103] Die zunehmende Eingliederung lokaler Eliten v.a. im Seleukidenreich, dessen Herrscherhaus seit der Thronbesteigung Antichos' I. ja sogar halb-iranischen Charakter trug,[104] ebenso wie die Bewunderung vor der hochstehenden Kultur der orientalischen Gesellschaften führten allerdings rasch zu einem Überwiegen einer rein zivilisatorischen Definition von Barbaren- und Griechentum im Denken der hellenistischen Philosophenschulen der Stoa oder des Kepos, wo es wesentlich der Respekt für die Rahmenbedingungen kosmopolitischen Humanismus war, der ausschlaggebend war,[105] und häufig zu Frustrationen bei den zu kurz gekommenen „ethnischen" Griechen führte, die sich angesichts des multikulturellen *koine*-Griechentums oft genug in antiquarische Schäferträume flüchteten.[106]

Identität wurde also, sehr verallgemeinernd ausgedrückt, zunächst als ethnisches Faktum konstatiert, dann durch zivilisatorische Überlegenheitsansprüche aufgeladen, welche sich schließlich von dem ursprünglichen essentialistischen Substrat lösten, das nur noch als eine allgemein zugängliche pädagogische Technik zur Erlangung des Status als „zivilisierter Mensch" beibehalten wurde, so dass das zwischenzeitlich zurückgetretene regionalistische Element griechischer Identität wieder verstärkt im Rahmen gesamtgriechischer kultureller Bemühungen hervortrat.

Auch die Sinisierung weiter Teile der südlichen und nördlichen Peripherie der Flussebene des Huang-Ho verlief unter ähnlichen Gesichtspunkten. Auch hier bestand die Fiktion einer gemeinsamen ethnischen, sprachlichen und politischen Identität der durch die Shāng- und später Zhōu-Dynastie beherrschten Völker der „hundert Familien", die „huá" (華), die sich nach außen hin von den Barbaren, den „yí" (夷), abgrenzten.[107] Dieser übrigens archäologisch durchaus nicht immer nachweisbare grundlegende Unterschied wurde im Laufe der Zeit auch zivilisatorisch aufgeladen, wie wir es etwa bei Konfuzius sehen, der ein höfliches und zivilisiertes Verhalten selbst inmitten barbarischer Länder einfordert[108] und den Barbaren per se jegliches Talent zu sittlich-staatlicher Zivilisation absprach.[109] Diese Dichotomie wurde freilich mit der zunehmenden Eingliederung außenliegender Gebiete in der Zeit der

---

[103]   Zu Alexanders Fusionsplänen (und dem Widerstand dagegen) vgl. Bosworth 1971, Stier 1973, Bosworth 1980, Heckel 1988. Allg. zum geistigen Umfeld Baldry 1965, Momigliano 1975.

[104]   Allg. hierzu Engels 2017b, 103–246.

[105]   Epict. 2,10,1–3.

[106]   Zum hellenistischen Antiquarianismus s. Pfeiffer 1968 (Kapitel Pergamum: Scholarship and Philosophy. A New Antiquarianism), Momigliano 1990 (Kapitel. The Rise of Antiquarian Research), Bravo 2007, und jetzt die Übersicht bei Engels 2014.

[107]   Zur Dichotomie Chinesen vs. Barbaren vgl. Pulleyblank 1983, Psarras 1994, Poo 2005.

[108]   Konfuzius, Analecta 13.19; ähnl. 15.6. Zu den konkreten Umsetzungen dieses Bilds vgl. Thote 1999.

[109]   Konfuzius, Analecta 3.5.

„Kämpfenden Staaten" wie auch des Aufstiegs selber als halb-barbarisch betrachteter Herrscher wie der Qín zunehmend infrage gestellt, wie es etwa Mèngzǐ zeigt, der betonte, dass es nicht die Herkunft, sondern vielmehr nur das Verhalten sei, das den wahren Weisen ausmacht;[110] eine vorübergehende kosmopolitische Öffnung, welche freilich in späteren Zeiten, als die Reichsbildung vollendet und durch den Bau der Mauern auch symbolisch zur Schau gestellt wurde,[111] zunehmend durch einen wieder unversöhnlichen Antagonismus von Innen und Außen verdrängt wurde, wie wir ihn dann etwa beim stereotypen, zwischen Romantik und kolonialem Dünkel schillernden Barbarenbild des Sīmǎ Qiān und der Hàn-Dynastie und der Idealisierung einzelner Regionalkulturen wie etwa der Chǔ finden, deren Liedkunst unter den frühen Hàn einen ungeahnten Aufschwung fand.[112]

Auch in Ostasien wurde also aus dem Selbstverständnis als ethnisch abgeschlossene Gruppe zunächst der Glaube an die zivilisatorische Überlegenheit über die Nachbarn, bis sich die angeblichen konkreten Begleiterscheinungen dieser Überlegenheit gewissermaßen verselbständigten und zum Ausgangspunkt einer neuen, kosmopolitischen Identität wurden, der *homo Sinicus* also zum Synonym für Zivilisation schlechthin wurde, gerade dies dann aber auch den Weg zu einer nostalgischen Neuentdeckung regionaler Traditionen ebnete.

Eine interessante, analoge Entwicklung finden wir dann auch im arabisch-islamischen Bereich. Auch hier überwog zu Beginn eine enge, wesentlich ethnische Definition arabischer Identität, wobei es dann in der Folge nicht der Gedanke des freien *polis*-Bürgertums oder der Respekt für den komplexen chinesischen Ritualismus, sondern die Unterwerfung unter die Offenbarung des Islam war, welcher zu einer ideologischen Aufladung ethnischer Identität, gleichzeitig aber auch ihrer potentiellen Öffnung nach außen hin führte. Die arabische Welteroberung schien den islamischen Herrschaftsanspruch ebenso wie das Auserwähltsein des arabischen Volkes zunächst auf beeindruckende Weise zu bestätigen[113], wenn auch zu betonen ist, dass jenes Superioritätsgefühl rein religiöser Art war und die Einsicht in die technologische und philosophische Unterlegenheit der arabischen Stammeskultur unter die byzantinische und sassanidische Zivilisation einschloss, welche zu einem Allgemeinplatz der islamischen Historiographie werden sollte. Das Phänomen der zunehmenden Bekehrung von Nicht-Arabern zum Islam wie auch der

---

[110] Mencius IB, 128.
[111] Zur Symbolik des Mauerbaus vgl. u.a. Waldron 1990, di Cosmo 2002, Rojas 2010, Spring 2015.
[112] Vgl. allg. Sukhu 2012.
[113] Vgl. z.B. die Einleitung des aṭ-Ṯaʿālibī zu seinem *Kitāb fiqh ul-lūġa*, wo der Prophet, der Islam das arabische Volk und die arabische Sprache als die endgültigen Höhepunkte der Heilsgeschichte interpretiert werden.

Hellenisierung, Sinisierung, Arabisierung

Kontakt mit den hochentwickelten Traditionen des byzantinischen und sassanidischen Reiches führte daher zu einer tiefen inneren Krise, die langfristig nach einer Phase der Ausschließung der Neubekehrten und des intellektuellen Kulturkampfes, der šu'ubīyya,[114] zugunsten der Auflösung arabischer in islamische Identität gelöst wurde, wie bereits bei Abū Ḥanīfa (699–767) deutlich wird, welcher sagte: „Der Glauben eines neubekehrten Türken ist derselbe wie der eines Arabers aus dem Ḥiǧaz". Dieser Prozeß, der eng verbunden war mit der Ausbildung der mentalen Trennung der Welt in ein dār al-harb und ein dār al-islām,[115] verlief freilich sehr zur Trauer der arabischen Oberschicht, welche angesichts des neuen, kosmopolitischen Islams und der allmählichen Vereinfachung der arabischen Hochsprache[116] zunehmend einer nostalgisch-puristischen Nomadenromantik nachhing und, wie später ibn Ḥaldūn, inmitten einer islamischen Welt dem verlorenen Imperium der Araber nachtrauerte oder, wie die Grammatiker Basras und Kufas, der Reinheit der Beduinensprache nachforschten.[117]

Gerade der Arabisierungsprozess ist also ein schönes Beispiel für die Dialektik zwischen ethnischem und universalistischem Identitätsverständnis, wurde doch auch im arabischen Raum aus einer ursprünglich rein ethnischen Selbstdefinition ein universalistisch (in diesem Fall: religiös) aufgeladenes Sendungsbewusstsein, das sich schließlich so weit verabsolutierte, dass es als Kategorie auch das zunehmende Zurücktreten des ursprünglichen Trägers überdauerte.

7. Schluss

Blicken wir nun abschließend unter einem vergleichenden Gesichtspunkt auf Hellenisierung, Sinisierung und Arabisierung, lässt sich tatsächlich feststellen, dass viele der komplexen, scheinbar widersprüchlichen Entwicklungen der ersten drei vorchristlichen Jahrhunderte im griechischen Osten weniger den spezifischen regionalen oder kulturellen Gegebenheiten geschuldet zu sein scheinen als vielmehr einer übergeordneten historischen Dynamik.

Als besonders überraschendes Charakteristikum können wir hier festhalten, dass jene komplexen Expansionsprozesse eigentlich nur in den wenigsten Fällen einem tatsächlichen Willen nach kultureller oder ethnischer Ausdehnung zuzuschreiben sind, sondern oft unfreiwillige, ja sogar ungewollte Begleiterscheinungen eines politischen Ausgreifens darstellen, welche häufig nachgerade den Interessen der jeweils dominanten Eliten und Ethnien

---

[114] Zur šu'ubīyya (dem Kampf der „Völker" um Gleichstellung mit den Arabern, basierend auf Q. 49,13) vgl. allg. Mottahedeh 1976, Larsso 2003, Jamshidian Tehrani 2014.

[115] Hierzu König 2015.

[116] Zur Herausbildung des "imperialen" Arabisch vgl. Ferguson 1959.

[117] Zu den Grammatik-Schulen Basras und Kufas, ihrer Beduinenromantik und ihrem Purismus vgl. etwa Versteegh 1993, Goldziher 1994, Van Gelder 1996, Touati 2010, 47f.

254 David Engels

zuwiderliefen, da sie eine langfristige Schwächung ihrer Monopolsituation bedeuteten, allerdings langfristig eine gewisse Eigendynamik entfalteten. Der „Middle Ground" als der halbwegs improvisierte Ort vorübergehenden Austauschs und Ausgleichs zwischen eroberter Bevölkerung und zumindest ursprünglich fremdstämmiger Reichselite gewinnt also, vereinfacht ausgedrückt, und dank der kräftigen Mitarbeit lokaler Akteure, ein Eigenleben und wird somit selbst zum Ausgangspunkt einer kulturellen Dynamik, welche die ursprünglichen Kräfte zunehmend als bloße partikulare Ausprägungen einer gemeinschaftlichen Identität an den Rand drängt. Hierbei ist freilich zu betonen, daß jener „Middle Ground" im Rahmen der hier untersuchten Fälle keineswegs eine gleichberechtigte Mitte zwischen den Interessen aller Beteiligten darstellte, sondern stark von der machtpolitischen Überlegenheit der Eroberer geprägt war, deren jeweiliges kulturelles Herzland trotz aller Synkretismen und Austauschphänomene weniger von jener kulturellen Annäherung beeinflusst wird als die jeweils dominierten Territorien. Erst im Nachhinein, als die Folgen der ursprünglichen Entwicklung klargeworden waren, kam es dann zur Konstruktion einer historischen Teleologie, die aus dem ursprünglich deutlich vorhandenen Wunsch nach politischer Beherrschung das Trachten nach einer völligen Anpassung der unterworfenen Bevölkerungen an die jeweils leitenden und inhaltlich voneinander jeweils grundverschiedenen Ideale der neuen Elite konstruierte, sei es nun das Konzept der griechischen *polis*, der chinesischen Ritualistik oder der islamischen Frömmigkeit.[118]

Überall beginnt die Phase breiten und nachhaltigen kulturellen Ausgreifens mit einer halbwegs improvisierten Sicherung vereinzelter Stützpunkte unter breiter Einbindung lokaler Kräfte, aus denen dann rasch neue Metropolen werden, deren jeweils unter verschiedenen inhaltlichen Gesichtspunkten ausgehandeltes Zusammenleben Vorbildwirkung für das Umland gewinnt und schließlich unter diesen Voraussetzungen zum neuen Ausgangspunkt regionalen Eigenlebens wird. Dementsprechend gestaltet sich auch die Umprägung der gesellschaftlichen und politischen Strukturen, welche ebenfalls von einer tastenden Anpassung an die Vorgaben der neuen Elite bestimmt sind, allerdings rasch von den örtlichen Gegebenheiten beeinflusst werden, so dass sich ein gewisser Konsens entwickelt, der dann die Blaupause

---

[118] Das soll nun freilich nicht bedeuten, dass ebenfalls alle anderen großflächigen Akkulturations- und Assimilationsvorgänge der Weltgeschichte ähnlichen Bedingungen unterlagen und somit an die Stelle der terminologischen Auflösung des Hellenisierungsbegriffs aufgrund seiner Komplexität nunmehr seine Auflösung in eine gewisse Beliebigkeit treten soll. Es würde hier natürlich zu weit führen, aus dem hier nur oberflächlich berührten Horizont interkultureller Vergleichsmöglichkeiten eine systematische Kategorisierung zu entwickeln; festgehalten sei nur, dass beispielsweise die große griechische Kolonisation der archaischen Zeit ganz klar einem anderen Schema verpflichtet war, dem man, sucht man nach vergleichbaren Maßstäben, etwa die langsame Ausdehnung des Herrschaftsbereichs des Zhou-Königreichs oder die allmähliche Durchdringung der Ganges-Ebene durch die einwandernden vedischen Völker an die Seite stellen könnte.

für die spätere Durchgestaltung der auf jener Grundlage errichteten jeweiligen Weltreiche liefern sollte. Selbst die religionspolitische Entwicklung, obwohl doch auf den ersten Blick so unterschiedlich, verläuft in analogen Strukturen: Auf eine erste Phase der Abgrenzung folgt eine wechselseitige Anpassung unter den Vorgaben der dominierenden Kultur, um dann nach Episoden forcierter Vereinheitlichung in einen breit geteilten Konsens zu münden. Besonders deutlich wird die parallele Dynamik schließlich auf dem Feld des Selbstbilds: Auf eine ethnische Selbstdefinition erfolgt überall eine exklusive Selbsterhöhung, deren universalistischer Grundzug dann zur Ausgangsbasis einer eher kosmopolitischen und inklusiven Identität wird, deren ursprünglichen ethnischen Grundbedingungen gleichsam ins Pädagogische überführt werden.

Freilich handelt es sich bei dieser Darstellung um eine grob vereinfachte, zeitlich und räumlich stark zu differenzierende Synthese, welche nur ein sinnvolles Grundgerüst für weitere komparatistische Überlegungen bieten soll. Hierbei würde vor allem die hier nur gelegentlich angerissene Frage nach einer Klassifizierung der verschiedenen Akteure von Hellenisierung, Sinisierung und Arabisierung eine systematische Analyse verdienen, ebenso wie die nach dem Widerstand gegen jene Prozesse, welche ebenfalls nur punktuell vermerkt werden konnte. Trotzdem dürfen wir daher vorsichtig festhalten, dass unter dieser komparatistischen Beleuchtung „Hellenisierung" nun doch wieder als ein semantisch sinnvolles historisches Gesamtkonzept erscheint; und das nicht unter reduktionistischer Ausschaltung, sondern vielmehr expliziter Einbeziehung seiner zahlreichen inneren Widersprüche, die eben nicht dazu verführen sollen, den Begriff zugunsten seiner einzelnen Bestandteile aufzugeben, sondern vielmehr, aufgrund ihrer Analogien zu Assimilationsprozessen in anderen Kulturen als innerlich zusammengehörend zu begreifen und zu beschreiben.

Bibliographie

Abou Al-Fadl, K. 2002. The Place of Tolerance in Islam. Boston.

Abu-Lughod, J. 1987. The Islamic City: Historical Myth, Islamic Essence, and Contemporary Relevance, in: International Journal of Middle Eastern Studies 19, 155–176.

Adang, C. und S. Schmidtke and D. Sklare. 2007. A Common Rationality: Mu'tazilism in Islam and Judaism. Würzburg.

Al-Sayyad, N. 1991. Cities and Caliphs: On the Genesis of Arab Muslim Urbanism. New York.

Andrade, N.J. 2013. Syrian Identity in the Greco-Roman World. Cambridge.

Aperghis, G.G. 2011. Antiochos IV and his Jewish Subjects: Political, Cultural and Religious Interactions, in: K. Erickson and G. Ramsey (Hgg.), Seleucid Dis solution. The Sinking of the Anchor, Wiesbaden, 67–83.

Arnold, T. 1896. The Preaching of Islam. A History of the Propagation of the Mus lim Faith. London.

Auyang, S.Y. 2014. The Dragon and the Eagle. The Rise and Fall of the Chinese and Roman Empires. London.

Bagley, R.W. 1990. A Shang City in Sichuan Province, in: Orientations 21.11, 52–67.

Baldry, H.C. 1965. The Unity of Mankind in Greek Thought. Cambridge.

Bang, P.F. und D. Kolodziejczyk (Hgg.). 2015. Universal Empire. A Comparative Approach to Imperial Culture and Representation in Eurasian History. Cambridge.

Barakat Ahmad, S. 1980. Non-Muslims and the Umma, in: SI 17, 80–118.

Barfield, T. 1989. The Perilous Frontier. Nomadic Empires and China. Cambridge (Ma.)

Baron, R.A. und A. Cara (Hgg.). 2011. Creolization as Cultural Creativity. Oxford (Miss.)

Bernard, P. 1973. Fouilles d'Aï-Khanoum I. Campagne 1965–1968. Paris.

Bernard,P. 1987. Le Marsyas d'Apamée, l'Oxus et la colonisation séleucide en Bactriane, in : Studia Iranica 16, 103–115.

Berry, J.W. und M. Segall und C. Kagitcibasi (Hgg.). 1997 Handbook of Cross-Cultural Psychology. Bd. 3, Social Behaviour and Applications. Boston et al.

Bichler, R. 1982. Hellenismus. Geschichte und Problematik eines Epochenbegriffs, Darmstadt.

Biegel, L.C. 1972. Minderheden in Het Midden-Oosten: Hun Betekenis als Politieke Factor in de Arabische Wereld. Deventer.

Bikerman, E. 1938. Institutions des Séleucides. Paris.

Bikerman, E. 1966. The Seleucids and the Achaemenids, in: RANL 76, 87–117.

Billows, R.S. 1995. Kings and Colonists: Aspects of Macedonian Imperialism. Leiden.

Boiy, T. 2004. Late Achaemenid and Hellenistic Babylon. Leuven.

Bopearachchi, O. 1994. L'indépendance de la Bactriane, in : Topoi 4, 519–531.

Bosworth, A.B. 1971. The Death of Alexander the Great: Rumour and Propa ganda, in: CQ, 112–136.

Bosworth, A.B. 1980. Alexander and the Iranians, in: JHS 100, 1–21.

Hellenisierung, Sinisierung, Arabisierung   257

Bosworth, C. E. 1982, The Concept of Dhimma in Early Islam, in: B. Braude und Lewis (Hgg.), Christians and Jews in the Ottoman Empire, Bd. 2, 37–51. New York.

Boyce, M. und F. Grenet 1991. A History of Zoroastrianism, vol. 3, Zoroastrianism under Macedonian and Roman Rule. Leiden.

Bravo, B. 2007. Antiquarianism and History, in: J. Marincola (Hg.), A Companion to Greek and Roman Historiography, Malden (Mass.) et al., 515–27.

Briant, P. 1978. Colonisation hellénistique et populations indigènes. La phase d'installation, in: Klio 60, 57–92.

Briant, P. 1990. The Seleucid Kingdom, The Achaemenid Empire and the History of the Near East in the First Millenium BC, in: P. Bilde et al. (Hgg.), Religion and Religious Practice in the Seleucid Kingdom, Aarhus, 40–65.

Briant, P. 1994. Institutions perses et institutions macédoniennes: continuités, changements et bricolages, in: H. Sancisi-Weerdenburg et al. (Hgg), Achaemenid History VIII, Leiden, 283–310.

Bringmann, K. 1980. Die Verfolgung der jüdischen Religion durch Antiochos IV, in: A&A 26, 176–190.

Bringmann, K. 1995. Kleine Geschichte der Antike. München.

Brodersen, K. 2001. In den städtischen Gründungen ist die rechte Basis des Hellenisierens. Zur Funktion seleukidischer Städtegründungen, in: S. Schraut und B. Stier (Hgg.), Stadt und Land. Bilder, Inszenierungen und Visionen in Geschichte und Gegenwart. Wolfgang Hippel zum Geburtstag, Stuttgart, 356–371.

Bulliet, R. 1979. Conversion to Islam in the Medieval Period: an Essay in Quantitative History. Cambridge (Mass.)

Burbank, J. and F. Cooper (Hgg.). Empires in World History. Power and the Politics of Difference. Princeton.

Cahen, C. 1999. art. Dhimma, in: EI2 2, 227–231.

Cai, L. 2014. Witchcraft and the Rise of the First Confucian Empire. New York.

Capdetrey, L. 2007. Le pouvoir séleucide: Territoire, administration, finances d'un royaume hellénistique (312–129 avant J.-C). Paris.

Chin, T. 2012. Antiquarian as Ethnographer: Han Ethnicity in Early China Studies, in: T. Mullaney et al. (Hgg.), Critical Han Studies. The History, Representation, and Identity of China's Majority, Berkeley, 128–146.

Chin, T. 2014. Savage Exchange. Han Imperialism, Chinese Literary Style and the Economic Imagination. Cambridge (Mass.)

Chin, T. 2017. Colonization, Sinicization, and the Polyscriptic Northwest, in: W. Denecke und W.Y. Li und X. Tian (Hgg.), The Oxford Handbook of Classical Chinese Literature (1000 BCE-900CE), Oxford, 477–493.

Ching, J. 1993. Chinese Religions. London.

Chokr, M. 1993. Zandaqa et zindiqs en Islam au second siècle de l'Hegire. Damaskus.

Cohen, G.M. 1978. The Seleucid Colonies: Studies in Founding, Administration and Organization. Wiesbaden.

Cohen, G.M. 2006. The Hellenistic Settlements in Syria, the Red Sea Basin, and North Africa. Berkeley.

Cohen, G.M. 2013. The Hellenistic Settlements in the East from Armenia and

Mesopotamia to Bactria and India. Berkeley.

Collins, J.J. 1999. The Hellenization of Jerusalem in the Pre-Maccabean Era, in: International Rennert Guest Lecture series 6.

Coloru, O. 2009. Da Alessandro a Menandro. Il regno greco di Battriana. Pisa und Rom.

Colpe, C. 1954. Der Manichäismus in der arabischen Überlieferung. Göttingen.

Cook, C.A. und J.S. Major 1999. Defining Chu: Image and Reality in Ancient China. Honolulu.

Cooper, R.S. 1976. The Assessment and Collection of Kharaj Tax in Medieval Egypt, in: Journal of the American Oriental Society 96.3, 365–382.

Coşgel, M. et al. 2009. Law, State Power, and Taxation in Islamic History, in: Journal of Economic Behavior & Organization 71.3, 704–717.

Crone, P. 1987. Roman, Provincial and Islamic Law. Cambridge.

Crone, P. 2009. Art. Mawlā, EI² 7, 874–882.

Dauge, Y.A. 1982. Le Barbare. Recherches sur la conception romaine de la barbarie et de la civilisation. Brüssel.

de Lafayette, M. 2017. Etymology, Philology and Comparative Dictionary of Synonyms in 22 Dead and Ancient Languages, Bd. 2. New York.

Debord, P. 2003. Le culte royal chez les Séleucides, in: F. Prost (Hg.), L'Orient Méditerranéen de la mort d'Alexandre aux campagnes de Pompée, Rennes, 281–310.

Denecke, W. 2014. Classical World Literatures: Sino-Japanese and Greco-Roman Comparisons. Oxford.

Dennett, D.C. 1950. Conversion and the Poll Tax in Early Islam. Harvard.

Di Cosmo, N. 2002. Ancient China and Its Enemies: The Rise of Nomadic Power in East Asian History. Cambridge.

Diesenberger, M. and R. Corradini and H. Reimitz 2003. The Construction of Communities in the Early Middle Ages. Leiden.

Dihle, A. 1994. Die Griechen und die Fremden. München.

Djait, H. 1986. Al-Kufa. Naissance de la ville islamique. Paris.

Donner, F.M. 1981. The Early Islamic Conquests. Princeton.

Donner, F.M. 1984. Tribal Settlement in Basra during the First Century A.H., in: T. Khalidi (Hg.), Land Tenure and Social Transformation in the Middle East, Beirut, 97–120.

Eddy, S.K. 1961. The King is Dead. Studies in the Near Eastern Resistance to Hellenism. Lincoln (Neb.).

Engels, D. 2013. Entre tolérance, désintérêt et exploitation: Les relations christiano-musulmanes en Sicile du 9ème au 13ème siècle, in : Les Cahiers de la Méditerranée 86, 273–300.

Engels, D. 2013. Le déclin. La crise de l'Union européenne et la chute de la République romaine, Paris. (Dt. Übers. Unter dem Titel: Auf dem Weg ins Imperium. Die Krise der Europäischen Union und der Untergang der Römischen Republik, Berlin, 2014).

Engels, D. 2014. Polemon von Ilion. Antiquarische Periegese und hellenistische Identitätssuche, in: K. Freitag und Chr. Michels (Hgg.), Athen und / oder Alexandreia? Aspekte von Identität und Ethnizität im hellenistischen Griechenland, Köln und Wien, 65–98.

Engels, D. 2015. Romanisation and Globalisation. Some Reflections on Martin Pitts' and John Miguel Versluys' 'Globalisation and the Roman World' (note de lecture), in: Latomus 74, 1073–1077.

Engels, D. 2016. s.v. Aristocracy and Kingship, in: J.M. MacKenzie (Hg.), Encyclopedia of Empire, vol. 1, 136–148.

Engels, D. 2017a. Construction de normes et morphologie culturelle. Empire romain, chinois, sasanide et fatimide – une comparaison historique, in: T. Itgenshorst und Ph. LeDoze (Hgg.), La norme sous la République romaine et le Haut Empire. Élaboration, diffusion et contournements, Bordeaux, 53–73.

Engels, D. 2017b. Benefactors, Kings, Rulers. Studies on the Seleucid Empire between East and West. Leuven.

Engels, D. 2017c. Neue Studien zum hellenistischen Osten – ein Forschungsüberblick, in: Latomus 76, 481–496.

Engels, D. 2018a. Zwischenstaatlichkeit und Herrscherideal in militärisch-politischen Sachbüchern. Ein komparatistischer Versuch über Sūn Zǐ, Kauṭilya, Aeneas Tacticus und Machiavelli, in: Electrum 25, 209–241.

Engels, D. 2018b. The Revolution of 1917 from the Perspective of the Morphology of History, in: A. Máthé (Hg.), 1917–2017. Memory and Legacy. Perception of Communism in Europe, Budapest, 27–44.

Engels, D. 2018c. Kulturmorphologie und Willensfreiheit. Überlegungen zu einer neuen komparatistischen Geschichtsphilosophie, in: D. Engels und M. Otte und M. Thöndl (Hgg.), Der lange Schatten Oswald Spenglers. Einhundert Jahre „Untergang des Abendlandes", Lüdinghausen und Berlin, 79–101.

Engels, D. im Druck a. Historical necessity or biographical singularity? C. Iulius Caesar and Qin Shi Huang Di, in: H. Beck und Gr. Vankeerberghen (Hgg.), Global Antiquities. Montreal.

Engels im Druck b. The Peach Blossom Land and the Sacred Isles: Utopias and Ideal States in Classical Antiquity and Ancient China - a Comparison, in: P. Destrée und J. Opsomer und G. Roskam (Hgg.), Ancient Utopias.

Engels im Druck c. "Reinheit" als Herrscherqualität im ideologischen Narrativ der großen Universalherrscher der alten Welt, in: L. Clemens und B. Eckhardt und K. Zimmermann (Hg.), Purity and Authority.

Engels, D. and K. Erickson 2016. Apama and Stratonike. Marriage Policy and Legitimacy, in: A. Coskun und A. MacAuley (Hgg.), Seleukid Royal Women. Creation, Representation and Distortion of Hellenistic Queenship in the Seleukid Empire, Stuttgart, 41–68.

Engels, D. and C. Grigolin 2018. Edition, Übersetzung und Kommentar der Fragmente von Pausanias von Antiocheia (FGrHist 1777). Leiden.

Fattal, A. 1958. Le statut légal des non-musulmans en pays d'Islam. Beirut.

Faurot, J. L. 1992. Ancient Chengdu. San Francisco.

Feissel, D. 1985. Deux listes de quartiers d'Antioche astreints au creusement d'un canal (73–74 après J.-C.), in: Syria 62, 77–103.

Ferguson, C.A. 1959. The Arabic Koine, in: Language 25, 616–630.

Fludernik, M. und H.-J. Gehrke (Hgg.). 2004. Normen, Ausgrenzung, Hybridisierungen und „Acts of Identity". Würzburg.

Francfort, H.-P. 1984. Le sanctuaire du temple à niches indentées. Paris.

Franz, E. 1978. Minderheiten im Vorderen Orient: Eine Auswahlbibliographie.

260 David Engels

Hamburg.

Fu, Z. 1996. China's Legalists. The Earliest Totalitarians and their Art of Ruling. London.

Funck, B. 1991. Herrscherkult der Seleukiden – Religion einer Elite oder Reichsideologie? Einige Bemerkungen zur Fragestellung, in: Klio 73, 402–407.

Funck, B. (Hg.) 1996. Hellenismus. Beiträge zur Erforschung von Akkulturation und politischer Ordnung in den Staaten des hellenistischen Zeitalters. Tübingen.

Gehler, M. und R. Rollinger (Hgg.). 2014. Imperien und Reiche in der Weltgeschichte, Epochenübergreifende und globalhistorische Vergleiche. Wiesbaden.

Georges, P. 1994. Barbarian Asia and the Greek Experience. Baltimore.

Giorgi, J.-M. 1989. Pour une histoire de la zandaka. Pavia.

Goddard, H. 2000. A History of Christian-Muslim Relations. Edinburgh.

Goldziher, I. 1994. On the History of Grammar among the Arabs: An Essay in Literary History. Philadelphia.

Gorre, G. und S. Honigmans 2014. La politique d'Antiochos IV à Jérusalem à la lumière des relations entre rois et temples aux époques perse et hellénistique (Babylonie, Judée et Égypte) , in: C. Feyel und L. Graslin-Thomé (Hgg.), Le projet politique d'Antiochos IV, Paris, 301–338.

Grenet, F. 1984. Les pratiques funéraires dans l'Asie Centrale sédentaire de la conquête grecque à l'islamisation. Paris.

Grenet, F. 1991. Mithra au temple principal d'Ai Khanoum, in: P. Bernard und F. Grenet (Hgg.), Histoire et cultes de l'Asie centrale préislamiques. Sources écrites et documents archéologiques, Paris, 147–151.

Gruen, E.S. 1993. Hellenism and Persecution: Antiochos IV and the Jews, in: P. Green (Hg.), Hellenistic History and Culture, Berkeley, 238–264.

Guidi, M. 1927. La lotta tra l'Islam e il Manicheismo. Rom.

Hakim, B.S. 1979. Arabic Islamic Cities Rev: Building and Planning Principles. London.

Hall, E.M. 1989. Inventing the Barbarian. Greek self-definition through tragedy. Oxford.

Hall, J.-M. 2002. Hellenicity. Between Ethnicity and Culture. Chicago.

Hawkes, D. 1985. The Songs of the South: An Anthology of Ancient Chinese Poems by Qu Yuan and Other Poets.

Heckel, W. 1988. The Last Days and Testament of Alexander the Great. Stuttgart.

Heidemann, F. und A. de Toro (Hgg.). 2006. New Hybridities: Societies and Cultures in Transition. Hildesheim.

Held, W. 2002. Die Residenzstädte der Seleukiden: Babylon, Seleukia am Tigris, Ai Khanum, Seleukia in Pieria, Antiochia am Orontes, in: JDAI 117, 217–249.

Held, W. 2005. Kult auf dem Dach. Eine Deutung der Tempel mit Treppenhäusern und Giebeltüren als Zeugnis seleukidischer Sakralarchitektur, in: IstMitt 55, 119–160.

Held, W. 2008. Seleukid Temples of 'Iranian Type', unpubl. conference held in Exeter 2008 (Seleukid Dissolution. The Sinking of the Anchor) and in Brussels 2008 (invited conference).

Held, W. 2014. Seleukidische Tempel „babylonischen Typs, in: Marburger Winckelmannprogramm.

Hengel, W. 1996. Jerusalem als jüdische und hellenistische Stadt, in: B. Funck (Hg.), Hellenismus: Beiträge zur Erforschung von Akkulturation und politischer Ordnung in den Staaten des hellenistischen Zeitalters, Tübingen, 525–542.

Hillenbrandt, R. 1999. Anjar and Early Islamic Urbanism, in: G. P. Brogiolo und B. Ward-Perkins (Hgg.), The Idea and Ideal of the Town between Late Antiquity and the Early Middle Ages, Leiden, 59–98.

Hodgson, M. 1974. The Venture of Islam. Conscience and History in a World Civilization (3 Bde.). Chicago.

Horden, P. and N. Purcell. 2000. The Corrupting Sea: A Study of Mediterranean History. Malden (Ma.) et al.

Hoyland, R. (Hg.) 2004. Muslims and Others in Early Islamic Society. Aldershot.

Hurlet, F. (Hg.) 2008. Les Empires. Antiquité et Moyen Âge. Analyse comparée. Rennes.

Jamshidian Tehrani, J. 2014. Shu'ubiyya: Independence movements in Iran. Teheran.

Juda, J. 1983. Die sozialen und wirtschaftlichen Aspekte der Mawālī in frühislamischer Zeit. Tübingen.

Jüthner, J. 1923. Hellenen und Barbaren. Aus der Geschichte des Nationalbewußtseins. Leipzig.

Kah, D. und P. Scholz (Hgg.). 2004. Das hellenistische Gymnasion. Berlin.

Keel, O. und U. Staub. 2000.Hellenismus und Judentum. Vier Studien zu Daniel 7 und zur Religionsnot unter Antiochus IV. Fribourg.

Keightley, D.N. 1969. Public Work in Ancient China: A Study of Forced Labor in the Shang and Western Chou. New York.

Kern, M. 2000. The Stele Inscriptions of Ch'in Shi'huang: Text and Ritual in Early Chinese Imperial Representation. New Haven (Conn.).

Khoury, A. T. 1980. Toleranz im Islam. München.

Kleeman, T.F. 1998. Great Perfection: Religion and Ethnicity in a Chinese Millennial Kingdom. Honolulu.

König, D.G. 2015. Arabic-Islamic Views of the Latin West. Tracing the Emergence of Medieval Europe. Oxford.

Kosmin, P. 2014. The Land of the Elephant Kings: Space, Territory, and Ideology in the Seleucid Empire. Cambridge (Mass.).

Kosmin, P.J. 2018. Time and its Adversaries in the Seleucid Empire. Cambridge (Mass.)

Kuhrt, A. 1996. The Seleucid Kings and Babylonia: New Perspectives on the Seleucid Realm in the East, in: P. Bilde et al. (Hgg.), Religion and Religious Practice in the Seleucid Kingdom, Aarhus, 41–54.

Lagerwey, J. (Hg.) 2004. Religion and Chinese Society, 2 Bde. Hongkong.

Lagerwey, J. und M. Kalinowski (Hgg.). 2008. Early Chinese Religion: Part One: Shang through Han (1250 BC-220 AD), 2 Bde. Leiden.

Lambton, A.K.S. 1953. Landlord and Peasant in Persia: A Study of Land Tenure and Land Revenue Administration. London.

Lapidus, I.M. 1972. The Conversion of Egypt to Islam, in: Israel Oriental Studies

2, 248–262.

Lapidus, I.M. 1981. Arab Settlement and Economic Development of Iraq and Iran in the age of the Umayyad and Early Abbasid Caliphs, in: A. L. Udovitch (Hg.), The Islamic Middle East, 700–1900: Studies in Economic and Social History, Princeton, 177–208.

Larsso, G. 2003. Ibn García's Shu'ūbiyya Letter, Ethnic and Theological Tensions in Medieval Al-Andalus. Leiden.

Lau, U. 1999. Quellenstudien zur Landvergabe und Bodenübertragung in der westlichen Zhou.Dynastie. Nettetal.

Lawton, T. (Hg.) 1991. New Perspectives on Chu Culture. Princeton.

Leriche, P. 1974. Ai Khanoum, un rempart hellénistique en Asie Centrale, in : RA 2, 231–270.

Levtzion, N. (Hg.) 1978. Conversion to Islam. New York.

Lévi-Strauss, C. 1966. The Savage Mind. London.

Levy, R. 1957. The Social Structure of Islam. Cambridge.

Lewis, B. 1980. L'Islam et les non-musulmans, in : AESC 35, 784–800.

Lewis, M. 2007. The Early Chinese Empire: Qin and Han. London.

Litvinskij, B.A. et al. 1985. The Votive Offering of Atrosokes from the Temple of Oxus in Northern Bactria, in: VDI 4, 84–110.

Lloyd, G.E.R. und J.J. Zhao (Hgg.). 2017. Ancient Greece and China Compared. Cambridge.

Loewe, M. 2006. The Government of the Qin and Han Empires, 221 BCE–220 CE. Indianapolis.

Løkkegaard, F. 1950. Islamic Taxation in the Classic Period, with Special Reference to the Circumstances in Iraq. Kopenhagen.

MacKenzie, J.M. und N. Dalziel (Hgg) 2004. The Encyclopedia of Empire. Oxford.

Mairs, R. 2010. An 'Identity Crisis`? Identity and its Discontents in Hellenistic Studies, in: Bolletino di Archeologia Online 1, 55–62.

Major, J.S. 1999. Characteristics of Late Chu Religion, in: A. Cook und J.S. Major (Hgg.), Defining Chu: Image and Reality in Ancient China, Honolulu, 121–143.

Marranci, G. 2008. The Anthropology of Islam. London.

Massignon, L. 1935. Explication du plan de Kûfa. Paris.

Masson, V. 1982 Das Land der tausend Städte. Eine Wiederentdeckung der ältesten Kulturgebiete in Mittelasien. München.

Mazzucchi, R. 2009. A Gymnasium in Jerusalem, in: I. Xydopoulos et al. (Hgg.), Institutional Changes and Stability. Conflicts, Transitions, Society, Pisa, 19–34.

Mehl, A. 1992. Erziehung zum Hellenen – Erziehung zum Weltbürger. Bemerkungen zum Gymnasium im hellenistischen Osten, in: Nikephoros 5, 43–73.

Millward, A.E. 1973. The Ruler Cults of the Seleucids.

Mittag, P.F. 2006. Antiochos IV. Epiphanes. Eine politische Biographie. Berlin.

Momigliano, A. 1975. Alien Wisdom. The Limits of Hellenization. Cambridge.

Momigliano, A. 1990. The Classical Foundations of Modern Historiography. Berkeley.

Morimoto, K. 1981. The Fiscal Administration of Egypt in the Early Islamic Period. Kyoto.

Morony, M.G. 1981. Landholding in Seventh-Century Iraq: Late Sasanian and Early Islamic Patterns, in: A.L. Udovitch (Hg.), The Islamic Middle East, 700–1900: Studies in Economic and Social History, Princeton, 135–175.

Mottahedeh, R.P. 1976. The Shuʿûbîyah Controversy and the Social History of Early Islamic Iran, in: IJMES 7, 161–182.

Musti, D. 1966. Lo stato dei Seleucidi. Dinastia, popoli, città da Seleuco I ad Antiocho III, in: SCO 15, 60–197.

Mutschler, F.-H. und A. Mittag. 2008. Conceiving the Empire: Rome and China Compared. Oxford.

Nadeau, R.L. (Hg.) 2012. The Wiley-Blackwell Companion to Chinese Religions. Malden (Ma.).

Noth, A. 1978. Möglichkeiten und Grenzen der Toleranz im Islam, in: Saeculum 29, 190–204.

Nrowder, M.H. 1992. The Formulation of Manichaeism in Late Ummayad Islam, in: G. Wiessner and H.-H. Klimkeit, (Hgg.), Studia Manichaica. II. Internationaler Kongreß zum Manichäismus, 6-10 August 1989, Leiden, 328–333.

Oelsner, J. 1986. Materialien zur babylonischen Gesellschaft und Kultur in hellenistischer Zeit. Budapest.

Panaino, A. 2003. The BAΓĀN of the Fratarakas: Gods or 'Divine' Kings?, in: C.G. Cereti et al. (Hgg.), Religious Themes and Texts of pre-Islamic Iran and Central Asia, Wiesbaden, 265–288.

Paret, R. 1970. Toleranz und Intoleranz im Islam, in: Saeculum 21, 344–365.

Pellat, C. 1953. Le milieu baṣrien et la formation de Ǧāḥiẓ. Paris.

Peters, H. 1985. The Role of the State of Chu in Eastern Zhou Period China: A Study of Interaction and Exchange.

Pfeiffer, R. 1968. History of Classical Scholarship: From the Beginnings to the End of the Hellenistic Age. Oxford.

Pines, Y. 2009. Envisioning Eternal Empire: Chinese Political Thought of the Warring States Era. Honolulu.

Pines, Y. et al. (Hgg.) 2014. Birth of an Empire. The State of Qin Revisited. Berkeley.

Pitts, M. und J.M. Versluys (Hgg.). 2015. Globalization and the Roman World. World History, Connectivity and Material Culture. New York.

Plischke, S. 2014. Die Seleukiden und Iran: Die seleukidische Herrschaftspolitik in den östlichen Satrapien. Wiesbaden.

Poliak, A.N. 1940. Classification of Lands in the Islamic Law and Its Technical Terms, in: The American Journal of Semitic Languages and Literatures 57.1, 1940, 50–62 und 248–262.

Pollock, S. 2013. Cosmopolitism, Vernacularism, and Premodernity, in: S. Moyn und A. Satori (Hgg.), Global Intellectual History, New York, 59–81.

Poo, M. 2000. Enemies of Civilization: Attitudes toward Foreigners in Ancient Mesopotamia, Egypt, and China. Albany.

Portal, J. (Hg.) 2007. The First Emperor: China's Terracotta Army. Harvard.

Psarras, S.-K. 1994. Exploring the North. Non-Chinese Cultures of the Late Warring States and Han, in: Monumenta Serica 42, 1–125.

Pulleyblank, E.G. 1983. The Chinese and Their Neighbors in Prehistoric and Early Historic Times, in: D.N. Keightley (Hg.), The Origins of Chinese Civilization, Berkeley, 411–466.

Rapin, C. 1992. La trésorerie du palais hellénistique d'Ai Khanoum. Paris.

Reitemeyer, E. 1912. Die Städtegründungen der Araber im Islam nach den arabischen Historikern und Geographen. Wiesbaden.

Rey-Coquais, J.P. 1991. Institutions hellénistiques des cités de Syrie et de Phénicie, in : OESA 407–416.

Roberts, R. 1925. Social Laws of the Qorân. London.

Rojas, C. 2010. The Great Wall: a Cultural History. Cambridge (Ma.).

Sage, S. F. 1992. Ancient Sichuan and the Unification of China. Albany.

Sarkisian, G.K. 1976. Greek Personal Names in Uruk and the Graeco-Babyloniaca Problem, in: J. Harmatta und G. Komoroczy (Hgg.), Wirtschaft und Gesellschaft im alten Vorderasien, Budapest, 495–503.

Sartre, M. 2007. Le nom ambigu. Les limites de l'identité culturelle dans l'onomastique de la Syrie gréco-romaine, in: Old and New Worlds in Greek Onomastics, 199–232.

Scharrer, U. 1999. Seleukos I. und das babylonische Königtum, in: K. Brodersen (Hg.), Zwischen West und Ost. Studien zur Geschichte des Seleukidenreichs, Hamburg, 95–128.

Scheidel, W. (Hg.) 2009. Rome and China. Comparative Perspectives on Ancient World Empires. Oxford.

Scheidel, W. (Hg.) 2015. State Power in Ancient China and Rome. Oxford.

Scheiner, J. J. 2004. Vom Gelben Flicken zum Judenstern? Genese und Applikation von Judenabzeichen im Islam und christlichen Europa (849–1941). Frankfurt a.M.

Schipper, F. 2006. Jasons Gymnasium in Jerusalem, in: M. Frass et al. (Hgg.), Akten des 10. Österreichischen Althistorikertages, Wien, 113–126.

Schmitt, H.H. und E. Vogt (Hgg.) 2005. Lexikon des Hellenismus. Wiesbaden.

Shemesh, A.B. 1967. Taxation in Islam (Including Translation of Kitab al-Kharaj, 2. Auflage. Leiden.

Sherwin-White, S. 1983. Aristeas Ardubeltaios. Some Aspects of the Use of Double Names in Seleucid Babylonia, in: ZPE 50, 209–221.

Sherwin-White, S. und A. Kuhrt. 1993. From Samarkand to Sardis: A New Approach to the Seleucid Empire. London.

Shryock, J.K. 1966. The Origin and Development of the State Cult of Confucius. New York.

Sina, M. (Hg.) 1991. La tolleranza religiosa. Indagni storiche e riflessioni filosofiche. Rom.

So, J.F. 2000. Music in the Age of Confucius. Washington (D.C.).

Spring, P. 2015. Great Walls and Linear Barriers. Barnsley.

Stevens, K. 2014. The Antiochus Cylinder, Babylonian Scholarship, and Seleucid Imperial Ideology, in: JHS 134, 66–88.

Stevens, K. 2019. Between Greece and Babylonia. Hellenistic Intellectual History in Cross-Cultural Perspective. Cambridge.

Stier, H.E. 1973. Welteroberung und Weltfriede im Wirken Alexanders des Großen. Opladen.

Stoneman, R. und K. Erickson und I.R. Netton (Hgg.) 2012, The Alexander Romance in Persia and the East. Groningen.

Hellenisierung, Sinisierung, Arabisierung 265

Strootman, R. 2013. Babylonian, Macedonian, King of the World, in: E. Stavria
nopoulou (Hg.), Shifting Social Imaginaries in the Hellenistic Period. Narrations, Practices, and Images, Leiden, 67–97.

Sukhu, G. 2012. The Shaman and the Heresiarch: A New Interpretation of the Li
sao. New York.

Tarn, W.W. 1951. The Greeks in Bactria and India. Cambridge.

Tcherikover, V. 1927. Die hellenistischen Städtegründungen von Alexander dem
Großen bis auf die Römerzeit. Leipzig.

Thote, A. 1999. Intercultural Relations as Seen from Chinese Pictorial Bronzes of
the Fifth Century BCE, in: Res 35, 10–41.

Touatui, H. 2010. Islam and Travel in the Middle Ages. Chicago.

Treistman, J.M. 1968. China at 1000 B.C.: A Cultural Mosaic, in: Science 160,
853–856.

Treistman, J.M. 1974. The Early Cultures of Szechwan and Yunnan, Cornell University East Asia Papers 3. New York.

Tritton, A.S. 1930. The Caliphs and their non-Muslim Subjects: a Critical Study of
the Covenant of `Umar. London.

Tuplin, C. 2008. The Seleucids and Their Achaemenid Predecessors: A Persian Inheritance?, in: Ancient Greece and Ancient Iran: Cross-Cultural Encounters.
1st International Conference (Athens 11–13 November 2006). Cambridge.

Twitchett, D. und M. Loewe (Hgg.) 1986, The Cambridge History of China, vol. 1,
The Ch'in and Han Empires, 221BC–AD220. Cambridge.

Van den Berg, G. 2013. Alexander in het Perzische Boek der Koningen, in: D.
Burgersdijk und W. Henkelma und W. Waal (Hgg.), Alexander en Darius. De
Macedonier in de spiegel van het Nabije Oosten, Hilversum, 195–208.

Van Gelder, G. 1996. Kufa vs. Basra: the Literary Debate, in: Asiatische Studien
50, 339–362.

Van Nuffelen, P. 2004. Le culte royal de l'empire des Séleucides: une réinterpréta
Tion, in : Historia 53.3, 278–301.

Versteegh, C.H.M. 1993. Arabic Grammar and Qur'ānic Exegesis in Early Islam.
Leiden.

von Hesberg, H. 1995. Das griechische Gymnasion im 2. Jh. v.Chr., in: M.
Wörrle und P. Zanker (Hgg.), Stadtbild und Bürgerbild im Hellenismus,
München, 13–28.

Wagner, C. 1991. Die Entwicklung Johann Gustav Droysens als Althistoriker.
Bonn.

Waldron, A. 1990. The Great Wall of China: from History to Myth. Cambridge.

Waley, A. 1955. The Nine Songs: a Study of Shamanism in Ancient China. London.

Watt, W.M. 1980. Islamic Political Thought: The Basic Concepts. Edinburgh.

Webster, J. 2001. Creolizing the Roman Provinces, in: AJA 105.2, 209–225.

Wenghofer, R. 2018. Rethinking the Relationship between Hellenistic Baktria and
the Seleukid Empire, in: K. Erickson (Hg.), War Within the Family: A Reassessment of the First Half-Century of Seleukid Rule, Swansea.

Wiesehöfer, J. 1994. Die 'dunklen Jahrhunderte' der Persis. Untersuchungen zu
Geschichte und Kultur des Färs in frühhellenistischer Zeit (339–140 v. Chr.).
München.

Wolski, J. 1982. Le problème de la fondation de l'État gréco-bactrien, in: IA 17,

131–146.

Zheng, D. 1945. An Ancient History of Szechwan, in: Journal of the West China Border Research Society 16, series A, 1–15.

Zheng, D. 1947. An Introduction to Szechwan Archaeology. Chengdu.

Zheng, D. 1947. Archaeological Chronology in Szechwan, in: Antiquity 21.81, 46–50.

Zheng, D. 1957. Archaeological Studies in Szechwan. Cambridge.

Indices

Sources

Inscriptions

AE
1982, 877: **120**

BCHP
14: **187–188**

BE
1973, 286: **90**
1977, 537: **93**

CIS
I 349: **152**; 350: **156**
II 197: **161**; 349: **154**; 354: **151**

I. Beroia
1:**184**

I. Didyma
49: **24**

I. Erythrai
II 207,10: **22**

I. Iasos
II 222f.: **22**

I. Magnesia Sip.
1 I: **19, 22**; 12f.: **23**; 34–36: **24, 26**

I. Mylasa
I 203,5: **22**; 204,3: **22**

I. Salamis
XIII 135: **165**

I. Smyrna
1, 574: **19**; 21f.: **23**

ID
1593: **165**

IG
XI 2,203: **93**

XII 4,1,206f.: **25**; 208f.: **21, 27**; 210:
20, 25; 211: **21, 25, 27**; 212: **21, 26**;
213: **21, 25, 27**; 220: **27**; 621: **165**
Suppl. 116,117: **184**

IGLS
VII 4001: **91**
XIII/2 9675: **120**; 9825: **121**
XV 24–25: **124**; 242: **118**
XIV 532: **121**; 548: **120**; 554–555:
119; 561a: **119, 120**; 561b: **120**; 565:
120-121; 567, 569: **120**
XVI 122, 123, 124: **123**; 393: **122**;
414: **120**; 565: **118**; 567: **120**; 685:
123–124

IGUR
1702: **165**

IGUR
IV 685: **165**

ILS
4995: **165**

IOSPE
II 357: **165**; 358: **165**

OGIS
I 195: **165**; 230: **105**; 246: **162**; 253:
187; 258–260: **163**; 283: **165**; 339: **103**;
741: **148**
II 247: **69**

RES
83: **156**; 527: **150**; 1423: **151**

Rey-Coquais
1989, 2.2: **92**
2006, 1: **91**; 57–75: **92**

SEG
7, 39: **187**
26, 1646: **93**
35, 1483: I **192, 252**

SEG
39, 1283: **182**; 1285: **183**
41, 1003: **27**, **30**, **33**
47, 1745: **185**
48, 785: **21**, **31**
55, 1251: **184**
56, 931: **165**
58, 1756: **188**
61, 1236: **183**

StV
III 492: **24**

Waddington
1870, 1866c: **93**

Coins

A. Tkalec AG
Auktion Mai 2005, Nr. 92: **54**

Alram 1986
no. 491: **48**; 496: **49**; 498: **49**

Assar 2006
fig. 5: **44**; 22: **45**; 30: **46**

BMC
302, 2: **50**

Bop. Ser.
12: **48**

CNG
auction 103, 14.9.2016, no. 444: **46**
electronic auction, 8.4.2015, no. 385:
50
mail bid sale 58, 19.9.2001, no. 805:
49
mail bid sale 63, 21.5.2003, no. 871:
55
Triton
V, 15.1.2002, no. 1561: **44**, **54**
VI, 14.1.2003, no. 505: **47**
VII, 12.1.2004, no. 518: **39**
XIII, 5.1.2010, no. 502: **41**; 507: **42**;
529: **43**; 534: **44**
XVIII, 6.1.2015, no. 165: **39**

XX, 10.1.2017, no. 418: **45**

Donner and Röllig 1962
1–2 Nr. 1: **71**; 4–7 Nr. 7: **1**; 9–11: **71**
2–3 Nr. 13–16: **71**
3–4 Nr. 18: **69**

Gorny and Mosch
Auktion 215, 13.10.2013, Nr. 918: **48**

Hellenistic Petra Project
III, 2007, no. 1: **176**

Hess-Divo AG
Auktion 320, 26.10.2011, Nr. 253: **50**
327, 22.10.2014, Nr. 81: **42**
328, 22.5.2015, Nr. 69: **45**

HGC
9, 1312: **107**

Hirsch
Auktion 323, 22.9.2016, Nr. 2234: **40**

Hoover 2010
30 Nr. 105–107, 109: **70**
30–31 Nr. 105–109, 111–112: **77**
31 Nr. 114–115: **70**
37–39 Nr. 130–131: **71**; 133–134: **71**;
136–140: **71**
39–40 Nr. 141–144: **67**
77–80 Nr. 281–285: **74**; 288–294: **74**;
299: **74**
78 Nr. 287: **74**
78–79 Nr. 284: **78**; 286: **78**; 290: **78**
80 Nr. 296: **74**
98 Nr. 360–361: **76**; 364: **76**
98–99 Nr. 360-364: **76**; 366–368: **76**
98–99 Nr. 360–365: **75**; 367: **75**

Houghton, Lorber, Hoover 2008
80 Nr. 1443–1447: **67**
81 Nr. 1447: **67**; 1448: **68**
83 Nr. 1453–1144: **70**; 1455–1456: **71**
84 Nr. 1457–1460: **71**
86 Nr. 1463–1466: **74**; 1467–1469: **75**
87 Nr. 1470–1471: **75**
135 Nr. 1578: **76**

Houghton, Lorber, Hoover 2008
136 Nr. 1579: **77**
177–178 Nr. 1666–1668: **77**
177–178 Nr. 1667: **76, 78**
179 Nr. 1668: **78**
179–180 Nr. 1671–1675: **78**
235 Nr. 1822: **76**
237 Nr. 1825-1826: **77**
239 Nr. 1833: **77**
299 Nr. 1957: **77**
303–304 Nr. 1968–1969: **78**
379 Nr. 2099: **76**
380 Nr. 2100: **77**
382 Nr. 2104–2106A: **77**
387–388 Nr. 2112–2114: **78**
426 Nr. 2185–2186: **77**
427–428 Nr. 2189–2192: **78**
431 Nr. 2198–2199: **78**
462 Nr. 2250–2252: **77**
512 Nr. 2326–2328: **77**
514 Nr. 2333–2334: **78**
542 Nr. 2387: **78**

Lanz
Auktion 162, 6.6.2016, Nr. 178: **40**

Le Rider 1965
Nr. 442f.: **54**; 485f.: **54**

Lichtenberger 2008
160 Abb. 28: **73**

Lindgren
I, 2134A: **116**
III, 1227: **116**, 1232: **116**

Meshorer 2001
207–209 (Group H, I, J): **205**
209–210 (Group K): **205**
210 (Group L): **205**
211 (Group N): **205**

Müller
III 1862, 53–57 Nr. 63–65: **72**

Peus Auktion
368, 25.4.2001, Nr. 330: **39**
376, 29.10.2003, Nr. 595: **45**

386, 26.4.2006, Nr. 373: **48**
405, 2.11.2011, Nr. 2371: **50**
413, 29.10.2014, Nr. 139: **44**

Rauch, GmbH
94, 9.4.2014 Nr. 494: **46**

Roma Numismatics Ltd
Auktion XII, 29.9.2016, Nr. 409: **49**;
413: **40**

RPC
4124: **37**

Sachs und Hunger 1996
124 B rev. 12'–14': **39**; rev. 17'–18':
39; obv. 19': **39**
125 A obv. 20: **48**
126 A obv. 6'-9': **48**
132 B Rev. 18-20: **47**; D ,obv.' 8'–
10': **38**
140 rev. 30'–35': **38**; C obv. 35–38:
39
144 obv. 18': **38**; rev. 20–22: **38**

Sawaya 2008
63–74 série. 1–8, 12: **70**

SC
855: **57**; 914: **57**; 1396f.: **51**; 1443f.:
53; 1472–75: **51**; 1635: **45**; 1866: **48**;
1867: **39**; 1868: **40**; 1984: **54**; 1992:
57; 1993f.: **48**; 1995: **39**; 1995A: **40**;
2345–2400: **57**; 2346 f.: **45**; 2456.2:
107; 2459–2470: **37**

Sellwood
1.1: **42**; 1.1–4.1: **41**; 2.1: **41**; 5.1–6.1:
42; 6.1: **42**; 6.2: **53**; 7.1–8.1: **43, 53**;
8.2–8.3: **53**; 9.1: **43**; 10: **43**; 10.1: **42**;
11.3: **43**; 11.6–11.7: **53**; 12.9–12.49:
53; 13: **44**; 13.10: **44**; 13.2: **44**; 14: **45**;
14.2: **44**; 14.3–14.6: **53**; 15.5–15.7: **53**;
16: **45**; 16.26–16.30: **53**; 16.6: **45**; 17:
45; 17.1: **44, 54**; 17.5: **53**; 18.3: **53**;
20.7: **53**; 21: **46**; 21.1: **45**; 21.5–21.9:
53; 23.4–23.10: **53**; 24.1: **46, 47**;

Sellwood
24.33–24.46: **53**; 26.25–26.33: **53**;
27.14–27: **46**; 27.6–27.28: **53**; 28.18–
23: **46**; 28.21: **46**; 28.8–28.23: **53**; 30:
46

SNG Kop.
42, 672–675: **72**
414: **116**

Sylloge³
1065: **165**

van't Haaff
2.1: **39**; 2.10–2.11: **40**; 2.3–2.9: **40**;
3.2: **40**; 4.2–4.5: **40**; 5.2–5.7: **40**; 6.1:
39; 7.1: **40**; 7.1–8.3: **41**; 8.1: **40**; 9.1:
40; 9.1–9.2: **41**

Literary Sources

Ael.
VH
7, 8, 12, 7: **221**

Aischin.
1,1–2; 116: **224**; 2,1–4: **216**; 2,22: **224**;
2,78: **224**; 2,180: **224**; 3, 152: **224**;
3,156: **224**; 3,172–173: **224**; 3,210:
224; 3,244: **216**; 3,247: **224**; 3,253:
216, **224**

Apol.
5: **215**

App.
Syr.
8,50: **104**; 45: **161**; 69: **161**

Arist.
Pol.
1252b8: **250**

Arr.
An.
1,12,1–5: **223**; 1,12,6: **221**; 1,12,7:
225; 2,13–15: **88**; 2,15: **88**; 2,18,1: **90**;
2,24,5: **90**; 2,24,6: **90**; 4,8,2–4: **218**;

9,9: **218**; 5,24,6–7: **220**; 7,13,1: **220**;
14,4: **221**, **225**; 14,9: **220**; 23,6: **224**;
25,1: **224**
Pr.
1,1: **218**
Per.
21,1–3: **224**

Athen.
4,167B: **224**; 6,249D–E: **218**; 250F–
251: **218**; 251C–D: **218**; 253B–E: **218**;
260B–C: **224**; 7,323B: **219**; 10–434B:
220; 12,538F: **218**; 196–202 = FrGH
627 F2: **159**

2 Cor.
11,32 **239**

Curt. Ruf.
4,1,6: **88**; 15–26: **88**; 4,2,2: **88**; 4,2,10–
12: **90**, 4,3,19–23: **90**; 5,10,3: **221**;
6,9,34–36: **219**; 7,9,19: **221**; 8,1,35–
36: **221**; 8,2,15–18: **221**; 8,4,25–30:
221; 10,6,13–14: **221**

Dem.
1,1: **216**; 3,1: **216**; 3,33: **216**; 18,1: **216**;
18,72: **216**; 18,88–89: **216**; 18,247:
216; 19,196–198: **224**

Deut.
32,14: **121**

Dio Cass.
49,32: **123**; 60,5: **165**

Diod.
2,30,3–4: **106**; 48,4–5: **147**; 16,4,5:
215; 17,40: **88**; 17,46–47: **88**;
17,115,6: **224**; 20,46,2: **218**; 33,4: **102**;
40,1b: **101**; 49,32,4–5: **102**

Diogenes Sinopensis
Epist.
24,1: **221**
Douris of Samos
BNJ
76 F36: **215**

Epict.
2,10,1–3: **251**; 22,17: **221**

Euseb.
HE
9,1,3–6: **121**

Exodus
28,2–39: **208**

Ezek.
39,18: **121**

George of Cyprus
Op.
1076: **121**

Hdt.
2,44: **88**; 3: **220**; 5,58: **96**; 8,144: **250**

Hyp.
6,20: **224**

Isocr.
Pan.
4,50: **250**

Jeremiah
50,19: **121**

Jos.
ant. Jud.
3,159–178: **208**; 3,184–187: **208**;
3,215–218: **208**; 12,119–120: **239**;
12,186: **193** ; 13,5: **123**; 13,15,1–2:
102; 13,39: **207**; 13,45: **200**; 13,83-85:
201; 13,123–125: **202**; 13,145–146:
202; 13,191: **153**; 13,213–214: **203**;
13,255–256: **207**; 13,301: **203**; 13,318:
205; 13,374: **205**; 13,375: **153**;
13,377–378: **205**; 13,387–391: **152**;
13,391: **153**; 13,392: **109f.**; 14,3,2:
102; 14, 39: **110**; 14,125–126: **110**;
14,129: **111**; 14,297: **110**; 15,10,2: **102**;
16,3–4: **102**; 16,12–26: **165**; 16,157:
165; 16,200: **152**; 16,294–299: **157**;
16,315–360: **157**; 17,23–29: **121**;

17,287:**157**;17,296: **157**; 18,17: **165**;
18,27: **165**; 18,91: **208**; 20,24: **203**
bell. Jud.
1,63: **207**; 1,70: **205**; 1,90: **153**; 1,99–
102: **152f.**; 1,101: **153**; 1,103: **109**;
1,185–186: **110**; 5,231–236: **208**
Contra Ap.
1,157: **94**

Just.
7,6,14: **215**; 11,10: **88**; 12,12,11–12:
221; 13,2,5–6: **221**; 30,10,5: **60**;
36,1,4: **60**

Konfuzius
Analecta
3,5: **252**; 13,19: **252**

Liv.
31,29,15: **219**

Luke
3,1: **123**

Luk.
Alex.
1: **214**; 2: **223**; 6: **214**; 7: **214**; 16: **214**;
41: **214**, **220**
Bis Acc.
14,25: **213**; 26: **216**; 27,34: **213**; 31:
215
Calumn.
2–4: **214f.**; 16: **215**; 17: **221**, **224**; 17–
18: **214**; 20–21: **224**
de Dea Syria
34: **107**
Din.
1,41: **224**
DM
1,1: **217**; 12,3: **214**; 13,1-2: **214**; 4: **214**;
13,5–6: **214**; 14: **214**, **217**; 14,1: **214**;
14,2: **217**; 14,4: **214**
Dom.
1: **214**, **210**; 5–6: **221**; 20: **214**
Eun.
4: **214**; 9: **214**

Luk.
Fug.
25: **214**
Gall.
25: **214**
Hdt. siv. Aet.
4–6: **220**; 5–6: **214**
Herm.
4: **214**
Hist. Conscr.
1: **214f.**; 3: **214f.**; 4: **215**; 7–10: **215**;
12: **214, 218**; 13: **215**; 13,59–60: **215**;
14–20: **215**; 22: **215**; 26: **215**; 27–28:
215; 32: **215**; 34: **215**; 35: **214f.**; 38:
214f.; 38–39: **215**; 40: **214, 218**; 42:
215; 45: **215**; 47: **215**; 49: **215**; 54: **215**;
56–57: **215**; 59–60: **215**; 62: **214f.**
Icar.
15: **214f.**
Ind.
4: **215**; 19: **214**; 20: **215**; 21: **214f.**; 27:
214–216
J. Trag.
14: **214–216**; 15: **215f.**
Laps.
8: **214f., 219**; 9: **214f.**; 10: **214**; 11: **215**
Merc. Cond.
5: **216**; 24: **214**; 25: **215**; 41: **214**
Nav.
28: **214f., 223**; 33: **214**
Nec.
1: **214**; 17: **214, 217**
Par.
35-36: **214**; 42: **214–216**; 43: **214, 216**;
56: **215, 217**
Peregrin.
2: **214**; 3: **214**; 12: **214**; 25: **214f.**
Phars.
10,20–21: **248**
Pisc.
19: **214**
Pr. Im.
5–6: **215**; 9: **214**; 20: **214, 216**; 27: **214**
Prom. Es
4: **221**; 4–5: **214**

Pseudol.
29: **214**
Rh. Pr.
1: **215**; 5: **214**; 9: **215**; 10: **214f.**; 17:
215; 21: **215**
Salt.
4: **214**; 37: **215**; 58–59: **214f.**
Somn.
12: **214–216**
Syr. D.
17-26: **215**
VH
II 9: **214**; 17: **214**; 31: **214**
Zeuxis
8-11: **215**; 11: **161**

1 Macc
10,20: **200**; 10,48–60: **201**; 10,62–63:
201; 10,65: **201**; 11,20–24: **202**;
11,26–27: **202**; 11,57–58: **202**; 13,36:
203; 13,41–42: **203**; 14,42: **207**; 14,44:
203; 14,48: **203**; 15,32–36: **203**

2 Macc
4,7–10: **179, 200**; 4,11: **190, 192**; 4,12:
184; 4,13: **179**; 4,18–20: **92, 180**; 4,19:
190; 4,24–25: **200**; 5–7: **180**; 14,3–14:
200

Micah
7,14: **121**

Nahum
1,4: **121**

Paus.
4,29,3: **219**

Plin.
nat. hist.
6,139: **47**; 35,78: **237**

Plut.
Alex.
23,4: **218**; 24,5–6: **90**; 28: **218**; 28,2:
218; 41,3–4: **220**; 47,1–2: **220**; 47,5–6:
220; 49,6: **218**; 51,4: **219**; 52,4: **218**;
55,4–5: **220**

Plut.
Ant.
54: **148**
Demetr.
10,4: **218**; 27,2: **224**
Demosth.
29: **153**
Eum.
1,2: **220**; 2,1–5: **220**; 14,5: **219**
Mor.
60C: **218**
65C–F: **218**
180D–E: **218**
292E: **219**
307D–F: **215**
737A: **218**
Pyrrh.
2,1: **219**; 11,4: **219**

Polyb.
34,14,1–6: **239**

Porph.
Abst.
4.21.22–27: **246**

Psalms
22,13: **121**

Qur'an
49,13: **253**

Ps-Skyllax
Peripl.
106: **69**

Sen.
De ben.
1,13,3: **223**
Ep.
94,62: **223**

Stephanus of Byzantium
Eth.
FGrH 675 F 4: **150**; 675 F25: **153**;
781 F5: **158**

Strab.
7,7,8: **219**; 16,2,18: **109**; 4,24: **152**;
2,40: **203**; 16,2,10: **123**; 18,20: **123**

Suet.
Claud.
11,2: **165**

Tib.
51: **165**

Tac.
Ann.
2,157: **157**

Theopomp
BNJ
115 F52: **215**

Names

Abd al-Malik: 245
Abinergaus II.: 50
Abu Hanifa: 253
Achaeus: 182
Achilles: 222, 224, 225
Agathocles, son of Lysimachos: 215
Agenor: 96
M. Agrippa: 165
Agrippina the Elder: 157
Aischines: 215, 216, 224
Alcimus: 200
Alexander I. Balas: 39f., 48, 76–77, 200-202, 215
Alexander II. of Epirus: 21, 25, 27
Alexander II. Zabinas: 77
Alexander III. the Great: 11, 88–90, 92, 95–97, 118, 153, 210, 214–229, 237, 246, 251
Alexander Jannaeus: 153, 203–208
Alexandra: 110
Al-Uzza: 156
Amat-Allah: 151
Amynander of Athamania: 21
Amyntas: 214
Anaxarchos of Abdera: 214
Andriskos: 215
Antigonos Gonatas: 21, 25, 27, 33, 238
Antigonos Mattathias: 199, 200
Antinoos 224
Antiochus Hierax : 22, 24, 26, 28, 57, 183, 215, 251
Antiochus II.: 19, 22–25
Antiochus III.: 20, 27, 29–33, 91, 162, 182, 183, 186, 187, 193, 200
Antiochus IV.: 14, 20, 41, 47, 51, 53, 60, 65f., 67–76, 77–78, 80, 84–86, 179, 180, 186, 187, 191, 200, 247
Antiochus IX.: 57, 67, 78
Antiochus V.: 76–78
Antiochus VI.: 202
Antiochus VII.: 47, 76–78, 108
Antiochus VIII.: 78, 163
Antiochus X.: 108

Antiochus XII.: 152–153, 163
Antiochus XIII.: 101
Antiochus, son of Antiochus II. and Berenice Phernophorus: 22
Antipatros: 230, 235
Aphrodite: 19, 22f., 55, 159
Apion: 159
Apodakos, king of Charakene: 49, 59
Apollo: 24, 39–42, 45f., 48, 51, 58, 71, 93, 107, 158, 163
Apollonius: 201
Arados: 91, 107
Archalelaos: 214
Archelaos of Cappadocia: 161
Aretas III.: 152–154, 156, 158, 161, 178
Aretas IV.: 151, 154–157, 160, 178
Aretas I.: 109
Aristobulus (philosopher): 214, 218
Aristobulus I.: 199, 203, 205, 207, 208
Aristobulus II.: 110
Aristotle: 190, 214, 249
Arrian: 89, 218, 221–225
Arsaces I.: 41–42, 59
Arsaces II.: 42–43, 59
Arsaces X.: 46, 48, 59
Arsinoe I.: 147
Arsinoe II.: 154, 159
Arsinoe III.: 147
Artabanus I.: 45–46, 53, 59, 60–61
Artabanus II.: 39
Artabazos I.: 59
Artagatis : 107
Artemis : 29, 40, 48, 103–104, 106–108, 116
Astarte: 93
Asklepios: 93
Athena : 19, 21, 48, 104, 106–108, 116
Attalus I.: 21, 28–30
Attambelos I.: 49–50, 59, 158, 161
Attembelos II.: 59
Aurelian: 130
Azizos, phylarch: 109, 101
Baal: 88–89, 106–107

Indices

Bagsis: 59
Batrachion: 223
Berenice II.: 147
Berenice Phernephorus: 22f.
Cadmos: 96–97
C. Ceasar: 111, 119
G. Caesar: 158
Claudius: 165
Cleopatra I.: 158
Cleopatra II.: 158
Cleopatra III.: 147f., 158–159
Cleopatra VI.: 163
Cleopatra VII.: 102, 160, 231
Cleopatra Thea: 201
Commodus: 119
Confucius: 247–248, 251
Constantine II.: 119
Cronus-El: 53
Q. Curtius Rufus: 89
Dareios, king of the Elymaïs: 38–40, 59
Datames, Achaemenid Satrap of Cappadocia: 43
Demetrius I.: 45, 54, 74, 76, 78, 108, 200, 230, 234
Demetrius II.: 38–39, 47–48, 54, 57, 60, 76-78, 162, 201-203
Demetrius III. Eukarios: 107
Demochares: 234
Demosthenes: 215, 216, 224
Dio Cassius: 123
Diodoros: 89, 101–102, 106
Diodotos Tryphon: 202
Diogeitos, envoy of Kos: 25
Diogenianus: 158
Dionysos: 30, 55, 71, 148f., 156–161, 163, 166, 176
Dionysos, ruler of Tripolis: 110
Dioscuri: 103f., 107–110, 116
Douris: 215, 218
Dushara: 155–156, 158–159, 177
Epiktetos: 222
Eshmoun: 93
Eumenes II.: 21, 27, 185, 186
Eumenes of Cardia: 215, 219, 220
Euripides: 214

Europa: 70–71, 73–75, 78–79, 85–86
Euthydemus I., king of Bactria: 48
Frataraka: 239, 242
Gamilat: 156
George of Cyprus: 120
Germanicus: 157
Gotarzes I.: 49, 59
Hadrian: 224
Hagiru: 156
Han Wudi: 248
Harpocrates: 67
Hathor: 159
Hecate: 108
Helios: 106–107, 160
Hephaistion: 214, 219–221, 224
Heracles: 44, 49, 53, 60, 88–93, 95–96, 107, 180
Hermes: 91, 103–104, 106, 110
Herod Agrippa I.: 13
Herod Antipas: 165
Herod I.: 102, 121, 157
Herodotos: 88, 224, 220, 250
Hesychinus: 158
Huldu: 156, 178
Hymenaios: 221
Hypereides: 216
Hyspaosines, king of Characene: 39, 47–48, 53, 59, 60
Iamblichus of Arca: 111
Ibn Haldun: 253
Inanna-Ishtar: 55
Indupane: 48
Isidore of Charax: 158–159
Isis: 67, 84, 108, 148–150, 156–160, 166, 176–177
Isocrates: 215, 250
Jason, high priest of Jerusalem: 15, 92, 179–197, 200
Johannes, diplomat in Jerusalem: 192, 193
John Hyrcanus, Hasmonean ruler: 199, 203, 206, 207, 208
Jonathan, Hasmonean ruler: 199–209
Fl. Josephus: 109–111, 121, 123, 152–153, 207
Juba of Mauretania: 158

Judah Maccabee: 199, 200
Jupiter: 106, 118
Justin: 89
Kallistenes: 230
Kamnaskires I.: 39, 47, 51, 59, 60
Kamnaskires II. Nikephoros: 38–39, 59
Kamnaskires III.: 40–41, 59
Kamnaskires IV.: 40, 59
Kamnaskires V.: 40–41, 59
Kassander: 214, 213
Kephalon of Uruk: 181
Kronos/El: 53, 106–107
Kynaithos: 218
Laodice I.: 22, 27, 31
Laodice III.: 162
Licinius: 119
Livia: 165
Lucian of Samosata: 15, 213–225
Luke: 123
Lykourgos: 215, 216
Lysanias, ruler of Ituraea: 102–103, 105–106, 112
Lysimachos: 214
Malichus I.: 157–159
Malichus II.: 155, 178
Marc Antony: 105, 160, 165
Marcus Aurelius: 165
Marian, ruler of Tyre: 110
Maximinus Daza: 121
Meleager: 95
Melqart/Heracles-Melqart: 69, 72, 88–93, 180
Menelaus: 180, 193, 200
Mengzi: 252
Menippus, envoy of Antiochus III.: 31
Mercury: 106, 110
Meredates: 48
Miriam: 215
Mithridates I.: 42–44, 59, 60
Mithridates II.: 46–47, 49, 58, 59, 61
Mithridates III.: 59
Monimos: 109
Nero: 165
Nike: 49, 54–55, 103–104, 106, 116

Ninos: 221
Noaros, ruler of Ituraea: 111
Obodas ‚the God‘ of Nabataea: 150–151, 153–155, 166
Obodas I.: 15, 152
Obodas II.: 148, 152, 156–158, 176, 178
Obodas III.: 152, 178
Octavian, C.: 106, 110, 157–158, 164–165
Olympias: 230
Okkonapses, usurper in Susa: 38, 59
Onesikritos: 214, 218
Onias: 179, 187, 191, 192, 200
Orobazes II.: 48
Orodes I.: 59
Orodes II.: 59
Osiris: 148f.
Pamphilius: 159
Pan: 165
Patroklos: 224, 225
Perdikkas, envoy of Philip V.: 21, 31
Perdikkas II.: 214
Perdikkas III.: 214
Perdikkas, general of Alexander: 214, 223
Phanokrates, gymnasiarch: 183
Philip I. Philadelphus: 37
Philip II. of Macedon: 88, 214–229
Philip II. Philoromaeus: 101
Philip V.: 21, 29–33
Philokrates: 216
Phraates I.: 59
Phraates II.: 44–46, 54–57, 59, 60
Phraates III.: 59
Phraates IV.: 59
Phriapatios: 59
Pindar: 95
Cn. Piso: 157
Plato: 213
Plutarch of Chaironaea: 89, 220
Pluto: 106
Cn. Pompey 102, 105, 111, 123, 245
Poseidon: 68, 77, 84, 86
Pseudo-Scylax: 68f.
Ptolemy I.: 221, 222

Ptolemy II. Philadelphus: 26, 147f., 154, 159, 215

Ptolemy III. Euergetes: 21–23, 25–27, 147

Ptolemy IV. Philopater: 21, 29, 147, 159, 215

Ptolemy IX. Soter: 147

Ptolemy V. Epiphanes: 108, 156

Ptolemy VI.: 201

Ptolemy VI. Philometor: 162

Ptolemy XII. Auletes: 148

Ptolemy, son of Iamblichus, ruler of Ituraea: 111

Ptolemy, son of Mennaios, ruler of Ituraea: 14, 102–112, 116, 123

Pyrros of Epeiros: 215, 223

Qín Shǐhuángdì: 247

Rabbel I.: 152–154, 178

Rabbel II.: 151, 155–156, 161, 178

Roma: 165

Roxane: 220

Sagdodonakos, father of Hyspaosines: 48

Sampsiceramos I. of Emesa: 101

Sarapis: 135, 149

Saturn: 106

Sauromates I.: 165

Sauromates II.: 165

Selene: 108

Seleucus I.: 163, 214, 238

Seleucus II.: 19f., 22–28, 31–32, 43

Selucus III.: 192

Seleucus IV.: 69, 91, 179

Semiramis: 221

Sha'udat: 155

Shaqilat, wife of Aretas IV.: 151, 156, 178

Sima Qian: 250

Simon: 199, 202, 203, 207, 208, 209

Sinatrukes: 59

Sosimos: 111

Sostratos of Knidos: 215

Spartokos IV. of the Bosporan Kingdom: 21, 25, 27

Stephanus of Byzantium: 150

Strabo: 123, 203

Stratonice, mother of Antiochus II.: 22, 216

Syllaeus: 158

Taym-Dushara: 151

Theodorus of Athamania: 21

Theonesios I.: 59

Theopompos: 214

Theokrit: 108

Thucydides: 213, 215

Tiberius: 165

Tigraios, usurper in Susa: 38, 59

Tigranes II. of Armenia: 102–104, 242

Tilloboros: 222, 223

Timarchos: 215, 224

Timarkusu: 48

Tiraios I.: 49, 57, 59

Tiraios II.: 49–50, 59

Trajan: 124, 132

Tyche: 45–46, 49, 54, 60, 65, 107, 119, 148, 156

Tychiades : 216

Umar II. : 245

Uranius : 150, 153–154

P. Varus : 157

Venus: 106

Verethragna : 53

Zakkur: 108

Zenodoros, tetrarch of Ituraea : 102–103, 106, 112

Zeus: 39–41, 44, 51, 96, 103–104, 106–107, 116, 150, 157, 160, 162–163, 180, 193, 216

Zeuxis: 215

Ziaelas of Bithynia: 21, 25, 27f.

Zoilos: 151

Places

Abel-Beth-Maacah: 69
Abila: 102, 106
Actium: 102
Aegean Sea: 33
Ai-Khanoum: 241, 246
Ake-Ptolemais: 51, 108
Alexandria: 92, 165, 232, 238, 241, 251
Al-Gaia: 151, 159
Allaria: 31
Amphipolis: 27, 90, 191
Amyzon: 20
Antigoneia: 238, 241
Antilebanon: 109
Antiochia: 190-192, 238
Antiochia in Persis: 29, 48, 57–58, 62
Antiochia on the Orontes: 45, 51, 66, 101
Apamea on the Silhu: 38
Apamea   186, 238
Aqrabat: 122
Arabia: 117–118, 120–121, 149–150, 159, 164
Arados: 89
Arca: 102, 109–111
Argolis: 96
Argos: 94
Arsakeia → Rhagai
Ascalon: 95
Asia Minor: 11, 13, 19, 24, 28, 32, 104, 186, 204, 223
Athens: 165, 247, 191, 216, 231
Atil: 123
Avdat: 150, 153–154, 166
Ba: 240, 244
Baalbek/Heliopolis: 106–107
Babylon: 15, 23, 37, 47–48, 186–189, 190, 242
Babylonia: 33, 38, 47
Bactria: 37, 54, 161, 221, 231, 238, 239, 245
Baidha: 159
Baitokaike: 107
Balkans: 204

Banias: 165
Bashan: 121
Basra: 241, 253
Batanaea:117, 119–124
Beroia: 184
Beka-Valley:101, 109
Bertyos: 65, 67, 68–70, 74–75, 77, 80, 86, 108
Bethramphtha: 165
Bethsaida: 165
Bir En-Suba: 103
Boeotia: 19, 96
Bostan esh-Sheikh: 93
Bostra: 117–118, 121, 124
Breikeh: 122
Byblos: 65, 67–68, 71, 74, 76, 89
Caesarea Maritima: 165
Cappadocia: 43
Carthage: 72–73, 231
Chalcis: 21, 30,
Chalcis on the Lebanon: 106
Chaironaea: 216
Characene: 13, 47–50, 53, 58, 59, 60, 62, 158, 161
Chengdu: 240
China: 234, 235, 237, 248
Chu: 237, 247
Cilicia: 43, 105
Crete: 31
Cyprus: 73, 165
Cyzicus: 13, 20f., 28–32
Dabiq: 241
Damascus: 102–103, 107, 109–110, 152-153, 161, 163
Dead Sea: 121, 153
Decapolis: 149, 155, 158
Dera: 119, 123–124
Delos: 93
Delphi: 19, 23
Dion: 21, 31
Dura-Europos: 163
East Asia: 16, 235–236, 239, 246, 251, 252
Ecbatana: 43
Ed-Deir: 151
Edessa: 108

Egypt: 15, 33, 68, 121, 147–178, 221, 239, 242
Ekron: 201
el-Mreriyye: 149
Elymaïs: 13, 38, 53, 57, 59, 62
Emesa: 108f.
Ephesus: 22, 108, 120
Ezra: 122
Falahat: 151
Forat: 48
Fustat: 240
Gadara: 95, 153, 188, 191
Galaaditis: 153
Gamala: 103
Gaza: 95, 153, 188
Gerasa: 149, 155, 191
Golan: 117, 153
Greece: 11, 220, 251
Hades: 217
Hauran: 14, 117–119, 122–124, 158
Hekatompylos: 42, 58
Hermonassa: 165
Hiera Nesos: 27
Higaz: 251
Hindukush: 11, 243
Hippo: 71–74, 85
Hippos: 191
Huang-Ho: 236, 247, 251
Indus: 96
Inkhil: 122
Ira: 120
Iran: 236
Iraq: 242
Issos: 219
Istron: 31
Jabal al-Druze: 117, 123, 124
Jabal al-Madbah: 156, 177
Jericho: 207
Jerusalem: 15, 92–93, 118, 179–197, 200, 201, 202, 203, 206, 207, 208, 209, 239, 243
Jiangzhou: 239
Jordan: 109
Judaea: 157, 199–209
Kafr: 120
Kafr Nasij: 121–122

Kairuoan: 240
Kambe: 71–74, 85
Kamid el-Loz: 109
Kana: 153
Kassandreia: 27
Kidron Valley: 118
Kition: 71–74, 85
Kolophon: 184
Koroneia: 19
Kos: 13, 20f., 22–28, 32, 165
Kufa: 241, 253
Laodicea in Phoenicia → Berytos
Larissa: 165, 223, 224
Lato: 31
Lato pros Kamara: 31
Lebanon: 121, 135
Lesbos: 165
Leuke: 224
Levant: 157, 188, 236
Limyra: 15, 182–185
Linqiong: 240
Lydia: 162
Macedonia: 90, 96, 184, 240
Maghreb: 242
Magnesia ad Sipylum: 19, 22–24
Magnesia on the Meander: 13, 20f., 28–32
Majdal Anjar: 106
Media: 48
Medion: 31
Mesene → Characene
Mesopotamia: 37–38, 43–44, 57, 58, 60–61, 107, 239
Methone: 215
Methymna: 184
Miletus: 24
Mismiyyeh: 122
Moab: 153
Motho: 153
Mount Gerizim: 207
Mount Ida: 222
Mysia: 222
Mytilene: 165
Nabataea: 15, 148, 150, 154–155, 159, 166
Negev: 153–154

Nemea: 94–96
Nicaea: 123
Nisa: 41, 43, 45, 58, 158
Nuqrah: 117
Oaxos: 26, 31
Olba: 105
Orontes: 45, 51
Palestine: 147, 149f., 164–165
Palmyra: 14, 108, 124, 129–146
Parthia: 13, 129, 158
Pella/Apameia: 239
Pella: 207
Peraea: 165
Pergamon: 21
Persis: 29, 243
Persepolis: 246
Petra: 148–153, 154–155, 156, 159, 166, 177
Phanagoreia: 165
Philippi: 27, 105
Phoenicia: 65–66, 79–80, 87–89, 96–97, 123
Phrygia Paroreios: 185
Pi: 239
Ptolemaïs: 201, 202
Qalat el Hosn: 109
Qasr al-Bint: 154–155, 166
Raïfa: 122
Rdeimeh Sharquiyyeh: 123, 124
Rhagai: 58
Rhodes: 31, 95
Rome: 11, 16, 104, 119, 121, 123, 129, 132, 137, 157, 160, 162, 166, 200, 234, 237
Samaria: 149
Sanamein: 119–122
Sardis: 15, 182–185
Scythopolis: 124, 150, 158
Sebaste: 165
Seleucia on the Hedyphon: 37
Seleucia on the Tigris: 37, 43–49, 53–58, 60–62, 187, 241
Sestos: 103
Shu: 240, 244
Si'a: 118
Sichuan: 237, 240, 244

Sidon: 65, 67, 69, 70–74, 75–76, 77–78, 89, 93–96
Smyrna: 13, 19f., 22–28, 31–32
Spasinu Charax → Antiochia in Persis
Stratonicea: 24
Sur: 122
Susa: 37–40, 43–46, 52, 57–58, 61f.
Suweida: 118, 122, 124
Sybrita: 31
Tadmor → Palmyra
Tel Anafa: 103
Teos: 13, 20f., 27, 28–32, 162, 184
Thebes: 95
Thessaly: 165
Thracia: 120
Tiberias: 13
Toriaion: 15, 185–187, 189, 191
Trachonitis: 117, 121–122, 124
Tripolis: 108
Tyre: 65–67, 69, 71–73, 74–76, 78, 85, 88–93, 95, 176
Umm al-Ahmad: 134
Umm al-Jimal: 149
Umm el-Awamid: 69
Uruk: 181, 242
Wadi a-Qina: 153
Wadi es-Siyyagh: 149
Wadi Musa: 151, 159
Wasit: 240
Xanthos: 20
Xianjang: 240
Yanouh: 109
Yarmuk: 124
Zhou: 247, 254